D1606379

Pinero

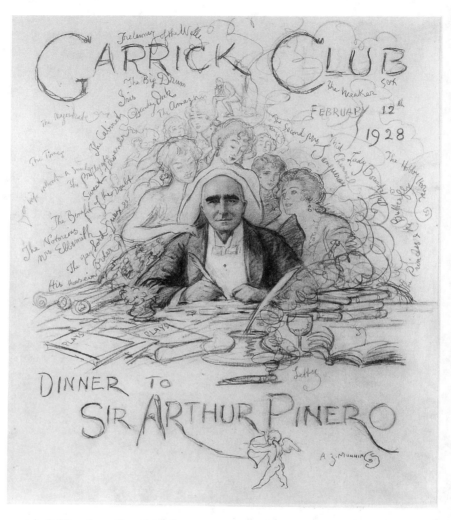

A. J. Munnings, Royal Academy, menu cover portrait of Sir Arthur Pinero (E. T. Archive photograph, by permission of the Garrick Club)

Pinero

A THEATRICAL LIFE

by

John Dawick

UNIVERSITY PRESS OF COLORADO

Cover: Phil May, sketch of Pinero (*Cassell's Magazine*, 1899)

ISBN: 0-87081-302-1

10 9 8 7 6 5 4 3 2 1

To George Rowell
and
Peter Wearing

Contents

Contents

Illustrations

Illustrations

Acknowledgements

I have been helped in my work on this biography by many people, but most of all by the two scholars to whom it is dedicated. Mr George Rowell and Dr J. P. Wearing have been generous with their assistance far beyond the call of duty. Both have provided me with access to primary sources without which I could hardly have begun, let alone completed, my task: the former told me of the Pinero papers now held in the Garrick Club library and smoothed my access to them; the latter handed over to me the large store of transcripts and microfilms of letters and manuscripts he had painstakingly assembled for his invaluable edition of Pinero's letters. Nor did their kindness and help end there. Both have subsequently read and commented on drafts of every chapter in the book, making many valuable suggestions and saving me from some embarrassing errors. Despite the book's inadequacies (which are mine alone), I hope that George Rowell and Peter Wearing will be pleased with the biography at least as a detailed and accurate narration of the career of a dramatist whose reputation they have done much to preserve and restore.

I also wish to record my particular gratitude to Major Philip Daniel, Lady Pinero's nephew, who provided me with significant details of family history that would otherwise have remained unknown to me. The dinner he gave me (and my wife and daughter) at Myra Pinero's birthplace, Ye Olde Cheshire Cheese, remains a highlight of my field research.

Many friends and colleagues have read and helpfully commented on draft chapters. In addition to George Rowell and Peter Wearing, I would especially like in this regard to thank my former professor Adrian Roscoe and my colleague John Ross, together with Michael Holroyd, who read early drafts of two chapters involving George

Acknowledgements

Bernard Shaw and gave kindly encouragement to a fledgling biographer. On a still more personal level, I owe more than I can say to my wife, Anona, and to my mother, Mildred Dawick, who not only read my drafts and revisions but gave unfailing support over the book's long period of gestation.

I also gratefully thank the following people for their help: Kay Hutchings, formerly librarian of the Garrick Club; Mary M. Huth and the staff of the Department of Rare Books and Special Collections at the University of Rochester Library; C.W.S. Sheppard, P. S. Morrish, M. Davis, and Ann Farr of the Brotherton Library of the University of Leeds; Carolyn Harden and other staff at the Theatre Museum, London; Cathy Henderson and the staff of the Harry Ransom Humanities Research Center of the University of Texas at Austin; Christopher Robinson of the Theatre Collection, University of Bristol; the staff of the Students' Room of the British Library Department of Manuscripts and of the Newspaper Library at Colindale, London; J.F.L. Bowes of the Cheltonian Society; Patricia Chute of the Royal Society of Literature; Mrs M. E. Gordon; Joel H. Kaplan; C. L. Kernahan; Lewis Sawin; and the late Marie Ney and Murray MacDonald.

I am also most grateful to the Council of Massey University, Palmerston North, New Zealand, for grants and periods of overseas leave while I was working on the biography, for the support of my colleagues in the Department of English, and also for much practical help from the department's secretaries, Ruth Filbee and Julie MacKenzie. Finally, I wish to record my appreciation of the assistance and support given by Luther Wilson, Jody Berman, Terri Eyden, Pam Graves, and other staff at the University Press of Colorado, with a special acknowledgement to my copy editor, Alice Colwell, for her keen eye and thoroughness.

For permission to publish letters and other writings of Arthur Wing Pinero and his friends and colleagues, as well as various photographs and illustrations, I am pleased to recognise: Samuel French Ltd; the Garrick Club; the Royal Literary Fund; the British Library; the Brotherton Library of the University of Leeds; Cambridge University Press; E. T. Archive; Mary Evans Picture Library; Jennifer Gosse; the Harry Ransom Humanities Research Center, University of

Acknowledgements

Texas at Austin; University of Minnesota Press; Random House UK Ltd; the Department of Rare Books and Special Collections, University of Rochester Library; the Society of Authors on behalf of the Harley Granville-Barker Estate and the Bernard Shaw Estate and © 1993 The Trustees of the British Museum, the Governors and Guardians of the National Gallery of Ireland and the Royal Academy of Dramatic Art.

Portions of Chapter 10, "*The Second Mrs Tanqueray*," first appeared in a somewhat different version in my article "The 'First' Mrs Tanqueray" in *Theatre Quarterly IX*, 35 (Autumn 1979): 77–93. I am grateful to the editors of the *Theatre Quarterly* and *New Theatre Quarterly* for permission to make use of this material.

As this is a biography of a playwright who lived and worked in the England of Queen Victoria and King Edward VII, I have retained the formal use of capital letters customary during this period for official titles such as the Lord Chamberlain, the Duke of Beaufort, or the Queen. Similarly, I have used the professional names by which actors and actresses of the period chose to be known rather than their real surnames or first names: for example, Arthur Cecil instead of Arthur Cecil Blunt and Mrs Patrick Campbell instead of Beatrice Stella Campbell.

John Dawick

Prologue: The Drama of Respectability

'The modern English drama was ushered into being on the night of May 27th 1893, when *The Second Mrs Tanqueray,* by Arthur Wing Pinero, was acted for the first time on the stage of the St James's Theatre, London,'[1] wrote an American editor of the play in 1917. A century after its first performance, however, it is difficult to see what was so revolutionary about what seems to us merely an effective period piece. By contrast, *Mrs Warren's Profession,* written by George Bernard Shaw in response to Pinero's success, is far more provocative in its social analysis, if less convincing in its characterisation. To understand the sensation that *The Second Mrs Tanqueray* created on its memorable opening night, however, we need to view it in its proper context: as the most daring challenge from within to what can be called the drama of respectability.

The leading ideal of the Victorian age was respectability. The prosperous citizens who occupied the stalls of theatres such as the St James's considered it an appropriate acknowledgement of the effort, willpower, and moral worth that had made England the workshop of the world and the heart of a great empire. That their wealth was also due to the sweated labour of millions of working-class poor did not unduly disturb them. Success was both a proof of merit and a sign of God's approval. The worthy Victorian businessman's duty was to acquire wealth and bequeath it to his children; therefore respect for property and marital fidelity (especially by wives) were the guiding principles of 'decent' society. When he condescended to patronise the theatre, or allowed his wife to do so, he insisted that the offerings presented should uphold these principles. Appreciating and meeting this demand brought success to managements such as those of the Bancrofts at the Prince of Wales and Haymarket theatres and the

German Reeds at the Gallery of Illustration — too respectable a venue even to be called a theatre!

The entertainments manufactured for respectable managements by the playwrights of the 1860s and 1870s, though, were usually insipid or woodenly melodramatic or plagiarised from the French. When a genuine satirical talent arose, like W. S. Gilbert's, the prevailing taste for blandness obliged it to dress up as fantasy, preferably accompanied by music. The consequence, as Pinero himself later remarked, was that 'people were drawn to the theatre by the performer rather than the play. If the piece was a good vehicle for the display of the actor's talents, the public were satisfied.'[2] But as time went by, an increasing number of critics (Matthew Arnold, Henry James, and William Archer among them) pointed out the shoddiness of the local product. 'Made in England,' theatregoers were repeatedly reminded, was not a sign of quality when it came to plays.

This was the situation Pinero sought to change when he assumed the role of theatrical chronicler of the age of respectability. He was well suited to the task, as he had been passionately attracted to the theatre from childhood but was also ambitious for material success because of his early experience of genteel poverty. Even more important were his typically Victorian values of earnestness, industry, and morality, though in Pinero they were leavened by a keen sense of humour and an observant eye. The theatre seemed to offer him the hope of escape from law office drudgery into a magical world of glamour and excitement, together with the prospect of fame and fortune. That this new world would turn out to be a reflection of the one he had left and that he would help to make it almost as respectable are just two of the ironies of his life and work. He did, however, acquire fame and fortune, though the latter was a modest one, and the former, like respectability itself, was vulnerable.

Most of Pinero's plays, nearly sixty in total, are concerned with the ideal of respectability, sometimes viewed comically, sometimes sentimentally, sometimes satirically, and sometimes with almost tragic force. But he did not attack the ideal itself — unlike Henry Arthur Jones, who scorned it as hypocrisy; Oscar Wilde, who mocked it as privilege; and Bernard Shaw, who dismissed it as a purchasable commodity. Pinero took respectability seriously, emphasising the danger of losing it. His plays show individuals in conflict with 'respectable' society, usually because of a combination of the protagonists' weakness and the intolerance of a society obsessed by appearances rather than substance. Indeed the gap between facade and reality is the essential focus of his Victorian work. As the Victorian age merged into the Edwardian, however, his drama responded to the changing moral climate by becoming more darkly satirical and consequently less popular. His vogue finally ended after World War I, when Victorian values were not merely discarded but discredited. He continued writing plays — some of them technically innovative — until his death in 1934, but he had effectively lost his theme and his audience.

Nevertheless, Pinero's achievement was significant. He dominated the British stage for more than a quarter of a century at a time when the theatre was more widely popular than it had been since William Shakespeare's day or would be again. He did much to raise the standard of drama for the playwrights who came after him, and even if he has proved to be not for all time but of an age, several of his plays are often revived successfully and others could be. The humanity, humour, and dramatic skill of his best work still appeal, and his keen observation of late-Victorian and Edwardian life vividly recaptures a world whose legacy remains. Whatever else may be said of Pinero's drama, it amply fulfilled Hamlet's final dictum on the purpose of playing: 'to show . . . the very age and body of the time his form and pressure.' As for his life, that (as I hope to show) had its own drama, which can be appropriately presented in four acts, the form he himself deployed so expertly in the theatre.

Pinero

.. ACT 1 ..

Preparation
(1855—1881)

...1...
Outside the Garrick Club

i. The Pineros

A London policeman regularly on duty in the vicinity of Lincoln's Inn Fields during the early 1870s might well have noted with suspicion the strange lunch-hour routine of an undernourished law clerk. Promptly at 1 p.m., the youth — identifiable by a tam-o-shanter perched above bushy black eyebrows and a long nose — would rush out of his office and round the corner to a bootmaker's shop in Great Queen Street (the part now called Remnant Street), from which he would emerge seconds later with a piece of bread and cheese. Then he would dash along Great Queen Street, across Drury Lane, down the length of Long Acre and into Garrick Street, where he would suddenly come to a halt opposite an imposing greystone-fronted building. There he would stand gazing intently through its elevated ground-floor windows at immaculately clad gentlemen enjoying much more substantial luncheons than his. Eventually, at about five minutes to two — or sometimes, when he had become particularly rapt in his vigil, even as the hour was striking — he would hurry back to the chambers from which he had set out.

Nearly sixty years later, the owner of the nose and eyebrows, known formally as Sir Arthur Pinero but as "Pin" to his friends, stood in the main dining room of the Garrick Club replying to a toast at a dinner in his honour. Recalling the strange behaviour of his former self, he explained that as a youth he had been severely stagestruck,

3

and hearing that the club now honouring him numbered among its members the most eminent actors of the day, he would often spend his lunch hours outside it in the hope of catching sight of some of them. It was quite likely, he admitted, that through eagerness he "often mistook a learned judge or barrister for a popular comedian." Nevertheless, though he could scarcely believe that he was once that youth — whom in his mind's eye he could still see wistfully gazing at their windows from the opposite side of the street — the visions he had seen and the dreams he had dreamt had more or less materialised, "one of the most joyous of those visions, one of the most fantastic of those dreams, being that one day he would have the right to enter the portals of the Garrick Club."[1]

For actors and playwrights, membership in the club, founded in 1831 with the aim of bringing together "the patrons of the drama and its professors," was ultimate proof not merely of eminence but respectability. "I would rather be a member of the Garrick than receive a peerage," Beerbohm Tree is said to have told Brandon Thomas, the author of *Charley's Aunt*, on the occasion of the latter's election.[2] That a poor, half-educated clerk could rise to this distinction — and become the most successful English playwright of the late nineteenth century — suggests a good deal of determination under that tam. It is also indicative of the goals and values that drove him.

Perhaps his Jewish ancestry had something to do with it. The Pinheiros, as the name was originally spelt, were a distinguished family of Sephardic Jews who rose to prominence in medieval Portugal before suffering the persecutions of the Inquisition. In the early eighteenth century some of them migrated to England. Despite acquiring citizenship, they maintained their separate Jewish identity until the playwright's grandfather altered the spelling of his surname when he married into an English family and, it would appear, joined the Church of England.[3] Thereafter the Pineros regarded themselves as totally English and, though acknowledging their part-Jewish descent with some pride, no longer subscribed to Jewish religious beliefs and customs.

Mark Pinero (born 1762) became a wealthy London solicitor with a house in Cavendish Square and a country residence at Kingsbury in

Middlesex. His bride was Margaret Wing, daughter of a deputy teller of the Exchequer and sister of a sea captain who as a lad had served on board the *Victory* at Trafalgar and can still be viewed among the background figures in Benjamin West's famous painting of *The Death of Nelson*. (In the fullness of time Captain Thomas Wing's dress sword and cocked hat — the latter somewhat moth-eaten — were passed down as treasured family relics to the playwright.)[4] Mark appears to have taken his connection by marriage to the Exchequer very much to heart, suggesting in a series of letters to the Right Honourable William Pitt a number of new taxes, including one on carriages (which was adopted), another on ladies' hats (which wasn't), and a third on theatre tickets (which, to the later satisfaction of his grandson, was also declined).[5]

Perhaps to reward this concern for the financial well-being of the state, Mark's younger son, John Daniel Pinero, was at the age of twenty appointed a steward for George IV's coronation. He proved of service by preventing the king's rejected consort, Queen Caroline, from entering Westminster Abbey and subsequently picking up and returning a handkerchief dropped by the king's mistress, Mrs Fitzherbert. His reward was a handwritten letter of thanks from the monarch.[6]

Thereafter John Daniel's career proceeded gently downhill. In 1823 he followed his father and his elder brother, Thomas, into the legal profession but with less success. He frequently neglected even to take out his annual certificate,[7] perhaps because he could not always afford the fee. By 1851, after moving his business address several times, he was practising at 6 South Square, Gray's Inn. The seven other solicitors and solitary barrister with chambers at the same address all had residences elsewhere, but John Daniel lived on the premises with his ailing wife, Nancy, until her death later that year.[8]

On 6 January 1852, however, after the briefest possible period of mourning, John Daniel married again. According to the marriage certificate, both he and his bride were "of full age." At fifty-four he certainly was, but she was barely sixteen.

Her maiden name was Lucy Daines, daughter of "Thomas Daines, Pilot," and (again according to the marriage certificate) she was at the time living at the same address as John Daniel. Perhaps she was the housekeeper's daughter — like the title character in *Sweet Lavender,* the popular sentimental comedy her son would later write — and the marriage offered her the chance to better herself. Unlike little Lavender, however, Lucy was a lively girl, fond of outings, family picnics, and visits to the theatre. She appears to have insisted on a full church wedding, being married after the due calling of banns in the Parish Church of St Andrew, Holborn, "according to the Rites and Ceremonies of the Established Church."

Despite the considerable age gap between the couple, the marriage was quite successful. John Daniel bestirred himself in his legal work, moving within a month to new chambers at 9 Gray's Inn Square, where he employed two clerks. His practice, however, remained a modest one, as his will, drawn up several months later, indicates. In this he named his "dear wife Lucy" as the sole beneficiary of his estate, except for "a small book or article as a token of love to my dear brother Thomas Wing Pinero and dear sister Margaret Elizabeth Bunn, regretting I have not in my power to give more." The following year Lucy bore John Daniel a daughter, Frances Lucy (usually known as Fanny), and some two years later, on 24 May 1855, their only son, Arthur Wing Pinero.

At the time of Arthur's birth, his parents and small sister were living at Mrs Sarah Ebdell's lodging house, 21 Dalby Terrace, Islington, the largest of six similar establishments in the street.[9] He later claimed to remember the area as being "then a pleasant enough locality,"[10] but he in fact lived there only four years. In 1856 his father moved his practice once again, this time to 8 Princes Street, Bedford Row, where it remained until 1868. Nearby premises housed two wastepaper dealers, a French polisher, a carpenter, a tailor, a builder, a law-stationer, a chandler, a haberdasher, and a cowkeeper.[11] But for a time John Daniel's practice did well, and by 1859 he was able to move his family to a house of their own at 1 Cumberland Terrace in Bayswater,[12] adjacent to Regent's Park — if on the unfashionable side.

The following year John Daniel acquired a more impressive address. Now he could point with pride to the *Law List* of 1860 — he had taken out his certificate in time that year — which stated that his residence was situated at 4 Hans Place, an exclusive Chelsea street where the neighbours, apart from a stray colonel, were all solicitors and surgeons and their families.[13] Less than a year later, however, he and his family had to retreat to a cheaper dwelling.

But this brief Chelsea sojourn made a lasting impression on his young son, who recalled it thirty-six years later in the first act of a comedy, *The Princess and the Butterfly*. Here, the Princess Pannonia, recently widowed after twenty years of marriage to a man forty years older, receives a visit from a tactless young admirer, Edward Oriel:

> PRINCESS. (*Giving her hand*). Mr Oriel. I believe I saw you once when you were a very small boy.
> EDWARD. In Hans Place. Strange to say I remember you.
> PRINCESS. (*Smiling*). Older people than yourself don't make me such speeches.
> EDWARD. (*Stiffly*). Pardon me. I mean I was a child of five — six—
> PRINCESS. Of course. What do you remember of the occasion?
> EDWARD. I remember that our visitor was exceptionally tall and slender, that it hurt my neck to stare up at her. (*Thoughtfully, not looking at her*). I remember comparing you, after you had gone, with my mother.
> PRINCESS. (*With a slightly elevated brow*). Really?
> EDWARD. My poor mother was youthful-looking to the last.
> PRINCESS. Yes, yes, very delicate and willowy —
> EDWARD. As you were then. (48–49)

That Pinero recalled the Hans Place house so long after this brief stay as one where a princess might have been received is significant: from then on his family occupied progressively poorer dwellings. And Edward's odd linking of the princess with his mother comes shortly after the princess has stated that her elderly husband had always been a good father — to *her*! It appears the playwright was recalling the relationship that had existed many years earlier between his own parents.[14]

ii. Two Worlds

After Hans Place the Pineros moved to 2 Rydon Crescent,[15] a small street of several houses and a dozen or so shop-buildings occupied by superior tradespeople — jewellers, watchmakers, and a linen draper[16] — on the opposite bank of the New River from the old Sadler's Wells Theatre. This move may have represented a step down for his parents, but to young Arthur it opened up a new world of fantasy and romance. The theatre became his playground. Its manager, Robert Edgar, was tolerant of small boys and allowed Arthur and a friend, H. Chance Newton — later "Carados," the *Referee*'s theatre columnist for nearly sixty years — to explore behind the scenes where they recklessly investigated the mysterious pools and springs far beneath the stage.[17]

They also fished in the river, and while doing so one day, Arthur met an old actress called Mrs Loveday, whose son later became the actor Henry Irving's stage manager. She had acted with Edmund Kean and described the star in words the stagestruck boy carefully wrote down and preserved: "He was mostly a barnstormer in his methods. Always virile, sometimes far from sober and on these occasions very ordinary, he seldom failed in some portions of his impersonations to be not merely *tremendous*, but TERRIFYING."[18] No doubt Pinero remembered the old lady's description many years later when he wrote the pivotal scene of *Trelawny of the "Wells"* in which the crusty old vice-chancellor, who calls actors "gypsies," suddenly lights up at the mention of Kean's name: "Ah, he was a *splendid* gypsy!"

Arthur had been taken as an infant to a pantomime at the Grecian Theatre in City Road, but it was as a frequenter of the old Wells that his lifelong addiction to the stage really began. Near the end of his career, in the 1920s, when an appeal had been launched to restore the derelict second Sadler's Wells Theatre, Pinero reminisced about the old theatre of his boyhood:

> It was a smallish house with a few rows of stalls and an eighteen-penny pit in which one sat on a bare plank with nothing to rest one's back against. In the intervals of the performance a man in a white apron, carrying a basket, pushed his way between the lean rows of people in

the pit, crying, "Ginger beer, lemonade, bottled ale or stout, almond cake." The words "almond cake" were always uttered in a coaxing, seductive voice. I never tasted this particular delicacy, my resources having been exhausted by the payment of the admission-money, but I often glanced longingly into the basket. I fancy the cake was a puffy sort of macaroon, but without a macaroon's crispness and shine, and in the light of a later wisdom I am convinced that it was thoroughly indigestible and unwholesome. The proscenium was fairly deep, and on either side of it was a door through which the actor entered to take his "call.". . . There was a green baize curtain and an act-drop of classical design, the lowering of the former signifying the end of the play. In the interior scenes the stage was covered, also with green baize, and in a woodland scene the covering was allowed to remain; but in a street-scene, or in a scene where a "trap" was used, the boards of the stage were as naked as the pit seats. A "front" scene was composed of a pair of "flats", and these were run on from opposite wings by a couple of stage-carpenters — a propelling-force not always invisible. Sometimes the flats failed to come together properly — hence the advice frequently offered to the literary novice, "Be sure to join your flats", and sometimes, through an error on the part of a careless stage-hand, half a street went out to meet half a landscape. The audience were never disturbed by these mishaps, perhaps because they were too unsophisticated to notice them, perhaps because — as in my case — the feeling of enchantment was too deeply rooted to be shaken.[19]

The great period of Samuel Phelps's Shakespearian seasons at the Wells had ended several years earlier, and the theatre was entering a long period of decline and decay. For a few more years the legitimate drama was kept going by the kindly Robert Edgar and his wife, who acted under the name of Miss Marriott. She became Arthur's first heroine: "She played, although already a somewhat mature lady, the leading juvenile characters, and, with no consideration for Mr Edgar, I, being at that time about ten years of age, fell deeply in love with her."[20] For the rest of his life he kept several playbills announcing Miss Marriott's appearances in various roles: Mrs Heller in August Kotzebue's five-act drama *The Stranger* (one of Mrs Siddons's great parts) and, on the same bill, Pauline Deschapelles in Edward Bulwer-Lytton's hoary old perennial, *The Lady of Lyons*; Rosalind in *As You Like*

It ("Lords and Foresters by a Host of Auxiliaries"); and Portia in *The Merchant of Venice*, followed by Margery, the country wife of J. B. Buckstone's farce *The Rough Diamond*. Nor did such appearances exhaust Miss Marriott's versatility and endurance. Another playbill announces the production at the Sadler's Wells Theatre ("The Home of Pantomime") of "an entirely New, Grand and Original Burlesque Pantomime, abounding with Gorgeous Scenery, Splendid Pageantry and Magnificent Spectacle . . . entitled LITTLE RED RIDING HOOD, or, Harlequin, Prince Hopeful, Baa Baa Black Sheep and the Cruel Wolf. The Pantomime produced under the immediate Superintendence of MISS MARRIOTT." This production (in eight scenes, concluding with "THE GRAND TRANSFORMATION SCENE conducting to THE GOLDEN VALLEY OF THE SCENTED MAGNOLIAS") was preceded on the bill by "the Splendid Comedy of THE WAY TO GET MARRIED" and followed by a final "Harlequinade in Four Scenes."[21] Like most nineteenth-century managers, the Edgars gave their pantomime customers value for money.

By now the pressures of real life were closing in upon the growing boy. Despite the decline of his father's practice, Arthur had not until then been unduly conscious of hardship. He had had enough pocket money for the occasional one-and-sixpenny place in the Wells pit and quite frequent purchases of the large and shiny half-penny buns sold at Doig's bakery in Red Lion Street.[22] His formal education, however, had been done on the cheap at the Spafields Chapel Charity School in Exmouth Street, Clerkenwell[23] — a fact he glossed over in later life. Then when he was only ten even this free schooling had to be discontinued. The extra strain on the declining family income caused by the birth in March 1865 of a third child, Mary, compelled John Daniel to set his son to work in his office.

Arthur appears not to have minded entering the work force at such an early age. "I was always a very old little boy," he later remarked,[24] hardly a surprising attribute, considering the difference in age between his father and mother, but one heightened by his new responsibilities. He took his work seriously, attending to accounts, answering letters, and acquiring business habits (perhaps in reaction to his father's more careless ways) that he never lost. This was the origin of the mania for order that was both his greatest fault and a positive virtue in his later career. The office served him too as "a school for the observation of character," as he once said.[25] Here again the experience was not without its drawbacks. The cynicism which is often apparent in Pinero's later plays was probably derived, in some measure, from his early exposure to the daily business of the law.

At night, however, he went to the theatre as often as he could. It was in this alternative world of lights, glamour, and excitement that he felt really alive. Throughout his life he was to display the contradictory traits of public formality and private enthusiasm — a dichotomy that no doubt derived from the contrasting influences of his elderly father and young mother and that eventually would be manifested in the frequent alternation between serious and farcical pieces in the Pinero canon. But for young Arthur the theatre simply offered life, vitality, and, above all, release from the constraint and tedium of his father's business. Furthermore, as he entered adolescence, there was also the lure of pretty actresses demonstrating on stage the reward of true worth by true love.

Not that Arthur was constant in his love for them. Miss Marriott was summarily displaced as an object of adoration by a notorious dark-haired beauty, Adah Isaacs Menken, when she appeared at the Wells for three weeks in May 1868 with her "World-renowned impersonation of Mazeppa." In this show — a scandalous success at Astley's Royal Amphitheatre three and a half years earlier — she created a nightly sensation careering round the stage lashed to a black steed that jumped over and over a series of "Stupendous Platforms erected expressly at Enormous Expense."[26] According to the actress Genevieve Ward, "the rich and glossy flesh-coloured silk tights that encased her [Menken's] splendidly moulded lower limbs, and the snowy-white, close-fitting drapery that she wore round her body (all unsoiled by the ghastly ride) contrasted well with the dark colour of the horse and produced a fine effect. But the crowning moment came when, after she was released from the courser, she stood upright and cried, 'Once more I stand erect; once more do I assume the god-like attitude of Freedom and of Man!' "[27]

Thirteen-year-old Arthur was quite overwhelmed. During Menken's engagement at the Wells he regularly stationed himself outside the stage door to see her as she entered the theatre. Just three months later her brief but extraordinary life came to an end when she died of lung disease in a Paris hotel. Heartbroken, Arthur composed an anguished elegy he later hoped for the sake of his literary reputation would never be recovered. Not that she was unworthy of the verses, he added, for it was his belief that she had at heart been "a good woman who knowing better did worse."[28] The same might be said of Paula Tanqueray and most other Pinero heroines, but it was a feeble tribute to Menken's desperate courage.

By 1870 John Daniel, who had been progressively losing his hearing and his clients, was completely deaf and generally unwell.[29] A sketch done by his son at this time shows the old man seated in his frock coat and squinting through *pince-nez* at his newspaper.[30] The family resemblance can be seen in the high forehead, bristling black eyebrows, and long nose — though, in addition to his furry moustache and muttonchop whiskers, John Daniel still had a good deal more hair on his head than his son would have at the same age. For the previous two years the old man had conducted what remained of his practice from rooms he occupied with his family above a linen draper's shop at 329 High Holborn,[31] but now he had to retire. His health worsened, and on 27 May 1871 he died of what the death certificate terms "Natural Decay." Arthur was present at the death but left no record of how it affected him. Because of his father's age (John Daniel was seventy-three when he died) and comparative lack of interest in him as a child, Arthur had always felt closer to his mother.

John Daniel's estate yielded less than £100,[32] and by the time all the bills had been paid, his widow, at the age of thirty-five, was left with little money to support herself and her young family. Lucy Pinero could hardly be blamed if, like the Princess Pannonia, she sometimes wondered aloud what had happened to her youth. But she soon set about coping with her new situation, helped by her older daughter and son. Arthur had worked briefly in a Wigmore Street circulating library after his father's retirement,[33] and then resumed law clerking "in a very dull, dirty room in Lincoln's Inn Fields"[34] for a pound a week.

A. W. Pinero (aged fifteen), sketch of John Daniel Pinero (Cassell's Magazine, *1899*)

Most of this — "so desperate was the need" — went into the common purse at home.[35] The family now moved into cheap rooms above a bootmaker's shop at 69A Great Queen Street, close to Arthur's work.[36]

Being a solicitor's clerk had long lost its novelty; Arthur attended to his duties mechanically and daydreamed about the stage. Since he was fifteen he had been attending evening classes in elocution at the Birkbeck Scientific and Literary Institution (later Birkbeck College of the University of London).[37] The tutor of the class was a Mr Ohlson, who encouraged his students in mutual criticism of the recitations they prepared each week, pointing out each other's faults in pronunciation, posture, and gesture. Arthur took part in these sessions with an enthusiasm that in July 1872 won him the institution's prize for elocution: a handsome set, bound in half calf, of three Dickens nov-els.[38] But the greatest attraction of the elocution class was the chance to act in the plays the group staged from time to time.

Arthur took the lead in organising these performances and tried to swell audiences by inviting his mother, sisters, and any other available friends or relatives — notably a favourite aunt, Mrs Eliza Schneider, and her daughters Lilly and Chrissy. A letter to Aunt Eliza on 8 November 1872 appears to refer to one of these productions with an engaging candour: "My mama has requested me to send you a Programme of next Wednesday's Entertainment. It has been said that the anticipation of an event is more pleasing than the event itself, and as I am certain it will be so in the present instance, I beg of you to expect a very great deal of us on Wednesday next, because the delight you will experience in so doing, will in a great measure compensate for yr. discovery that we are a miserable set of people who can do next to nothing."[39]

Apart from appearing in plays, Arthur was also trying to write them. Over the next two years he churned out a dozen or so (all, it is perhaps fortunate, now lost or destroyed) with titles such as "Achil-les," "Heir at Law," "A Hundred Thousand Pounds," and "The Castle Spectre."[40]

This activity eventually got him into his employer's bad books for a while. Having only a limited practice, the solicitor often left him in charge of the office. Able therefore to style himself "managing clerk," Arthur suborned the younger lad who made up the remainder of the staff into delivering copies of his plays around the various theatres. Because the manuscripts were invariably ignored or returned, he then hit on the idea of impressing theatre managers by writing to them on his employer's letterhead. One day, however, the solicitor accidentally opened an envelope addressed, care of the firm, to his clerk, and with some astonishment read: "Dear Sir, Your stuff is no earthly use to me. For God's sake fetch it away as soon as possible." On being sent for, Arthur confessed his crime and was sternly admonished not merely for purloining the firm's notepaper but for associating it with bad plays. That was the end of the affair, though, and over the next year or so his weekly salary was increased to twenty-five and, ultimately, thirty shillings.[41]

Pinero later claimed that finding himself in those days with half a crown to call his own "was an experience as exciting as it was rare."[42] But a letter to Aunt Eliza suggests he was more often out than in at night:

> 69A Great Queen Street, WC.
> April 7th, 1873.
>
> My dear Mrs Schneider
> I repeat,
> My dear Mrs Schneider
>   I write amidst the din of children. Pardon therefore, the apparent wandering of a usually brilliant & imaginative intellect. On Thursday night last (3rd day of April A.D. 1873) I abstained from seeking pleasure abroad, & settled down quietly by the fireside of my humble though honest home. "Ah!" said I to myself, "visitors will surely come tonight to alleviate the hongwe (French) which oppresses me" — but nobody comed. I merely mentn. this to show that you & your three little girls (two of whom I address by this post) have not been absent from my mind — "Though lost to site, to memory deer" (Poetry). On Saturday evening I attended the first performance of *Fleur de Ly*s a detailed account of which I send your eldest daughter (Lilly). . . .[43]

Whatever his reputed lack of funds, Arthur contrived to see an astonishing range of performances, including each new role by Irving, who a year or so earlier had suddenly blazed forth at the Lyceum with his spellbinding portrayal of the conscience-stricken murderer in Leopold Lewis's *The Bells*. In another letter to the Schneiders (20 April 1873), Arthur describes a similar Irving vehicle, *The Fate of Eugene Aram*, as "a very fine play — rather melancholy and ghastly," adding that in order to see it he had "waited from 5.30 at the doors & even then only sat in the 3rd row."

Some four months later he experienced a key event in his theatre-going life: a performance at an East End theatre of T. W. Robertson's celebrated comedy *Caste*. It was given by the Prince of Wales's Theatre company, which, led by the brilliant comedienne Marie Wilton (Mrs

Bancroft) and her husband, was establishing a high standard of realistic acting and presentation in England. Many years later, after the death of the actress who became Lady Bancroft, Pinero evoked the occasion in a nostalgic letter to her husband, by then his oldest and closest friend:

> That red-letter night in unsavory Shoreditch! Outside the theatre, the thick air of a warm evening, presently to be fouled by the naptha lamps of the gutter tradesmen; the incessant bawling of those gentry; the garish display of cheap wares in the shop-windows; the jostling and shoving of the loiterers on the pavement; and the sensation of complete happiness, almost choking in its intensity, because one was going to the play! And the fight for a front seat in the pit; the contentment, after a terrific struggle resulting in a torn jacket and the limpest of shirt-collars, at finding oneself in possession of about eight inches of bare board; and then settling down to enjoy the blended odours, peculiar to the popular theatre of that day, of gas and stale orange-peel, than which no more agreeable smell could greet the nostrils of a stage-struck youth! Then the tuning-up by the orchestra — joyful discord — and the unheeded playing of a "selection"; and the rising of the curtain, the sudden hush of voices, and lo! there is the poor shabby room on the ground floor of the lodging-house at Stangate! "George" appears, followed by "Hawtree"; they talk and I wonder that their talk should be so different from the talk that I have heard in other plays; then comes "Papa Eccles" who can "tell a real gentleman with half a sov"; then when Papa, the half-sovereign in his dirty fist, has shuffled away to meet a friend round the corner, "Esther" steals in; and then — oh then — "Enter Polly, D.R.H." as the stage-direction says, and in a moment the audience is enraptured by the brightest, freshest, sweetest little woman that ever gladdened ears or eyes in or out of a playhouse![44]

Marie Wilton's acting had been a revelation to Arthur because of its combination of apparent naturalness with a professionalism that enabled her, "while keeping strictly within the picture-frame, to button-hole, as it were, each individual member of the audience. The man on the farthest bench of the gallery, as well as the man in the stalls, was flattered by her skill into believing that she was acting specially for him."[45] And he was equally impressed by the genteel revolution in dramatic style implicit in Robertson's comedy, dealing as it did with "the merest everyday stories — stories of the joys and sorrows of ordinary, unromantic people, stories of youth and age, love, parting and reunion, of quarrels and reconciliation, of modest acts of chivalry and self-sacrifice, the whole stippled with a thousand humorous and pathetic touches, yet narrated in language devoid of ornament and set in surroundings of the most commonplace description."[46]

In short, the performance of Wilton and the company, the realistic mounting of Robertson's play, and its artful simplicity of plot and dialogue inspired Arthur with a vision of a new style of drama that, rather than relying on rhetoric and sensationalism, would faithfully reflect everyday life. But Robertson's comedies — often sentimental and even melodramatic despite the realistic detail — had not made much impact on British drama. Indeed, with the exception of one or two pieces, such as James Albery's *Two Roses* (1871), the development of genteel realism would have to wait until Arthur was ready to take up and greatly advance on Robertson's work. Near the end of his career, Pinero summed up in unflattering terms the general condition of British theatre during the 1860s and 1870s:

> It was a theatre, so far as the higher aims of the drama were concerned, of faded outworn tradition. Shakespeare was acted pretty regularly in a plodding, uninspired way; but for modern poetic drama audiences were still asked to listen to the jog-trot rhetoric of James Sheridan Knowles and to the claptrap of Edward Bulwer Lytton. For the rest the staple fare at our playhouses consisted mainly of pirated versions of pieces of foreign origin and the works of Dion Boucicault, Byron and a few others of smaller talent. The cribs from the French and German were lurid melodramas, comedies unfolding intricate plots with a stilted verbosity of dialogue, and farces emasculated in the process of translation till nothing remained but humour of a boisterous and elementary kind. Boucicault's vast output was for the most part of the ultra-sensational school, while Byron and his compeers contented themselves with rapidly turning out burlesques and extravaganzas, which were found amusing in proportion to the number of puns they contained, and those domestic dramas which had no more semblance to life than in stature a flea has to an elephant.[47]

Birdseye view of Gravesend at the present moment.

Gravesend from another point of view

Portrait of the only person at present out of doors

The Doors of Gravesend Theatre — as they appeared last evening at the time for opening

A. W. Pinero, *sketches of Gravesend, included in a letter to Lilly and Chrissy Schneider (University of Rochester Library)*

As a stagestruck boy, however, Arthur was not at all put off by the blatant artifice and exaggeration of the contemporary theatre. In fact, he fancied his own acting powers and longed for applause. At the end of September 1873, he went on a brief tour with his Birkbeck group, presenting a programme of recitals and short plays in Ilfracombe, Gravesend, and Bristol. Their opening engagement, as he frankly confessed to Aunt Eliza (1 October 1873), was less than a resounding success: "We suffered in consequence of the evening being fine. Everybody went on the promenade. Therefore, although we have certainly cleared something, it is not sufficient to warrant our staying longer in this detestable place of enjoyment. We therefore leave precipitately." He was still cheerful enough, nonetheless, to pose for his aunt the following conundrum: "Why are we like the lady whose remains were found in the Thames? Because we are cut up, but in excellent spirits."

On his return Arthur was rewarded for his efforts by being appointed reader to the elocution class, "to act on alternate nights with Mr Wright," according to an entry in the institution's minutes for 20 October 1873. The group's next production was *Plot and Passion* by Tom Taylor, a playwright Arthur later rated more highly than others of the period. Arthur was cast in the lead comedy role of the shady detective Maximilian Desmarets. He informed his aunt (6 November 1873) that the elaborate makeup he was planning for the part involved shaving off his moustache, but despite this sacrifice, he modestly declined to recommend the production: "I haven't any idea whether it will be amusing or not — in addition I do not like to cry my wares too loudly. Still, if you care abt. coming to the Institution on Wednesday next, there will be a knife & fork ready (on the stage in the farce). So please write and let us know."

Meanwhile, as letters to the Schneider menage indicate,[48] his theatregoing continued unabated: Bulwer-Lytton's *Richelieu* at the Lyceum ("It is the finest perfce. Irving has given"); Robertson's *School* at the Prince of Wales's ("words fail to describe it. Coghlan will send you away delirious."); the singer Emily Soldene ("You must see Soldene at the Gaiety. There is no comparison betw. Julia Mathews and her. She is immensely superior. There now!"); Mary Elizabeth Braddon's *Griselda; or, the Patient Wife* at the Princess's Theatre; Mrs

John Wood in Charles Reade's *The Wandering Heir* at the Queen's Theatre; the comedian J. L. Toole in Isaac Bickerstaff's *The Hypocrite* at the Gaiety ("I have been in a most unsettled state all day, suffering from a complaint called Toole."); Andrew Halliday's *Heart's Delights* at the Globe; and (provoking a sequence of awful puns) even the circus: "I went to *Sangers* on Thursday. A man *sang us* a song. It gave us *sangersfaction* & we applauded, but the fellow did not *thankus* for our kindness. (Play upon words). I witnessed the evolutions of a Mlle. Di Kostki in her wonderful bare backed performance. (This requires a little explanatn. — I should say, wonderful bare backed *steed* performance — pardon me). It was announced to have been given before all the crowned heads of Hoxton, so you may judge it was good."[49]

But he was becoming increasingly restless and dissatisfied. Writing to Aunt Eliza (12 March 1874) to apologize for not having visited her during a recent illness, he explained, "You know when you were too ill to see me I *did not* come — & when you got better I *could not* come. You don't know how full of bother and anxiety I have been about one thing & the other. *I have not been to a play for about three weeks.*"[50]

The cause of his depression was simple: he had determined to go on the stage but did not know how. Amateur theatricals seemed increasingly futile. A recent performance by the elocution class at Greenwich, for example, had ended in bathos when the curtain jammed and the corpse of the leading character walked off in full view of the audience.[51] Somehow the family income had increased to a point where his weekly wage was no longer essential, and his mother was prepared, if tearfully, to let him go. But how could he, lacking theatrical connections or influence, make a start?

The answer seemed to be through a theatrical agent, so every week — while still prudently continuing with his job — Arthur climbed the stone staircase leading to the office of one of these gentlemen. More than forty years later, when introducing a theatrical novel by another writer, he confessed that he had neither forgotten nor forgiven the agent's treatment of him: "He sits before me at this moment . . . a most shocking bully. I can see myself standing in his awful presence . . . and can hear myself asking him, perhaps for the third time within a month, if he "had anything for me"; and his contemptuous reply, "Look heah! Would yer like yer money back?" cuts into me now, as I recall it, almost as sharply as if I had only just felt the lick of the whip."[52]

And so the days dragged on for Arthur, his dream of a professional career seeming no more than a mirage, as remote and unapproachable as the portrait-lined dining room on the far side of the ground-floor windows of the Garrick Club.

...2...
"General Utility"

i. Rebirth

On Sunday, 26 April 1874, the following small advertisement appeared in the *Era*, a weekly paper shared by the theatrical profession and the licensed victuallers" trade:

THEATRE ROYAL, EDINBURGH. WANTED an entire COMPANY, for the Summer Season, under the direction of Messrs NEVIN, ARCHER and DALY. Good Burlesque *Artistes* please state lowest terms.

It seems likely Arthur had replied to similar advertisements without success, for though he duly wrote off to the Edinburgh Theatre Royal stating his lowest terms, he did not bother to mention his doing so in a letter written three days later (during office hours) to the Schneiders. He was thinking of leaving town in early June, he told them, and there was some prospect of his playing "for one night, under a nom de plume, at the Victoria, or some other 11th rate theatre, for the purpose of shewing an Agent fellow what I can do." At the moment, though, the main excitement in store was taking his mother and Fanny the following Saturday to see Irving's terrifying performance in *The Bells* — a prospect that so alarmed them that he anticipated "awful difficulty" even getting them into the theatre. And after threatening to advertise in the paper to find a fiancé for Lilly ("Personal applicatn. can be made to L.S., 14 Kingsdown Road, N."), he ended the letter abruptly, explaining "my Governor is hovering restlessly about and I must perforce conclude."[1]

A week later (6 May 1874) Aunt Eliza must have been astounded to receive a jubilant letter from her nephew featuring a sketch of himself in Highland dress playing the bagpipes: "Here you see represented your humble servant as he will appear in a very short time. You will be pleased to know that on the 4th inst. I concluded an engagement with the Lessee of the Theatre Royal Edinburgh where I 'open' on the 22nd of next month." Arthur went on to say that as the Theatre Royal was considered next to a London theatre in position, he considered himself not altogether unfortunate, that he intended in future to restrict his diet "exclusively to the native porridge of 'the land of my adoption' " and that Ma and Fanny had been "paralyzed" by *The Bells*.

Now that he had secured an engagement as a professional actor — if only as a "general utility" (or bit-part actor) for some six weeks — he formally resigned his post as honorary reader to the elocution class. The Birkbeck Institution's general committee noted Mr Pinero's resignation "with great regret" in its minutes, adding that he had "distinguished himself by the ability he has displayed" and that the committee wished "to convey to him its sincere thanks for the valuable service he has rendered to the Institution."[2] To mark his retirement Arthur gave the class a farewell performance, modestly choosing the role of Hamlet for the occasion.

For a few weeks he continued to bask in the admiration of his former classmates, particularly that of a friend, Tom Tolman, with whom he viewed the latest exhibition at the Royal Academy, admired a new tenor at the opera, and watched Irving play the title role in Hamilton Aide's *Phillip* at the Lyceum. On this last occasion the behaviour of the new recruit to the professional stage was, as he admitted to his aunt (1 June 1874), less than seemly: "When Irving made his entrance (finding he wore the same clothes as on the production of the piece) we quietly said, loud enough to be heard all over the house, 'What! those clothes not worn out yet?' The effect was electrical — Irving seemed overcome by his feelings for a moment."

Arthur was conscious, however, that he would soon have to find his own costumes — not to mention board, lodgings, and everything else — on a pound a week from the Theatre Royal, so he kept on his clerk's job until a few days before leaving for Edinburgh. In the meantime Lucy Pinero, once she had recovered from learning that her son really was "going upon the stage," busied herself searching the suburbs for a more "suitable habitation" for herself and her daughters than the shoemaker's rooms. She also bought her son a huge travelling trunk that left a permanent imprint on his memory:

> It was of oak, and was bound in massive iron clamps which rusted and wounded the fingers; and it was the most obstinate and cruelly-disposed box my existence has ever brought me into contact with. For instance, when open its lid would hang lazily back, supported by a chain, at an angle which apparently made it impossible that it should close without human aid. Yet whenever I was unwary enough to trust my head within its jaws in search of some article or other lying deep down in the swallow of the beast, down would come the lid to strike me upon the neck and nearly kill me after the fashion in which a rabbit is slain by a keeper.[3]

Lucy's intention seems to have been to provide her boy with some respectable ballast in an otherwise unstable profession. He did his best to appear grateful for the gift, knowing she felt some comfort that it was going with him on his journey.

At last the fateful day arrived — a day Arthur was later to describe, only half-jokingly, as that of his rebirth. At King's Cross, Lucy, Fanny, and little Mary bid him a tearful farewell as he struggled on board the train with his trunk. Nor were the omens on his arrival at the Waverley Railway Station more favourable. It was raining, and a large tip was needed to bribe a porter to consign the trunk to the left luggage department. Then, weary and miserable, Arthur trudged off towards Prince's Street in search of a hotel he had been told was comfortable and cheap. Years later he recalled his disillusionment:

> I entered it dog-tired and in the dark, and when I left it I was thoroughly shaken and demoralized. It may have possessed all the advantages my friend claimed for it — I was totally without experience, as

became one newly-born, in such matters. I am inclined now to think it was even a ridiculously cheap establishment. But it was dear to me, poor simple infant that I was — horridly, unexpectedly, overwhelmingly costly. The first shock of discovery had passed when I paid my bill, and I handled my few gold pieces like a man in a dream. I knew at that moment exactly how a great speculator feels upon receiving news of utter ruin; and, oddly enough, I have never since then found myself able to give a first glance at an hotel bill without feeling the same sensations, the painful catch in the breath, the icy spine, the chill tingling in the legs, which I endured upon discovering my liabilities at my first hotel.[4]

He next took shelter at a Leith Street temperance hotel that proved no more welcoming. It was run by a scarlet-faced landlady who claimed to offer "special terms." These turned out to be an undertaking "for which no extra charge was to be made": to allow Arthur to take the place in her affections formerly occupied by a nephew who had drowned in Greenock Harbour. Most of the work at the hotel, however, was done by the woman's thin, dry, hard-featured daughter, who always wore her sleeves rolled up above the elbow, enabling the new lodger to note that "the skin of her poor arms was not in the least degree a perfect fit."[5]

It was a place of "awful barrenness and frigidity." According to the only other guest, however, it had one merit: that, in common with other Scottish "palaces of temperance," if one went to bed early and then rang the bell noisily, the landlady was obliged according to the law of the land to produce a bottle of whiskey and leave it by the bedside.[6] No doubt had Arthur had to stay there for more than a short time he would have been driven to this expedient or, alternatively, tempted to emulate the landlady's nephew. After a week, however, he was able to leave for much more satisfactory lodgings.

ii. The Theatre Royal

Despite this discouraging start, the young actor — whom I will now refer to either by his theatrical nickname of "Pin" or, more formally,

Pinero — soon warmed to Edinburgh. "The place is really magnificent," he enthused in his first dispatch to Aunt Eliza (18 June 1874), adding that the city exceeded his expectations and that the people were very polite and well behaved — except for the police, who were "either fearfully stupid or confoundedly cautious." Probably the latter regarded him with the suspicion minor Scottish officials traditionally applied to persons associated with the stage. That there were many citizens who did support the drama was amply demonstrated by the grandeur of the Theatre Royal. This was the third theatre to have been built on the same site in Broughton Street during the previous twenty years, the earlier ones having been destroyed by fires that local zealots attributed to the wrath of God. The present building, erected in 1865, featured a splendid vestibule decorated with statues and valuable engravings, and a handsome auditorium seating more than 2,500 people.[7]

The backstage facilities were equally impressive. The large stage, which extended from the proscenium arch to the back wall of the building, had an elaborate system of traps and a three-storey fly-tower, and on either side there was ample space for all the necessary service areas: dressing rooms, wardrobe, carpenters" and painters" shops, a gas room where the tanks of oxygen and hydrogen required for the limelights were stored, and business offices for Mr Nevin, the treasurer, and Mr R. H. Wyndham, the manager. Moreover, not to tempt providence, special precautions had been taken against fire with the installation of a massive iron safety curtain behind the proscenium arch and a 2,000-gallon water cistern above the stage.

With the sole exception of young Pinero, the company engaged for the six-week summer season consisted of experienced actors, most of them well known to the city's theatregoers. The season was being directed by Nevin (assisted by Mr Daly, conductor of the theatre orchestra, and John Archer, a popular local actor) to give Wyndham a well-earned rest before he undertook his last season of management.

As in other provincial theatres of the time, the resident company provided the supporting cast required by visiting stars who performed with them for a week or so before moving on. The work was demanding, calling for almost instant recall of many standard roles and a good

"swallow" (the ability to learn a dozen new parts in a week if necessary), though the task was somewhat eased in that each actor specialised in a particular line of business or type of role, such as "leading
gentleman," "first old woman," "singing chambermaid," "light comedian," or "second old man."

As a "general utility," Pin was, of course, at the bottom of the
company hierarchy, but the on-the-job training he received was valuable for the novice who was observant and eager to learn. Indeed, he
was lucky to have such an engagement, because the stock company
system was dying out. Within a decade the growing practice of assembling full casts to tour London successes around the provinces would
kill off nearly all of the old stock companies. Later, when as a successful
playwright-producer he found himself directing untrained actors in
his plays, Pinero would recall his time at the Edinburgh Theatre Royal
as a vanished golden age.

If at first he felt rather lonely at the theatre, Pin soon struck up a
friendship with a young actor called Garside who had also been
engaged for utility work. The two took long walks, attended rehearsals, and made props together during the days leading up to the opening
of the season. Garside was horrified to learn where Pin was staying;
only stars ever thought of putting up at hotels, even of the temperance
variety. Ordinary actors dwelt in modest lodgings under — if they were
lucky — the watchful care of sympathetic and tolerant landladies.
Garside claimed to reside with the most perfect of these: a generous
soul who even indulged his craving for smoked herrings at breakfast
provided he kept his window open the rest of the day. With a husband
and two little girls to look after, she had no room for a second lodger,
but Garside was able to recommend a landlady of almost equal benevolence. Pin accordingly left the temperance hotel with great relief and
took up residence at 20 Alva Place, just off the London Road en route
to Portobello.

Alva Place, as Pinero later described it, was

> a small colony of six or seven regular little streets . . . formed of
> neatly-built, somewhat dwarfish, stone tenements. The construction
> of these little houses was peculiar. They were obviously houses

possessing one storey but this advantage was for the eye only, for the ingenious architect had so contrived it that the first floor of one of these cottages was not accessible to the ground-floor tenant, unless that tenant put himself to the trouble of walking round into the next street, where he might gain admittance by means of a tiresome flight of stairs built outside the back of his premises. As a matter of fact, however, the first and second floor had nothing to do with each other but were as twins, held together by a vital unseverable ligature, who were not on speaking terms.[8]

The neighbourhood was rather gloomy, especially in bad weather, when the distant roaring of the sea mingled with the beating of wind and rain on the roofs of the tenements, but Pin was happy with his lodgings because of the kindness of his landlady, a silver-haired woman who had been in service at Dalkeith Palace:

She had the soft tread and subdued voice of one accustomed to move about vast chambers and to seek to avoid the echoes lurking upon broad staircases. Sometimes she would talk to me of the Palace, especially when, upon a show-day, I had been viewing its rich stores; and then she would tell me, in her habitual half-whisper, where that door, or that, closed against such as I, led to. And standing in the middle of my little room as she talked, a light would come into her grey eyes which seemed to make my walls recede, to enable her to look beyond them.[9]

This gentle woman not only fed and sheltered him but looked after his clothes and instructed him how to get the best value out of his pound a week so as to emerge, "even at the week's end, with a modest balance to the good." Pin was conscience-stricken when, a few days after his arrival, she received a vicious blow from the lid of his travelling trunk while she was tidying it up for him. He immediately arranged to sell it to a dealer in secondhand goods who offered him "an absurdly low figure . . . on account of the expense of cart-hire for a removal" but collected the trunk on foot, aided by several members of his family, while Pin was busy at the theatre. Though he felt some remorse for disposing so cheaply of his mother's gift, the shared relief at finally having got rid of the thing cemented good relations with his landlady.

Meanwhile the theatre's summer season was under way, featuring a typical selection of visiting celebrities: Wybert Reeve, a sinister Count Fosco in Wilkie Collins's thriller, *The Woman in White;* the popular American musical comedian J. K. Emmet; and two rising young actresses, Ellen L. Wallis, who specialised in standard serious pieces (such as Knowles's *The Hunchback* and Bulwer-Lytton's *The Lady of Lyons*), and Marie Rhodes, whose range extended from bur- lesque to melodrama. Pin made his debut in the tiny part of a groom in *The Woman in White*, got on quite well with Emmet (who offered only one play, *Fritz, Our Cousin German*), was kept busy by Miss Wallis (who changed her bill every night), and was even busier during Miss Rhodes's fortnight "swallowing" new parts, one or two of which (such as Radamanthus, the Lord Chancellor of Hell, in H. J. Byron's *Orpheus and Eurydice*) were reasonably demanding. His best role, however, came at the end of the season when he was cast as the lust-stricken Captain Crosstree in Douglas Jerrold's famous nautical melodrama, *Black Ey'd Susan*, played on Saturday, 1 August 1874, as a benefit for the retiring management team of Nevin, Archer, and Daly.

"Taking a retrospective view of my doings for the last six weeks you will be glad to hear that I am *very satisfied*," Pin told Aunt Eliza in a letter written on 2 August. "I have been put forward very much by the management, & the other day, Mrs Wyndham (the manageress of *next season*) sent me a message that 'she was very pleased with me & that it would be my own fault if I did not get on' — so far so good." In reply to a query from his aunt as to whether he had found any unpleasant- ness through envy or jealousy from his fellow actors, he admitted that "such feelings do make themselves apparent, but if you look at it as a mere matter of business, it is of no consequence." He had been engaged for the next season but without any raise in salary — an omission he described in his next letter (13 August) as "rather mangy" but that he put down to the fact that the company for the coming season had been hired during his second week at the theatre, when he had only played a groom and a policeman. "Next season," he added, "I shall get an engagement specifically for walking Gents. At present I am merely in my *novitiate*."

For the next month or so, however, he was out of a job. An attempt to fill in the time with some law clerking ended ignominiously when the solicitor who engaged him saw Pinero named on a Theatre Royal playbill and sacked him forthwith.[10] (This was not the only example of prejudice against the stage he encountered in Edinburgh, a more comical one being the refusal of an old fishwife to supply his landlady with fish because of the vendor's deadly hatred of "play-arkers," as she called them.) So for two or three weeks before the autumn season, Pin had, as he put it, "to do the gentleman."[11]

While "resting," he took the chance to observe "Mdlle Beatrice and her celebrated company" fulfil their customary engagement at the Theatre Royal prior to appearing at the Haymarket Theatre for the start of the London season. Pin was particularly impressed by their performance of Octave Feuillet's drama *The Sphinx*. "It is intensely interesting from beginning to end and well acted throughout," he reported to Aunt Eliza (13 August 1874). "It has, however, in common with most French pieces, a rather unhealthy tone about it, and you leave the theatre after seeing it with a nasty taste in your mouth. The death of the woman at the end is distressingly horrible. Nevertheless it is a wonderful piece & shd. be seen without fail." He added that the lead actress was "one of the few women who wear handsome dresses (really handsome dresses) on the English stage" and that (for women in the audience, at least) her costumes alone were worth the price of admission. Twenty years later similar remarks would be made about his own plays — *and* their costuming.

The Theatre Royal's autumn season began splendidly when "a brilliant and enthusiastic audience" welcomed the return of Edward Sothern from his latest tour of the United States. Sothern had made himself into a star of the first magnitude some sixteen years earlier when he had created the role of Lord Dundreary in the New York premiere of *Our American Cousin*, a mediocre Tom Taylor piece. And *created* is the appropriate word: as an almost unknown young English actor, Sothern had refused to play what was then a quite insignificant and dull part unless he was allowed entirely to rewrite it. He had his way (the author being safely out of reach in England), and the hilarious caricature of the bewhiskered English swell he invented so delighted

American audiences that it made his reputation in the States. Two years later Sothern's Dundreary enjoyed a run of nearly 400 performances in London at the Haymarket, and he had since repeated the role thousands of times in the United States and Britain without, it was said, ever appearing stale or mechanical.

For this appearance at the Theatre Royal, Sothern was playing both Dundreary and another of his famous parts, the title role in Robertson's early play *David Garrick*. Each year he was welcomed as eagerly by the theatre staff and company as by the public because of his high spirits, his excellent cigars (he was one of the very few actors Mr Wyndham allowed to smoke backstage), his tolerance of the crochets of old actors, and his encouragement of young ones. When Pin asked him what the most valuable attribute was that an actor needed, Sothern told him "repose" and then smilingly advised him the surest way to gain it: "Play 'second heavies,' my boy, for five years as I did. When you have to stand listening night after night to the long, dreary, deep-voiced utterances of the 'first heavy man' you will in the course of years acquire 'Repose'!"[12]

During Sothern's season Pin played an alderman in *David Garrick* and, with the zeal of the novice, piled on the makeup until he looked a shocking sight. Sothern made no comment but two or three nights later entered the greenroom looking, as Pinero later recalled, uncharacteristically annoyed.

> Glancing in my direction he said, "The presumption of modern audiences is getting unbearable. The latest mode of criticism takes the form of impertinent letters from the front. Tonight I rant, tomorrow I'm inaudible. And now some presuming person says that your face reminds him of Vesuvius in eruption! It's unendurable." I agreed cordially with Sothern, played my scene, and then in my dressing-room examined my face in the glass. The next night Alderman ——— was an altered being. "Good Gracious!" said Sothern when he met me, "You've actually bowed to the writer of that d——d impudent letter! If I were you I should stick to my colours. However I dare say you are wiser than I." I replied magnanimously that I thought I had done the right thing, and then caught sight of Sothern's face in the greenroom mirror. He was winking at my manager, who was dressed for Squire Chevy. With that wink a light burst upon me.[13]

Pin was sorry when Sothern's brief visit ended. He had been jolly company and not in the least stuck-up; instead always ready to have a chat with a young "fellah" while waiting in the wings. Such liberties could not be taken with the next star, Mary Frances Scott-Siddons — a granddaughter of the great Sarah Siddons — who for twelve nights presented her impersonations of Juliet, Rosalind, Katherine, Lady Teazle, and Pauline Deschapelles. On her departure Pin confessed in a letter to Aunt Eliza (20 September 1874) that the "fortnight's harassing labour at the 'Legitimate' " had left him thoroughly exhausted.

He had acted in all seven of Scott-Siddons's pieces (not to mention the farces that followed them) and had been especially nervous about the long leading part of Sir Geoffrey of Orange in a historical drama called *King René's Daughter*. He had been rather proud, however, of his depiction of Le Beau as a young fop in *As You Like It* and of his role as Snake in *The School for Scandal*. Despite his experience with Sothern, he was still plastering on the makeup and had given this last character "a very sallow complexion, red eye-brows and very weak-looking eyes." So pleased was he with the result that he had bowed approvingly several times to his reflection in the greenroom mirror before removing his makeup.[14]

Scott-Siddons was followed by the popular comedienne Mrs John Wood ("the Queen of Burlesque"), who excelled in playing boisterous female characters. (Some ten years later she was to star in several notable Pinero farces in London at the Court Theatre.) Pin, not needed onstage during Mrs Wood's season, watched from the audience her appearances in well-mounted productions of Byron's *An American Lady* and Boucicault's *London Assurance*. In the second of these she played a lively Lady Gay Spanker, and it may well have been her performance in this role that sowed the seed in Pin's mind for the character of the horsy Georgiana Tidman in *Dandy Dick*. She was followed by Kate Josephine Bateman (Mrs Crowe), the eldest of the four daughters of "Colonel" H. L. Bateman, Irving's manager at the Lyceum. With her was John Clayton who, coincidentally, would later play opposite Mrs John Wood in *Dandy Dick*, creating the role of Georgiana's brother, the hapless Dean of St Marvells. However, both Mrs Wood and Clayton were eclipsed for the moment in Pin's eyes by the next star who visited the Theatre Royal — the legendary Charles Mathews.

Nearly forty years earlier Mathews and his first wife, Lucia Elizabeth Vestris, had pioneered a new style of scenic realism in the English theatre during their remarkable tenure of the Olympic Theatre. Mme Vestris had now been dead for twenty years, but Mathews — author of more than thirty farces and light comedies, mostly written to display his inimitable gifts as a performer — remained the outstanding light comedian of the age. Pin had greatly looked forward to meeting him, but found the gap between the man and his stage persona disconcerting:

> As I walked down to the theatre one sharp leaden morning in October I smacked my lips at the prospect of meeting the delicately fashioned little gentleman with the perfect hands, slim nether limbs, and the elegant sloping shoulders. I expected, I suppose, to renew my acquaintance with the familiar yellow or fawn-coloured kid gloves; the folded handkerchief, with its corner peeping from the pocket; the dapper little shirt-collar, and all the other characteristics so well-known to the public. I almost expected to see the well-shaped little foot being flourished in the air, the owner's custom when he desired to express the recklessness of the spendthrift or defiance of a domineering mother-in-law. What I did find was a rather shabbily-dressed old gentleman — very cold and a little peevish — sitting at the "prompt" table and smoking an evil-smelling cigar.[15]

Mathews never rehearsed when on tour. This did not trouble the old hands at the theatre but helped to thoroughly unnerve Pin when he acted that night with the veteran in *A Game of Speculation*.

> The quaint-looking, white-stocked, incisive gentleman I found on the stage was so appallingly unlike the Mathews of the morning that my small share of self-possession quite deserted me. I failed to take up my cues. Accustomed, as a country actor used to be, to hear the last few words of every speech given with peculiar stress as a sign that the speaker had nothing more to say, I was simply floored when the short crisp sentences fell glibly and naturally from Mr Affable Hawke's lips. I had, of course, studied the cues, and I recognised them in my mind, but they came upon me in so novel a manner that my tongue

absolutely declined to acknowledge them. Mathews quickly saw through the state of affairs, and with a reassuring wink slipped his finger through the button-hole of my coat and led me down to the footlights. Gradually my courage returned. When my cue came Mathews tugged at my coat; if I spoke he listened; if I failed to speak he went on. I apologised afterwards for my shortcomings. "Capital, my boy, capital!" said he, patting me on the shoulder. "Capital; a *quiet, unobtrusive* performance."[16]

Several nights later Pin was again caught out by inexperience. It was "fast week" in Edinburgh, a time when respectable citizens were expected to forgo worldly pleasure. In a vain attempt to lure audiences back into the theatre, Mathews presented a different programme of plays every night. Standing in the wings with him before the star made his entrance in yet another farce, Pin was taken by surprise when Mathews suddenly called out in a loud voice, "Where on earth is my umbrella?" Concerned that a vital prop was missing, Pin cried, "I'll fetch it, sir!" and rushed to the star's dressing room. "Quick, quick," he ordered the dresser, "Mr Mathews is waiting for his umbrella!" The man looked at him with a grin and replied, "Lor bless you, sir, that's all right. He *always* says that at the door before he goes on in this piece."[17]

And so, as the nights grew longer and colder, visiting stars came and went at the Theatre Royal. Ada Cavendish stayed a fortnight playing Mercy Merrick in a Collins piece, *The New Magdalen,* and a selection of Shakespearian heroines. Pin found her "a delightful creature" with "not a sensation of pride about her" and told Aunt Eliza (22 November 1874) that everybody in the theatre had been sorry when she left. The Drury Lane tragedian Henry Talbot played Shylock, Othello, and Richard III as Pin struggled with Lorenzo, Montano, and Catesby, finding Catesby, with no fewer than twenty-five entrances, particularly demanding. "It is the most difficult (though a bad) part I have ever played," he informed Aunt Eliza (22 November 1874). "We pull'd it off last night, and I was never so nervous in all my life." Next came John Clarke, who had been in the original cast of Robertson's Crimean comedy *Ours* and was now presenting the play on tour. Pin was entrusted with the major role of Prince Perovsky, originally created by the masterly John Hare. After this, the theatre's autumn season ended with a ten-night run of the popular Boucicault melodrama *Arrah-na-pogue*, with Wyndham himself playing Shaun the Post.

iii. End of an Idyll

Pin had been at the Edinburgh Theatre Royal six months. Although the increasingly important roles allotted to him suggest he was developing into a useful supporting actor, his failure yet to be noticed in the *Era* hints that he was unlikely to become a star. He was, however, gaining a detailed knowledge of working conditions in the professional theatre and acquiring useful contacts with a number of leading actors. All this was to be of enormous value to the later dramatist.

For the moment, though, he was enjoying himself immensely. Freed from the tedium of the law, he felt in his element. And if Edinburgh was not yet impressed by his talents, he had admirers back in London — his family, the Schneiders, and Tolman and Wright of the Birkbeck group — who all received fairly regular letters and in return kept him up-to-date on the London theatre scene. He was, too, enjoying a lively, if economical, social life with the younger members of the Theatre Royal company. Years later, imagining himself back in Edinburgh telling the son he never had about his youthful acting days, he waxed lyrical:

> I would push on to the edge of the broad Loch upon whose sapphire surface it was my wont in times of prolonged frost to venture timorously, and here I would tell of certain nocturnal excursions in midwinter in the company of boon companions, recalling nights which stained the whole countryside with their azure; breathless nights whose still air had in it, nevertheless, the sting of the nettle, but whose silence was so profound that till the comparative riot of our own breathing made us presumptuous, we walked, talked and essayed to laugh in solemn measure. And thence I could drag my weary charge along the homeward road my friends and I followed on those long ago winter nights, and I would gently hum to him snatches of the songs

and carols which I and those choice spirits once sang to the ring of the hard soles upon the frozen paths.[18]

Not that this happiness was unalloyed. Pin was distressed when the two little daughters of Garside's landlady suddenly fell ill and died of scarlet fever during an epidemic in early November. He and his friend had often played with them and given them presents of oranges and toys. After the girls' deaths the house and the little garden that had been their playground felt bleak and empty. Such grief was exceptional, but a shadow — which might perhaps have been taken as an omen — had been cast. Though Pin did not know it, his idyll was nearing its end.

For Christmas and New Year the Theatre Royal had prepared a grand pantomime of *Jack and the Beanstalk*, which, according to the *Era*, was "in its splendour of scenery and magnificence of appointments a fitting last to a brilliant series of Christmas entertainments" annually produced by the Wyndhams for the past twenty years. The review praised a succession of "brilliant performances" and eventually noted that "the other chief characters" had been played by "Messrs Henderson, Garside, Pinero and a host of clever juveniles."[19]

This was Pin's first mention in the *Era*, but he was not much excited about it or by his role of Count Tiptopa, for which he wore fake Dundreary whiskers so the clown could shave them off with "foul soapy water and a wooden razor."[20] Writing to Aunt Eliza (16 January 1875), Pin observed: "The monotony of the pantomime precludes my having any startling news to communicate. It is getting rather tiresome — the only enjoyable thing about it is the laughter of the little children in the front of the house." Three weeks later his news was to be startling in the extreme.

On Saturday, 6 February, the members of the Theatre Royal company collected their wages as usual between one and two o'clock in the afternoon from the treasury and after a few minutes' friendly chat went on their way. As there was no performance of the panto that afternoon, the fireproof iron safety curtain had been drawn up ready for the evening's performance. By five past two no one was left in the theatre except for the wardrobe mistress, two assistants attending to costume repairs, and the boxkeeper in his front lobby office.

Suddenly there was an explosion in the backstage gas room followed by a violent rush of air that swung open the glass doors into the foyer and brought several large framed engravings crashing to the floor. Outside, passersby saw a dense cloud of black smoke pouring through the stage roof, which had been partly blown away. The shops had closed a few minutes earlier, so a huge crowd quickly filled every available vantage point, while detachments of police and militia tried to clear them back to a safe distance. By the time the two local manual fire engines arrived on the scene, flames were roaring into the sky, accompanied by thick clouds of smoke and steam, the great water tank over the stage having exploded and vaporized its contents in the intense heat. Only the surrounding buildings could be saved; the Theatre Royal was clearly doomed.[21]

By half past five the building had been reduced to a burnt-out ruin, though this fire, unlike the last one, had involved no loss of life. Wyndham, who had immediately been called from his nearby home, had organized a group of volunteers to save the pictures and statues in the foyer, which for a while was protected from the flames by a solid brick wall. The stock in the theatre tobacco shop was also rescued (the firemen were also especially careful to protect barrels of whiskey valued at £1,000 in the adjoining pub). But nothing survived from inside the theatre except the money and papers in the safe.

The Wyndhams lost £7,000 worth of scenery, not including sets and properties being made for a spectacular production of *Rob Roy* intended as the grand finale of their management. Their entire wardrobe had been destroyed, along with valuable books and papers, including a set of promptbooks that had once belonged to the noted Shakespearean producer Charles Kean. Because of their approaching retirement, they had greatly reduced their insurance cover. The fire was a financial disaster for them.

For their 500 employees the consequences of the fire were no less serious. They were not only out of work, but many had in effect lost the tools of their trade. Daly's entire stock of sheet music had been burnt as had nearly all of the orchestra's instruments, and most of the actors had lost their stage clothes and personal properties.[22]

It was ironic, as Pinero later recorded, that the fire had occurred on a gloriously fine afternoon. As dusk fell he and his stricken companions watched the flames die out in the ill-fated theatre and at last silently turned their backs on its smouldering shell.[23]

...3...
A "Walking Gentleman"

i. Liverpool

The burning of the Edinburgh Theatre Royal brought Pin's first theatrical engagement to an abrupt and shocking end that affected him deeply. It did not weaken his commitment to the stage, but a sense of loss remained long after — a feeling that among the ashes of the gutted building lay part of his youth. Some five years later he wrote several short stories, derived from his Edinburgh days, about members of a stock company in an imaginary town called Chucksford. The disastrous fire that destroys the town's theatre and disbands its company is touched on in each of these tales. "A Theatrical Art Union," for example, tells how an ill-conceived attempt by the actors to form a trade union against their manager (Boother) leads to the accidental burning down of the Chucksford Theatre. The story is mostly fictional, but the ending, with its description of the actors' reaction to the fire, was taken from life:

> The alarm soon spread; but when the rest of us reached the theatre we saw that our winter season was over. There was only one engine in the town (a wretched little thing worked by hand) and within two hours of the outbreak there was nothing of the poor Chucksford Theatre but four white walls bleached by the heat of the flames. Ah! we had no thoughts but kindly ones for the old place then. All its discomforts, our bickerings and quarrels with Boother, and our own little jealousies and squabbles, were forgotten, and we felt as if we had lost a home. One of our fellows, who had been engaged there for

eleven successive seasons, said it seemed to him that he had just buried his mother. Standing with the crowd contemplating the ruins I saw Boother. "Are you satisfied now?" he asked.[1]

Another of these stories, "Capel and Capello,"[2] portrays two friends — a young actor and a violinist from the theatre orchestra — who, after the fire, trudge through winter snows to a town ninety-five miles away in the hope of finding work there. Pin, however, was spared such an ordeal. He was fortunate at this crisis in his career to be offered an engagement in Liverpool at the Royal Alexandra Theatre, managed by Mrs Wyndham's brother-in-law, Edward Saker. Several others of the Theatre Royal company were also going there on the recommendation of the Wyndhams, who, despite their own difficulties, were doing their best to find work for their former employees.

The Liverpool engagement was to begin on 1 March 1875. In the meantime, as the following letter to Aunt Eliza shows, Pin and his colleagues did what they could to help themselves:

> 28 Greensides,
> Edinburgh.
> Feby. 15th 1874 [*sic*]
>
> My dear Aunty,
>   We are busy getting up a benefit concert for next Wednesday night at a large hall in town, and another for Saturday at Leith. I think they will be successes, but there are so many to share the proceeds that very much cannot result from them.
>   As regards the things that I have lost, I shall only replace what I absolutely require — till I reach London, when I can get things so much better than in Edinburgh or Liverpool.
>   I am not very well. After the fire I rushed about a little too much consoling (or trying to) and getting up meetings &c. — and in the end I rather knocked myself up.
>   I think of going to Liverpool about Monday or Tuesday next.
>   With Love and kisses.
>   Dear Aunt,
>   Ever your affecte. Nephew
>   Arthur W. Pinero[3]

Next day he wrote more cheerfully to Tolman. Though he had lost an "enormous amount of clothes and belongings" in the fire, he was pleased about Liverpool and hoped to be back in London for a few days before Easter. During the summer he expected to tour with Emmet, playing "first walking gents" and "dabbling in the juveniles and light comedy," after which he would return to the Alexandra for the winter.[4]

Meanwhile he had to say good-bye to Garside and other Edinburgh friends. Not the least poignant of these partings was from his kindly Alva Place landlady. Twenty years later it was still fresh in his memory: "I can see her now standing at my cab door — with her apron to her eyes if you please — bidding me goodbye and God-speed. As the flyman whipped up his horse, she threw an old silver brooch into my lap — a brooch fashioned like the Arms of a great family, and bearing the motto, 'Amo'. I recognised it as one of her few treasures."[5]

The weather was so cold on his arrival in Liverpool he could hardly hold his pen as he wrote his first letters from digs centrally situated at 8 Gill Street, Pembroke Place. Though he had not had much time to look around, he reported to Aunt Eliza (24 February 1875) that Liverpool seemed "a very fine town, in fact *London the 2nd.*" The previous night he had called at the Alexandra, which he considered the equal of any London theatre, "a kind of cross between the Opera Comique and the Haymarket" with "landings and vestibule . . . very much like those of the London Gaiety."

The enforced move to Liverpool proved helpful to his career. As a newcomer to the Alexandra, Mr A. W. Pinero was immediately noticed in reviews, the *Era* listing him "among the notables of the cast"[6] in his first play, a production of *London Assurance* featuring Charles Mathews as Dazzle. Pin played the insolent manservant, Cool, a small but effective part with some amusingly dry lines. The *Era* also praised him for contributing to the "effective ensemble" in the local production of Boucicault's *Arrah-na-pogue* that followed.[7] The comments did not amount to much, but they encouraged Pin and helped him get work elsewhere when he was not required at the Alexandra. Indeed, where the Edinburgh Theatre Royal had been his second home, the Alexandra proved more of a base from which he ventured forth when opportunities arose.

Just before Easter he did have the hoped-for few days in London. Since the previous November his mother and sisters had been living at 4 Faulden Road in the north London suburb of Stoke Newington — a change of address Pin had greeted with mock horror, claiming that he didn't even know where Stoke Newington was.[8] It was almost nine months since he had seen them. Apart from catching up on family gossip, visiting friends and relations, and shopping to replace clothing lost in the fire, Pin made sure of seeing the Lyceum's "Hundred-Pound *Hamlet*," the production that established Irving as the greatest actor of the age. Shortly afterwards, Pin happened to pass Irving's manager, Colonel H. L. Bateman, in the Strand and noticed how "white and thin and worn out" he was looking.[9] A day or so later Bateman died, leaving his wife to run the theatre where Irving was now the undisputed star. Though Pin had no suspicion of it, his future career was to be decisively influenced and assisted by Irving. Slowly but surely destiny was bringing them together.

Returning to Liverpool, Pin was caught up in intensive rehearsals for the Alexandra's grand Easter production — "An entirely New Spectacular Drama in Five Acts, entitled *Round the Globe, or A Well-Won Wager*." This was an illegal adaptation by a local writer, one J. F. McArdle, of the Jules Verne novel *Around the World in Eighty Days*, which was already enjoying a major success in an authorized stage version at the Princess's Theatre in London. According to the Liverpool *Daily Post*, the Alexandra production was "on a scale of grandeur and magnificence" perhaps never equalled in the city.[10] But as Pin informed Tolman (31 March 1875), there were unfortunate technical hitches on the opening night, such as "when the train knocked down a cottage (which caused me to remark that it had *"brought down the house"*) & when, after the explosion, the top part of the steamboat funnel, instead of dashing into the air, rose gracefully at a speed of about ten yards an hour."

A week or two later the managers of the Princess's Theatre brought an injunction against the Liverpool production, and Saker had to dash off to London to make peace with the rival management. His role in the show was taken over by another actor (whose part was then added to the two Pin was playing already), and the company had to re-re-hearse whole scenes McArdle had hastily rewritten to distance them further from Verne's novel. As a result everyone got thoroughly muddled at the next performance, but all ended happily when the Princess's management accepted a cash payment from Saker and dropped the injunction. After this the production went smoothly except for a last minor mishap. Writing to Tolman (18 April 1875) after the final night, Pin reported that a pea had "got caught in one of the Rifleman's guns and shot a lady (who had been sitting in the dress circle) in the face. Great panic. Doctor sent for and infuriated husband came round to see the governor, etc., etc." Whether Saker had to resort once more to his chequebook is not recorded.

The remainder of the spring season saw Pin appear as "King Dick" in a tableau of "Shakespeare surrounded by his principal creations" to honour the Bard's birthday, and in half a dozen roles during a thinly attended fortnight of serious drama featuring Miss Wallis. Mr Pinero, according to the *Daily Post*, gave "an effectually-sustained Tybalt," and the *Era* praised him for "his powerful Franciscan monk" (Friar Dominic) in *Love's Sacrifice*.[11] During Miss Wallis's engagement he also appeared as Le Beau in *As You Like It*, Lord Tinsel in *The Hunchback*, Timarch in *Ingomer,* and the substantial role of Beauséant, the scorned lover in *The Lady of Lyons*. Small wonder, as he made clear to Tolman (13 May 1875), he was delighted by Emmet's subsequent arrival at the theatre:

> Miss Wallis departed to Dublin on Saturday after giving a fort-night's very hard work and doing bad business.
> Mr Emmet, who gives no trouble at all, playing only one piece during the whole fortnight, is drawing tremendous houses. I calculate he will take about a thousand pounds for his trouble — Mr Saker the same.
> With Emmet we terminate the season, after which my arrangements are — blank. I am not sure whether I will go on tour with him as originally intended. Will however let you know my movements when settled.

I fancy I go to Glasgow in August to assist in the production of *Round the Globe*, thence to Newcastle, opening in Liverpool in September in a grand revival by Calvert of *The Winter's Tale*. We also produce in December, Mr Wilkie Collins' *Armadale*, the rehearsals of which he is coming down to superintend himself. Miss Ada Cavendish has purchased the work.

ii. Various Engagements

A month later, however, Pin found himself in Belfast with a speculative company that was touring a double bill of *The Two Orphans* by the *Times* drama critic John Oxenford and *The Chevalier of the Moulin Rouge*, adapted from the French by C. H. Hazlewood. Pin informed Tolman (22 June 1875) that Belfast had an especially large body of police "in consequence of the riotous disposition of the populus [*sic*]. On the occasion of any disturbance here the men shoot each other like dogs." But there had been no such trouble at the theatre, where "a very enthusiastic house" had given him an extra bow for his fencing in the *Chevalier*'s duel scene. Despite this promising beginning, he had no idea where the tour was going next. "The future arrangements of the company I cannot tell you, and may not know myself until the last moment. They are in the hands of a Mr Weston at Bolton, and whether we go anywhere, or where we go, if we do go, is a matter which time will solve."

In fact they did not go anywhere. Pin fell ill and as soon as the Belfast engagement ended returned to Liverpool, where he recovered in new and more spacious digs. On 5 July he wrote again to Tolman:

> Gladstone Road,
> Edge Hill.
>
> My dear Thomasio,
>   Ma writes me you have called upon her which I am very glad to hear. I dare say you wanted to hear what had become of me. I have not been at all well. The weather here is fearful.
>   I dare say you heard from home that *The Two Orphans* did not go further than Belfast. I had a most enjoyable fortnight there — paid me very well for the time being but nothing further. I am now doing

nothing till about 2nd August, when I think I shall play in *The Two Orphans* here for a fortnight. After that I am uncertain whether I shall open on the 16th at the Alexandra or not. I can if I like, but I have two capital offers from Glasgow, one from the Gaiety & one from the Theatre Royal there. I am dubious as to what to do. The only thing is, I *am* in Liverpool and I am *not* in Glasgow.

I saw *Our Boys* at the Alexandra, last week, capitally played by a good company. Young Garden (Chaucerian Comique) play'd Talbot Champneys and was immense. I saw *Giroflé Giroflá*, also at the Alexandra, last night. It is capitally done on all hands. Kate Lewis is charming.

I perceive there is rather a dearth of theatrical matter in London, and with the bad weather you must feel depressed.

All I ask is — is this July?

My friend John Archer of Edinburgh goes to the Lyceum to play the 2nd Witch. I have seen him do the 1st Wtch. and he used to be immense.

Send me a budget.

> Dear Tom,
> Sincerely yours,
> Arthur W. Pinero.

During his "rest" before the Liverpool season of *The Two Orphans*, Pin sampled the entertainment on offer in the city. He informed Aunt Eliza (26 July 1875) he had seen Mrs John Wood in *The School for Scandal* at the Royal Amphitheatre, an Offenbach opera at the Prince of Wales's, a performance (interrupted by a fire alarm) from George Hamilton and his London Standard company at the Theatre Royal, and "at an obscure place of recreation," Young Sankey, the Negro revivalist, who "sang all M & S's [Moody and Sankey's] hymns to an accompaniment of the bones, tambourine, &c." Pin had emerged from the last of these feeling, he claimed, much improved in his religious tendencies.

He had decided to go to the Gaiety for the month after he finished with *The Two Orphans* as it was not only offering "more coin" but also the bait of his first engagement as "Juvenile Lead." Soon after arriving in Glasgow, he wrote Tolman an interesting letter revealing his increasingly critical judgement of plays and performances — and (in the postscripts) an eye for the main chance:

Mr Whitesides
122 Renfrew St.

August 17th 1875.

My dear Tom,
    Business has prevented my writing.
    I opened last night as Valentine in a revival of *Faust and Marguerite:*
        Faust. E.H.Brooke
        Mephisto. T.Mead
        Marguerite. Rose Leclercq.
    I think I told you in my last that I am here for *four weeks*.
    The Gaiety is a charming little theatre, and embraces now the whole of the patronage of the Glasgow folks. It is nearly new and is small. The "Royal" here is a perfect wilderness in size. Hare and his lot are there now. I saw them play *Nine Days' Wonder* last week in Liverpool. Mrs Vizier and Clayton now take the place of Mr and Mrs Kendal. Clayton is an improvement on Kendal, but Mrs V. being an actress of the *old* school cries and sobs in excess, & though very fine is a little out of the picture — the acting is appreciated in the country, but Everybody says "Is *this* the piece London calls a success?"
    By Jove, they're quite right. It will not stand taking from place to place as a great thing.
    Mr Mead goes back to the Lyceum for the First Witch — Irving is resting.

Dear Tom,
Yours ever,
Arthur W. Pinero

P.S. Rose Leclercq — a delightful woman.
P.S.(2) I make up fair as Valentine, to match the Marguerite — Standing in the entrance with Miss Leclercq last night, she said, "Well, I have a *very* pretty brother." — (always on the lookout for an opportunity) I replied, "It is only a weak attempt to be worthy of such a sister." — She said, "Thanks very much for the compliment, but I'm out of sorts tonight in looks and in temper. My face is spotty and I feel wicked." — Original, eh?

Pin quite enjoyed his spell at the Gaiety, but finding Glasgow "very wet and very dull," occupied his off-stage hours reading all of William Thackeray's novels in turn. Meanwhile, in London, Irving was about to open his controversial production of *Macbeth*. In letters to Aunt Eliza and Tolman written on the same day (9 September 1875), Pin expected they would be at the Lyceum on the first night, repeated that he had friends in the cast, and regretted Irving's intention to omit Matthew Locke's music from the production, as it was "always such a feature, and relieves the gloom of the play."

A week later he was back at the Alexandra, rehearsing for a grand production of Byron's historical tragedy *Sardanapalus* under the direction of Charles Calvert, an actor-manager noted for lavish revivals of classic drama. Pin's role was a major one: the traitor Arbaces, who plots to poison the corrupt king — the latter to be played, of course, by Calvert himself. Drawing on materials recently unearthed at the original site of ancient Nineveh where Sardanapalus once reigned, Calvert aimed "to give in the production . . . as truthful and exact a representation of the manners, habits, architecture and costume of this memorable time as the Assyrian sculptures, tablets and records in the British Museum render possible."[12]

But even in the midst of these rehearsals, the Lyceum's *Macbeth* was a major topic of conversation. Writing to Tolman (15 September 1875), Pin remarked that "the reason the music of *Macbeth* is not to be done is that it is an interruption to the interest of the piece," adding that Calvert had told him that Phelps in his Sadler's Wells revival had also dispensed with it. Irving was determined to banish once and for all the witches' songs inserted into the play by the dramatist William Davenant shortly after the Restoration. In any event, the production proved too innovative for the Lyceum audience when it opened, a week later than originally planned, on Saturday, 25 September. Not only had Locke's music been dropped, but Irving had dared to interpret Macbeth as a fearful assassin rather than the traditional valiant warrior. This radical reassessment upset the preconceptions of both audiences and critics.

Sardanapalus, in contrast, was pronounced a triumph: the *Era* began a full-column review with the claim that the revival was the most

magnificent ever seen on the Alexandra stage and went on to describe
the spectacular settings, culminating in the Hall of Nimrod:

> Huge winged lions, with human heads, support the columns on which
> the roof rests, while receding in the background are the regularly
> jagged outlines of the boldly hewn interior. Banqueting tables of
> ancient form, illuminated by Assyrian lamps, surround the hall;
> while in the centre is built up a sort of pyramid, on the summit of
> which the throne is placed. Here Sardanapalus is seated, with his
> slave-girl Myrrha at his feet, and grouped on the steps of the pyra-
> mid, as well as round the hall, are fan-bearers, dancing-girls, courti-
> ers &c. The sudden change here from dazzling brightness to lurid
> shade, with pealing thunder, flashing lightning, and cowering revel-
> lers is very thrilling. But all pictures fade before the great final
> catastrophe. A vast heap of combustibles is placed round the throne,
> and when fired by Myrrha with lighted torch the flames burst forth
> in flashes, the smoke ascends in thick clouds, and all the genuine
> effects of a terrible conflagration are realised. The splendid pillars
> topple to their fall, the throne and its two occupants disappear amid
> the burning mass, and in a short time what was lately a magnificent
> Court, radiant with barbaric splendour, is reduced to a heap of
> ashes, and the curtain descends upon a scene which is terrible in its
> realistic grandeur. [13]

In the light of this climax, the reviewer's comment that "Mr A.W.
Pinero threw the requisite fire into the role of the impetuous Arbaces'
appears faint praise — he could hardly have competed with Myrrha!
Indeed, some critics were distinctly unflattering about the acting
compared with the scenery and effects. Writing to Aunt Eliza near the
end of the run (15 October 1875), Pin cheerfully referred to "the
remarks of a Liverpool satirical paper called the *Wasp*, which said 'as
for Messieurs Calvert and Pinero, we should like to pin-a-row of such
actors up to a post to show the public to what a level mediocrity can
sink'!!!."

After the spectacle of *Sardanapalus*, it was business as usual again
at the Alexandra. The genial low comedian J. L. Toole (later to give
Pin encouragement as a playwright) appeared for a week at the theatre
in *Our American Cousin* and *David Garrick* before being succeeded
in the same plays by Edward Sothern. Pinero was commended for his

playing of Lieutenant Vernon in the first and Mr Smith, the vulgar tradesman, in the second[14] but could hardly have been at his best, suffering as he was from a severe bout of flu.

His health did not improve during the following fortnight when the stock company played at the Rotunda Theatre in a poor area of Liverpool while an Italian opera company graced the Alexandra. The weather remained thoroughly miserable, but this, as Pin told his aunt (16 November 1875) with a certain snobbish glee, did not deter their audience: "our advent has created some excitement and the houses have [been] crammed to excess nightly. On Saturday the people broke the barricades down 20 minutes before the opening. After the place was full there still remained a crowd outside, and to quiet them, an undertaking was given to repeat the bill the following (this) week. The fun of it was, that it was a pouring wet night and the multitude that did get in simply sat and *steamed*. It looked, from the stage, like a thick fog. The people were like potatoes — boiling in their jackets."

iii. Miss Gwilt

During this visit the cast list for the Alexandra's forthcoming production of *Miss Gwilt*, dramatised from Collins's mystery novel *Armadale*, was posted backstage amidst keen interest. Not only would the author be attending rehearsals, but the play was expected to transfer to London. Ada Cavendish, whom Pin had met and liked in Edinburgh, was financing the production and would play the title role. Everything pointed to a success.

Pinero's name was not on the cast list, but soon after rehearsals began he was given the small part of Mr Darch, an elderly solicitor entrusted with much of the lengthy background exposition in the first act. The chance to create a role — even a minor one — in a new play destined for London was a leg up for Pin. He was duly grateful for it but amazed at the famous author's humble acceptance of his star's demands:

In the course of rehearsals Collins was extremely kind to me. I remember his appearances at rehearsal very clearly. He used to sit, his manuscript before him, at a small table near the footlights, and there he made such additions and alterations as Miss Cavendish deemed necessary. He did this with the utmost readiness and amiability, influenced perhaps by her habit of calling him "Wilkie," a familiar mode of address which I recollect, surprised and shocked me not a little. . . . His goodness to me, so flattering from an eminent man to a mere youth, was ever in my mind, and to this day I feel grateful to him.[15]

Collins's complaisance about his work and status, however, was not an example Pinero chose to follow when he became a successful dramatist.

The opening night of *Miss Gwilt* at the Royal Alexandra Theatre on Thursday, 9 December, was all that had been hoped for. Collins's enormous popularity as a mystery writer drew a capacity audience to see what the *Era* described as "*the* theatrical event of the season" and hailed as "a genuine triumph." The house had been "attracted and fascinated almost at the rise of the curtain by an air of mystery thrown round the principal characters" that had gone on "increasing till the bitter end, enchaining the audience by the careful evolvement of what at first had seemed a tangled plot." The reviewer did note that some climaxes seemed "over-elaborated" and that the curtain had not fallen until half past eleven. Nevertheless, "the whole audience, spellbound, as it were, by the genius of the author, remained until the close" and gave Collins two enthusiastic curtain calls. The acting, too, deserved the highest praise in the critic's opinion. Cavendish had made full use of her opportunities as the passionate ex-governess coerced into deceit and attempted murder by the sinister Dr Downward, "artistically embodied" by Arthur Cecil (later one of Pin's closest friends). And after applauding the other important actors, the reviewer added that the smaller parts had been "admirably filled by Mr A. W. Pinero, Mr R. Brough, Mr Sympson, Mr Sainsbury, &c."[16]

Miss Gwilt played to excellent houses for the remainder of its Liverpool season, and the London transfer was accordingly confirmed. Before the play opened there, however, Pin received an invitation from Mrs Bateman to join her company at the Lyceum. Though the chance to act with Irving was desperately hard to refuse, he decided he had to honour his commitment to Collins and Cavendish.

Meanwhile the Alexandra was preparing its Christmas panto, *Sinbad the Sailor*. As usual, the spectacular scenes, effects, and transformations involved a succession of late-night rehearsals until the opening on 26 December, followed by two months' tedious repetition of the performance. "Although it is a long time since you have heard from me, you have not lost much 'news,' " Pin wrote gloomily to Aunt Eliza (27 February 1876). "The pantomime has been (& indeed still is) dragging along its weary length. We manage to endure it, however, by playing whist during our waits in the Dressing Room, and a few practical and other jokes on the stage." He was, however, looking forward to his final few weeks at the Alexandra, for, in addition to "a dose of the 'legitimate,' " there was to be a season of six nights with "that wonderful man Charles Mathews."

But Mathews was in poor health when he turned up at the theatre. Years of touring had finally taken their toll, though his mind was as sharp as ever:

> On some nights he was almost inaudible — the beginning of the end — on others he was brisk and bright, acting with as much enjoyment to himself as to others. One night while playing Cool to his wonderful Dazzle I found myself on the Right side of the stage, when my cue had been given to enter with a letter on the Left. To work my way round would have occupied two or three minutes; there was no door on my side, so without hesitating I squeezed myself through a small opening in the scene where two flats had been imperfectly joined. I stood before Dazzle flushed and breathless. He gave me a smile, and turning to Charles Courtly, who was looking for me in the opposite direction, observed, "Here's Cool; *he has just walked through a brick wall.*"
>
> On the last night of this Liverpool engagement he passed me at the stage door on his way out. It was mid-winter and he — poor old gentleman — was to play in Dundee the following Monday. I said, "Goodbye, Mr Mathews," and held out my hand. His thoughts seemed far away — perhaps in Dundee where the snow lay rather thickly, but he absently gave me two fingers to shake. I wished at the time they had been four, but for all that I look back on those two little fingers with pleasure, for I never saw their owner again.[17]

So while the veteran who had helped pioneer realism on the British stage trudged off into the night, the young man who would bring a new realism to British drama waited impatiently for his chance to impress London.

...4...
Irving and Authorship

i. On Tour with Irving

As Pin had once remarked to Aunt Eliza, anticipation is often more pleasing than the event itself. So it proved when the new Collins play opened in London on 15 April 1876. The *Globe*'s review began ominously: "To the long list of plays that have lost in London the reputation they have brought from the provinces must now be added *Miss Gwilt*."[1] Most of the other papers agreed. The late finish of the performance (after midnight) undoubtedly prejudiced reviewers against it, but by then even the most indulgent spectators had been numbed into silence.

But the production did not turn out badly for Pinero. The *Era* praised his "clever performance," Clement Scott of the *Daily Telegraph* commended his "useful services,"[2] and several other critics mentioned his name. Moreover, *Miss Gwilt* managed to "lumber along like a brewer's dray" (*Globe*) for two and a half months, keeping him in work until the end of the season.

He then approached Mrs Bateman, who was assembling a company to support Irving on a four-month nationwide tour. At the beginning of his career, the star had laboured for ten years in the provinces without recognition. Now, five years after succeeding in *The Bells*, Irving was about to return in triumph as the leading actor of the London stage. The plays chosen for the tour were his greatest successes to date: *The Bells*, *Charles I* (a made-to-measure study in noble

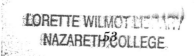

suffering by W. G. Wills), and *Hamlet*. These were to be toured with full scenery, but Mrs Bateman had no intention of wasting money on expensive supporting actors. So it was that at the age of twenty, Pinero, after two years' utility work in the provinces and a bit part in London, found himself engaged to play the president of the court in the nightmare scene of *The Bells*, the Marquis of Huntley in *Charles I*, and — implausible as it seemed — Claudius to Irving's Hamlet!

If he anticipated instant stardom, he was rapidly disillusioned. The tour opened in Manchester, where the critics slated the entire company apart from Irving and were especially severe on the callow Claudius, whom one reviewer condemned as the worst he had ever seen.[3] That nearly 18,000 people crammed the theatre for a fortnight to see Irving did nothing for Pin's wounded pride, and, to complete his misery, the Manchester rain never stopped falling.

Though weather and critics were kinder in Birmingham, both again turned nasty a week or two later when Pin found himself back in Liverpool for a fortnight at the Royal Alexandra. Affecting an air of indifference, he remarked in a letter to Aunt Eliza (4 October 1876): "There is always a certain amount of jealousy of a London company in these provincial towns. It, however, does not affect the business one jot." Nevertheless, it felt odd to be playing again in the old theatre, and at times the change in his circumstances was hard to credit. Despite the trials of touring, the company was "a very jolly one — both ladies and gentlemen," Pin told his aunt. Apart from Mrs Bateman and her daughters ("very, *very* nice people"), the senior lady was the veteran actress Georgiana Pauncefort, who played Gertrude to Pinero's Claudius, though old enough to be his grandmother. She and her daughter, touring as her companion, were lodging at his old Edge Hill apartments, where they were very comfortable but had to suffer endless anecdotes about Pin's former "manners and customs" and exhortations to eat his favourite meals. He himself had been rooming in Manchester and Birmingham with R. C. Lyons, another former member of the Edinburgh Theatre Royal company who had also transferred to Liverpool after the fire and thence to London with *Miss Gwilt*. However, finding that their "tastes and habits" did not "assimilate," they had dissolved partnership. Pin was now staying at his old digs in Gill Street and sharing his sitting room with the Edinburgh veteran John Archer. After Liverpool, however, he would share with a young couple, the Cartons (both "nice quiet people"), and expected this to be "a very happy arrangement."

Barely a year later this couple would launch Pinero's true career as a playwright. Carton — whose real name was Richard Claude Critchett — was a doctor's son who had fallen in love with an actress, married her, and gone onstage himself. At the time Pin met him he was only twenty, but within two or three years he would venture first into management and then into playwriting. His wife, Kate, came from a theatrical family; her father was the veteran actor Henry Compton. Three years older than her husband, she acted under the name of Miss Compton and later made her reputation playing elegant (if sometimes unscrupulous) society women in her husband's comedies. Pin became a close friend of them both.

But the member of the company destined to have the strongest influence on him was, of course, Irving. Despite a seventeen-year age gap, they had much in common. Both had become stagestruck by frequenting the old Sadler's Wells Theatre (Irving on his first visit having seen Phelps play Hamlet). Irving, like Pinero, had been removed from school to become office boy to a solicitor but had then moved on to a clerkship with a firm of East India merchants. At fifteen he, too, had joined an elocution class and become an obsessive, word-perfect reciter and amateur actor before throwing in his job to join a provincial stock company. After a two-and-a-half-year apprenticeship — most of it in Edinburgh under Wyndham — he had secured a London engagement that turned out badly, forcing him back to the provinces for seven more years before he made another — this time successful — attempt on the capital.

There was little likelihood that further grinding in the provinces would have polished young Pinero into a leading actor, let alone another Irving. But the similarity of their early careers contributed from the first to mutual sympathy and respect. For each, the theatre was the most important — almost the only — thing in the world, and each was prepared to devote himself utterly to its service, Irving seeking to elevate the profession from social ostracism to pride and dignity, Pinero to raise the equally despised British drama to respectability.

The end of the tour provided proof that Irving was already being seen as the saviour of the British stage. Everywhere crowds had been large and enthusiastic, but his reception in Dublin was extraordinary. He was invited to Trinity College to receive a congratulatory address praising him for making the stage "a school of true art, a purifier of the passions and a nurse of heroic sentiment" and for having succeeded "in commending it to the favour of a portion of society, large and justly influential" that usually held aloof from the theatre. In reply Irving thanked the audience for encouraging him to feel not merely pride in his own success but that "the far nobler work" he aimed at was "in truth begun."[4]

ii. First Plays

Pinero was retained in the Lyceum company at the end of the tour, but found himself relegated to lesser roles. As a stopgap while preparing *Richard III*, Irving revived his controversial *Macbeth*. Demoted to first murderer, Pin did not greatly impress in the part and was so terrified by Macbeth's glare at the news of Fleance's escape that he forgot his lines.[5] His performance as a scheming young lover in W. H. Murray's popular curtain raiser *Diamond Cut Diamond* was more successful, though, thanks in part to Carton, who played his conniving servant. In *Richard III* he was given yet another conspiratorial part — on the winning side this time — as Lord Stanley. Carton played Lord Rivers, then left the Lyceum at the end of the run to star in the Liverpool tryout of a new comedy. Pin would soon hear from him again.

Irving went on tour again in autumn 1877, but Pin remained at the Lyceum to appear in *The Dead Secret*, another stage adaptation of a Collins mystery novel. Featuring Isabel Bateman in the lead, it had been produced under Irving's personal supervision but was slated by the critics. Pinero, however, was praised for his acting in a small but striking character part, Shrowle, the misanthropic servant of a wealthy hermit,[6] and Collins's popularity kept the piece running until Irving returned in mid-November.

But *The Dead Secret* was not Pin's main reason for staying in London at the time. Circumstances had conspired to bring about an event of crucial importance to his career. A popular actor at the Globe Theatre, F. H. Macklin, had been looking for a new one-act comedy in which he could appear to advantage at his forthcoming benefit. He had consulted Carton, who, remembering Pin's stories of early attempts at playwriting, had asked his friend if he could write a piece for Macklin, preferably with a good part in it for Miss Compton as well. The result was a neat little comedietta called *£200 a Year* that Pinero, surprising himself, dashed off in an afternoon.[7]

The little comedy fitted the bill perfectly when it was presented as a curtain raiser for the benefit at the Globe on Saturday, 6 October 1877. Macklin had the sympathetic role of the kindhearted but idle Jack Meadows, who marries a pretty heiress and then discovers she has accepted him merely to get rid of her other suitors. Miss Compton had an equally good part as the feminist bride who orders Jack to leave her alone in return for an allowance and a billiard room, only to find that the loss of her deceased aunt's will has left her dependent on her husband's scorned pittance of £200 a year. And the audience applauded the conventional happy ending in which Jack's generous acceptance of the situation breaks down his wife's prejudice against him — just before the will is found again! The curtain fell, as the *Era* recorded, "amidst hearty cheers, bestowed equally between Mr Pinero's little work and the performers."[8]

The Cartons were delighted, as was Macklin, who expressed his appreciation by presenting the author with a set of gold studs and cuff links.[9] Nor was this the end of the comedietta. It was not only kept in the Globe's bill for several more weeks, but featured as the curtain raiser at a special matinee held at the theatre on Saturday, 20 October, in aid of the Royal General Theatrical Fund. The performance was attended by the Lord Mayor of London, the Duke of Beaufort, and other dignitaries and supported by many theatre notables. As the *Illustrated Sporting and Dramatic News* for 27 October 1877 reported, more than usual interest had attended

the revival at the Globe matinee for the benefit of the Royal General
Theatrical Fund of Morton's old comedy *Speed the Plough* which had
not been played in London since the last revival at the Haymarket,
twenty years ago. In addition to the comedy in which nearly all the
leading actors and actresses now in London appeared, either as
principals or as supernumary Plough Boys, and to which Mr Byron
furnished an original epilogue; Mr Macklin and Miss Compton appeared in the new comedietta, *£200 a Year*; Mr Herman Vezin recited
with great impressiveness Edgar Poe's poem, "The Raven"; and Mrs
Stirling delivered, with telling point and effect, an apropos address
written for the occasion by Mr Clement Scott.[10]

Once again Pin had been remarkably lucky. He could hardly have
dreamt that his first performed play would be staged on such an
auspicious occasion.

Irving returned to the Lyceum at the end of December and for the
next three months presented in repertory *The Bells, Charles I,* and
The Lyons Mail. This last was a melodrama, adapted from the French,
in which Irving appeared as a virtuous character and his villainous
double. Pin, kept busy with supporting roles in all three plays as well
as in the accompanying farces, somehow found time to write a full-
length play based on another kind of double act.

La Comète; or, Two Hearts (alternatively titled *Paul Marston's
Love*), designed to exploit identical twin actresses, is one of the most
artificial pieces ever contrived by an apprentice playwright. Only the
circumstances of its composition— and the author's deliberate intention of squeezing the last drop of theatrical effect from his totally
incredible plot — can be advanced in its defence. The action centres
on the semi-comatose form of Paul Marston, a callow youth who has
been accidentally shot in a hunting accident and can be revived only
by the sight of his former love, a Parisian cabaret dancer known as La
Comète. She loves Paul but is reluctant to go to him because she has
lived a life "of wickedness and sin" and is, in any case, married
already. To solve the dilemma she disguises herself as a nun and
prevails on her pure twin sister, Rose (who does not recognise her!),
to travel to England and give the wounded youth the kiss of life. The
play ends with the bogus nun standing upstage centre in the double

doorway of the Marstons' library pronouncing a final benediction: "From this time I leave the world with all its beauty, its gladness and its sin, far behind me. (*Pointing to Paul and Rose*) There are the two beings I have loved best on Earth. In expiation of my guilty life do I feel the tie that binds me to them. (*Holding her hands out to them*) Oh my loves, my loves! . . . We shall meet again. (*Pointing upwards*) There!"[11]

Despite its silly plot, stereotyped characters, and stilted dialogue, this first full-length Pinero play contains in crude and unsophisticated form several ingredients typical of his mature dramas of respectability. Above all, there is the loss of reputation by an erring but well-meaning young woman, her two sides here conveniently represented by twin sisters: one a fallen woman, the other pure and virginal. Further typical characters are Paul's father, Sir John Marston, who is obsessed with the preservation of his family's honour, and his friend Frank Sartoris, a worldly-wise bachelor who observes, comments on, and occasionally meddles in other people's affairs — the *raisonneur,* to use the French term. The play is essentially a technical exercise, with the plot being manipulated to create a hothouselike atmosphere of sexually charged emotion (what Shaw would later label the "Pinerotic" effect), but so blatantly as to be quite incredible.

La Comète opened on 22 April 1878 to enthusiastic applause from the suburban audience at the Theatre Royal, Croydon, but the *Era* (the only metropolitan paper to review the play) was not deceived. Noting that "Mr A. W. Pinero, an actor of considerable ability" had recently written "a modest little comedietta," the reviewer ridiculed his latest effort using an appropriate simile: "Now Mr Pinero's ambition soars, and, attempting to go up like a rocket, he succeeds only in coming down like the stick. We, of course, might expect, in the natural order of things, that a comet would be erratic, but *La Comète* introduced by Mr Pinero is the most erratic yet discovered. It would drive the Astronomer Royal mad and send the Curator of the Greenwich Observatory into a fit but for one thing, and that is the shortness of the tale."[12]

The review made an impression on the young playwright, who several years later used the rocket image for the plot and title of a popular farce, but it did not harm the production, the extraordinary physical resemblance between Amy and Louise Lionel (the twins for whom the play was written) easily outweighing the idiocy of the plot. *La Comète* blazed brightly for its fortnight in Croydon before shooting off around the secondary provincial touring circuit. During the following two months, audiences in Doncaster, Derby, Oldham, and Bradford marveled at the twins, though the prediction of one indulgent reviewer that they were "destined to speedily secure Metropolitan fame"[13] was not fulfilled.

The next Pinero piece was staged within a month of *La Comète*. A more modest effort, *Two Can Play at That Game* is a comedietta that (despite its title) has nothing to do with twins. Pin wrote it with the sole motive of giving himself a better part than had been allotted him lately at the Lyceum. Mrs Bateman liked the little comedy, agreed to produce it, and paid five pounds for the rights.[14]

Pin played Montgomery Clutterbuck, a forty-year-old hypochondriac who has recently married Kate, a girl of twenty, in the prudent expectation that she will nurse him in his old age. The most plausible explanation for the conception of this unappealing character and Pin's interest in playing him is that Clutterbuck is a comic version of his father. If this is so, the farcical events of the comedietta may hint at the spirited character of Lucy Pinero in her younger days. When Clutterbuck decides to test his young wife's devotion by saying he has lied about his age and is really an ailing sixty-year-old, she counters with a tearful "confession" of her own: that she is already married to another man — in fact to the old sea captain she has overheard putting her husband up to his trick! When she reveals the truth, however, Clutterbuck realises his folly and promises to love her honestly in future. "Ah," Kate replies, "Love is a little game that two can play at!"[15]

The comedietta went into the Lyceum bill as a curtain raiser on Monday, 20 May 1878, but because the main piece (*Louis XI*) had been running two months, reviewers did not notice Pinero's latest work. It was, however, sufficiently appreciated by audiences to be kept on for the next production, *Vanderdecken,* an ill-fated version of the Flying Dutchman legend that sank without a trace after a month. Irving then revived his famous double act of Mathias in *The Bells* and Jingle in Albery's adaptation of an episode from *The Pickwick Papers* — a lengthy programme that left no room for *Two Can Play at That Game.* But billed as "A. W. Pinero's Successful Comedietta," it reappeared in August for three weeks as curtain raiser to a revival of a Taylor drama, *Mary Warner,* which brought both the Lyceum season and Mrs Bateman's management to a close.

iii. The Chief

For some time it had been apparent that the sole reason for the Lyceum's recent success was Irving. It was also evident that he wished to assume full artistic and financial control of the productions in which he appeared and that he was no longer prepared to accept Mrs Bateman's daughters as his leading ladies. A parting with his manager was inevitable, but it was to Mrs Bateman's credit that she suddenly took the initiative, sold the lease of the Lyceum to Irving, and removed herself and her daughters to Sadler's Wells. Her timing took everyone by surprise. Pin had no chance to say good-bye, so he wrote her a warm note (27 August 1878) thanking her for many kindnesses he would not forget.[16]

During the following three months, while alterations and improvements were carried out in his theatre, Irving made another triumphal progress round the provinces, touring *Hamlet, Richelieu, The Lyons Mail, Richard III, The Bells,* and *Jingle.* Pin, who acted his usual supporting parts (except in *Hamlet,* in which he now played Horatio), later recalled his astonishment at the energy with which Irving attacked a demanding succession of roles: "As an example of his zest for work, I recall his acting, in Edinburgh, Hamlet at a matinee and at night Louis XI in the play of that name, followed by Jingle, in an excerpt from 'Pickwick'. At the final fall of the curtain I asked him if he was tired. 'Tired!' he replied, 'Not in the least. I should like to do it all over again.' And he acted invariably with an ever alert brain and with every nerve on fire."[17]

It is not surprising that the Chief, feeling in such fine fettle himself, expected almost equally superhuman feats from his subordinates. On one occasion during this tour, Pin, on stage with Irving during *Louis XI*, observed with horror that a huge stage tree was parting company with the metal rod that supported it from behind. Its collapse was imminent. He whispered this news to Louis XI, who calmly murmured, "Hold it up then, my boy, hold it up," and went on with the scene. Pin, looking like he was having a fit, grappled frantically with the tree for what seemed an eternity. Finally, he gasped out a warning as the whole thing tilted over and came crashing down across the stage. Irving then had a timely idea. "Where is the Dauphin?" he ad-libbed in the character of the French king. "I don't know," Pin croaked, not in character at all. "Then let us go and find him," said the monarch, and the two left the stage while the curtain was lowered and the scenery restored. Waiting in the wings, Louis XI's only remark to his minister was, "Why the devil didn't you hold it up, my boy?"[18]

When Irving returned to the Lyceum after this tour, he had scarcely two weeks left to organise the new production of *Hamlet*, which was to open his first season of management. There was much to be done: painters and decorators were still in the theatre, innumerable administrative details had to be resolved, and, above all, a new supporting company had to be rehearsed. Only Pinero and Miss Pauncefort remained from the old one, though the new people included veterans such as old Mr Chippendale, who had played Polonius to almost every Hamlet since Edmund Kean, and Tom Mead, whose resonant tones and splendid bearing made him (as four years earlier) an ideal Ghost.

But Irving's most important recruit was, of course, Ellen Terry, his leading lady for the next twenty-three years. Later she recalled her concern at the obsessive way he rehearsed every detail of this vital first production — except his scenes with Ophelia. "*We* shall be all right," he told her, "but we are not going to run the risk of being bottled up by a gas-man or a fiddler."[19] And among her other early memories of the Lyceum was that of "one very studious youth who could never be caught loafing. He was always reading, or busy in the greenroom studying by turns the pictures of past actor-humanity with which the walls were peopled, or the present realities of actors who came in and out of the room. Although he was so much younger then, Mr Pinero looked much as he does now. He played Rosencrantz very neatly. Consummate care, precision, and brains characterised his work as an actor always, but his chief ambition lay another way. Rosencrantz and the rest were his school of stagecraft."[20]

Her memory here is a little astray, as Pinero played not Rosencrantz but Guildenstern. Any distinction between these characters, however, had been obliterated in the Chief's heavily cut acting text. Pin would have been less than human if he had not been upset by this brutal reduction of his role, especially after having previously played Claudius and Horatio. There is a plausible, though perhaps apocryphal, tale about how Irving, having noticed at rehearsal that Pin was sitting on a piece of sharply profiled scenery, called out, "My boy, if you sit there you will cut yourself!" "It really doesn't matter, Mr Irving," Pin is said to have replied, "We are quite used to having our parts cut around here."[21]

Late in life Pinero indignantly repudiated this and several other anecdotes about him in an unauthorised biography by H. Hamilton Fyfe. Another of these tales had Pin, irritated by the frequency with which the Chief assembled his company to note minor alterations on stage, sticking up a notice ordering the cast to gather at noon to watch the property master drive a screw into a flat! In a letter to the critic (13 May 1930), the elderly playwright exploded:

> Reading the opening chapter of your book last night, I almost had a fit. Who has been imposing on you those stories of my Lyceum days? Utterly false every one of them. I had too great a regard for Irving — to say nothing of the awe in which I held him — to treat him with pertness or familiarity. And as for the sticking of an impudent notice on the call-board by a member of the company, such an outrageous proceeding would have brought disgrace upon the offender, and perhaps summary dismissal. The theatre was strictly conducted and its rules reverently obeyed.

Although this protest may have been prompted by the rectitude of old age, it was probably valid. Pinero strongly approved of the exacting standard of discipline the Chief imposed on his company as a measure of respect for the art they practised. It is also clear that if Irving did not overvalue Pin's abilities as an actor, he had a high opinion of the young man's intelligence and reliability. In his first month of management, Irving, seeking to foster an atmosphere of permanence at the theatre, set up the Lyceum Provident and Benevolent Fund with himself as trustee and Pinero as secretary.[22]

But Pin's promise as a playwright was probably his main asset in the eyes of his manager. Throughout his career, Irving was to seek — largely in vain — for dramatists who could provide new roles to suit his highly idiosyncratic acting style. It was one of Pinero's greatest regrets that he could not do this. "I felt about the Chief," he later confessed, "as a schoolboy feels after he has grown up, about his head master. I simply could not imagine the Chief acting in a play of mine. The idea overcame me!"[23]

iv. Daisy's Escape

Near the end of Irving's first season of management, Pinero completed a new comedietta for the Lyceum. Though it contained no part for him, Irving was delighted with the piece and paid fifty pounds for it (knowing full well that Pin would have given it to him for nothing).[24]

Daisy's Escape went straight into the bill on 20 September 1879, the opening night of Irving's second season. This time the new piece was well placed to attract favourable notice. Instead of coming first and therefore not being seen by the wealthier patrons who habitually arrived late after digesting their dinners, *Daisy's Escape* concluded the bill. Moreover, the main play at first was a revival of *The Bells*, a stopgap until the next major production was ready. After the familiar agonisings of Irving's Mathias, a little comedy was bound to go down well.

The comedietta shows the consequences of the ill-advised elopement of a young lady called Daisy White and a young bounder aptly named Augustus Caddel. Their train blocked by a snowdrift, they are forced to seek shelter at an inn, and by the time they reach it Daisy's shoes are sodden. After they quarrel, Augustus leaves her to smoke his "filthy pipe" in another room while she offers in soliloquy "two pieces of advice to any young lady about to elope. First, don't elope. Second, always elope in summertime." At this point a former suitor of Daisy happens to enter the room; when he leaves it she has altered her second piece of advice to "always elope with the right man!" Everything ends happily, however, when the arrival of her grumpy guardian encourages Augustus to give her up. She tells him he is rid of a bad bargain and everybody rejoices at "a very lucky escape!"[25]

Pinero's motive for writing the comedietta had again been to provide himself with a part, this time even contriving a legitimate excuse for smoking on stage! But he had taken care to make his plot and dialogue crisp and amusing, and the piece represented a step forward in his work. As the *Era* noted, the comedietta "pleased the audience thoroughly. At the close the author was called for amid hearty applause. The little piece was cleverly acted, the author as Augustus, the blighted lover, being decidedly droll . . . while Miss Alma Murray was a very attractive heroine, delivering some smart lines with much point. Mr Pinero may be congratulated upon the complete success of the little piece."[26]

Several days after the opening of *Daisy's Escape*, Pin wrote to his cousin Chrissy Schneider, who, it appears, was something of an artist. The letter offers a rare glimpse of his personal life at this time:

> London. Septr. 25th. 1879.
> 35 Alfred Place.
> Bedford Square.

Dear Old Chris,

Thank you very much for your kind note.

The piece continues to go extremely well and the people do *not* go out in the middle of it. However on and after Saturday next it will commence the Evening.

I have been very busy since my return to town &, some part of last week, extremely poorly. So I have had little time for calls. But I will come up north & see your Ma very soon. Give my best love to her.

I hope you have recovered from the fatigue of those little strolls in the country. I look forward to some more next year — I yearn already for Cobham Woods and the stimulant.

Some day a distinguished looking stranger may Enquire the price of a picture in Great James St. Bear up till then. My fondest love and kisses.

Affectionately yours,
Arthur W. Pinero[27]

The changed position of *Daisy's Escape* in the Lyceum bill came about when George Colman's old play *The Iron Chest* replaced *The Bells*. But Irving's portrayal in this revival of Sir Edward Mortimer — yet another murderer with a bad conscience — failed to please. "We are weary of this reiterated remorse," complained the Captious Critic of the *Illustrated Sporting and Dramatic News*.[28] The public agreed. *The Iron Chest* closed for good a month later to make way for one of Irving's most successful productions, *The Merchant of Venice. Daisy's Escape* remained in the bill until 3 January 1880.

Nor was that the end of the little comedy. It was revived again towards the end of the season and subsequently became a stock piece at the Lyceum, reappearing whenever something bright was needed to fill up a bill. All in all, Irving had good value for his fifty pounds. And Alma Murray also had reason to be pleased: as a result of her success as Daisy White she found herself playing Jessica to Ellen Terry's Portia. Fifteen years later she would help another new playwright achieve his first stage success when she played Raina in Shaw's *Arms and the Man*.

But for Pinero, the comedietta was to have unexpected and momentous consequences. During the last two months of its run, he found himself, as a result of Alma Murray's promotion, eloping with a different Daisy. This time, however, he was not content to give her up. He had fallen helplessly — and, it seemed, hopelessly — in love.

...5...
A Difficult Courtship

i. Myra Holme

Her stage name was Myra Holme, and her circumstances when Pin
first met her were tragic. Married six years, she was the mother of two
small children for whose sake she had recently gone on the stage. Her
husband had been invalided out of the army and was no longer able to
support his family. He was slowly dying of consumption.

But in May 1873, when Myra married him, Captain John Angus
Lushington Hamilton must have seemed a great catch. His grandfather, Sir Frederick Hamilton, Baronet of Silvertonhill, Lanarkshire,
was a member of the ducal house of Hamilton and head of a family with
a proud record of military service in India. John's father, Henry
Charles Hamilton, though only a fourth son, had seen to it that his
three boys were commissioned into the army according to family
tradition. The eldest, Henry, had become a lieutenant colonel in the
2nd Cavalry; the youngest, Robert, a lieutenant in the 65th Foot;
whereas John had gone from Cheltenham College to the 2nd West India
Regiment. Having enlisted as an ensign in January 1865, he was
promoted to lieutenant a year later. In 1867 he had seen service in
Africa, where he was commended in dispatches by the Administrator
of the Gold Coast "for the manner in which he performed the 'arduous
and dangerous duty of conducting King Armarkie to his country' in
February and March 1867, and for 'his courage and determination in
capturing the rebel chiefs' on which occasion, his party being attacked,

Myra Holme as Clara Dart in The Mighty Dollar *(The Theatre, February 1882)*

he saved the life of Mr Blenkinson, his interpreter, who was wounded."[1]

As a result of these exploits, Hamilton was promoted to captain in January 1868, but in October of that year, at the age of twenty-three, he was obliged to resign his commission, having contracted tuberculosis.[2] Four years later, convalescing in Maida Vale, he met Myra and fell in love with her.

She was beautiful, with long fair hair and a classical profile, but there was nothing aristocratic about her background.[3] Though her father, Beaufoy Alfred Moore, styled himself "gentleman," he was in fact the proprietor of a notable Fleet Street pub, Ye Olde Cheshire Cheese, in earlier times a favourite haunt of Dickens and Dr Johnson. Her mother, Sarah, also had a background in the trade, having been previously married to an innkeeper named Wood who had managed an establishment in Portugal Street (just off the Strand) until his death in 1851. By then she was thirty and the mother of three children, but she was still a beauty and remarried immediately, in the next few years giving birth to three more children, of whom Myra was the second. The "Cheese" proved a profitable business under their management, for by the time of Myra's marriage Beaufoy and Sarah no longer resided in the top rooms of the pub but at "Beaufoy Lodge" in St John's Wood Road.

Despite this indication of raffish affluence, it would seem that Beaufoy disapproved of Myra's marriage to a semi-invalid; the marriage certificate states that she was given away by her elder half brother, Oscar Wood Moore. This may explain why her parents provided no financial help when Hamilton's fragile health broke down two years later. His own parents were dead, and his elder brother was in India, so no help was available from that quarter. By this time the couple had two children, a little boy and a baby girl, both named after their parents. Somehow Myra had to find work so she could feed her infants and pay the doctor's bills for her husband.

It was probably Oscar who encouraged her to try the stage. He was a keen amateur actor and "general manager" of the Beaufoy Amateur Dramatic Club (later the Nomads), registered in 1869 and active until 1880. The performances he organised were given under distinguished patronage, supported by society, and reviewed in the leading papers. It seems likely he pulled a few strings to get Myra her first professional acting engagement.

Adopting the stage name of "Myra Holme" in order not to shame her relatives, she began with a bit part in *The Gascon* at the Olympic in January 1876. Later that year Miss Holme joined Charles Wyndham's company at the Criterion Theatre to play one of five daughters in a curtain raiser called *Mother Carey's Chickens*. Soon promoted to principal "walking lady," she appeared in several of Wyndham's productions at the Crystal Palace, including Tom Taylor's detective thriller *The Ticket-of-Leave Man*, in which she played Emily St Evremond (née Traddles). Later she appeared as Lady Greythorne in *Pink Dominoes* at the Criterion (between engagements at the Strand and the Vaudeville) before joining the Lyceum in September 1879 for Irving's ill-fated revival of *The Iron Chest*.[4] Its failure would have left her unemployed had not Alma Murray resigned the role of Daisy White in Pinero's new comedietta.

By then Myra was desperate. The winter that gripped London in November 1879 had produced freezing fogs so dense that sometimes audiences could barely make out the actors on stage. Captain Hamilton's diseased lungs finally collapsed, and he died on 16 December.[5] Though a tragic end to her marriage, his death must have come as a relief to Myra, who, in addition to nursing him and looking after her children, had been expected to sparkle on stage nightly and at matinees. She gave a fortnight's notice and left the Lyceum at the beginning of January, after which *Daisy's Escape* disappeared from the bill.

ii. Pin in Love

Moved by Miss Holme's courage, Pin's admiration of her beauty rapidly turned to love, but in the circumstances he could hardly declare such feelings openly. Instead, he put them into a short play written while Myra was acting with him in his comedietta.

Bygones is a one-act comedy with more pathos than humour. Its unlikely hero is an elderly music teacher, Professor Giacomo Mazzoni, who offers his hand in marriage to one of his pupils, an orphan called Ruby, when she is rejected by a lord's son because of her humble birth. No sooner has Ruby accepted the old man than her young lover returns to beg her forgiveness, thus setting up a touching finale in which the professor nobly releases Ruby and, giving her his mother's necklace as a wedding present, says: "It belongs to you for I shall never love again. Like the plant which bears one flower in a hundred years my love has blossomed once and for ever, and its bloom is as dead as this nosegay under our feet. Take it. Now go back to him — and remember, my secret belongs to you and the grave."[6]

Pin's devotion was made of sterner stuff, though his courtship was to be long and frustrating. Once Miss Holme emerged from mourning, she resumed her acting career with some success. She was therefore in no hurry to be married again, especially not to a mere supporting actor whose only claim to fame was authorship of several brief plays.

The love letters Pin wrote Myra over the next three years no longer exist, but it is on record that he also sent letters "filled with humour and sentiment" to her small daughter, who treasured them all her life.[7] Even these appear to have been destroyed, so all that remain of Pin's feelings during his courtship are hints in the plays and stories he wrote at this time. Such "evidence" is necessarily conjectural, but it is surely significant that Professor Mazzoni is merely the first of several self-sacrificing lovers in these writings.

There is, for example, "Tiny" Langdon, hero of a short story called "A Fallen Star."[8] An impressionable young actor in the Chucksford stock company, Tiny falls in love with Miss Clarissa Rosenbloom, a visiting "star," when he plays Orlando to her Rosalind, but she marries for money to support her dependent mother and sisters. The marriage turns out badly, and she runs off with a lover who deserts her when she falls gravely ill. The story ends with the faithful Tiny discovering her predicament just in time to rush to her deathbed and comfort her in her dying moments.

In "Confessions of a Theatrical Swindler,"[9] Pin tried a different tack. The narrator is a con man whose technique is to hire a provincial theatre, advertise for a company, run a short season — and abscond with the takings. His main victim in the story is a young widowed actress who, out of work and starving, sells her dresses to get the train fare to Chucksford and arrives with her baby at the theatre only to find that the swindling manager has decamped. She swoons and nearly dies but is nursed back to health by the wife of the cab driver, who has refused her last shilling. Six months later the swindler, under another alias, again hires her and leaves her in the lurch, this time with fatal consequences. But with poetic justice the decamping manager catches a chill on the train and is himself dying when he reads the widow's obituary in the *Era*.

Myra took no notice of these cautionary tales. She had accepted an offer from John Hollingshead, manager of the Gaiety, to appear in a season of plays with the famous American comedy actor W. J. Florence. Her roles included Clara Dart in Florence's most popular vehicle, *The Mighty Dollar,* and Edith to Florence's Captain Cuttle in *Dombey and Son*. Under the circumstances she saw herself not as a fallen star but a rising one.

Meanwhile Pin was playing a minor part in Irving's long-running revival of *The Merchant of Venice* and finding the task distinctly irksome. A few years later he sardonically identified it, in response to a questionnaire, as "the most Striking Incident in his Theatrical Experience":

> I played Salarino in *The Merchant of Venice*, justly accounted one of the most wretchedly depressing "responsible" parts in the Drama — on Two Hundred and Fifty consecutive occasions, at the Lyceum Theatre; a feat never accomplished or attempted by any other actor.
> I add, with Pride, that I acted the part with the same Earnestness, Absorption, and Zeal, on the last as on the first night. All my intervening performances however were extremely careless.[10]

The long run at least gave him more time to write plays. Irving had already accepted *Bygones* for production the following season and now conspired with his close friend J. L. Toole to give the young playwright further encouragement. Toole, who had recently taken over the Folly Theatre, was the most loved and popular low comedian of the time, though perhaps now past his best. As a young man he had been "discovered" by Dickens, who later admitted having written *Great*

Expectations with a view to a dramatic version in which Toole would play Joe Gargery. Pinero later described him as

> a thick-set man with a stiff leg. . . . He was not an impersonator, what we would call a character actor, but relied in every part he played upon the comicality of his face and manner. He had a hoarse voice and a wry mouth, looking as if he was always trying to bite his ear. The special quality of his acting, however, was an appealing spirit of wistfulness — almost of sadness — which came through his broad humour. . . . In private life Toole was one of the most lovable men it has been my good fortune to know — simple as a child and brimming over with fun.[11]

He was also the kindest of men. Though recently devastated by the death of his only son, he readily agreed to commission a comedietta for his theatre from young Pinero.

The result was "a new Original Comedy-Drama, in One Act" called *Hester's Mystery*, which ran for more than 300 performances at the Folly following its initial presentation at a matinee on Saturday, 5 June 1880. Much of its appeal came from the novel rural setting — "The Dairy and Stableyard of Nance Butterworth's Farm" — a ground plan of which was carefully drawn on the second page of Pinero's manu-script, alongside a note stating: "The whole scene to be quaint and old-fashioned and as bright as possible."[12]

The plot centres on the mystery of where Hester, Nance's daughter, has been for six unexplained weeks between her departure from Mr Owen Silverdale's Academy for Young Ladies and her arrival back at the farm. She is pursued there by the schoolmaster (originally a clergyman, but Toole had this altered), an unpleasant man who threat-ens to tell on her if she refuses to marry him. Hester's secret, however, turns out to be a baby that she produces — together with a young husband — to thwart the schoolmaster and melt her mother's frosty heart. How she had previously concealed her pregnancy and marriage from her schoolmates is not explained, and it seems the question was not one that any reviewer cared to raise.

Having demonstrated his worth to Toole, Pinero lost no time in submitting to G. B. Loveday, the Folly's stage manager, a synopsis of a proposed full-length comedy. Having heard nothing further about it for three months, he wrote to Loveday that although his scheme was "a very simple affair," he felt he could "work it . . . into a very effective play."[13] The synopsis was then shown to Toole, who was unimpressed, but the playwright refused to take no for an answer:

> Lyceum Theatre
> London, W.C.
> Oct. 5th. 1880.
>
> Dear Loveday,
>   Thanks for your note. I am however a little surprised at my Plan being "scarcely the thing for the present company," inasmuch as it is constructed *especially* to fit Mr Toole and your company individually and collectively.
>   I met Mr Toole on Saturday night when he seemed under the impression that the hero of my piece was a sentimental personage of the "Plummer" or "Uncle Dick" type. I did my best to remove this misunderstanding, and, as you are doubtless under the same bias, I subjoin two conditions on which I would write the piece for you or any other manager in London.
>   1. That the hero of my comedy shall get more genuine laughter than does Mr Barnaby Doublechick in "The Upper Crust."
>   2. That my Comedy shall turn out a better piece artistically and at least as good commercially as any yet produced under the present management of the Folly Theatre.
>
>   However, I don't urge the matter if you fail to see your way clear.
>
>   Truly yours,
>   Arthur W. Pinero

His brash self-confidence apparently paid off, for in an undated note to Loveday written shortly afterwards, he reported he was "dead on the job," having already written Act 1, and asked whether Toole would care to hear it at that stage or wait "till the entire thing is complete." Whichever course was followed, the play was rapidly finished and accepted for production at the Folly.

There was, however, an unexpected last-minute snag. The comedy, originally titled *Human Nature, A Village Love Story* but later re-named *Girls and Boys, A Nursery Tale*,[14] not only offered Toole the made-to-measure role of an old cobbler-schoolmaster but also contained a beautiful and mysterious heroine whom the author insisted should be played by Miss Myra Holme. By an unfortunate stroke, she had just been engaged to appear at the Prince of Wales's Theatre, under the management of Edgar Bruce since the Bancrofts' recent removal to the Haymarket. But the ever-obliging Toole agreed to hold over the comedy until Miss Holme was free (though he might not have been so accommodating had he known how long he would have to wait).

In the meantime Irving's third Lyceum season opened on 18 September 1880 with a new production of *The Corsican Brothers*, preceded on the bill by *Bygones*, with Pin playing his lovelorn professor to Alma Murray's Ruby. There was scarcely a dry eye in the house when Mazzoni, on finding his intended bride in her repentant lover's arms, slowly let the bouquet of flowers he had brought her slip from his fingers. Clement Scott, who liked nothing better than a good cry, noted in the *Daily Telegraph* that

> those who had taken the trouble to come early were rewarded with a great treat in the shape of a charming one-act play, full of gentle and refined feeling, tinged with an occasional flavouring of genial humour, and acted extremely well. Mr A. W. Pinero would have been pleased, could he have taken his attention from the character he was acting so well, to find he had touched the heart of his audience by the simple pathos of his homely story. . . . The applause that greeted the young author must have assured him that whenever he makes a bolder claim for fame, he will receive the sympathetic encouragement of those who have watched his brief career with interest, and see far more than average merit in his well-considered and conscientious work.[15]

That was not Pin's only moment of glory at the opening. Irving had prepared an impressive entrance for himself in *The Corsican Brothers* by instructing his designer to use the full depth of the Lyceum scene dock for the set in the first act. This would enable the actor-manager

Scene. The Lyceum.   Time - First Night of The Corsican Brothers.
            Enter Alfred de Meynard.
1st E. thusiast (in the gallery.) 'Bravo, Irving!'
2nd   do   . 'It aint Irving - it's only Pinero!'
1st   do   . 'Then what the douce does he mean by looking
            like that ? | Yaah ! Ssss ! Ooooh !'
                                    Arthur W. Pinero

A. W. Pinero, *sketch of himself as Alfred de Meynard in* The Corsican
Brothers *(Era Almanac and Annual 1881)*

to enjoy the audience's applause while he advanced a full seventy feet from the garden gate of the Villa dei Franchi to the footlights. Somehow no one had noticed that Pinero, in a minor role but an elegant costume, entered a little earlier by the same route. He was therefore able on the first night to make a slow and deliberate entrance that drew louder and more prolonged applause (until the audience realised their error) than he would ever again receive as an actor.[16] A month or so later he showed a deplorable lack of repentance by contributing a cartoon of the incident to a portfolio of sketches published in the *Era Almanac* under the aptly punning title, "How Actors Draw"!

But if Pin stole a little of Irving's applause, he more than repaid his manager that night. Irving's sons, Harry and Laurence, had been given permission by their mother to visit Irving backstage before the curtain rose on the melodrama. They were virtual strangers to him. Some nine years earlier their mother had asked Irving as they drove home after his triumphant debut in *The Bells* how much longer he intended to continue making a fool of himself in public. She was eight months pregnant and tired after a long night, but the effect of her acid enquiry had been devastating. Irving stopped the carriage, got out, and never spoke to her again, though he continued to provide for her financial support.[17]

On the opening night of *The Corsican Brothers*, when his sons came backstage to see him, Irving hardly knew what to say to them and was highly relieved when Pin offered to take them under his wing. Dressed incongruously in Eton jackets and tall hats, they sat in the playwright's dressing room and chattered away while he put on his old man's makeup for *Bygones*. Using the same room was an old, broken-down actor by the name of Arthur Matthison, whom Irving had out of pity engaged to be his double in *The Corsican Brothers*. Laurence, amused at the grotesque caricature of his father that Matthison presented in his double's costume, made an "unfeelingly cheeky" remark to the old actor, for which Pin, supported by Harry, insisted he apologise. Laurence did so good-naturedly, and the incident, far from creating any ill feeling, began a lifelong friendship between Pin and the boys. Over the years he was able to help them appreciate and understand their father.[18]

iii. Hare and the Kendals

On 5 November 1881 Pinero made the "bolder claim for fame" that Scott with inside knowledge had anticipated in his review of *Bygones*. This claim came in the form of a two-act comedy, *The Money-Spinner*, which was staged at the Prince's Theatre, Manchester, by a touring company managed by a William Duck. Nine days later a full column of extracts from the Manchester reviews was printed as an advertisement in the *Era*. All, of course, were highly complimentary, but the author was even more pleased by an announcement in the paper that *The Money-Spinner* would soon be produced in London by the new managers of the St James's Theatre, William Kendal and John Hare.

This was an exciting prospect. Though Kendal was a sound rather than inspired performer (he was known mainly for his legendary collection of cigars), his wife was the best all-round actress in England. Born Madge Robertson, Mrs Kendal was the twenty-second child of an actor-manager and the youngest sister of Pin's favourite playwright, Tom Robertson. Like her brother, she could claim to have been "nursed on rose-pink and cradled in properties." She had promised her father when she married Kendal that she would never appear on stage without her husband and had kept her word. As a result she was regarded by critics and playgoers as the "Ideal English Matron," a title she did not entirely relish — particularly when, as in the new Pinero play, she wished to act a character of dubious morality.

Hare had equally impressive credentials. After making his debut at twenty in Liverpool in 1864, he had spent ten years with the Bancrofts at the Prince of Wales's before becoming manager of the Court Theatre. A dapper, incisive little man with a quick temper, he had a meticulous eye for detail that made him a brilliant character actor, especially in roles as elderly men, and served him equally well when directing his own productions. Though successful at the Court, he was tempted by the much larger St James's when it fell vacant in summer 1878, and after some hesitation he had taken over the lease in association with the Kendals. Their joint management had begun successfully in October 1879 with a military drama called *The Queen's Shilling*, but this had been followed by a run of comparative failures.

The title of Pinero's new play must therefore have struck them as a good omen.

The Money-Spinner opened at the St James's Theatre on Saturday, 6 January 1881, and was an immediate success. The managers, however, worried about how the critics might view a heroine who cheats a former lover at cards to save her feckless husband, had presented the play as curtain raiser to a popular Taylor drama, *A Sheep in Wolf's Clothing*, in which Mrs Kendal played a wife who saves her husband from death in the wake of the Monmouth Rebellion. But after the opening night the order of plays was reversed, the new comedy proving so popular that the *Illustrated Sporting and Dramatic News* dubbed its author the "Moneyspinero."[19]

Most reviewers, though, qualified their praise with expressions of concern at the dubious morality of the plot and characters. Indeed, George Augustus Sala in the *Illustrated London News* considered the piece especially dangerous *because* of the author's dramatic skill: "Mr Pinero is an expert in ascertaining what situation will 'tell' on the stage. His scenes are capitally constructed; his characters come and go precisely as they should; the climax is most artistically led up to; and the consequence is that the piece is brilliantly successful, and that the playwright succeeds in extorting from the audience not only genuine sympathy but enthusiastic admiration for a peculiarly disreputable set of people who, properly, should be extremely repulsive."[20]

Clement Scott liked the characters no better than Sala but took a more broadminded view. Reviewing the play in his monthly magazine the *Theatre*, he stated he was "unable to agree with the verdict of those who consider that to sit out a play in which the subtlety of sin is elaborated involves a certain social disgrace on the audience," and he warned his readers that the drama "must be reduced to a pulp of sickly sentimentality if the mainsprings of action and interest are to be arrested in this fashion." He also noted that since the Manchester opening Pinero had made a significant improvement to the morality of his play and its dramatic effect. Originally he had shown Millicent Boycott as determined to cheat Lord Kengussie from the outset, but in the London production she did so only when her luck ran out in the climactic card game.[21]

"*Mr A. W. Moneyspinero*" (Illustrated Sporting and Dramatic News, *January 1881)*

William Kendal, sketch of John Hare as Baron Croodle in The Money-Spinner *(The Theatre, March 1881)*

This, the great scene of the play, had been planned in exact detail down to the identity of each card played.[22] Mrs Kendal brilliantly conveyed both Millicent's struggle with temptation and her shame when exposed as a cheat. But as the *Era* recorded, it was in the pathos of her subsequent confession to Lord Kengussie (played with appropriate magnanimity by Mr Kendal) that "her great triumph came, and that reached all hearts, touched all sympathies, and drew tears to many eyes."[23] For the more sympathetic reviewers, Mrs Kendal's acting removed any lingering doubts about the play's morality.

The other outstanding performance was Hare's portrayal of Baron Croodle, Millicent's old reprobate of a father. Though the character resembles Eccles in Robertson's *Caste* (and similar figures in Thackeray and Dickens), Hare made the baron an original creation still remembered years later as one of his finest. As T. E. Pemberton noted in his biography of Hare: "Every little detail of the character had been minutely studied, every little item of make-up and costume carefully thought out. When he surreptitiously lifted his brandy-flask to his lips or when he, in a half-lordly fashion, asked the naturally high-minded daughter he had trained to cheat if 'there was any little dispute at cards that dear papa could settle' we laughed at, but we pitied him. . . . The impersonation possessed the whimsical pathos of Newman Noggs and the irresistible but transparent bluster of Captain Costigan, and was in its way unique."[24]

The Money-Spinner's run suffered a setback on 22 February when Mrs Kendal was seriously injured in a cab accident on her way to the theatre. For the next three weeks Millicent Boycott was played by an understudy, and audiences fell away. On Saturday, 12 March, Mrs Kendal, declaring that "work was the best cure," returned to the St James's with "her arm in a silken sling and with a cruel scar on her forehead . . . to be pelted with flowers by her legion of friends."[25] But she had returned too soon to act with her usual vitality and after another month, during which it was alternated with *The Lady of Lyons*, *The Money-Spinner* had to be taken off.

iv. Farewell to the Lyceum

In early March 1881 Pin suffered a severe bout of flu. After several weeks of nursing at Gravesend by his mother and Fanny, he recovered sufficiently to resume his part in *The Corsican Brothers*.[26] He had been writing incessantly for two years, and the illness was a warning that he needed to slow down.

His recovery was helped by an invitation from the Bancrofts to join their Haymarket company in September at the start of the new season. He accepted without hesitation. Though grateful for Irving's generous encouragement, Pin was embarrassed by his inability to write starring roles for the Chief. The Bancrofts, for their part, had always prided themselves on their ensemble and were quite content to play minor roles when this suited a particular production. No doubt Pin imagined himself writing plays for them at the Haymarket that would eclipse the success of Robertson's comedies at the Prince of Wales's.

He also hoped his new engagement would impress Myra, who was enjoying a triumph at the Bancrofts' old theatre. On 2 February she had begun playing a lead role in *The Colonel* by F. C. Burnand, editor of *Punch*. Burnand had adapted the comedy from an old French farce into a skit on the aesthetic craze and the art-for-art's-sakers personified in the figure of Oscar Wilde, who had recently burst out of his Oxford cocoon and onto the London scene. Intending to play the lead, Bancroft had commissioned *The Colonel* for the Haymarket, then rejected the play because of a weak third act. Bancroft's loss proved Edgar Bruce's gain and an important step in the early career of Beerbohm Tree, who soon after the start of the play's run took over the Wilde-like role of Lambert Streyke.[27] As the run continued on and on, Pin must have viewed with concern Myra's proximity to the notoriously amorous Tree.

Meanwhile, the Lyceum season drew to an end with a revival of Mrs Hannah Cowley's old comedy, *The Belle's Stratagem*. Pin had a tolerable part in it but did not appear in the more important piece on the bill, Alfred, Lord Tennyson's *The Cup*. From the beginning of April until mid-May, however, this programme was alternated with a revival of *Othello* that Irving staged especially for the visiting American tragedian Edwin Booth, who had suffered a poor run at the Princess's Theatre earlier that season. Booth and Irving alternated Othello and Iago at successive performances. Pin contributed an excellent Roderigo, according to Ellen Terry, who later remarked that he "was always good in the 'silly ass' kind of part, and no one could say of him that he was playing himself!"[28] On 2 July 1881 he gave a final performance as Augustus Caddell to Alma Murray's Daisy White and then, after a few more nights of *The Belle's Stratagem,* packed up his gear and left the Lyceum.

He was aware that a new and promising phase of his career was about to begin. What he could not have anticipated was the price he would have to pay for success.

.. Act 2 ..

Development

(1881—1891)

...6...
The Madding Crowd

i. Pinero and the Biographers

Like most people, Pinero displayed different aspects of his personality in different contexts, which is why at times I use different names
for him: Arthur the stagestruck boy; "Pin" the young Bohemian and
(later) clubbable companion; and Pinero the professional actor, playwright, and public figure. It was in this last role that he deliberately
created difficulties for interviewers and prospective biographers.
There is no lack of liveliness and candour in the surviving letters by
Arthur or Pin, but Pinero was to become obsessively close and
guarded, the despair of all who attempted to question him about any
aspect of his work or private life.

Though much of Pinero's professional correspondence survives,
the only personal letters that remain are those to the Schneiders,
Tolman, and some later, less intimate friends. All letters to close family
members appear to have been deliberately destroyed either by the
playwright or at his request. Nor was he prepared to offer much
assistance to would-be biographers during his lifetime.

I have already referred to Pinero's repudiation of stories about his
Lyceum days in H. Hamilton Fyfe's *Sir Arthur Pinero's Plays and
Players* (1930). The publication of this attempt at a critical biography
elicited protests from Pinero that the book contained many basic
errors — including a fictional birthplace, the Old Kent Road.[1] In reply
Fyfe claimed that when he was researching an earlier biography,

Arthur Wing Pinero, Playwright (1902), Pinero had refused to supply any information for it and that he (Fyfe) had been "therefore driven back on other sources, mostly books of reminiscences and newspaper articles."[2] In a subsequent letter of self-justification, Fyfe stated, "When I set to work on the second book, I knew it would be no use asking you to alter your decision, for I was aware that your horror of 'publicity' had deepened in the interval," adding that though he regretted the mistakes, "the life of a book nowadays is little more than that of a newspaper article. Soon they are both forgotten and soon we all shall be. Which may be annoying or consoling, according to temperament."[3] This — as Fyfe was well aware — was not a particularly tactful remark to make to a playwright only too conscious of a fading reputation.

Because of this experience Pinero was slightly more cooperative when in November 1933 a persistent young American scholar named Wilbur Dwight Dunkel announced that he intended to devote his forthcoming sabbatical leave to researching another biography. Pinero showed Dunkel some correspondence, made marginal comments on the American's transcripts of old newspaper reviews, and let slip a few previously concealed biographical details, such as the street where his school had been situated — though not the fact that it was a charity school. The playwright, however, still withheld much basic information (for example, the age difference between his parents) and all letters of a personal nature, and Dunkel was too much in awe of him to press more closely. As a result, Dunkel's *Sir Arthur Pinero: A Critical Biography with Letters*, published some six years after its subject's death, added little of substance to the record beyond transcripts of several interesting professional letters that have since been lost.

Nor did the numerous interviewers from newspapers and magazines fare any better during the playwright's lifetime. After a session with Pinero in 1923, Carlton Miles noted in the American publication *Theatre* that

> it should be said at once that if you attempt an interview you fail. To interview Pinero is impossible. For years he has dodged the London

questioners. "If you see Pinero, it will be an achievement," said a British critic. "He is a miracle of secretiveness." Discretion rather than secretiveness. A conversation with the dramatist is a game of mental tennis. He has returned your serve with a quick, double twist that sends the ball of discussion out of bounds. Strive as you will, he reaches advantage at once and takes the game with a smile that comes of the surety of practice.[4]

Pinero's discretion — and secretiveness — had not always been a game. To some extent his extreme reticence about personal matters may have been a consequence of the conditioning he received from his father and from his own work in solicitors' offices. It was also typical of Victorian notions of respectability that one's private life be concealed from public view. But in large measure Pinero's fear of publicity was caused by a combination of private disappointments with public savaging of his work while a struggling young writer. When evidence from a variety of sources is pieced together, the "second act" of his story — a decade that included the end of his courtship, the beginning of his marriage, and his early years of full-time authorship — emerges as a time of trial that reshaped his personality and his later drama.

ii. The Commission

During summer 1881, before taking up his engagement at the Haymarket, Pinero was hard at work on another play for Hare and the Kendals. Mrs Kendal in particular was keen to follow up her success as Millicent Boycott with a new role written specifically for her by the same author. But the project did not go smoothly at first. For a while the young playwright laboured at a three-act comedy, provisionally called *Bound to Marry*, in which a wealthy young man in love with an artist promises to marry instead the gold-digging sister of a youth he has accidentally crippled.[5] Like *The Money-Spinner*, the piece combined humour, pathos, and drama, but the plot was hopelessly involved and contrived. Worse still, neither of the principal female characters was likely to appeal to Mrs Kendal, as the one was too naive and the other too unsympathetic.

Then Pinero remembered a plot idea he had jotted down some time earlier in an old notebook. The memorandum read: "The notion of a young couple secretly married — the girl, about to become a mother, finding that a former wife is in existence. The heroine amongst those who respect and love her. The fury of a rejected lover, who believes her to be a guilty woman. Two men face to face at night-time. Qy. — kill the first wife?"[6]

Pinero mentioned the plot idea to Hare and then discussed it in detail with Mrs Kendal. The problem was to give this "Pinerotic" puzzle (as Shaw would have called it) some dramatic flesh. When Pinero suggested the situation might fit into a play with a rural setting such as *Hester's Mystery*, it seems the actress offered some more ideas to round out the basic scheme. Why not make the heroine the owner of a farm, like Nance Butterworth, but younger and better bred — say, a squire in her own right following the death of her father? Suppose she were secretly married to an army officer — a lieutenant perhaps — and her farm manager or bailiff (who had been in love with her since childhood) found out that the lieutenant was visiting her at night. Would not that bring about the memorandum climax quite naturally? Of course, some suitably rustic minor characters would be needed to fill out the scene: perhaps an old gaffer, a pair of vengeful gypsies, a young country girl in love with a soldier who deserts her, and so forth. Encouraged by Mrs Kendal's interest and suggestions, the young playwright threw aside the script of *Bound to Marry* and eagerly set to work on the new play.

In the meantime another Pinero piece, *Imprudence*, a three-act farce dashed off before *The Money-Spinner*,[7] was playing a limited season at the Folly and doing excellent business. Toole was to have the theatre (which would soon bear his name) redecorated later in the summer, but as he was touring until December, he had let it at a nominal rent for two months to Carton, who was venturing into management with his friend's boarding-house romp.

Carton had put together a good company for *Imprudence*, keeping the leads for himself and his wife. He played Baines Durant, a plausible but feckless young man who sets himself up as an amateur matrimonial agent at "Mrs Lazenby's High-Class Boarding Establishment" and causes havoc amongst the guests; Miss Compton appeared as flirtatious Mrs Parminter Blake, the siren of the house. Both were warmly received, the *Era* commending Carton as "one of the best living representatives of what we may call the Charles Mathews school" and describing his wife's acting as "most satisfactory and pleasing" in her development from lighthearted vivacity in the first act to apprehension in the second and repentance in the third.[8]

The play also featured a gallery of amusing eccentrics, among them Mrs Blake's ridiculously jealous little husband, Parminter; a grumbling old sea dog called Captain Rattlefish; a peppery ex–Indian Civil Service official; and a landlady who sleeps in a sideboard to protect the dining-room silver. Although most reviewers thought the plot thin, nearly all enjoyed the characters. An odd exception was Scott, who took the piece as a serious study of contemporary manners and earnestly condemned the lodging-house's inhabitants as "the most objectionable that ever sat around a table"[9] — to which the usually Captious Critic of the *Illustrated Sporting and Dramatic News* sensibly replied in Pinero's defence, "Hoity-toity! What *has* the boy done? A three-act farce full of fun and unbounded good humour of dialogue, the only fault of which is its exuberance and good-natured boisterousness."[10]

Pinero had superintended the rehearsals himself — the first time he had directed his own work — and according to the *Weekly Dispatch*, the production "went with perfect smoothness on the first night."[11] The audience consisted largely of actors who gave their colleague a warm reception when he appeared in front of the curtain at the play's close in response to repeated cries of "Author!" Indeed, the playwright seemed carried away by their applause and, as the *Stage* noted disapprovingly,[12] actually blew kisses at them, perhaps really directed at Myra and his family. Enthusiastic audiences packed the Folly for the next two months until the production had to make way for Toole's carpenters and decorators. Carton then presented it at the Standard Theatre in northeast London for another fortnight and later that year took it on tour. Thereafter, despite some lively characterisation and homely wit, *Imprudence* vanished from the stage.

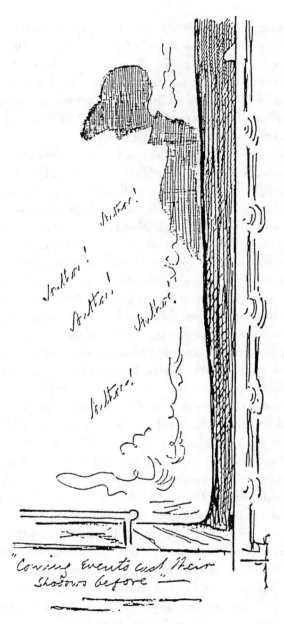

"Coming Events Cast Their Shadows Before" (Illustrated Sporting and Dramatic News, *August 1881*)

iii. Progress

At the end of August 1881, Pinero was the subject of a full-length article in a publication called the *Biograph*. The piece began by stating that readers who were interested "in the future of original dramatic work in this country" would be pleased that "in Mr Pinero's case we have an author who has not thought it necessary to seek his inspiration from foreign sources. Mr Pinero has relied on himself with the happiest results." The article then outlined his career and, after noting that the playwright was soon to join the Bancrofts at the Haymarket, summed up his accomplishments and aspirations in glowing terms:

> Mr Pinero has an acquaintance with literature, which is by no means confined to theatrical matters pure and simple. He has written several clever papers for magazines, which imply something more than mere dramatic power, but of late has been obliged to give up this work. His knowledge of theatrical history is accurate and sound, and he thoroughly appreciates the literary merit and poetry of a school of play-writers whose method is the entire opposite of his own as regards adaptability to stage requirements. He himself, however, knows where his own strength lies; he belongs most unmistakably to the school of actor-authors represented by Mr Byron and Mr Robertson, and he wisely seeks to obtain excellence in his own line, without aspiring to a domain in which he would not be at home.[13]

In pursuit of this excellence Pinero worked with more than usual care on *The Squire*, tightening the plot but leaving room for humour and for detail that would help "get the scent of the hay over the footlights."[14] When at last he was satisfied with the script, he travelled to Birmingham, where Hare and the Kendals were on tour. They listened to the play with enthusiasm, but Hare observed that the plot bore some resemblance to *Far from the Madding Crowd*. Pin replied that he had read Thomas Hardy's novel, but after he had conceived and planned his play. The managers then agreed to stage *The Squire* at the St James's at the end of the year.

Back in London Pin turned his attention to his part in Taylor's *Plot and Passion*, which the Bancrofts, lacking a new play, had selected to open their winter season. They were making a late start, as Bancroft had added a trip to Constantinople to his usual lengthy holiday and so was not back in London for the final rehearsals until November. These were conducted in a more gentlemanly manner than Irving's long and exhausting drill sessions at the Lyceum. Bancroft's rehearsals, which he ran jointly with his stage manager Edward Hastings, began punctually at ten with the supers (or "extra ladies and gentlemen," as they were called at the Haymarket), the principals came at eleven, and everyone finished precisely at one. No member of the public was ever allowed to intrude, so things generally got done with a minimum of fuss.

The Haymarket company for the new season was, as usual, a fine one. In *Plot and Passion*, Bancroft gave himself a change from his usual swells by acting Fouché, Napoleon's unscrupulous minister of police; Arthur Cecil, perhaps the best light comedy actor in London, played the crafty Desmarets (the part Pinero had sacrificed his moustache for eight years ago); and the handsome, well-tailored H. B. Conway was cast as the hero, Henri de Neuville, opposite Ada Cavendish's Marie de Fontagnes. Mrs Bancroft did not appear in the main play but was featured in the afterpiece, a comedietta by Burnand called *The Lesson*, with Conway and Charles Brookfield, a clever young actor who later metamorphosed into the Lord Chamberlain's examiner of plays.

It says something for Pinero's acting that in the midst of such a company he received good notices for his playing of the foolish Marquis de Cevennes when *Plot and Passion* opened on 26 November. (It was also a tribute to his diction, for outside the theatre that night a storm was threatening to blow the roof off.) But the piece, by then nearly thirty years old, had clearly outlived its popularity and played only six weeks or so to thin houses.

Tickets were at a premium, however, for one performance staged at the Haymarket during the run. The celebrated society beauty Lillie Langtry asked the Bancrofts if they would sublet their theatre for a charity matinee of *She Stoops to Conquer* in which she would play Kate Hardcastle, a role she had been coached in by Mrs Henrietta Labouchere. The Bancrofts agreed and on 15 December sat in their own

stalls savouring what they later described as "a remarkable performance of the small part of Diggory by Mr Pinero"[15] — while the Prince
of Wales gazed indulgently at his Jersey Lily.

But these were sideshows for Pin. His main concern was the
forthcoming premiere of *The Squire* arranged for a few days after
Christmas. Writing to Chrissy Schneider from new lodgings at 20
Buckingham Street, the Strand, on 22 December, he thanked her for
one of the prettiest Christmas cards he had ever received but confessed
to not feeling "at all Christmassy," being "borne down just now with
worry and bother." He would, however, get home to Gravesend for
Christmas Day, when he hoped "the sight of the Almonds and Raisins
and Ginger Wine" would animate him "with a proper sense of the
conviviality of the occasion."[16]

iv. Scandal

The premiere of *The Squire* at the St James's on Thursday, 29
December had every appearance of being a triumph. The picturesque
settings, the actors, and the author were all warmly applauded. Mrs
Kendal as the lady squire, Kate Verity, and Kendal as her secret lover
and husband, Lieutenant Thorndyke, made the most of their lead
roles, notably in the dramatic nighttime encounter at the end of Act 2.
Hare impressed as a misogynistic country parson, T. N. Wenman was
a vigorous and manly Gilbert Hythe (the farm manager whose love
Kate Verity rejects), T. W. Robertson (the playwright's son) was good
as a surly young gypsy, Brandon Thomas (the future author of *Charley's Aunt*) played a comic rustic, and William MacIntosh drew roars
of laughter with his verbal and facial expressions as Old Gunnion.

Next day the critics were almost unanimous in their praise. A long
review in the *Era*, after noting that the managers of the St James's had
enjoyed little success of late, went on to say:

> Now, however, we have to congratulate Messrs Hare and Kendal on
> the possession of a piece that will, probably, take playgoing London
> by storm, crowd the theatre for many months to come, bring fortune

The Kendals in The Squire (Illustrated London News, *January 1882)*

to the managers and fame with fortune to the author, and revive the
hopes of those who, after a long endurance of adaptations from the
French, had begun almost to despair of anything good, as well as
original, from an English author's pen. In *The Squire* Mr Pinero
more than fulfils the promise held out in his comediettas and in his
first ambitious attempts . . . and at once asserts his right to a place
among the best of native writers for the stage, a claim that will readily
be admitted.[17]

The only jarring note was the widespread observation that the play
was clearly indebted for its setting and leading characters to *Far from
the Madding Crowd*, published seven years earlier. Most of the critics
were not greatly concerned about the similarities between Pinero's
Kate Verity, Lieutenant Thorndyke, and Gilbert Hythe, and Hardy's
Bathsheba Everdene, Sergeant Troy, and Gabriel Oak, adaptations of
one kind or another being common on the London stage. W. Moy
Thomas of the *Daily News*, however, took a stern line, not only
detailing the "borrowings" at some length but implying that the playwright had been guilty of questionable conduct: "That Mr Pinero,
neglecting to acknowledge the sources of his inspiration, and permitting *The Squire* to be described on the playbill as simply 'a new and
original play,' has treated Mr Hardy with what in England is considered scant courtesy, and in other countries where author's inventions
are more strictly guarded would be downright illegal, cannot, we fear,
be denied."[18]

This was chastening enough, but on New Year's Eve Pinero discovered that he had, without his knowledge, been put in a far worse
situation. A year and a half earlier, Hare had been offered an author-
ised stage version of Hardy's novel, under the title of *The Mistress of
the Farm*, by the art critic and playwright J. Comyns Carr and had
promised to produce it at the St James's, subject to the Kendals'
agreement. Mrs Kendal, though, had decided against it.[19] After a long
delay, Hare, with considerable embarrassment and many expressions
of regret, had returned the manuscript. Now he was terrified that
when Carr read the reviews of *The Squire*, the rejected author would
believe that the St James's management had stolen his play and hired
their own man to rewrite it. Hare had therefore written to Carr that

morning protesting his innocence in the hope of forestalling a scandal and a possible claim for damages.[20]

Pinero's feelings at this dreadful revelation are not recorded but may easily be imagined. To have achieved the great success he had hoped and worked for only to have it immediately discredited must have been galling. Without Mrs Kendal's "suggestions," his play would have borne little similarity to Hardy's novel, let alone to Carr's adaptation. Even after the reworking, despite similarities of character and situation, there was little resemblance between the plots or their development.[21] Nevertheless, Pinero must have resented that neither Mrs Kendal nor Hare had forewarned him of the danger he was in. Under the circumstances the aggrieved playwright had no intention of passively waiting to be branded a plagiarist.

Mrs Kendal's part in the affair could not, of course, be mentioned, but in his best official manner, Pinero wrote to the *Daily News* outlining the origins of *The Squire*, referring to his notebook memorandum, his comedietta *Hester's Mystery*, and his as yet unstaged comedy, *Girls and Boys*. *The Squire* had not, he insisted, been even slightly influenced by *Far from the Madding Crowd*, read long after the idea for the play was thoroughly in his head and its scheme imparted to Hare. He was sure that any readers of the novel who witnessed his play would "have no difficulty in perceiving that my motive, characterisation and dialogue differ wholly from Mr Hardy's; I merely put my horse's head to the open country and take the same hedges and ditches with him, though perhaps my hack is a very sorry one and lacks the blood and muscle of my neighbour's one."[22]

On Monday, 2 January, the scandal became public property and proved even more embarrassing than anticipated. Letters to the *Times* and the *Daily News* from Carr and Hardy[23] revealed that *The Mistress of the Farm* had in the first instance been adapted from the novel by Hardy himself! Carr had subsequently "improved" the play in various ways, including introducing a vengeful gypsy to replace Mr Boldwood as the slayer of Sergeant Troy — an innovation now claimed as proof that *The Squire* (which contained a somewhat similar character) had been directly plagiarised from *The Mistress of the Farm*. Hardy further stated that he had suggested to Carr that in their play Sergeant

Troy be promoted to a lieutenant and that this idea had been conveyed to the managers of the St James's. As Pinero's heroine was in love with a lieutenant, this was a further proof of plagiarism. Hare and Kendal were therefore, in Hardy's opinion, guilty of conduct that "would be a discredit to the management of any theatre." The novelist ended his letters with the claim that his play had been rendered useless by Pinero's, "for it is obviously not worth while for a manager to risk producing a piece if the whole gist of it is already to be seen by the public at another theatre."

Nor had Carr been mollified by Hare's unsolicited letter of apology. In this, the manager claimed that at the first reading of *The Squire* he had confronted Pinero with its resemblance to the novel but had felt obliged to accept the playwright's emphatic assurance that he had never "read a line" of the book. Carr proceeded to quote this absolute denial in a letter that appeared in the *Daily News* alongside one from Pinero admitting that he had read the novel while writing his play.

Hare and Kendal decided to limit their defence to a brief but firm denial that "any hint, suggestion or act" of theirs had influenced the writing of *The Squire*,[24] a statement that was literally true, as Mrs Kendal was not a signatory to their letter. With this they retired from the fray, leaving their playwright with the dilemma of either letting the matter drop (thus tacitly admitting the plagiarism charge) or continuing to protest his innocence in spite of the circumstantial evidence against him.

Pinero unwisely chose not only to deny the charges (which were mainly levelled at his managers) but, in a further letter to the *Daily News* (3 January 1882), to attack his accusers. Hardy was pardoned for "gross inaccuracies" because he had remained in Dorset and relied on his collaborator for information, but Carr was treated to the full force of Pinero's scorn: "Mr Carr is the author of a rejected play, and shares with all authors of rejected plays the bitterness of ill-success. He is evidently an angry gentleman as well as a disappointed one, and for that reason I desire to answer him most temperately. Let me give Mr Carr my solemn assurance that I have never borrowed a suggestion nor an idea from any work in which he has had a hand. Let me further assure him, with equal solemnity, that I do not intend ever to do so."[25]

Pinero would later regret these ill-judged comments, but the playwright had been stung by a further accusation of plagiarism, made anonymously in the *Daily Post*, claiming that the plot of *Daisy's Escape* had been taken from a French comedy, *La Petite Pluie* by Edouard Pailleron.[26] Pinero, who had never heard of it, vehemently denied the charge, which he suspected Moy Thomas had slipped in to add fuel to the flames. Under the circumstances it was hardly surprising that Pin was beginning to feel like a stag at bay or that his temper was getting the better of his judgement.

In the meantime Hardy, after viewing *The Squire* on 2 January with Carr and a well-known stage and society lawyer, George Lewis, had decided to retire from the dispute.[27] Though Lewis believed the similarities between the plays constituted a case, Hardy felt the public wrangle was distasteful and demeaning, especially as it was now throwing up "uncomfortably plausible counter-charges of plagiarism"[28] against two of his own novels.

Carr, however, decided to prolong the controversy. In a clever letter to the *Daily News* (written on 3 January but misdated 2 January), he mocked his opponent's credibility by pointing out the contradictions between Hare's and Pinero's letters. In Carr's opinion the only original feature of *The Squire* was its dialogue, which would have been vastly improved if it, too, had been borrowed from Hardy. Pinero replied (4 January 1882) with the equally sarcastic jibe that if he was in possession of Hardy's plot, and Carr of Hardy's beautiful dialogue, surely their plays must be quits in terms of dramatic attraction. Why didn't Carr have his play produced under the billing "The Origin of *The Squire*"? This in fact was precisely what Carr had in mind.

During the next few days the controversy appeared to simmer down. There were no legal moves against the St James's management, Carr had ignored Pinero's last letter, and Carton had written to the *Daily News* stating that it was he who had casually recommended that Pinero read — among other books — Hardy's *Far from the Madding Crowd* and *The Trumpet Major*, and that this suggestion had been made long after his friend had planned *The Squire*.[29] Had Pinero let the dispute drop at this point he might have emerged with some credit, but having learnt of Hardy and Carr's visit to the St James's, with

Lewis in tow, five days earlier, he wrote again to the *Daily News* on 7 January asking why nothing had come of the inspection and suggesting that Hardy and Carr had not found *The Squire* "quite so much like 'Far from the Madding Crowd' as they had been led to believe." Carr immediately replied that his previous letter, though wrongly dated by the paper, had clearly been written after "the conviction of the wrong done to our work had been renewed and strengthened by witnessing the performance of *The Squire*. . . . And now I have done with the matter. Mr Pinero appears to think it extraordinary that I have not wearied your readers with daily repetition of our wrongs; but those who have remarked the tone of this gentleman's letters will be scarcely surprised if I have been unwilling to prolong the discussion beyond the limits of bare necessity."[30]

Pinero had fallen into a trap of his own making but tried in a final letter (10 January 1882) to excuse his error by blaming the strain he had been under:

> I should have avoided this stupid mistake by remembering that Mr Carr . . . had said unkind things about my dialogue. But, really, who can wonder at this slip of memory on my part? In what condition of mind must I be after this lengthy squabble? What misgivings must I have as to whether my very name belongs to me? What doubts must have arisen within me as to whether I am or am not even an adapted [*sic*] son? . . . I am sorry that Mr John [*sic*] Comyns Carr takes exception to the tone of my letters; but what on earth does Mr Carr expect from me in answer to his charges? — and such charges! The compliments of the season, and so on? That Mr Carr may be better able to appreciate the moderation of my replies, let him tomorrow call a man a thief at the street corner — the result, if not amusing, will be instructive.[31]

If Pinero was not amused, the theatregoing public considered the scandal over *The Squire* great sport. The playwright Sidney Grundy, writing on 17 January to the young theatre critic William Archer, remarked with glee that the row in the *Daily News* had made life deliciously worth living, adding that it would have been even better if Mrs Kendal had been dragged into it as "Madge in a fit of righteous indignation would have been a real happiness to me. . . . She is unreason personified and real jam!" As for *The Squire*, Grundy thought it "an amateur piece of work — a play of promise, not of performance" and, after ridiculing the climax, summed up his opinion of its author: "Pinero has some knowledge of theatrical effect & is good at superficial character. But he is a moral obliquity, and his literary power is only middling." Nevertheless, he added, the book Archer was currently preparing on contemporary English dramatists would have to include some consideration of Pinero.[32]

In the meantime the papers were having a field day. The *Era* reprinted all the letters written by the principals in the controversy, Scott organised a special symposium on it in the February 1882 issue of the *Theatre*, the gossip columnists scribbled away about it, and the satirical weeklies entertained their readers with displays of wit like the following piece in *Punch:*

INHARMONIOUS CONCERT AT ST. JAMES'S THEATRE

Solo (Mr KENDAL) — "*Maria and The Squire*"

Concerted piece (Messrs HARDY and CARR) — "Far From the Madding Crowd". Arranged for the St. James's Minstrels by Mr PINERO

Press-Gang Chorus (Conducted by W. MOY THOMAS)
"*There's another jolly row at Hare's*"

Solo (by Mr HARDY) — "*Moy que j'aime*"

Trio (Messrs PINERO, HARDY and CARR) — (*Mr PINERO aside*)
PINERO, PINERO! the robbers' pet!
We (I) wish that We'd (I'd) never
This gentleman (these gentlemen) met.

Ensemble — *Dance the PINERO!* — *Contrabandisto*, Act 1

Solo (Mr J. HARE) — "*The Kendals and Comyns!* Oh dear! Oh dear!"

Solo — (Mr PINERO)

The Good Young Man who tried it on!

The Good Young Man who tried!

The probable result of the above Inharmonious Concert will be:

Publisher's Advertisement — "*Far from the Madding Crowd*"
Mr HARDY's Celebrated Novel. New and Popular Edition just out!

Theatrical Managers Advertisement — Immense Success of *The Squire* — Madding Crowd every night. Seats can be booked a year in advance![33]

Punch was right. Whatever its effect on the participants, the controversy had been good for business. At the St James's, *The Squire* was playing to capacity houses and continued to do so until the end of the season. As for Hardy and Carr, the former enjoyed increased sales of his novel, and the latter was hard at work revising *The Mistress of the Farm*.

On 27 February Carr's play — now identical in title to the novel — opened at the Prince of Wales's Theatre, Liverpool, with a strong cast that included Marion Terry as Bathsheba Everdene and Charles Kelly (Ellen Terry's husband) as Gabriel Oak. Many London critics came up for the premiere to report on the reputed similarities between this play and Pinero's. As, however, Carr had deleted all of Hardy's first act, added a new final act of his own, and extensively reworked the rest of the play, little remained of the original on which to base comparisons. By and large the critics found Carr's piece old-fashioned and melodramatic when set against Pinero's, and most admitted that any similarities were superficial. Two months later, after a brief provincial tour, *Far from the Madding Crowd* opened in London at the Globe and played for some ten weeks, a longer run than it probably would have enjoyed on its own merits.

v. Consequences

The controversy over *The Squire* might well be regarded as a storm in a teacup, but it did Pinero a good deal of harm. Later playwrights like Shaw and Wilde who rejected Victorian notions of the sanctity of property — especially in the area of literary ideas — would have laughed at the charges of plagiarism levelled in this case and pointed out that literary originality is a matter of how a writer treats an idea, not where he gets it from. Judged from this standpoint, as William Archer was to point out,[34] the chief weakness of *The Squire* is not any possible indebtedness of situation to Hardy's novel but an ending that panders to sentimentality and theatrical convenience. Pinero, however, had reacted with moral outrage to what he — the son of a solicitor — regarded as a charge of theft and then had added to the damage by venting his spleen against another writer who had at least as much reason to feel wronged. Later he would make up with Carr, but for many years critics and rivals, knowing Pinero to be sensitive to imputations of plagiarism, would deliberately goad him in the hope of provoking another outburst.

Just how deeply the sense of injustice had entered Pinero's soul and soured his sense of humour was demonstrated a few days after the Liverpool premiere of Carr's play. Herman Merivale, a minor novelist and playwright, suggested in a letter to the *Times* that novelists would be well advised in future to produce dramatised versions of their novels to "save themselves from being Pinerized."[35] Pinero replied with unconcealed anger:

> In *The Times* of yesterday Mr Herman C. Merivale, a dramatic author, under the pretence of treating the question of novelists and their rights, insults me, a dramatic author, by attempting to cast a slur upon my honesty. I doubt whether the brilliancy of the pun which Mr Merivale makes upon my name will quite atone, in the eyes of the readers of *The Times*, for the utter absence from Mr Merivale's letter of any indication of the writer's good breeding. Mr Merivale should be careful to keep a schoolboy at his elbow to prompt him in the observance of those very elementary rules of politeness which are intuitive to men of culture and refinement.[36]

Yet there was one bright spot for Pin in the midst of all this strife. He was making progress in his courtship. Although Myra was still appearing with Tree in the seemingly unending run of *The Colonel*, she had eventually given in to Pin's entreaties and was now unofficially engaged to him. Tree, too, was engaged and was being kept jealously in line by his future bride, Maud Holt, who had been displeased when she learnt he had presented his leading lady with an expensive silk scarf from Liberty's on her birthday![37] But this little contretemps had no perceptible effect on Pin and Myra. On 17 May they appeared together in *Daisy's Escape* at a special matinee at the St James's in aid of "The Persecuted Jews of Russia." Among the distinguished actors and actresses who appeared in the other items were the Bancrofts, Mrs Kendal, Jessie Millward, Arthur Cecil, Toole, and Hare.[38]

As the season ended Pin made an important decision. The time had come for him to give up acting on a regular basis. His brief spell at the Haymarket had been enjoyable and furthered his friendship with the Bancrofts, but he had made little progress as an actor. His supporting roles in *Plot and Passion* and *She Stoops to Conquer* had been followed by similar parts in a revival of *Ours* and an undistinguished drama by Victorien Sardou called *Odette,* none of which had extended or even interested him very much. Next season the Bancrofts planned to open with yet another old Taylor comedy, *The Overland Route,* which offered more of the same. Though they were also hoping for a new play from him, Pin felt that he would make a better job of it if he freed himself from the distraction of having to appear on stage night after night.

Besides, he wanted to get away for a while. He had written little or nothing since the outbreak of the controversy and needed peace and quiet to clear his mind and get back to work. Despite the bitter aftertaste of the squabble surrounding it, *The Squire* had at least given him a measure of financial independence that seemed likely to continue for a while. Not only were Hare and the Kendals about to take the play on a long tour of the major provincial cities, but Edgar Bruce was organising two more companies to cover the smaller centres. Pin therefore wrote to the Bancrofts telling them of his decision, thanking them for many kindnesses, and expressing his appreciation of their unique style of management: "In one's early days, what was known as 'sentiment in business' flourished poorly. In the Haymarket Theatre, the actor's willingness to do as much as he can for his managers is more than matched by his managers' anxiety to do more for the actor. I carry away with me a regard for you both quite unbusinesslike, but which I am glad to acknowledge always and everywhere."[39]

Now he had to find whether he was capable of supporting himself — and before long a wife and family, too — by his pen alone.

...7...
Low Water

i. Archer

A month or two before Pinero became a full-time playwright, William Archer published his first book on contemporary drama. *English Dramatists of Today* (1882) was a pioneering study for the simple reason that virtually nobody at that time thought Britain had any worthwhile contemporary drama to speak of, let alone write a book on. Nor did Archer. His frankly stated aim was to show "by applying a moderately high standard of criticism to the body of our contemporary drama, how far it falls short of any literary merit, and, in so doing, to indicate possibilities of improvement and elevation."[1]

Archer, who was to exert a significant influence on Pinero's career and become a firm friend, was twenty-five — a year younger than the playwright — when he began this task. He had, however, already enjoyed a range of experience that gave his criticism a wider perspective than that of other theatre critics. Born in Perth, Scotland, in 1856, he was the eldest of a family that included five sons and four daughters. His father had been a farmer in Australia and a gold prospector in California, and his mother was the daughter of a Glasite Church elder who was also one of Perth's leading publishers. Archer appears to have inherited traits from both parents — a zest for adventure, a touch of wanderlust, intellectual curiosity, a love of literature, and, above all, a sense of mission. The family Mecca was Archer's grandparents' home at Tolderodden in Norway. Archer spent several years of his early childhood in the old house, which he later described as the first place he could remember and the last he would forget. During this time he spoke only Norwegian, though he lost most of it when his family moved back to Scotland. He was educated in Edinburgh and in 1872 won a four-year scholarship to the university. His father then returned with the rest of his family to Australia, but Archer stayed on, combining university study with some journalism to supplement his grant and spending his summer holidays at Tolderodden. He retaught himself Norwegian in order to read the early plays of Henrik Ibsen — at that time entirely unknown in Britain — and visited the Copenhagen Royal Theatre, an experience that was to inspire his later campaign for a British national theatre.

After acquiring an undistinguished M.A. in 1876, Archer sailed to Australia to visit his family. On his return a year later, he translated a recently published Ibsen play into English as *The Pillars of Society*, wrote a series of articles on the Comédie Française during a six-week visit to Paris, and, after a year as a journalist in Edinburgh, moved to London in January 1879. He became theatre critic for the *London Figaro*, his first article a discussion on the lack of worthy contemporary British drama. The next month he followed this up with a satirical poem on the same theme, and three years and many theatre reviews later, he launched a full-scale onslaught on the London stage, newspaper critics, and audiences in the opening chapter of *English Dramatists of Today*.

A lack of serious criticism informed by fundamental principles had, he believed, left the theatre in the hands of a public composed of "the most Philistine section of the middle classes and . . . the worse than Philistine, the utterly frivolous section of the upper class." Such people were prepared "to laugh always, cry sometimes, shudder now and then, but think — never." Above all they could be relied on to reject out of hand any play to which the word "unpleasant" could be applied. "The British public," he charged, "want sedatives and not stimulants in the theatre, and it is the essence of great and serious modern drama to be a stimulant and not a sedative. There lies the whole question in a nutshell."[2]

What he was looking for was the emergence in Britain of a play-wright who, like Ibsen in Norway, would lift the nation's drama to a new level of literary and intellectual achievement. But before "the coming dramatist" could hope to find a manager and a public, "the coming critic" (who would probably write for a serious magazine rather than a daily paper) would have to prepare the way. "When he appears," Archer told his readers, "I shall begin to have some hope that the day of regeneration is at hand."[3] Inwardly, no doubt, he saw himself as this critical John the Baptist. It was to be five years before Archer became personally acquainted with Pinero, but his influence on the playwright began with the publication of his book on English dramatists. Taking Grundy's advice, Archer had not only included Pinero amongst the contemporary playwrights discussed in his book but devoted a full chapter to analysing *The Money-Spinner, Imprudence,* and *The Squire.* Though Archer admitted his study was more detailed than the plays deserved, he felt they showed "sufficient promise to warrant a hope that we have in their author a playwright of genuine talent, whose more mature work will take a prominent and honourable place upon the stage in coming years."[4]

ii. Girls and Boys

Archer's public encouragement was probably a key factor in Pinero's decision to devote himself solely to writing. English drama, as the young playwright knew from firsthand experience, was indeed at a low ebb, thus creating the opportunity for a new playwright of ability to make his mark. But it is one thing to be hailed as a promising writer and another to fulfil that promise. Pinero had no political programme to promote or "views" to propound; his only cause was the desire to write better plays than his contemporaries. It is therefore hardly surprising that it took him some time to find his way as a playwright, let alone to achieve popularity.

"Such success as I have obtained," he was to remark many years later, "I attribute to small powers of observation and great patience and perseverance."[5] Finding he worked best late at night — this having been the only time available for uninterrupted writing while he was acting — he soon established a routine of sitting down at his desk at about six o'clock, writing for some three hours until supper, then resuming work around midnight for another three hours. In front of him as he wrote would be a detailed ground plan of the stage setting for the scene he was writing. He did not, however, remain continuously at his desk but did much of his thinking pacing back and forward in his room, smoking more than was good for him.

He had moved out of London to give himself peace and quiet, taking rooms at a place called Echo Lodge, downriver at Milton-next-Gravesend, not far from his mother's. After breakfast he would attend to his mail and then take a walk along the riverside. Afternoons were usually spent visiting or relaxing, his favourite pastimes being riding, cycling, walking, and playing cricket.

But he could not stay out of town for long. By early October 1882 he was back to supervise rehearsals for the long-delayed production of *Girls and Boys* at Toole's Theatre. *The Colonel* was at last about to be retired, and Myra was ready for a change after nearly two years of "flopping" and posing as an aesthetic wife in Burnand's successful but shallow comedy. Gillian West, the worldly-wise circus rider, though not an especially sympathetic role, at least offered Myra something different.

On 11 October Pin took a night off to see the opening of Irving's lavish revival of *Much Ado About Nothing* at the Lyceum. The production featured a strong cast, from Ellen Terry and Irving's Beatrice and Benedick to William Terriss's Don Pedro and Tom Mead's Friar Francis. Even the secondary lovers, Hero and Claudio, were exceptionally well played, the former by Jessie Millward and the latter by the rising young romantic actor Johnston Forbes-Robertson. Pin was so impressed with the performance that he immediately wrote to congratulate Irving on "as perfect a representation of a Shakespearian play as I conceive to be possible." "I think," he added, with perhaps a hint of gloom at the prospects of his latest piece, "that the work at your theatre does so much to create new playgoers — which is what we want, far more I fancy than we want new theatres and perhaps new plays."[6]

Satirical sketches of Girls and Boys (Illustrated Sporting and Dramatic News, *November 1882)*

Certainly neither the public nor the critics appeared to want what was offered by *Girls and Boys* when this "Nursery Tale" opened on 1 November 1882. The play, as Sala remarked in the *Illustrated London News*, was "a hodge-podge, in which comedy, farce, domestic drama, pastoral and burlesque extravaganza are confusingly intermingled."[7] Toole playing the village cobbler-cum-schoolmaster did his best to keep the audience amused by touches such as his lugubrious look on remarking that he wished he had known his breakfast herring before it had been cremated. But Myra's role was of a totally different order. Lines like Gillian West's opening remark, "I wish to live in a little village like Bassingdene. I have had a great deal of trouble in my life, and the seclusion of the place pleases me," suggested a sympathetic character study, but a clumsy plot made her appear, as Sala put it, "an unstable and cynical egoist" whom the audience found repellent. Toole gave the play every chance, keeping it on for fifty-three performances even though the houses were thin; a less indulgent manager would have changed the bill much sooner.

The play's poor reception depressed Pinero because he had hoped to direct it in the United States the following year, with himself and Myra playing the leads. Augustin Daly, who was presenting *The Squire* with an all-star cast at his own theatre in New York, had considered the proposition but after the unfavourable London reviews of *Girls and Boys* lost interest in it. The playwright made a forlorn attempt to keep the idea alive by suggesting a similar scheme to another New York manager, Lester Wallack, who declined it as well, having lost money earlier that year with a production of *The Money-Spinner*.[8]

iii. Marriage

By the end of 1882 Pinero had completed two new plays: a drama called *The Rector* for Arthur Cecil and a comedy entitled *Low Water* for Carton. Bancroft, too, wanted a new piece for the Haymarket, and on New Year's Day Pin began work on this commission. But best of all was that Myra, on the strength of these prospects, had agreed to marry him, though not to give up her career. He therefore had every reason to look forward to the year ahead. As it happened, the next two years were to prove mostly a time of trial, frustration, and disappointment.

The first setback was the failure of *The Rector*, which survived only fifteen performances after opening at the Court on 24 March 1883. The *Era* was almost alone in appreciating the effort that had gone into the play: "There will, of course, be contrary opinions as to the dramatic theories Mr Pinero has adopted in the working out of his story, but there can only be one opinion as to the cleverness the author has displayed in his novel sketches of character, and the refinement, ease and brilliancy of his dialogue. Seldom is a modern play so well written, or with so much earnestness of intention."[9]

But the plot had a fatal flaw. Not only was the audience denied important information in the earlier acts, but it was deliberately misled at the climax into believing the false testimony of a character later revealed to be suffering from sunstroke. The protracted agonisings of the central character — a clergyman made to suspect his young wife of causing the ruin and suicide of his best friend — thus turned out to be totally pointless. Pinero, as Joseph Knight remarked in the *Athenaum*, had mystified his audience for three acts only to enrage them in the fourth.[10] Not even a talented cast, which included John Clayton as the rector, Marion Terry as his wife, and Arthur Cecil and Kate Rorke among the supporting players, could save the piece after that.

Despite this debacle, Myra kept her word and married Pin at the District Register Office, Broadstreet, Bloomsbury, on 19 April. For the next two months the couple stayed at Pin's old Bedford Square lodgings, as Myra was to appear in a new Collins play called *Rank and Riches*. She fell ill during rehearsals and on 28 May Collins wrote to Pin to express his concern, adding that he well remembered "the funny actor who interested us" in times past and heartily congratulated him on the position to which he had risen as a dramatic author. As for his own play, Collins felt that the first half was beginning to "look alive" and hoped the second half would follow suit when they began work on it next day.[11] In the event, however, *Rank and Riches* failed completely when it opened at the Adelphi Theatre on 9 June; it ran only a week. Pinero later recalled standing beside Collins at the back of the dress circle that night: "We exchanged greetings, and I noticed that, expecting a call at the fall of the curtain, he wore a large camelia in his button-hole. Everything went wrong. The audience, amused by some awkwardly phrased expressions, tittered; then, as the play advanced, broke into unrestrained laughter; and finally, enraged by an indignant protest from one of the actors, hooted the thing unmercifully."[12]

Pin was soon to experience for himself what Collins had suffered that night, but the failure of *Rank and Riches* affected Myra more seriously because it effectively put an end to her acting career. Her ill health at this time enabled Pin to insist on her taking a long rest from the stage. He took a house at 10 Marlborough Crescent, Bedford Park, an artistic suburb sufficiently far from town to discourage Myra from undertaking further acting engagements. In time she came to accept the restrictions, but it was hard for her to return to a purely domestic existence after having enjoyed professional success and financial independence.

Pin, too, found that his marriage fell short of his hopes. He was to have no children of his own, though he had very much wanted to be a father. At the end of 1882 he had sent Clement Scott, in response to a request for some short items for the *Theatre*, several poems, including the following effort:

The Riddle — A Song

I've a wife who is fair as the down of the swan
And as sweet as perfume arabesque —
She is called Lady Gwendoline — I am plain John,
And a drone at a barrister's desk.
There's no maid who can laugh like my beautiful wife,
While I'm dull to the lowest degree —
So the riddle that puzzled me during my life
Is — why should my wife love me — love me?
Why should my wife love me?

When I'm weary with toil she is witty and bright,
And a slave to my every whim,
So my friends in propounding the riddle delight —
What can beauty and grace see in *him?*

Ah but look where she faces me beaming and glad,
As she dandles our boy on his knee,
She can hear her babe lisping the little word — dad!
And that's why my wife loves me — loves me,
That's why my wife loves me![13]

Whether or not the cause was Myra's ill health, Pin had to abandon this dream. He was later to remark that the wise course with disasters was to dismiss them from one's mind, adding that "after a while the process becomes a mechanical matter and it is possible to defy misfortune."[14] The lesson was not learnt easily. All he could do to combat his frustration at this time was immerse himself in his work. Marriage therefore made no difference to his regime of writing until the small hours of the morning.

He had, however, acquired two stepchildren, one of whom was to prove a great comfort to him. Little Myra Hamilton, eight at the time of her mother's remarriage, had been his principal ally during courtship, and their relationship remained close and affectionate. She called him "Ebe" and listened with delight and fascination to the stories he made up for her entertainment. Later she became a children's writer and published two collections of fairy-tales, the first of which is dedicated: "To my mother and stepfather, my two best friends . . . in loving gratitude for generous help and unfailing sympathy."[15]

Nine-year-old Angus Hamilton did not adapt so easily to his new circumstances. Though physically brave, he was shy and afflicted with a dreadful stammer that made conversation with strangers a nightmare for him.[16] Deeply attached to his mother, he probably resented Pin as an intruder. He took part in his stepfather's impromptu cricket matches but did not confide in him or ask for help in times of trouble. Longing to emulate the military heroism he associated with the fading memory of his dead father, Angus later became a war correspondent who revelled in physical hardship and danger but could not cope with the pressures of everyday life.

The difficulties Pin, Myra, and her children experienced in adjusting to each other were heightened by Pin's irregular income and lack of professional success at this time. Indeed, as J. F. Nisbet had recently noted in the *Times*, he currently enjoyed "the curious distinction of having won a reputation for cleverness mainly by means of dramatic failures."[17]

iv. "Up Like a Rocket . . ."

In the second week of July 1883, Pin was given a tantalising taste of the fruits of success when Bancroft included him among ninety actors invited to a special supper in the main dining room of the Garrick Club to bid farewell to Irving on the eve of his first American tour. Though Pin had yet to achieve his boyhood goal of club membership, he must have felt, as he dined with the leading actors and managers of the present surrounded by portraits of outstanding actors of the past, that he had come a long way in ten years.

The end of July found him in Liverpool for the final rehearsals and opening night of *The Rocket*, a three-act comedy he had written for the popular comedian Edward Terry — not a member of the famous theatrical family but a Londoner who had served his acting apprenticeship under Calvert at Manchester. Terry had subsequently become a key member of Hollingshead's celebrated burlesque quartet (with Nellie Farren, Kate Vaughan, and Edward Royce) at the Gaiety, where he became so popular that he commanded a salary of £100 a week from Hollingshead as well as the privilege of touring on his own account during the summer. Soon he would be managing his own London theatre.

The Rocket went off quite well at Manchester and at the end of the year made a good showing at the Gaiety for a limited run of fifty-one performances. But the playwright regarded it as a potboiler — if a necessary one — and was rather ashamed of it. It was, he frankly admitted, a one-part play, and that part merely an expanded version of Baron Croodle under another name. In response to a suggestion from the playwright Henry Arthur Jones that he should treat himself to a holiday in Cornwall after writing it, Pin replied jokingly:

A. W. Pinero, sketches of Edward Terry and Squire Bancroft (The Sketch, *March 1993)*

The moment a man has written a Farcical Comedy, or played Rosencrantz to Irving's Hamlet, his Doctor begins to talk about Brain Tissues and Nerve Centres — whereas *you* know very well, my dear Jones, that a play of the substance of

THE ROCKET

calls for little mental strain, while the construction of a work like

The Silver King

demands none whatever.[18]

The remark, of course, was a friendly dig at the recent success of Jones's popular melodrama, but Pin meant what he said about his own play.

He had far more pride invested in *Lords and Commons*, which the Bancrofts had commissioned for the Haymarket. The plot of this comedy was based on a Swedish romantic novel, *Mannen af Böes* by Maria Sophia Schwartz, which a friend of Bancroft had recommended as having the makings of an effective drama. In fact the story was not promising. It concerned an aristocrat who rejects his wife on her wedding night when he learns that her birth was illegitimate but fails to recognise her fourteen years later when she returns as a wealthy American lady intent on humbling his pride. Pinero did not bother to read the romance, but Bancroft's secondhand narration of the plot offered a suitable framework for a satirical comedy of manners.

Although he later claimed to have written the first draft in just ten days,[19] Pinero worked hard on revising and polishing the text before handing over the completed script. It appeared to offer significant parts for the central couple (Forbes-Robertson and Mrs Bernard Beere), rewarding roles for the Bancrofts, and effective parts for the rest of a strong company that included the famous old actress Mrs Stirling. According to Bancroft, Pinero directed the rehearsals with great skill and diligence, and no expense was spared in mounting the production. William Telbin the younger, who had devised a number of impressive settings for Irving's recent productions, was one of two designers called on to re-create the decaying splendour of Caryl Court. There seemed every reason to expect a great success.

Instead, the opening night on Saturday, 24 November proved a bitter disappointment. Audience reaction was lukewarm, and during the next few days the reviewers scorned virtually every aspect of the play except the acting. Even the programme note, in which Pinero carefully referred the critics and public to Schwartz's romance as the source of his plot, was taken by some, as Nisbet unkindly remarked in the *Times*, "as an ungracious pleasantry directed against that propensity for playing the literary detective which the furtive habits of certain dramatic authors have inspired in the critical mind." Indeed Nisbet found "it difficult to resist the conviction that if there had been anything worth borrowing in the Swedish romance, Mr Pinero had not been generous enough to share it with the public"![20]

Pinero and Bancroft had tried too hard. The plot's weaknesses had been compounded by overwriting and excessively elaborate staging. Even after substantial dialogue cuts, the production remained ponderous. The dominant feature of Telbin's grandiose setting for the hall of Caryl Court was a huge staircase that became the bane of old

Mrs Stirling's existence. Suffering from bronchitis and poor eyesight, she disliked staircases at the best of times, and to make her entrance down this one she had first to clamber up a precipitous flight of steps behind the set. Mrs Bancroft watched her nightly ordeal with sympathy and admiration: "I often felt anxious about her. One would imagine to see her slowly and cautiously ascend the flight of steps, stopping every now and then to murmur 'Oh, these stairs!', that she would scarcely be able to get through her part, but, although she had stood gasping for breath and terribly ailing, the moment her cue came to go on stage she seemed to become twenty years younger, vigour returned to her limbs and she walked with such a firm and steady gait that the change was extraordinary."[21]

Some critics were less charitable than the kindly manager. "Scrutator" of the *Truth*, after observing that Bancroft had a fondness for baronial halls and interminable staircases, remarked that the characters in the play were "perpetually ascending and descending like the angels in Jacob's vision," adding that, as one of the principal characters was "an infirm old lady of eighty, who has at periodic intervals to be helped downstairs, and helped upstairs again, followed by family processions with wraps, and shawls, and sticks, and footstools," he had found the process decidedly tedious.[22]

Mrs Stirling, even when ill, resolutely rejected any suggestion from the Bancrofts that she should make her entrances and exits by an easier route. At the end of the season she presented Pin with the walking stick she had used during his play and as the Nurse in Irving's revival of *Romeo and Juliet*. On it she had inscribed a quotation from her part in *Lords and Commons:* "I am of the old fashion."[23]

The main critical objection to the play, however, was neither the production's lack of pace nor the improbability of the plot but what had by now become a regular catchcry: that Pinero was much too cynical in the depiction of his characters. The *Daily News* considered the personages of *Lords and Commons* "all base, malicious and unmannerly."[24] The *Sportsman* found "the pride, not to say hauteur" of the Caryls "very phenomenal, and a not very artistic libel on the manners of gentle people,"[25] and Scott decided that the time had come to give the young playwright a stern lecture on the folly of his ways.

Reviewing the play for the *Daily Telegraph*, Scott noted that Archer had commended Pinero for daring to be original but warned that this originality, too, often took "the curious and unwise turn of almost persistently alienating the sympathies of . . . [the] audience."[26] A few days later, he developed this theme at length in an article for the *Illustrated London News:* "The majority in every audience is naturally more pleased when they are presented with the tender rather than the seamy side of life; and, as a rule, they are anxious to find men and women better and purer than they are outside the walls of a theatre. No doubt it is a very fine thing to tell the truth; but a man who habitually tells home truths to society is looked upon as a very disagreeable companion." Anticipating the countercharge that T. W. Robertson, "the most popular and original dramatist of this last quarter of a century," had also castigated the society of his time, Scott remarked that Robertson had nevertheless "looked upon the best side of human nature, hoped for the best, loved the best, encouraged the best." The article ended with a vehement peroration in which Scott exhorted Pinero "not to be led away by the heartlessness and emptiness of the age in which he lives. Let him rise superior to the youthful cant of the present day that whatever is — is wrong. Let him try to see some good in human nature. . . . The dramatist who forces his pessimistic doctrines on his audience makes a very great mistake."[27] Archer's opinion of audiences and critics could hardly have been more aptly illustrated!

Though *Lords and Commons* ran seventy nights and made a small profit, its critical reception frustrated Pinero's hope that it would repeat the success Robertson's *Society* had given the Bancrofts eighteen years earlier. Moreover, after the critical drubbing given to his mild satire, Pin feared the worst for Carton's forthcoming production of *Low Water,* a comedy that juxtaposed sentimental scenes about a girl's conversion of her aristocratic seducer with farcical ones involving her weak-willed father and his obnoxious companions. Not only was such a mixture bound to be unpopular with the critics, but playwright and manager were at loggerheads with each other. Carton wanted drastic cuts, whereas Pinero wanted the production cancelled or at least postponed until a more favourable time. Neither gave way, and the result was total disaster.

Low Water opened at the Globe Theatre on 12 January 1884 and closed a week later. According to Pin's boyhood friend H. Chance Newton — "Carados" of the *Referee* — the audience on the first night, "from being attentive and patient grew derisive, and well they might for they suffered much. No audience ever seized more gladly or applauded more vigorously such lines and business of a bright and clever kind as the play possessed; but matters rapidly got from bad to worse until the curtain fell amid a perfect hurricane of hissing and hooting, mingled with mock calls for the author who fortunately did not appear before the curtain."[28]

Ever since *The Squire* controversy, there had been a small clique who regularly appeared at Pinero's first nights to hiss the play, but this was the first time the entire house had turned against him. Even some of the actors demonstrated their sympathy with the protesters by giving deliberately careless performances. Pinero was so upset, disheartened, and disgusted that he took the unprecedented step of writing to the *Daily News* the following day to publicly dissociate himself from the production, which he stated had been staged against his wishes and in spite of his most earnest protests. As control of the play had passed out of his hands a long time earlier, he claimed he had been unable to prevent its performance "under conditions which I knew would result in the complete obscuring of the meaning of my work."[29]

If he had hoped to gain sympathy by this letter, he soon found he had made a serious mistake. Hostile critics seized on his remarks as a caddish attempt to blame Carton and the actors for his own shortcomings. Chance Newton agreed and wrote some verses entitled "How to Write a Play" satirising what he considered the playwright's arrogant dismissal of friendly advice:

> First, when you're making a kind of a footing,
> And critics point out certain flaws,
> Be obstinate — make those defects more glaring,
> Defy all the dramatist's laws.

At the start you may sometimes (unconsciously) copy —
"Coincidence" oft will occur —
'Twill bring you advertisement, and you'll discover
Your Pegasus onwards will spur.

When the critics point out that you've mixed up your pathos
With chunks of nonsensical mirth,
Don't heed them, pass by them, pooh-pooh them, ignore them —
Their statements you know have no worth —
Sketch your characters strangely — in fact make them stupid —
Let all their worst vices be shown,
Let your language be flippant, adopt when you're writing
A sort of Low Watery tone.

And so on for another five stanzas, concluding with the lines:

And if people should jeer, you can write to the papers,
And say 'tis your company's fault![30]

In the face of this chorus of derision, Pin must have wished he had
never chosen a profession so exposed to public rejection and humili-
ation. With the opening of *Low Water* he had had three original plays
running simultaneously in London; several weeks later all had been
withdrawn. It was the lowest point of his career. But because he had
a family to support, he could not afford to despair. All he could do was
to take a deep breath and, like old Mrs Stirling at the staircase, climb
painfully back up to confront his public and critics once again.

v. Final Bows

A year earlier Archer had ended his chapter on Pinero with the
advice that he learn how to tighten up his plots by adapting one or two
French well-made plays. An opportunity now arose to do so. The
current dramatic sensation in Paris was a drama by Georges Ohnet,
Le Maître des Forges, in which the aristocratic heroine, after being
spurned by a duke whom she loves, marries but refuses to sleep with
a foundry owner who loves her. The rift between the pair widens until

"Just before the Duel. Coming to Hattention." (Punch, *April 1884*)

the heroine's husband fights a duel to defend her honour and she intercepts with her body the bullet meant for him, after which all ends happily. The Kendals commissioned Pinero to adapt the piece, retitled *The Ironmaster,* for the St James's. Hare, who decided not to act in it, directed rehearsals with his usual efficiency.

Commenting on the production a week or so after the opening on 17 April, "Nibbs," theatre columnist for *Punch,* remarked that the piece had been staged with such total disregard of expense that everyone, except the lawyer, had worn a brand new hat. The effect of these hats in the duel scene, *"when they all went off at once"* before the pistols did, had been extremely striking. However, Nibbs added, there had been no cause for alarm or any danger as "on the first night the piece went off as well as the hats and pistols."[31] The play proved as popular at the St James's as it had in Paris, having a run of 200 performances.

In a postscript to his review of *The Ironmaster,* Nibbs informed his readers that a manifesto had just been issued announcing a forthcoming production of *The Rivals* at the Haymarket. Pinero was said to be helping Bancroft edit Richard Sheridan's script so as to avoid unnecessary scene changes. The columnist added that the moment Bancroft had determined on the revival, "he at once told his scenic artists to 'go to Bath'. Mr BANCROFT and Mr PINERO (temporarily escaped from being 'under the Direction of HARE') have also been staying there, in order to go through a course of waters and baths; and the manager has brought back a supply of the real Bath waters, bottled, which have been dealt out to all the actors and actresses concerned in the revival, regularly every morning at 10.30, half an hour before the rehearsal."

Though Nibbs's account of the preparations for the revival was slightly fanciful in detail, it was accurate enough in essence. In this production Bancroft allowed his passion for realism — an important element in the success of many of his past productions — to swamp Sheridan's play. When it was staged at the Haymarket on 3 May, the critics almost unanimously condemned the excessive scenic detail. The *Stage*, for example, considered it unfortunate

> that before setting this play of *The Rivals* in so gorgeous a frame Mr Bancroft had not remembered it is one of the very few comedies that can dispense with the aid of scenery altogether. . . . The first act looks more like the opening of a harlequinade than a play. It is very beautiful, it is mere pantomime in dumb show. Well-drilled supernumeraries cross and recross the stage, and are supposed to be representing the fashionable Bath of the eighteenth century. They go into shops and taverns, they enter circulating libraries, they pass before us in sedan chairs, fruiterers sell at their stalls, others await the arrival of the coach, bugles blow, bells chime, watchmen go their round; it is a picture of reality but the play is lost amid all the portentous realism.[32]

Pinero, as script editor, came in for more than his share of blame from the critics. "Can it be," one had sneeringly asked when Bancroft first announced the project, "that the Haymarket management believes it has succeeded in educating the taste of the public up to the pitch of requiring Pinero with their Sheridan?"[33] They had further opportunity for ridicule when Pin, having accepted an invitation from Bancroft to act in the production, tried to reinterpret the role of Sir

Anthony Absolute. Even the *Era*, which praised aspects of his performance, found it wanting in "the full, broad, genial, old comedy air"[34] usually associated with the part; whereas the *Stage* was utterly scathing: "Mr Pinero's Sir Anthony Absolute is a well-meaning but feeble effort. He cannot rise to the occasion or even fill the stage. Sir Anthony was a choleric, blustering, breezy, full-blooded old gentleman, loud of voice, assertive of manner, and with a whole-hearted chuckle ready to burst out from his waistcoat. Mr Pinero's Sir Anthony is a wizened, peevish, contradictory old scarecrow, who snarls at Jack, and hops about like a discontented rook."[35]

Despite the reviews, the revival lasted the ten or so weeks until the end of the season. Pin enjoyed participating once again in the friendly backstage atmosphere of the Haymarket. He was sharing a dressing room with Forbes-Robertson (who was playing Captain Jack Absolute) and amused the company by inventing conversations between two coster girls he claimed to have overheard discussing his roommate's handsome appearance. "Ooooh," the first girl was said to have exclaimed as she swooned over Forbes-Robertson's photograph in a shop window, "I do love that Robertson!" "Ah, so did I once," the other girl had supposedly replied, "till I seen 'im outside the stage door in a bowler 'at. That were enough for me!"[36]

It was probably not a coincidence that Myra soon emulated Pin's guest appearance as an actor. She accepted an invitation from the American actress Mary Anderson to play Cynisca, Pygmalion's wife, in Gilbert's *Pygmalion and Galatea* for a limited season at the Lyceum. But the engagement did not revive her career. Anderson's Galatea received most of the praise, and the little the reviewers said about Myra's performance was not encouraging. Her only consolation was a charming studio portrait of herself as Cynisca that Scott published in the December issue of the *Theatre*.

Meanwhile, Pin had revisited Edinburgh for the first time since his apprenticeship at the ill-fated Theatre Royal. His main purpose was to attend the first night of a new farce he had written for Edward Terry, but he also visited old friends. Garside was no longer in town, but Pin called on his friend's landlady, mother of the two little girls who ten years ago had died of scarlet fever, to ask how she was getting on. Her shoulders moved uncomfortably at the question, and with a faint, deprecatory smile, she replied in a whisper, "Weell, I'm just missin' ma bairns."[37]

The opening of *In Chancery* at the Edinburgh Lyceum on 19 September 1884 was a happier occasion. Terry excelled as a hapless traveller who loses his memory in a railway accident and, on assuming what appears to be his correct identity, finds himself hounded by a tenderhearted Irish barmaid who wants to marry him, by her belligerent innkeeper father who insists that he does so, by a pretty young ward in Chancery who claims she is married to him already, and by a detective who wants to arrest him for absconding with the ward. Eventually he and everyone else accidentally end up in a boarding house run by his real wife, whereupon the irate innkeeper exclaims, "Begorra, it's not Bigamy but Trigonometry he's been attemptin'!"

The audience enjoyed the farce immensely and insisted that the author make a speech when he appeared for his bow at the end. Recalling that it was only ten years since he had begun life as an actor on the Edinburgh stage, he stated (with some slight embellishment of the truth) that it had been the kind encouragement of the city's press and public that had led to whatever success he had subsequently enjoyed as a dramatic author. His heart, he said, was very full that night, and he thanked the audience warmly for once more giving him their kind approval.[38]

Soon after returning to London, Pin was surprised to receive a note from Bancroft stating that he and his wife would be retiring from management at the end of the following season. In his reply (29 October 1884) Pin expressed his hope "that nothing, no change in the Haymarket Theatre or out of it" would ever rob him of "two of the best friends I have ever had or can ever hope to have," and he went on to pay tribute to the Bancrofts' achievement, stating that it was his firm belief "that the present advanced condition of the English stage; throwing as it does a clear natural light upon the manners of life and people, where a few years ago there was nothing but mouthing and tinsel; is due to the crusade begun by Mrs Bancroft and yourself in your 'little Prince of Wales's Theatre'. When the history of the stage and its progress is adequately and faithfully written Mrs Bancroft's name and your own must be recorded with honour and gratitude."[39]

Pin's friendship with Bancroft was to endure until the end of the latter's very long retirement. But the announcement meant he would be losing the support of an important management — another disappointment in what had been another generally depressing year. On 23 December he wrote a gloomy note to Scott remarking that it was "folly to wish men a Happy Christmas — one can only wish for a happy oblivion to its *dismal* memories and a freedom from its accompanying train of forebodings." It was far more sensible, he added, "to hope for a prosperous New Year," and he desired most sincerely that 1885 might "be a golden number" for Scott.[40]

In fact 1885 would prove a golden year for Pin. At long last his fortunes were to take a decisive turn for the better.

...8...
The Court Farces

i. The Magistrate

On 20 October 1884 Pinero ended a business letter to the American manager Augustin Daly with the following note: "I have just finished an original three act comedy of modern English manners — I think a good play. It is written for the St. James's and is approved of, *but* (between ourselves) there is a little hitch. The part (a fine one) intended for Mrs Kendal is that of a woman of 35 or thereabouts with a grown up daughter. You guess the difficulty? Oh, vanity of woman! I will let you know the result of things, as the play, which, at present, I believe in, might turn out to suit you."

In the event *The Weaker Sex*, another "Pinerotic" hybrid — in this case combining satire of the "votes for women" movement with a contrived plot about a mother and daughter who find themselves in love with the same man — was for various reasons not staged by Mrs Kendal (or anyone else) until five years later. But her reluctance to appear in it inspired Pinero with a marvelous comic idea that became the mainspring of *The Magistrate*. Whether Mrs Kendal recognised herself as the model for Agatha Posket, who in order to conceal her true age from her second husband tries to pass off her nineteen-year-old son as fourteen, is not recorded. If, however, Pinero still harboured any lingering feelings of resentment because of her conduct over *The Squire*, he must have experienced a delicious feeling of satisfaction as he set about immortalizing her vanity in what was to become a classic farce.

He completed *The Magistrate* in January 1885 and, not having written it for anyone in particular, began to look around for a producer. His first thought was that it might suit Wyndham or perhaps Terry. But at that moment John Clayton and Arthur Cecil, whose comanagement of the Court Theatre had been going badly, asked if he had a play that might revive their flagging fortunes. As they had recently been associated with serious work, Pinero first read them *The Weaker Sex*, but Clayton feared the mother-daughter rivalry would cause offence. When, however, Pinero mentioned his new farce, the managers decided it was exactly what they needed — though soon afterwards, in announcing their forthcoming production of *The Magistrate* to the public, they felt obliged to apologise for lapsing into frivolity.[1]

They need not have bothered. As Scott remarked in the *Illustrated London News* after the triumphant opening night on Saturday, 21 March 1885, all the public wanted was good entertainment, and Mr Pinero's play was "a very excellent farce indeed."[2] Even Chance Newton admitted in the *Referee* that the piece was "written with much ingenuity and a strong sense of humour," though he added a characteristic jibe: "The method is that of Palais Royal farce as rendered familiar to London audiences at the Criterion, but Mr Pinero declares that it is original, and we know that he always speaks the truth in these matters."[3] Scott countered this charge by noting that "the rare cleverness of Mr Pinero consists of utilising the very scenes so popular at the lower French theatres and never once tasting the forbidden fruit. A West End supper-room on the stage without so much as the rustle of a gown, the fall of a veil, or the sight of a domino that could raise a blush on the face of Mr Gilbert's 'young lady of fifteen' is in itself a very remarkable achievement."

Pinero later told an interviewer that his aim with *The Magistrate* had been "to raise farce a little from the low pantomimic level" and treat it as artistically as possible in the belief that "farce should have as substantial and reasonable a backbone as a serious play. Instead of relying on adulterous automata, he had tried to create probable characters in possible situations.[4] Whether or not he had really set out with such worthy intentions, the play gave splendid opportunities to the excellent Court Theatre cast. Clayton shone as an ex–Indian army colonel and Mrs John Wood as the prevaricating Mrs Posket, while Marion Terry was delightfully amusing as her ever-hungry sister.

But the play's outstanding role is Posket, the hapless magistrate whose naive rectitude plunges him into a series of increasingly compromising situations. Though Arthur Cecil played the part with considerable skill and subtlety, Scott could not help speculating what other notable comic actors — one in particular — might have made of it:

> Mr Posket is simply one of the best comic characters that has been introduced into farce since the days of Buckstone, Compton and Charles Mathews. It has tragic possibilities in it that would have delighted Robson. With what a cold sweat of agitation, with what a sense of nervous exhaustion, would not Robson of the Olympic days have described the flight of the police-magistrate from Leicester-square to Kilburn! This is the highest vein of elevated comic writing. Who might not have played Mr Posket? Toole, Terry, David James might well have given their heads and ears for such a character. But there is one actor I should like to have seen playing it, though I shall be laughed at for saying so. I should like to have seen Irving's idea of this terror-haunted magistrate.[5]

It is perhaps unfortunate that this idea, which might have involved Irving in the development of contemporary British drama, was never taken up.

The opening night immediately established *The Magistrate* as an outstanding farce and its author as no longer merely "promising" but in the front rank of contemporary English playwrights. The play recorded an unbroken run at the Court of 363 performances, with Tree briefly taking over Posket when Cecil took his usual summer holiday. No fewer than three companies were engaged to tour the British provinces with the play; Australian, Indian, and South African managements swiftly mounted their own productions.[6]

Pinero was especially concerned to see that *The Magistrate* was produced and promoted effectively in the United States. Three days after it opened at the Court, he wrote to Daly saying that his new comedy was "an enormous success" and that he was already besieged with offers from other American managers. Because Daly had presented most of his earlier plays in New York (and usually lost money on them), Pinero was happy to offer him the New York rights, subject to certain conditions. In addition to his usual fee (7 percent of the gross plus an advance of £150), he asked Daly to open his next season with *The Magistrate* and to pay the return fares for "some suitable person" to come over and instruct the New York cast in the intricate business of the play. In a follow-up letter (7 April 1885) Pinero explained, "As the play is produced here under my sole direction and is animated with the life and character I have instilled into it, I think it of vital moment that the same spirit should be infused into the New York production."[7] Daly took the hint and invited him to do the job himself.

Meanwhile Pinero basked in the warm glow of success. On 2 April he wrote to Moy Thomas, who had questioned Clayton's decision to produce a farce, suggesting that the critic might care to inform his readers of "the nature of the public response to our 'new departure' (if it be one) at the Court Theatre." The playwright went on to observe that the demand for seats had been quite unprecedented in the history of the Court and "that even during this passion [Easter] week (one of the worst in the theatrical season) the theatre is nightly crammed to its utmost capacity."

Having achieved an unequivocal triumph, Pin could afford to laugh at the desperation he had felt during his recent bad patch. For the 1886 *Era Almanac* he wrote a story called "Consulting the Oracle"[8] in which the narrator, an eager young playwright, seeks advice from the leading dramatist of the day about the best moment to produce a new play. The young man is received by Mr Blank "in the imposing stranger's room of his magnificent grey-stone fronted club" and is advised of the "three golden rules" to be observed when arranging a premiere. "First: your play must follow a dismal, disastrous failure at the theatre where it is produced; a series of disastrous failures if possible. . . . Second: the first performance of your play must immediately succeed a fiasco by another author at another house. . . . Third and last: you must not produce a new play in an east wind."

To the narrator's delight all three rules are obeyed by the time his new play opens, and on entering the theatre for the first performance he is congratulated by Mr Blank on the favourable auguries. But as the end of the story demonstrates, theatrical predictions are notoriously unreliable:

> I cannot dwell upon this matter. *The play was irretrievably damned!* Walking home from the theatre, angry, wretched, disconsolate, with my head down, I jostled against somebody who was walking along smoking a cigarette. I muttered a vindictive apology. It was Mr Blank. "This is the result of your three golden rules, Mr Oracle!" said I, with an artificial laugh. "My dear young friend," said Mr Blank, "you are unjust. Recollect Rule Number 1. You have contributed to the series of dismal disastrous failures which will unfailingly contribute to the success of some other work." He was right. The play which succeeded mine was by — Mr Blank. It was triumphantly successful, and is running now.

So, too, of course, was *The Magistrate.*

As the end of 1884–1885 season approached, the attention of the London theatre world focussed on the Bancrofts' farewell. From the moment the date — 20 July 1885 — was announced, the Haymarket Theatre was besieged with requests for tickets. The occasion was to be graced by the presence of the Prince and Princess of Wales, Irving would deliver a valedictory ode by Clement Scott at the conclusion of the performance, and Toole would add a few words in his inimitable style. Amongst actors, however, everyone wanted to know who would be invited to appear in the evening's first two items, Act 1 of Lytton's *Money* and a scene from *London Assurance.* These were to be cast from past members of the Bancroft companies, but as they numbered well over 100 for some twenty parts, most would have to miss out.

Pin was delighted to be asked to play Dolly Spanker in the Boucicault scene. This turned out to be his last appearance as an actor. Mrs Kendal played Lady Gay Spanker, while Kendal appeared as Dazzle,

Terriss as Charles Courtly, and Hare as Sir Harcourt Courtly. When to these names are added those appearing in the first act of *Money* — Alfred Bishop, Charles Wyndham, John Archer, Arthur Cecil, David James, Mrs Stirling, Ellen Terry, Lillie Langtry, John Clayton, and Mrs John Wood — it can be seen that Mr A. W. Pinero's exit from the acting profession was made in distinguished company.[9]

But it was the Bancrofts' night. The applause was overwhelming when Mrs Bancroft appeared as the great actress Peg Woffington and Bancroft as the broken-down playwright Triplet in Taylor's theatrical comedy *Masks and Faces*. Next day Pin wrote to Bancroft saying how much he and Myra had appreciated being present at this great occasion, adding that he did not think it possible "for any theatrical event of like importance and impressiveness to again occur in our lifetime."[10]

The following night the playwright took part in another function organised by Bancroft, who as chairman of that year's annual Royal General Theatrical Fund dinner had invited him to reply to the toast to "The Drama," the first of many speeches he would make on similar occasions. His theme was the thoughtlessness of the "Spirit of Ridicule," sometimes found in the gallery, sometimes in the pit, but more frequently, and "in his most mischievous form," in the stalls. Pinero went on to appeal for sympathetic treatment for those attempting to advance English drama, claiming that "what English actors and English playwrights require is a wholly undivided sympathy, a knowledge that the audience is eagerly watching for the virtues rather than for the vices of a performance. . . . I think we have to appeal to the flippant playgoer that the future of the drama is in his hands, and that it rests with him to raise and ennoble it with patience and sympathy or to destroy its best shape by a sneer or a thoughtless smile."[11]

Another speaker at the dinner was Comyns Carr. It may well be that the kindly chairman used the occasion to reconcile the once rival playwrights. Their future relationship was to prove far more cordial than their previous exchanges.

After this dinner Pin called a halt to social engagements. Before his departure for New York in mid-September he had to complete for Hare and the Kendals a new English version of a Sardou comedy called *Maison Neuve* (in an odd coincidence, at the same time he was keenly observing the progress of a new house being built for him at 64 St John's Wood Road). Turning down an invitation to an end-of-season supper organised by Irving and Toole, Pin wrote to his former chief (26 July 1885), "I am more disappointed than I can express to you, and ask you to believe that nothing but the stern necessity of work could induce me to forgo so much real pleasure as I shall lose by my absence from your gathering." The following month, while Myra went off on her own for a holiday, he pleaded the combined pressure of completing his play and superintending "the subterranean arrange-ments — or rather *de*rangements — of the new Mansion at St John's Wood" to excuse his refusal of a dinner invitation from a Miss Helbert and her father. "All this is the truth," Pin assured her, "and that you have surprised me into telling it is the surest proof I can afford you of my terribly unhinged state of mind."[12]

Embarking for New York at Liverpool on the SS *City of Chicago*, Pin found that his newly won fame brought a crowd to the dockside to see him off. By chance another ex-member of the Haymarket company happened to be a passenger. Old Odell, as he was known, habitually wore a shabby frock coat and had long, straggly hair. As no one knew he was going, no one had come to bid him farewell. "Why, what on earth are you doing here?" Pin asked when they met on deck. "I'm seeing myself off," Old Odell replied with a wry smile.[13]

Reaching New York on 25 September, the playwright was met by his manager and taken to the Clarendon Hotel for a press conference, where he impressed the *New York Times* with his "ruddy complexion and dramatically shaven face." Pinero told reporters that his trip was a brief visit to make the New York production of *The Magistrate* similar to the London one. He was concerned, however, that the play might prove too English for American audiences, dealing as it did with "a little question of the licensing laws in London," and he added that past American productions of his plays had run into difficulties be-cause of their English character. He had a plan to overcome this. Although obliged to leave New York on 10 October to produce a new play in London for the Kendals, he intended "to return and study attentively the manners and customs of the American people" so he could write a play for the American public and appeal directly to them.[14]

The following day he and Daly took a train to Philadelphia, where the company was waiting to start rehearsals. Daly's top stars, James Lewis and Ada Rehan, were to play the Poskets. Earlier there had been a disagreement between author and manager over the latter's suggestion that Rehan be cast as Mrs Posket's allegedly fourteen-year-old son. Pinero had vetoed this idea and arranged for the importation of a suitable young English actor, Hamilton Bell. Now, however, rehearsals went smoothly, with the final intensive work being done back in New York.

Two nights before the opening on Wednesday, 7 October 1885, Pin took a few hours off for an unusual sight-seeing excursion. Henry Arthur Jones was also making his first visit to New York to produce a play, a religious melodrama called *Saints and Sinners*, which had provoked a disturbance at its London premiere, members of the audience objecting to the villain's quoting of Scripture. This outcry had moved Jones to publish an article defending the right of dramatists to deal with the whole of life — and perhaps that was why Pin now invited him on a tour of the Chinese quarter to inspect the opium dens. Daly, however, had arranged a police escort to ensure that his guests did not get into trouble.[15]

Pin probably would have appreciated a pipe of opium himself for the New York premiere of *The Magistrate*. The tensions of his own first nights had become unendurable to him, and during the performance he was generally to be found pacing nervously outside the theatre or chain-smoking in a nearby hotel or coffee shop. On this occasion his nerves caused him to miss his author's bow, as he had not been told that in New York playwrights were called in front of the curtain after the *penultimate* act of the play. When, therefore, he appeared in front of the curtain at the end of the performance, the audience were already leaving their seats, but they turned to applaud him warmly and called for a speech.[16] In this he remarked that it was not the custom in England for an author to do more than take his bow and retire. Indeed, sometimes it was advisable for even this ceremony to be omitted to allow his escape via the back door! But the kind reception given to *The*

Magistrate and the tolerance shown his previous efforts required him
to express his gratitude. He repeated his wish to some day stay long
enough to write a play based on his personal experience of America
and Americans. Until that time, he respectfully and gratefully bade
them farewell.[17]

Three days later Pin boarded a fast steamer for England and
watched the New York waterfront recede into the distance. It was to
be his last sight of the United States. Though he considered returning
on several occasions, he never did so. Perhaps he felt embarrassed
about his rash promise to write an American play, realising that his
talent and temperament were, for better or for worse, essentially
English. Indeed, even though a number of his plays (including *The
Magistrate*) were to achieve good runs in New York and adequate
support on tour in the States, American response to his work tended
to be respectful rather than enthusiastic.

ii. The Schoolmistress

Back in London Pin barely had time to tumble into his new house
before attending the opening night of his adaptation of Sardou, *Mayfair* at the St James's on 31 October. The evening was not a success.
The *Graphic* described Pinero's attempt to update and transplant the
French play as "a comedy with a hero and heroine so perverse and
contemptible that they exhaust the patience, while they never for a
moment secure the sympathies, of the audience."[18] Indeed some spectators chattered so noisily during Mrs Kendal's big scenes that Hare
publicly rebuked them at the conclusion of the performance. The
play's length — a full five acts — counted against it, but the main
problem was the audience's unwillingness to accept Mrs Kendal in the
role of a disaffected wife who compromises herself with a would-be
lover. As Pinero dryly remarked in a letter to Daly (8 November 1885),
the public had been "rubbing its eyes in wonder at Mrs Kendal playing
a woman who was not absolutely circumspect. Mrs Kendal, as you
know perhaps, occupies a peculiar position with us as a personification
of all the virtues." Only Hare's performance as Nicholas Barrable, the

heroine's kindly old uncle, saved the piece from total disapproval —
thereby enabling wits in the satirical weeklies to observe that the play
had enjoyed "a Hare-breadth escape!"[19] But *Mayfair*'s limited success
as a "Hare-piece" could not prolong its run beyond a couple of months.
Again theatregoers had confirmed what Archer and Scott from their
different perspectives had been saying all along; Pinero, too, now
admitted to Daly: "Success depends on whether or not the play is too
'unpleasant' for the audience."[20] But he was not unduly concerned.
Royalties for *The Magistrate* were flowing in from productions in the
United States and the dominions, and he was hard at work on a second
farce for the Court.

In *The Schoolmistress* Pin sought to create characters to fit the
company's leading actors, a task he accomplished with considerable
success. The fiery Admiral Rankling, whose temper fails to distinguish
between his quarterdeck and the drawing room, fitted Clayton's formidable presence; Miss Dyott, the headmistress of Volumnia College
who embarks on a secret career as a comic-opera star, appealed to Mrs
John Wood; Arthur Cecil was precisely suited as the dapper little Vere
Queckett, Miss Dyott's aristocratic but impecunious husband; and
even young H. Eversfield, who had joined the company to play the
"boy" in *The Magistrate*, was provided with an effective part as
Reginald Paulover, the seventeen-year-old suitor of Admiral Rankling's daughter.

In contrast to *The Magistrate*'s plot, which was developed from a
single premise, the plot of *The Schoolmistress* is much more complex
because of the conflicting preoccupations of its characters. Despite its
title, which suggests another authority figure in trouble, *The Schoolmistress* focusses less on Miss Dyott's concern to conceal her extracur-
ricular activities from her pupils and her newlywed husband than on
what they on the one hand and he on the other get up to during her
absence.

Indeed, by the time Pin came to write the final scene, it was obvious
that the real heroine was Peggy Hesslerigge, the shabbily dressed
student teacher who tries to manipulate events for the benefit of the
young lovers, but whose well-meaning efforts go disastrously wrong.
She was accordingly given the play's final speech but subsequently lost

Alfred Bryan, sketch (Illustrated Sporting and Dramatic News, *April 1886*)

it when Mrs John Wood objected that the honour properly belonged to Miss Dyott as the title character. The change made little difference, for when the play opened on 27 March 1886 the hit of the evening was the actress who played Peggy. Rose Norreys, a slightly built young woman with large, haunting eyes and burnished-copper hair, had earlier impressed playing a minor part in *The Magistrate*. Following her success as Peggy, she created two more Pinero characters — including the title role in *Sweet Lavender* — and acted for a time as Tree's leading lady before a mental breakdown brought her career to a sad and premature end.[21]

It was perhaps inevitable that the critics' response to the second Court farce was less enthusiastic than to the first — Chance Newton, for one, remarking that *The Magistrate* had been "a masterpiece of dramatic art compared with the wild nonsense of *The Schoolmistress*."[22] But all agreed that the audience had begun laughing with the opening lines and not stopped until the final curtain. Writing to Daly a few days later (1 April 1886), Pinero reported that thus far *The Schoolmistress* had been "a greater go than *The Magistrate*." He was concerned, however, that Mrs John Wood had suffered an accident the previous night that would not only prevent her playing at the next performance — "a full house and Royalty coming" — but might affect future bookings. Though Daly decided not to take up his option, *The Schoolmistress* proved almost as popular at the Court as its predecessor, achieving a run of 291 performances.

iii. Dandy Dick

On 20 April John Hare proposed Pinero for the distinction he coveted above all others: membership in the Garrick Club. The proposal was seconded by Bancroft. Its success — already virtually assured by the eminence of the sponsors — was rapidly confirmed by the signatures more than thirty other members added to the nomination form during the following months. The backers included Irving, Toole, Kendal, Tree, Edward Terry, George Alexander, Hollingshead, Arthur Blunt (that is, Arthur Cecil), the critics Joseph Knight and Percy Fitzgerald, the publisher Walter Lacy, and even Herman Merivale, the novelist and playwright whom Pinero had castigated in the *Times* for casting a slur on his honesty during *The Squire* controversy. This strong support proved that he had been fully accepted by the theatrical establishment as one of their own.[23]

During the summer Hare invited Pin to stay at a country house the actor and his family had taken for the holidays. Hare doted on his children and was inordinately proud of everything they did. One morning after breakfast he was looking out a window at a paddock when he suddenly called to his guest, "Here, Pin, quick!" The playwright duly hurried to the window. "Look at Bertie!" Hare exclaimed with pride, referring to his son Gilbert, "He's riding! Wonderful seat, what? Part and parcel of the horse, eh! . . . Damn it, he's off!"[24]

Whether or not this incident (one of Pin's favourite anecdotes) suggested the idea for his next St James's play, Hare's part in it was that of an avid horse-fancier called Spencer Jermyn whose decision to convert part of his property into a home for retired jockeys brings him into conflict with his childless young wife (played by Mrs Kendal), who wants to establish a home for orphans. Pin had difficulty deciding what the piece, intended as a gentle satire on sentimental do-gooders, should be called. He eventually settled on a witty suggestion from Daly, *The Hobby-Horse*.[25]

The playwright's hopes for the comedy encouraged him to discuss a New York production with Daly and send over set models before he began rehearsals for the London production. But the opening night at the St James's on Saturday, 23 October 1886, was not a success. Once again the mixing of satirical comedy and emotional drama puzzled the audience, provoking some hostility at the final curtain. The display not only shocked Hare, who was expecting applause after speaking the last lines of the play, but moved Scott to castigate the offenders in the *Daily Telegraph*:

> Such artistic faults as the new piece contains are amply atoned for by its ingenuity and daring. Each thoughtless hiss that fell upon the ears of the astonished audience last night conveyed to their ears the presumption of ignorance or the existence of illiberality. . . . The notion that one play is for one theatre, and another for another, is as idle as it is childish, and to suggest that those who, coming for seriousness, found satire, and vented their displeasure by a sudden outburst of anger, were justified in doing so is to ring the death-knell of all enterprise and check the impulse of originality.[26]

Pin was upset, too, but replying to a letter of good wishes from Jones made light of his distress: "The play is out, thank goodness, and this morning I am a frivolous light-hearted creature. What the work is worth, commercially, the Box Office alone can show — last night the better parts of the house applauded, the gallery boo-hooed — in the same style the *Observer* notices us appreciatively, and a paper called *Reynolds* says the piece is *Rot*. However, the dear thing is a favourite child of mine — though perhaps like many favourite children it may die young."[27]

Writing to Daly (29 October 1886), he reported that though the early houses had been nearly full, he was uncertain how the play would appeal to the public. From a literary point of view he felt the piece had done everything he intended, but Mrs Kendal as Diana Jermyn on the first night had been "alternately tragic and broadly comic," where the part simply required "acting with a high comedy earnestness from start to finish." He felt, however, that Ada Rehan would be admirable in the role, as her "spirit of unconscious drollery" was just what was needed. But by 22 December Pinero's enthusiasm had waned, and he wrote suggesting that if the manager had doubts about a New York production, he should abandon the idea, as it was in both their interests that they "only play pretty sure cards." Daly accordingly cancelled *The Hobby-Horse*, though it had achieved a respectable run of 109 performances at the St James's.

It seems likely that elements of this play gradually reshaped themselves in Pinero's mind to provide the basis for his next farce. In his October letter to Daly he had mentioned that he was about to start another play for the Court but had no idea what he would write. In early November he took a house in Brighton and began work on a replacement for *The Schoolmistress*, which was nearing the end of its run. But when Clayton came down a month later to hear the first two acts, he was alarmed to find that Pin had torn them up, having had a more promising idea for a completely new play about an excessively respectable dean who finds himself accused of horse-doping. (*The Hobby-Horse* also contains a controversial episode about an unjustly compromised clergyman.) Clayton liked the new plot (especially as he would be playing the lead) and hurried back to London with sketches for the settings. Three weeks later the scenery was ready and so was the script of *Dandy Dick*.[28]

Though nearly exhausted, Pin had to deal with a tricky casting problem before beginning rehearsals: Clayton was delighted to be given the dean, but Arthur Cecil was less than happy with Blore the butler. When Cecil wrote asking to discuss the matter, Pin replied:

64 St John's Wood Road,
Saturday.

My dear Blunt,

I wish I could say come up tomorrow, but I have been very queer — almost quite ill — and as I want to bring the last scene with me on Monday morning I must work at it all day on Sunday.

After all I wd. rather you acted on your own impulses & desires than allow yourself to be persuaded by me. I admit that Blore is next to nothing in Act I and III — perhaps I over-estimate his importance in Act II. At any rate if you can't recognise his value on paper do not be influenced by any argument of mine: They may be selfish and inconsiderate, for an author in urging an actor to play a part distasteful to him is too apt to forget that the one leaves town for a holiday the day after production while the other groans under his burden, embitters his life, ill-treats his wife and children (if he has any, or in default his next-of-kin) and is altogether a blasted Being for perhaps hundreds of nights. Therefore, my dear Blunt, pray forget me entirely; please yourself and I promise never to revile your grave should I have, at any time, the opportunity of doing so.

If you don't see Blore in the right light I think Mr Allan who writes the enclosed wd. be the best engagement for it we cd. make. Miss Leighton is of no use for our purpose. She is a weird caricature of Ellen Terry. Miss Lottie Venne is the only lady discussed by us, at present, who is at all like Hannah. Pray mention these matters to Clayton.

You need not rehearse on Monday, in any event.

Yrs. A.W.P.[29]

The letter proved effective, for Cecil not only accepted the role but, as the *Era* remarked in its review of *Dandy Dick*'s opening performance on 25 January 1887, "contrived to make much of the small part of the wicked butler, with a face full of benevolence and a heart full of guile."[30]

The play was well received despite first-nighters" having to brave a violent storm to reach the theatre. Writing to Jones the next day, Pin remarked his friend had done well not to come to town, as he could not remember such an hour as they had endured the previous night between seven and eight o'clock. "However, with a somewhat curtailed

Alfred Bryan, sketch of John Clayton as the Dean of St Marvell's (Illustrated Sporting and Dramatic News, *November 1887*)

but very good tempered audience at the Court, we got safely through our difficulties."

Indeed, the audience had laughed heartily throughout the play — and especially at the exchanges between the horsy Georgiana Tidman (played with great spirit by Mrs John Wood) and the pompous Dean of St Marvells. The reviewers also enjoyed themselves but on reflection felt obliged to be censorious, objecting to the plot as "outrageously silly" (*Graphic*), the characters as "violent daubs" (the *Times*), and the dialogue as sometimes "coarse and vulgar" (the *Era*).[31] Scott in the *Illustrated London News*, though admitting that "Mr Pinero's latest farcical folly" was "unquestionably an excellent specimen of its class," saw the play and its reception as a sad reflection of the times: "An age steeped in irreverence and careless of respect could alone permit the liberties that are at present tolerated in the guise of fun. A very few years ago the mere presence of a clergyman on the stage, even in the shape of a grave and reverent pastor, would have been resented by his flock, who, to use an old-fashioned phrase, 'respected his cloth'. But we have changed all that with a vengeance." What was more, all the cleverness expended on such plays would ultimately be in vain: "The pity of it is that it is bound to be so ephemeral — that it will disappear and be heard of no more when the curtain has fallen on the success of so many hundred nights; for it is as certain as anything can be that your 'Magistrates' and 'Schoolmistresses' and 'Hobby-Horses' and 'Dandy Dicks' will never be heard of again when their first popularity is exhausted. They are for the moment, and the moment only."[32]

Though Scott's prediction would prove to be one of the most wrongheaded assertions in the history of theatrical criticism, *Dandy Dick* did bring to an end the brief but glorious reign of farce at the Court. Because of improvements about to be made in Sloane Square, the theatre had been sentenced to demolition. On 22 July 1887, after the curtain had fallen on the final performance at the old theatre, John Clayton stepped forward to make what he claimed was his first public speech in his twenty-one-year career. His purpose for troubling the audience on this occasion was to give an assurance that, despite the forthcoming demolition of the building in which they sat, the Court

Company — and indeed the Court Theatre — would not long remain in a state of suspended animation: "What I believe will happen is this — that on the 10th of September, *Dandy Dick*, having been allowed a brief interval to recover his wind, will resume his prosperous gallop at Toole's Theatre, and early in the year 1888, a theatre, not many yards from the building in which we are now assembled, will be opened to the public under my management. This theatre will be known as the Court Theatre. It will be a house for what you have known as the Court Company, and it will, I trust, be under the patronage of those who are in this building tonight." After paying tribute to Cecil, who was retiring from the management, Clayton went on to what he described as his most difficult task:

> to find words sufficiently strong and simple to express our deep indebtedness to Mr Pinero. For nearly three years without a break the walls of this theatre have nightly echoed and re-echoed with hearty laughter and innocent mirth, called into existence by his healthy, honest, pure English wit, and I think we may be justly proud in having been instrumental in putting before you his Trilogy of *The Magistrate*, *The Schoolmistress* and *Dandy Dick*. I hope you will feel as elated as I do when I tell you that he has promised me to write the opening play for the new theatre.[33]

But it was not to be. The first play at the new Court Theatre when it opened more than a year later was not by Pinero, nor was the theatre under Clayton's management. The burly actor who had lent his substantial weight and talent to the luckless Colonel Lukyn in *The Magistrate*, convulsed audiences as the eccentric Admiral Rankling in *The Schoolmistress*, and — to quote the author himself — acted the Dean of St Marvells with "such unction and irresistible good humour that the notion of an eminent cleric in trouble never offended his audiences," died unexpectedly five months before the new theatre was ready.

iv. Pin Triumphant

Time has proved *The Magistrate, The Schoolmistress,* and *Dandy Dick* not merely the most popular of Pinero's plays (with the sole exception of *Trelawny of the "Wells"*) but among the best farces of all time. Only the lowly status criticism generally gives farce has denied their author full recognition of his achievement. His original Court farces are more than marvelously funny plays; they have a distinctive flavour and point of view that amounts to a lighthearted but perceptive critique of Victorian respectability. In them the playwright's youthful energy, sharp powers of observation, and keen sense of the ridiculous combined with an ease he was able to recapture only once in his later work. The trio of farces (along with *Trelawny*) represent the quintessence of the lively Pin as opposed to the earnest and ambitious Pinero who later strove to make his mark as a serious dramatist.

The Court farces more or less conform to the formula of respectability in danger — *The Magistrate* and *Dandy Dick* more, *The Schoolmistress* less. In all three the characters are preoccupied with maintaining appearances. When Agatha Posket's lie about her age puts her not only in a socially compromising situation but in the dock of her husband's court, he — though equally guilty — promptly sentences her to seven days in jail. The Dean of St Marvells, after abandoning his official principles and gambling on his sister's race-horse with all the humiliating consequences that follow, nevertheless adopts a high tone when he discovers that his butler has put the money on another horse:

THE DEAN. Oh! (*to Blore*) I could have pardoned everything but this last act of disobedience. You are unworthy of the Deanery. Leave it for some ordinary household.

BLORE. If I leave the Deanery, I shall give my reasons, and then what'll folks think of you and me in our old age?

THE DEAN. You wouldn't spread this tale in St Marvells?

BLORE. Not if sober, sir — but suppose grief drove me to my cups?

THE DEAN. I must save you from intemperance at any cost. Remain in my service — a sad, sober and, above all, a silent man! (156–157)

For her part, Miss Dyott, headmistress by day and comic-opera star by night, finds release in the final act of *The Schoolmistress* when her secret is exposed and her school burnt down: "Tyler has rendered me a signal service. He has demolished Volumnia College. From the ashes of that establishment rises the Phoenix of my new career. Miss Dyott is extinct — Miss Delaporte is alive, and, during the evening, kicking"(165).

If respectability is thus shown to be predominantly a male obsession, the female characters of the farces are not idealised. They tend to pay lip service to the conventions while behaving quite unscrupulously to achieve their own ends. The Dean's daughters, in desperate need of money to pay for costumes to a forbidden fancy-dress ball, provide a typical example:

> SHEBA. We must get Papa in a good humour and coax him to make us a present of money. He knows we haven't been charitable in the town for ever so long!
> SALOME. Poor dear Papa! He hasn't paid our proper dress-maker's bill yet, and I'm sure he's pressed for money.
> SHEBA. But we can't help that when *we're* pressed for money — poor dear Papa!
> SALOME. Suppose poor Papa refuses to give us a present?
> SHEBA. Then we must play the piano when he's at work on his Concordance — poor dear Papa. (5–6)

In some of his other plays Pinero is occasionally sentimental about young women, but not here. Indeed, the above passage may be a sketch from memory of the tactics Pin's sisters employed with his elderly, respectable, but impoverished father.

Another characteristic feature of the Court farces is the comic emphasis placed on material objects such as clothing. As Alexander Leggatt has remarked, the characters

> have a consistent habit of mind: a concern for the proprieties that affects their reactions even in situations where respectability is not the issue. . . . This constant deflection away from immediate business to the social code by which the characters judge themselves make the plays not just farces of situation, but depictions of a special mental

state in which a social gaffe becomes virtually a spiritual disaster, and disaster of more real and dangerous kind is likely to find a character worrying about whether he is properly dressed. When Mr Posket's world falls about his ears, as he finds that the prisoner at the bar is his own wife, not the least of his misfortunes is that through a series of misunderstandings he is wearing "*a very common gaudy neckerchief.*". . . The characters of these plays live a trivial, material half-life, in which money, clothing and social position are the things that matter.[34]

The focus is generally on middle-class characters who lack sufficient money to maintain the social status to which they aspire; this is the source of the special flavour of these plays. Young Reginald Paulover's letter to his would-be bride in *The Schoolmistress* is typical of the confusion of romantic sentiment with underfunded gentility: "Please assure Dinah that I shall love her till death, and that the piano is now moving in. Dinah is my one thought. The former is on the three years' system. Kiss my angel for me. Our carpet is Axminster, and, I regret to say, second-hand. But, oh! our life will be a blessed, blessed dream — the worn part going well under the centre table" (16). This of course was a state of affairs with which Pin had been uncomfortably familiar from his early childhood and during the first years of his marriage. But it is one thing to write from experience and another to rise above it and create hilarious and pointed social comedy out of personal misery.

It is unlikely, however, that Pinero would have persisted further with this formula. His success — and the wealth it had brought him — had rekindled his ambition to advance the cause of higher drama in England. Two letters he wrote at this time confirm his new bent. In the first, to Daly (3 November 1887), written shortly after *Dandy Dick* had received a lukewarm welcome in New York, Pinero stated that the comedy he had been asked to create for the opening of the new theatre would be less farcical and "more natural and refined" than its predecessors. Though this commission was abandoned after Clayton's death, the farces Pinero later wrote for the second Court Theatre did indeed prove more genteel in style and design.

In the second letter Pinero informed Scott (16 December 1887) of the profitable business *The Magistrate* was doing in Germany, business the playwright claimed was not important for its own sake but for the possibilities it might open up: "I hope the time will come — is coming — when the Englishman, like the Frenchman, will write his plays for all nations. The consciousness, when a man is writing a play, that he is working for the amusement of a few thousand middle-class English people is not favourable to the development of Dramatic Art. That's why this German business seems of some importance — if the English writer's reach spreads, his thoughts might run with his arm."

Nor was it only in comedy that Pinero wished to break new ground. Even as *Dandy Dick* was hitting its stride at the old Court, its author was planning a more daring challenge to audiences than had been ventured by any recent English playwright. He would strive to write a truly serious drama.

...9...
New Directions

i. The Profligate

Soon after *Dandy Dick* opened at the Court, the Pineros left London for a holiday in Italy. Pin was run down, and it was no surprise when he suddenly fell ill, turning the holiday into a period of convalescence. While recuperating in a Venetian hotel, he received a chatty letter from Henry Arthur Jones, who was also holidaying on the Continent. Jones was enthusiastic about a successful production at the Comédie Française of *Francillon*, a new play by Alexandre Dumas fils, claiming it proved that French audiences, as opposed to English ones, were prepared to "listen, respect and learn from a serious play." Pin in his reply (17 April 1887) was not convinced:

> But given the existence of such an audience, is *Francillon* worthy stuff to face them with? Clever! To its very backbone, of course — but what else? Nothing more than any of our English plays — an Entertainment. Try to dignify it by a moral; it can't be done. A woman maintains that a wife is justified in meeting her husband's infidelity with her own. The provocation is given, the lady affords but two hours' entertainment — mostly of a conversational kind — and the curtain is rung down. The only moral here — a trite one — is that a woman never means what she says. For the play to have done something — to have taught something — the lady should have kept her word, lived happily ever afterwards or have ultimately died in the gutter: I haven't worked out the natural consequences of such an act.

Several days after writing this, Pin — now feeling quite himself again — returned home with Myra, eager to resume work. Jones's letter had suggested a play that would mark a new departure for contemporary British drama. It was time to find whether a London audience was prepared to "listen, respect and learn from" a serious English play, one that would not merely flirt with moral issues but unflinchingly pursue their consequences to the bitter end.

Whatever its defects to modern eyes, *The Profligate*, the four-act drama Pinero wrote during the next two months, was resolutely designed to enforce the stern moral spelt out in verse (bad enough to be his own) he prefaced to his printed text:

> It is a good and soothfast saw:
> Half-roasted never will be raw;
> No dough is dried once more to meal,
> No crock new-shapen by the wheel;
> You can't turn curds to milk again,
> Nor Now, by wishing, back to Then;
> And having tasted stolen honey,
> You can't buy innocence for money.[1]

Every detail in the first three acts is designed to prepare or reinforce the climax when the profligate's past catches up with him, and the last act (as originally written) ensures that all ends miserably for everyone concerned, especially the rejected sinner who drinks poison and dies. Though its credibility is gravely strained by the incestuous economy with which the small cast of characters is made to interact and by the incredible coincidence that sets up the climactic scene, *The Profligate* in its unremitting earnestness made no concession to the taste of contemporary London audiences.

It took several months to find a manager for the play. Eventually Hare agreed to produce it if Pinero would wait for the completion of the new Garrick Theatre that Gilbert was financing out of his Savoy opera profits. Hare, who would be the sole lessee, needed a new play for the opening and was prepared to risk some controversy — though not, as it turned out, too much.

Pinero had already sent a promptbook of *The Profligate* to Daly, but on receiving Hare's offer he wrote to the American manager (18 September 1888) that "rather than risk a very delicate play amidst uncongenial surroundings," he had agreed to leave it on the shelf for about a year until he would have the chance for it to be produced under favourable circumstances. He asked Daly to keep the play's existence secret, which of course made the manager keen to produce it, though he did suggest curtailing the "sermonising propensities of the heroine" and hurrying up the climax. Pinero acknowledged the advice (19 October 1887), and there for the moment the matter rested.

ii. Sweet Success

Edward Terry also had a new theatre and wanted a new play. Although he did not want to write another one-part farce like *In Chancery* for Terry, Pinero knew Terry's audience would reject anything too heavy. The play he finally devised proved the biggest money-maker of his career, but his experience of writing it resembled advice he later offered to an aspiring playwright: "You take a good old stock story about a will found under a sofa cushion or something of that sort and design a set of characters to fit it. You spend three months developing them and then fling away your story in disgust and despair. Then you spend three more months developing a new story to your characters — and there's your play."[2]

Sweet Lavender began as a "comic drama" but evolved into what Pinero later described as "a domestic drama with a distinctly serious interest."[3] In fact the play is an almost cynical blending of scenes of undiluted sentimentality with others in Pin's distinctive comic vein. The interrelated stories of Clement Hale's unworldly love for poor little Lavender and of the humbling of his rich foster father, Geoffrey Wedderburn, who had previously deserted her mother, were calculated to draw tears from audiences who in real life were more likely to emulate Wedderburn than Lavender. But the setting of the barrister's chambers Clement shares with his dissipated but goodhearted colleague, Dick Phenyl, was totally authentic and Phenyl a comic creation of the first order. Whether claiming to feel "none the worse" (in fact "about the same") after a night's indulgence in a Fleet Street pub[4] or identifying himself professionally with Clement's interests ("This is, in point of fact, the first time we have offered ourselves in marriage"), Phenyl is a constant source of delight.

The role that became Edward Terry's most famous was not in the original version of the play but arose from a bit part in a discarded draft Pinero resurrected when he decided the manager needed something better. As the finished play was read to him, Terry listened in silence, expressing no opinion on the play or his part. Wishing to satisfy his curiosity, Pin one day asked Terry's business manager if he knew what his employer thought of the piece. "No," came the reply, "the only remark the Gov'nor has ever made to me about it was, 'This is a nice drunkard Pinero has given me to play!' "[5]

Once committed, Terry made major company changes for the play. Rose Norreys — with her dark, wondering eyes — was engaged to play little Lavender, and Maude Millett — a beauty with a peaches-and-cream complexion — the second heroine, Minnie Gilfillian. Two notable veteran actresses, Miss M. A. Victor and Carlotta Addison, were cast, respectively, as the domineering widow, Mrs Gilfillian, and the unhappy housekeeper, Ruth Rolt. Pin, who had admired the two in his early theatregoing days, watched with fascination during rehearsals as these heroines of his youth merged into the creations of his imagination. The leading men included Brandon Thomas, who played Wedderburn with a grave and ponderous dignity; Bernard Gould (offstage Bernard Partridge, a well-known artist) as Clement Hale; Alfred Bishop as a kindly Irish doctor; and Fred Kerr as the amorous American, Horace Pinkley Bream, who relentlessly pursues Minnie Gilfillian.

Sweet Lavender opened on Wednesday, 21 March, at Terry's Theatre in the Strand, where it ran continuously until 25 January 1890, a total of 684 performances. The day after the opening Pin replied to a telegram of good wishes from Jones with an unduly modest note: "The play went well enough with its first audience — whether it will attract the public in a substantial way I can't guess. But it escaped immediate annihilation and I am thankful for small mercies."[6] In fact

Alfred Bryan, caricature of Edward Terry (The Entr'Acte, *March 1888*)

the audience's applause had been rapidly and almost unanimously endorsed by the reviewers.

For Scott, the piece summed up everything he most cherished in the old Robertsonian drama:

Sweet Lavender is, as its happy title implies, a wholesome, pure, refreshing, and a charming play; one of the very best of the many clever works Mr Pinero has given to the stage. Only a simple story of London life, its scene a set of chambers in the Temple, its hero a brave young barrister, its heroine the daughter of a widowed housekeeper [Scott here glosses over the fact that Lavender's mother, Ruth Holt, was unmarried]; only a tale of man's sure trust and woman's gentle confidence; only a record of the hope of youth contrasted with the repentance of age — it passes before us with its alternate ripples of honest laughter and its tears of sympathy, with its genuine humour and its wholesome manly sentiment.

After suggesting the playwright had drawn his inspiration for the play from Dickens, Thackeray, and Anthony Trollope, Scott went into ecstasies about the portrayal of Minnie Gilfillian, whom he described as "a sweet, pure-minded English girl, redolent of roses and buttercups." On the page, however, Minnie's dialogue has a more materialistic frame of reference. Releasing Clement Hale from any obligation to marry her, for example, she says: "Hush! Well then, dear, as we grew up we grew out of our love, as boys and girls outgrow their clothes. Your love, as it were, got too short in the waist, and mine wouldn't meet at the buttons. And at last, one fine day we yawned, Clem, and the seams of our affection parted"(67). Later in the play, when she decides she has been wrong to refuse Horace Pinkley Bream's proposal of marriage, she explains that "at a big dinner the sweets are always brought round twice" but that she had forgotten that if they did come round again "other ladies have been digging spoons in"(161). Though Minnie's words are not always "redolent of roses and buttercups," Millett's charm in the role persuaded Scott that "since Robertson was lost to us and Albery laid down his pen, no such pure and perfect specimen of English girlhood has been given to us to oppose the feverish, excited, unwholesome creature called woman on the modern stage."[7] Five years later these words would acquire a bitter irony, for in *The Second Mrs Tanqueray* Pinero brought another pure-minded English girl — also played by Millett — into direct conflict with the ultimate dramatic embodiment of the type of woman Scott most detested.

What Terry thought of Scott's eulogy of the second heroine compared with Scott's more moderate praise of his own performance is unknown, but he was probably not greatly concerned. For him, *Sweet Lavender* simply represented money in the bank. A Poor Law guardian, a magistrate, and a churchwarden, he had a passion for social work and cared more for a play's profit than its artistic effect. The furniture for his new play was hired by the week from a well-known theatrical firm that had subtly and delicately matched the colours of the materials even though the general appearance was deliberately shabby. When Terry saw he was in for a run, though, he replaced all this carefully chosen stuff with a job lot from a secondhand shop in Tottenham Court Road.[8] By such penny-pinching he made such a huge profit from *Sweet Lavender* over the next two years that he was able to buy his theatre outright, despite the exorbitant price his backers asked. But he missed out on a second fortune when he failed to invest in the touring rights, which, fittingly, were acquired by the younger T. W. Robertson.

Sweet Lavender also ran well in New York; Daniel Frohman presented it at the Lyceum Theatre on 13 November 1888 and later claimed special credit for the success. Noticing an uneasy first-night response to the heroine's illegitimacy, he cabled for permission to make "a slight change in the relationship of the parents." Pinero grudgingly agreed, with the result (according to Frohman) that the play ran the whole season and was subsequently toured with great success throughout the United States.[9]

Indeed, it was difficult to find playgoers anywhere who did not enjoy *Sweet Lavender,* however embarrassed some of them were to say so in public. Even William Archer, who had just published his translation of Ibsen's *Pillars of Society* and was preparing a new version of *A Doll's House,* liked it — though he wanted more substantial work from its author.[10] As a professional critic, Archer avoided meeting actors but had no such scruples about playwrights, believing his literary judgement independent of any possible friendship or enmity. Several years earlier he had sought out Henry Arthur Jones as an ally in his campaign for the advancement of British drama. Now that Pinero was no longer an actor Archer decided it was time to enlist him, too. Their first meeting had been in 1887 as the critic was soliciting theatre people's views on acting for his book *Masks or Faces.* Real contact began in June of the subsequent year, when he asked Pinero for seats to a revival of *The Squire* that Hare and the Kendals were staging as their final presentation at the St James's. In his letter Archer admitted that his comments on the play in *English Dramatists of Today* had been influenced by his brother, who had attended the original first night while the critic was holidaying in Rome. Amused by the confession, Pin sent the tickets, commenting (11 June 1888) he was sure the review had been written with Archer's blood if not with his ink but doubting if the critic would enjoy seeing the play again as (its own faults apart) it was being given "a rough and hasty revival."[11] After the performance Archer wrote a long letter to the playwright appraising *The Squire* as he now saw it. This was followed a few days later by a note suggesting a small change to a speech in *Sweet Lavender,* an amendment Pinero agreed to adopt in later editions of the play. Thus began a close personal and professional friendship that lasted until the critic's death in 1924.

Archer's faith in Pinero as the potential leader of a renaissance of English drama received a setback, however, when on 16 March 1889 *The Weaker Sex* was staged by the Kendals at the Court. The critic later remarked how amazed he had been "to find that the phrase, The Weaker Sex, was not used ironically, but that the play deliberately set forth to prove, by the most barefaced psychological jugglery, that women were incompetent to take any serious part in the non-domestic work of the world. It seemed to me even then that such a title simply begged the whole question on which the play turned."[12]

The play by then was more than five years old, but the following letter to the feminist publisher and lecturer Emily Faithful, written a few days before a tryout at the Manchester Theatre Royal six months earlier, indicates that Pinero's views on women's rights were as reactionary as the play suggested:

> Queen's Hotel, Manchester.
> 23rd September, 1888.

Dear Miss Faithful,

   I have to be so very busy in the theatre next week that I fear I shall not have an opportunity of calling on you, but I shall try to do so.

   It is true that the Women's Rights Movement is satirised in my new play, and, like most satire, perhaps mine deals with only one side of the question. *The Weaker Sex* merely points the old moral that with all her longings for what is called Equality with Man, Woman remains a tender, sympathetic, dependent, and — where her heart is touched — an occasionally weak creature. I scarcely think that this — inferred I hope not impolitely — can offend the strong-minded sisterhood, amongst whom I have the happiness of numbering some very good friends.

I tell you almost as much about the play as I myself know, and you are at liberty to use this in any way you please. With kindest regards, believe me,

> I am, Dear Miss Faithful,
> Most faithfully yours,
> Arthur W. Pinero[13]

Miss Faithful's reply — if she bothered to make one — has not been preserved.

The only change made to *The Weaker Sex* following a mixed reception in Manchester was to the ending, in which the middle-aged heroine (Mrs Kendal) settled for marriage with an old family friend after learning that her former suitor was courting her daughter. At the Court both mother and daughter remained unmarried. This alteration was not the result of objections from "the strong-minded sisterhood" but from Manchester critics who considered the original dénouement in doubtful taste. The new ending made little difference at the Court, the play being withdrawn after sixty-one performances, though the Kendals retained it for a while in their touring repertoire.

iii. A Great Play?

The comparative failure of *The Weaker Sex* was soon totally eclipsed by the outstanding success of *The Profligate*, which opened Hare's management of the Garrick Theatre on Wednesday, 24 April 1889. Nothing had been spared to make the production effective; an incidental song, for example, was composed for the occasion by Arthur Sullivan. The cast included Forbes-Robertson in the central role of the rake Dunstan Renshaw; Kate Rorke as his innocent wife, Leslie; Olga Nethersole as the woman he has wronged; Lewis Waller as an upright Scottish solicitor; and Hare as the callous and cynical Lord Dangars. On the first night the applause at the final curtain was tumultuous, and next day the reviewers were ecstatic. "A REAL PLAY AT LAST!" was the headline in the *Pall Mall Gazette*, which described the first night as "not a success but a triumph, not a judicial hearing but a verdict by acclamation!"[14]

Most enthusiastic of all was Archer; he not only regarded the play as the strongest original piece seen on the London stage for many years but saw its first night as a potential landmark: "The next few weeks at the Garrick Theatre will be full of significance for the future of the English drama. If *The Profligate* succeeds — really and solidly succeeds — we shall know there is in England a public of men and women ready and even eager to accept the serious treatment of serious themes."[15]

As might have been predicted, Scott ridiculed this analysis:

> My friend Mr William Archer, who is not often very enthusiastic, throws his cap in the air, claps his hands and shrieks with delight because Mr Pinero has dared to write such a play as *The Profligate*. He thinks that now the barrier has been broken down, and that we shall worship dolls and dummies no more. . . . Well, we are all rejoiced that Mr Pinero has written *The Profligate*; it is a charming and delightful work, a play that would have succeeded any time these twenty years; a play that would succeed no doubt these twenty years to come; but is there anything so strange and wonderful in the ethics of the new play?[16]

In fact its impact had been softened. After the first night Hare confessed he had persuaded the author to change his ending, making Renshaw dash the poison from his lips and then be forgiven by his wife. Pinero found Hare's revelation embarrassing and, in a letter to the *Theatre* (7 May 1889), claimed he had changed the ending willingly without any sacrifice of his convictions. He admitted sparing Renshaw's life to enable the play to reach a wider public but said this in no way "distorted my original scheme as it affected the other characters of the play." The letter ended with a strong, but not entirely convincing, peroration: "I am aware that in dealing with the destinies of many of the characters in *The Profligate* I have not been guided by the usual and often valuable mechanism of stagecraft; but it has been my purpose to yield unresistingly to the higher impress of truth, and from the truths of life as they appear to my eyes I have never wavered in any degree."[17]

The Profligate was the first of three plays produced in London in 1889 that attracted widespread critical attention as forerunners of a new dramatic realism. Henry Arthur Jones's *Wealth*, produced by Tree at the Haymarket three days later, was the second; and the third — and by far the most controversial — was *A Doll's House*, presented by Charles Charrington and his wife Janet Achurch at the Novelty Theatre on 7 June 1889. As Archer (the play's translator) later remarked, *A Doll's House* threw the entire country into a state of "moral epilepsy."[18] In fact, as the *Stage* pointed out in an editorial entitled "A New School" (14 June 1889),[19] the plays had little in common. Jones's old-fashioned melodrama scarcely qualified as "new," whereas Ibsen's play, in the writer's opinion, was intolerable to a British public that would not have "discussed in the theatre questions of morality that are almost too private for the closet, nor tolerate before the eyes of man, woman and child, diseased personalities which are fit only for a very different theatre — the operating theatre of the hospital." The author of *The Profligate*, however, had not "distorted the mechanism of the stage to suit his ends" but had remained purely "the dramatist treating a powerful phase of morality in a purely dramatic spirit." As such, his play seemed to mark the beginning of a reaction against the "bad influences . . . of the so-called 'tea-cup and saucer' school of serious drama." The editorial concluded: "We are not prepared to say that by this single effort Mr Pinero has made a new school — that future school in which the robustness and fearless strength of the older dramatists shall find being, and have movement in the freer, far more perfected mechanism of the modern stage, and in which the relations of man and wife shall have equality with, perhaps precedence over, those of lover and lass. At least he has taken the first step towards such a school, and, having taken it, he is likely to go forward, gathering followers as he goes."

Such praise was bound to provoke reaction, not least among other playwrights. A fortnight after the opening, Sidney Grundy, whose critical sense was sharper than his comedies, informed Archer with malicious glee that *The Profligate*'s capacity audiences nightly tittered at the play right up to the big situation, even though they left the theatre saying it was the finest play they had seen. "But," declared Grundy, "they don't think so. They think as I do — and as you do — that it is a fine situation set in a puerile play, written in the language of journalism. Someday somebody will dare to say so, and there will go up to heaven a mighty chorus of assent."[20] Archer himself was having second thoughts about the play, though he still insisted it had dragged English drama "out of the toyshop and put it in touch with adult art." Ten years hence, he admitted, critics might "look back upon it as a tentative, immature, adolescent work," but he would still have "a sneaking fondness for *The Profligate* in memory of the novel emotion of one exhilarating evening."[21]

Time has confirmed Grundy's verdict and Archer's second thoughts. The excessive praise accorded to *The Profligate* at its first performance was due in part to the theatrical excitement generated by strong acting and a brand-new theatre but mainly to public and critical awareness of the lack of serious — let alone tragic — drama from contemporary British playwrights. No doubt the play touched a nerve with its stern denunciation of male philandering, but stylistically the piece is little more than earnest melodrama. Apart from its overreliance on coincidence and contrivance — acceptable in farce and sentimental comedy but not in serious drama — the play's effect is marred by characters who constantly adopt postures rather than express their emotions naturally. Pinero's penchant for metaphorical writing — again, acceptable in farce but not here — is largely to blame for the play's forced and unreal tone. A notable example of this is a warning given to the profligate that his wild oats will one day (to mix the metaphor) come home to roost:

> Tomorrow, next week, next month, you may be happy — but what of the time when those wild oats thrust their ears through the very seams of the floor trodden by the wife whose respect you will have learned to covet! You may drag her into the crowded streets — there is the same wild growth springing up from the chinks of the pavement! In your house or in the open, the scent of the mildewed corn always in your nostrils, and in your ears no music but the wind's rustle

MR. JOHN HARE (*loq.*):—" THANK YOU, MY DEAR PINERO! YOU HAVE MADE THE
GARRICK A SUCCESS !"

Alfred Bryan, sketch of Pinero and John Hare following the success of The
Profligate (The Entr'Acte, *April 1889*)

amongst the fat sheaves! And worst of all, your wife's heart a granary
bursting with the load of shame your profligacy has stored there! (39)

Pinero himself shared in the initial euphoria generated by *The
Profligate* and for several years continued to believe he had achieved
a notable breakthrough. His consciousness of the new standing the
play had brought him is evident from his attitude toward requests for
permission to stage it in the United States. Immediately after the
London opening he had escaped into the countryside for a touring
holiday with Arthur Cecil, ignoring several letters and cables from
Daly. Then on 15 May 1889 Pinero began a lengthy reply by politely
refusing a request to write a comedy especially for the manager's
company, explaining that he could barely meet the home demand for
his plays even by writing them at the rate of two or three a year. In
future, because of the standard of work now expected of him, he
intended to restrict himself to no more than one play annually. As for
The Profligate, it was "a favourite child" he feared would not travel
well, and he was reluctant to expose it to the risk of "ignominious
failure in New York" after its "complete success in London."[22]
Daly refused to be put off. He persisted for more than a year in his
attempts to stage the play, until finally, in June 1890, he lost patience
and returned the promptbook with a curt note stating that Pinero had
evidently lost faith in him. Their relationship never really recovered
after this. Pinero, however, also discouraged requests for *The Profligate* from other American managers, including Richard Field, who
regularly staged his new plays at the Boston Museum Theatre.[23] As a
result *The Profligate* was not seen in the States until Olga Nethersole
included the play in her touring repertoire in 1899; she gained little
praise or success with it.

The same attitude is present in a letter of advice Pinero wrote to
Jones (15 October 1899) about royalty rates for productions of their
plays in Germany and the Netherlands. After stating he would receive
45 percent of the translator's fees for *The Profligate* and rather less
for *Sweet Lavender* (which was said to require more "adapting" for
German audiences), Pinero remarked that *Sweet Lavender* could be

adapted until it was "sage and onions" for all he cared, but he had insisted that *The Profligate* be faithfully translated.

The initiative for these Continental productions came from Jacob Thomas Grein, a young Dutch journalist with a passion for theatre who had settled in London four years earlier and was already energetically fostering the interchange of innovative British and European drama. In appreciation of his efforts on their behalf, Pinero and Jones presented him with a grandfather clock bearing the inscription: "From Arthur W. Pinero and Henry Arthur Jones to J. T. Grein in recognition of his efforts on behalf of the British drama abroad, and especially in remembrance of the performances of *The Profligate* and *The Middleman*."[24]

But Grein, whom Pin regarded benignly as "a most enthusiastic and good-natured little gentleman,"[25] had scarcely begun his work. Inspired by André Antoine's Théâtre Libre, which had given its first performance in Paris just six months earlier, he published on 10 November 1889 in the *Weekly Comedy* (one of several short-lived theatre journals he edited) a proposal for a "British Théâtre Libre" that he believed would provide opportunities for "a small but daily-increasing number of younger authors, whose aim in the first place is not money, but art; whose notion of playwriting is not that it should merely cause tears to flow, or laughter to roar, but that real human emotion should be aroused by the real presentment of human life."[26] The next (and last) three issues of the *Weekly Comedy* contained letters to the editor for and against the proposal, including one from Pinero declaring that any scheme for the protection of serious drama had, and always would have, his "warm sympathy."[27] He could hardly have suspected how much Grein's Independent Theatre project would affect his own career.

Pinero was now taking his role of serious dramatist very much to heart. A few weeks earlier he had been at the centre of a newspaper controversy after protesting in the *Daily Telegraph* against a proposal for licensing music halls to present short plays with their other entertainments. He was concerned that the recently awakened public taste for worthwhile plays might be debased by untrustworthy managers' sandwiching drama "between the dance and the ditty."[28] His stand, however, was widely condemned in the press as mean-spirited. One theatrical weekly, for example, depicted him grimly wielding an axe against a tree labelled "Music-Hall" in a full-page cartoon captioned "Mr A. W. Pinero. It Is When He Attacks the Music-Hall That This Superior Person Shows Temper."[29] Even Henry Arthur Jones argued that there were enough committed theatre managers to ensure the drama's survival despite what his colleague had termed "the roll of the great wave of vulgarity." Pinero's reply was to challenge his friend to join with him in urging "the subsidising for the service of the serious drama but one English theatre." This done, he would "regard with greater equanimity the prospect of entrusting the people's play to the care of . . . managers of music-halls."[30]

iv. Relaxing

Despite his new reputation, Pinero had not turned his back completely on comedy. Outside of theatrical matters his sense of humour was easily provoked by displays of solemnity. One day, for example, a hushed discussion took place at the Garrick Club about the horrific crimes of Jack the Ripper. "What would the mother of this monster say, did she know of her son's deeds?" a member piously enquired. "Well," Pin replied, "I've no doubt she would say, 'Jack may 'ave 'is faults, but 'e's been a good son to me!' "[31]

In fact he found the effort of working on a serious drama something of a strain and after finishing one — or even before — generally felt the need to relax by writing something lighter. Thus while he was rehearsing the earnest histrionics of *The Profligate* he had begun *The Cabinet Minister* for Arthur Cecil. Though intended for the new Court Theatre and labelled a farce, the piece was not as outrageously undignified in its treatment of the central character as *The Magistrate* and *Dandy Dick* had been, being more akin to a lighthearted comedy of manners. Indeed, when it was presented at the Court Theatre on 23 April 1890, Cecil as the Right Honourable Sir Julian Twombey, Secretary of State, had little to do beyond play the flute, deliver some witty lines, and look resplendent in his ministerial dress uniform. Mrs John

Wood, the manager of the new theatre, had a more rewarding role as Twombey's kind but weak-willed wife who allows herself to be blackmailed by Joseph Lebanon, a ridiculously vulgar Jewish moneylender with social pretensions, a part played with relish by Weedon Grossmith.

The play received a half-hearted reception on its opening night because, as Malcolm Salaman later remarked, the audience "found itself laughing at seemingly serious situations which it felt should provoke tears, feeling sympathetically interested in passages of sentiment one moment only to mock at them the next, and, in fact, experiencing constant perplexity as to its emotional duties."[32] Next morning the reviews reflected this confusion, and Pin informed Archer (24 April 1890) that having seen one newspaper he had no intention of opening another for the next fortnight — and then it would be "only the *Mining Journal,* or something of that sort." Before long, however, audiences (including many leading politicians) were flocking to the theatre. The play went on to achieve a run of nearly 200 performances, and it was still attracting capacity houses when Mrs John Wood decided to take it off.

It is ironic that two days before the opening of *The Cabinet Minister* Pinero had written a letter to Boucicault agreeing with the old dramatist's claim that modern audiences lacked discrimination: "Your feeling about the trash with which the stage is flooded, and the ready acceptance given to it, finds a response in my heart. It is this state of affairs which makes one sometimes feel *tired.* Just now, on our side of the water, *everything* is succeeding — or at any rate is being listened to with a sort of respectful apathy. In my bitter moments I often say that it will take a very good play to fail now-a-days!"[33]

Perhaps to rekindle his zeal to write another "very good" play, Pinero gave a solo reading of *The Profligate* on 16 May at the Birkbeck Institution in aid of its Library Fund. According to a report in the June number of the *Theatre,* "From the opening of the reading, by the recital of the quaint piece of poetry giving the motive of the drama, to the close, Mr Pinero was very successful, and, what is more to the point, each character was individualised by excellent dramatic effect."[34] Three years later the institution returned the compliment by appointing him an honorary examiner in elocution.

At the beginning of July, Pin and Myra took up residence at Highercoombe, a country house near Haslemere in Surrey that they had leased until the end of the year. Situated on a hilltop commanding a fine view into three counties, the house was surrounded by trees that screened from sight the adjacent properties, except for the chimneys belonging to their nearest neighbour, the novelist Mrs Humphrey Ward. This prospect was to torment Pinero's most famous heroine and the handsome residence (its name unchanged) she would regard as a prison. But Paula Tanqueray had not yet disturbed Pinero's thoughts, and he simply revelled in the country life. So, too, did Myra, who was not only an expert horsewoman but reputedly one of the best lady whips in England, whether driving tandem, four-in-hand, single, or double. Only two dozen miles away, near Ockham, Archer and his family had a cottage (named Walden after Henry David Thoreau's retreat), and from time to time Pin enjoyed long walks and talks with the critic. But the highlight of his stay was a chance meeting with Tennyson one day at Haslemere. Later asked by Salaman how he had liked the poet, Pin confessed to having been frightened out of his life. "It was overwhelming," he said, "like meeting Milton face to face!"[35]

At the end of November a sour episode intruded on this country idyll and hastened its end. The *Era* published a long letter from one Austin Fryers claiming that in March 1886 he had shown a one-act play of his to Pinero who had subsequently used its plot as the basis of *Sweet Lavender*. Because he thought the borrowing was unintentional, Fryers said he waited until the Pinero play had completed its long run at Terry's Theatre before making his statement, but now that he had done so he was sure that "Mr Pinero's . . . sense of fairness [would] dictate to him how to proceed."[36] In fact Pinero was so incensed by what he described as "a most mendacious attempt to discredit a successful work"[37] — not to mention the implied blackmail — that on discovering Fryers belonged to the Playgoer's Club (another of Grein's promotions), he promptly terminated his own membership on the grounds that he could not be associated, however distantly, with such a man.[38] The accusation, though soon forgotten by most people, had an unfortunate side effect. Hitherto Pinero had been prepared to read and comment on plays by aspiring writers. Now he instructed his secretary to return unopened any unpublished scripts sent to him, thus gaining an undeserved reputation for hostility to young playwrights.

v. The Challenge

On 10 December 1890 Pinero returned to London and promptly set about casting a new serious play called *Lady Bountiful,* written for Hare's Garrick Theatre company during his last months at Higher-coombe. The principal roles were designed for Hare, Forbes-Robert-son, and Kate Rorke, but there was some difficulty finding an actress to play the second female lead. After attending performances at several other theatres in the hope of spotting a suitable lady, Pinero, accompanied by Hare and Forbes-Robertson, found one in a drama Wilson Barrett was staging at the Globe. During an interval they went backstage to see the actor-manager, who refused to release the actress but begged them to stay for the rest of his performance. The theatre had just been redecorated and the plaster was still moist. Back in their box, Hare with his overcoat collar turned up and grumbling about the damp, Pin whispered to Robertson, "After one of Wilson Barrett's wonderfully-delivered emotional speeches it was discovered there was not a dry wall in the house!"[39]

There was not a dry eye in the house during the third-act climax of *Lady Bountiful,* which opened at the Garrick Theatre on 7 March 1891. In this tear-jerking scene Forbes-Robertson as the hero, Dennis Heron, sat talking sentimental nonsense over the cradle of his newborn baby, unaware that the wife he had married out of pity was quietly expiring in the background. Though Robertson did his best with the part, as did Rorke in the title role, neither they nor Hare, who played Dennis's father (modelled on the childishly irresponsible Harold Skim-pole in Dickens's *Bleak House*), was able to prevent the play from annoying most reviewers. Scott found the heroine disagreeable and overbearing, and Archer felt the play, which he later described as the last work of Pinero's Robertsonian period, began well but was let down by lapses in taste and a tedious and overcontrived final act.[40]

The piece, which ran a mere two months and was never revived, did have a few admirers. In the *Times*, Nisbet — usually one of Pinero's sternest critics — claimed that it possessed something of the force of Greek tragedy and had the potential to become one of the great English dramas: "It is a play illustrative of cross-purposes, of thwarted aim, of unblushing selfishness and noble endeavour, with an all-pervading suggestion of a divinity that shapes our ends, rough-hew them as we will. . . . Pessimism of the narrow Ibsen kind is depressing on the stage when it is not merely irritating. But this of Mr Pinero's has a wholesome influence; it is not so much depressing as chastening."[41]

Pinero was not so easily deceived. Any lingering hopes he might have momentarily harboured that *Lady Bountiful* would enhance his standing as a serious playwright were obliterated just six nights later. On Friday, 13 March 1891, he, together with many leading theatre people, attended the inaugural production of Grein's Independent Theatre at the Royalty. The play chosen was Ibsen's *Ghosts* — the flag bearer of avant-garde theatre throughout Europe. After seeing it, Pinero could not escape the realisation that if he were ever again to be regarded as a serious dramatist, he would have to begin his work anew.

.. Act 3 ..
Climax
(1892—1909)

...10...
The Second Mrs Tanqueray

i. Preparing

When Pinero began writing *The Second Mrs Tanqueray* in February 1892, he was aware that his career had reached a turning point. Writing to his friend Salaman, who was editing a selection of his earlier plays for Heinemann, he exclaimed with unusual passion and frankness, "How I hate the ghosts of these dead and gone plays! I am too full of my new work just now to bear with other things patiently. Heavens! I pray that some of my work in the future may be better, more truthful, more sincere than the old stuff!"[1]

During the previous year the Ibsen controversy had climaxed with the production in London not only of *Ghosts* but of *Rosmersholm*, *Hedda Gabler*, *The Lady from the Sea*, and a revival of *A Doll's House* — mostly at special matinees to avoid financial risks. On 7 June 1891 the London edition of the *New York Herald* tried to sum up their impact by publishing a symposium of views from prominent British playwrights, managers, and critics on: "(1) the type of drama likely to prevail in England in the immediate future; (2) the nature and extent of Ibsen's influence on the English drama; and (3) the extent to which "realism' is permissible on the stage." Most of those asked were inclined to be dismissive. Charles Wyndham, for example, succinctly replied "(1) Domestic Comedy. (2) Not a bit. (3) Till it becomes obtrusive," and Clement Scott claimed Ibsen would never influence English

OVER IBSEN THE DOCTORS DISAGREE.   WHAT IS MEAT TO MR. WILLIAM ARCHER
IS POISON TO MR. CLEMENT SCOTT.

Alfred Bryan, caricature (The Entr'Acte, *April 1891*)

drama until there was "a general taste for inhaling sewage instead of smelling dew-covered roses."

Pinero's replies, though guarded, were more thoughtful:

(1) A drama based wholly upon observation and experience, which lays aside the worn-out puppets and proverbs of the theatre, and illustrates faithfully modern social life.

(2) English playwrights now working may fairly claim to have already laid the foundations of such a drama in this country. The coming of Ibsen is not likely to disturb the settled views and methods of these writers; but it is probable that Ibsen will find a following of unformed dramatists who will readily make themselves believe that men and women are precisely as the Scandinavian author depicts them.

(3) In recording what is sweet and generous and beautiful in life, there need be no limit to realism; beyond this the question is one to which I am unable to make any brief reply.[2]

The seriousness of Pinero's intentions is apparent from his first answer, his concern not to be thought a disciple of Ibsen from the second. Writing to Archer a year later (25 May 1892), he repeated his claim that English writers had been working with every prospect of success to popularise "a rational, observant, home-grown play" when the Scandinavian drama "held up by the New Critics as the perfect drama and used by them as a means of discrediting native produce" had knocked everything askew with the result that "the English dramatist has little influence and the public, urged to witness *A Doll's House*, patronises the Empire Theatre of Varieties!"[3] Although he acknowledged Ibsen's power, he was by no means uncritical of the Norwegian's workmanship. In a much earlier letter to Archer (30 June 1889), for example, he had gently mocked the portrayal of Dr Rank's relationship with Nora in *A Doll's House*, claiming that Rank had apparently "inherited ambiguity among other dreadful complaints."[4]

Nevertheless, Pinero could see that his own attempts at serious drama were shallow and clumsy by comparison and admitted that even *The Profligate*, the play of which he was most proud, had become old-fashioned in the wake of Ibsen. During the months following the production of *Ghosts*, he made a thorough study of the works of the leading European dramatists, especially the French playwrights Emile Augier and Dumas the younger, concluding that "a really earnest English play — conceived in accordance with the social intention of Ibsen and executed with the developed technique of Dumas *fils* — would stand a chance of achieving at least an honourable *succès d'estime* in the current English theatre."[5]

Before embarking on this project (which would in effect answer the *Herald's* third query), he had to rehearse a comedy he had written earlier in the year for Edward Terry. Called *The Times*, it was produced at Terry's Theatre on 24 October and went on to achieve a creditable run of 155 performances despite lukewarm reviews from the critics, who disliked its satirical portrayal of the central characters, a social-climbing linen draper and his wife. The objections were understandable, for the tone is sometimes almost bitter in its denunciation of the various hypocrisies associated with getting into and making an impression in society:

> BERYL. I have been answering invitations for mamma — look! What a wearisome affair is a Season, isn't it?
> DENHAM. A Season?
> BERYL. I don't mean either of the four seasons sent by Heaven; I mean the fifth, made by Man.
> DENHAM. The one Season honoured by a capital letter.
> BERYL. And called *the* Season. Ugh!
> DENHAM. I know you care very little for gaiety.
> BERYL. The gaiety of climbing a flight of stairs to clutch at a haggard hostess on the landing! Do sit; we both have to tread a great many stairs tonight, I expect. (6)

The play's main significance, however, lay in Pinero's decision to publish the text simultaneously with its first performance, something that had not been done in England since William Macready staged Robert Browning's *A Blot on the Scutcheon* in 1843. Following the U.S. Senate's recent ratification of the International Copyright Act (1887), it was at last possible for British playwrights to publish their work without inviting unlicensed production in the United States. To celebrate the event, handsomely printed copies of the comedy were given to the first-night audience and thereafter sold at the theatre. For several years Pinero had been having his new plays privately printed in advance of rehearsals so that his actors each had a complete copy of the text instead of a mere "part" consisting only of a character's words and cues. In extending this practice to including the audience, he took the opportunity to observe in a preface to the play that "such a course . . . were it adopted as a custom, might dignify at once the calling of the actor, the craft of the playwright. It would, by documentary evidence, when the play was found to possess some intrinsic value, enable the manager to defend his judgement, while it would always apportion fairly to actor and author their just shares of credit or of blame. It would also offer conclusive testimony as to the condition of theatrical work in this country."[6]

Pinero's ambition to be taken seriously as a writer instead of being regarded as a mere entertainer is the most important point here, but the innovation was both successful and influential. Within a month, the first edition of 5,000 copies of *The Times* had been exhausted and a second edition printed.[7] Over the next few months other Pinero plays were published by Heinemann in a similar library format — vastly superior to the old cheap acting texts — beginning a vogue for publishing reading editions of new plays that other playwrights soon followed — most notably Bernard Shaw, who several years later used the practice virtually as a substitute for theatrical production.

Immediately after the first performance of *The Times*, Archer wrote Pinero a note congratulating him on his publishing venture and apologising for a tepid review of the play. The playwright replied (25 October 1891) that he had for years believed Archer to be "absolutely honest" and this belief had taken much of the sting out of his reproofs without lessening their value. But the remainder of Pinero's letter shows he had in fact hoped for a greater measure of appreciation:

> With your present aims believe me I fully sympathise though it has struck me that in your earnest, persistent search for one object you run the risk of missing all others, and that you and the school you have created are perhaps too inclined to accept the latest formula in art, whatever that formula may be, as the only true one.

As for myself, I am sadly conscious that I disappoint you and many good friends. You speak of the tastes or traditions which influence me and I feel the censure which is here implied. Yet when some years ago I started my attempt to purge the popular comic play of something worse than mere vulgarity I had little tradition to guide me; while my tastes, in this connection at any rate, though they may have been simple hardly deserve to be more severely described. I thought the work would be really serviceable to the theatre and I set out upon it with some, very likely misdirected, enthusiasm. As far as I can judge my reward is only this — blame for not having done something else. However I hope I shall by and by turn out work which may rank upon a different platform. Of one thing I am certain, that you and many others wish me well and for this I am unaffectedly grateful.[8]

By now the outline of *The Second Mrs Tanqueray* was taking shape in his mind, though he did not begin writing the play for another two months. Some years later Salaman recalled how fully Pinero had realised his characters and plot in his imagination before committing them to paper:

I shall never forget the night in the winter of 1891, when, as we sat late over the fire in his old house in St John's Wood Road, he told me the story of the play, as it had then developed in his mind, and from which he found occasion to deviate in only the most trifling details. Rising every now and then from his armchair, energetically to pace the room, puffing the while at his pipe, he would draw the characters of Aubrey and Paula Tanqueray, and Ellean, and the rest, until they actually lived for me, and the drama already seemed a vital thing, stirring my emotions, although not a line of it was written.[9]

Soon afterwards, Pinero spent two or three days in the neighbourhood of the Albany, noted for its expensive bachelor apartments, and one night announced jubilantly to Salaman, "I've seen Aubrey Tanqueray's chambers in the Albany." Now that he could visualise the first-act setting (Highercoombe had already provided him with the others), he was able to sit down with a detailed ground plan and begin writing in January 1892. By early March he had finished Act 1 and read it to Hare who, though impressed, responded with a wry grimace and the remark, "We shall have to cut a lot of that out."[10]

Work on the play proceeded slowly and was interrupted in July when Pin and his family moved from St John's Wood Road to a large and handsome brick house with stone facings, built to his own design in nearby Hamilton Terrace. Now, however, he had a really spacious study with plenty of room for his books and pictures instead of the narrow and inconvenient room known as "The Tunnel" he had worked in previously. The new house was still close enough to Lords for Pin and Myra to continue with the garden parties they were in the habit of giving after the annual cricket match between Eton and Harrow, the large back lawn providing a suitable pitch for less formal games.

Whenever possible Pin escaped to a cottage he had rented in Westgate-on-Sea to get on with his play. Although it was taking him far longer to complete than any of his earlier pieces and had, he believed, not the slightest chance of making money, he could think of nothing else until it was finished. At the end of August, after ten months' solid work, the script was finally sent to the printers.

ii. Casting

The Second Mrs Tanqueray tells the story of a disastrous marriage experiment between a middle-aged widower and a young woman who has successively been the mistress of several wealthy men. After his unhappy first marriage and the decision of his only child, Ellean, to become a nun, Aubrey Tanqueray resolves to cut himself adrift from society in order to rehabilitate Paula Ray by marrying her. He gives a farewell dinner party at his bachelor flat in London for his closest male friends, Frank Misquith, Gordon Jayne, and Cayley Drummle, but fully confesses his intentions only to Drummle, who as a bachelor will not be forced by a wife's pressure to abandon Tanqueray socially after his marriage.

Tanqueray has no sooner committed himself irrevocably to marrying Paula and retiring with her to his country house in Surrey when Ellean decides to return to him instead of entering the convent. There is an irreconcilable clash of temperament between Paula and her prim stepdaughter. Cut off from almost all other human contact, Paula becomes passionately jealous of Tanqueray's protective concern for Ellean. When society, represented by the Tanqueray's neighbour Mrs Cortelyon, eventually deigns to call, it is with the ulterior motive (encouraged by Drummle) of removing Ellean from her stepmother's influence by taking her off on holiday to Paris. Tanqueray agrees to Ellean's departure in defiance of desperate pleading from Paula, who in revenge invites as houseguests two of her "old set" — George Orreyed, a pathetic young baronet who drinks heavily because of his ostracism by society, and the cause of his trouble, Mabel, his vulgar chorus-girl wife. But Paula finds that she can no longer stand the Orreyeds; all she has achieved is to alienate herself still further from her husband.

The climax of the play comes when Ellean returns unexpectedly from Paris after becoming engaged to a handsome army officer, Captain Hugh Ardale. She has received no reply to the letters she has written to her father because Paula, out of jealousy, has intercepted (but not opened) them. Ellean, in love, is now prepared at her father's behest to be kind to her stepmother and offers to introduce her fiancé, who has called secretly and is waiting outside. Ardale, however, turns out to be one of Paula's former lovers, although this is not immediately apparent to Ellean. Paula sends him away and then prepares to face the consequences.

In the fourth and final act there is a series of dialogues between Paula and the characters who remain, each encounter emphasising the hopelessness of her position. The most dramatic scene is with Ellean; aware of the nature of the former relationship between Ardale and Paula, she tells her stepmother, "I have always known what you were." In Paula's last desolate scene with her husband, he feebly asserts that they can elude the consequences of the past by going abroad, but she replies they will never forget or escape from what has happened. Tanqueray bitterly tells Drummle that this miserable situation has come about because men like Ardale and themselves have led "a man's life" without considering the outcome. Then Ellean, shocked and hysterical, enters with the news that Paula has committed suicide. "I know I helped to kill her, Ellen cries. If I had only been merciful!"

The Second Mrs Tanqueray, with its indictment of "respectable" society's double standard of sexual morality for men and women, was a very different proposition from Pinero's previous work, which theatre managers had usually snapped up quickly. His first refusal came from Hare, who condemned it as "not only bad art but commercially hopeless."[11] Bancroft's son, George — a favourite of Pin's — later claimed the real problem had been Mrs Hare's disapproval, but whatever the cause, the refusal was a severe blow to Pinero's confidence.[12]

Pinero next offered the play to George Alexander, the youngest theatre manager in London. Only thirty-five and after a mere ten years on the London stage, Alexander had recently taken a lease on the St James's and was currently enjoying a major success with Wilde's first comedy, *Lady Windermere's Fan*. But though eager for new plays and flattered to be approached by Pinero, his initial response was a polite but discouraging "Sorry; I daren't do it." Dejectedly leaving the manager's office, Pinero suddenly turned and, putting his pride in his pocket, asked if Alexander would "do the thing at a matinee for nothing." "Oh that puts a different complexion on the affair," said the manager and promptly accepted the proposal.[13]

Alexander soon had second thoughts. "If you are going to produce this, God help you!" a friend told him after glancing at the script, increasing the manager's concern that the play might alienate the fashionable audiences he had succeeded in attracting back to the St James's.[14] But to give only a single matinee performance of what was clearly an important play by a leading London dramatist would have been insulting. Alexander spent his summer holiday at a seaside cottage pondering the script, and on his return he placed the following announcement in the *Times* of 25 October 1892: "Mr Alexander has much pleasure in further intimating that at some time during the season, commencing with a series of afternoon performances, a new modern serious play by Mr Pinero will be presented."

Although no starting date had been set down for the proposed matinees, discussions on casting began almost immediately. Alexander himself was the natural choice for Aubrey Tanqueray, his natural gravity and sympathetic bearing easily compensating for his being somewhat younger than the part. Others already in his company who

"THE SECOND MRS. TANQUERAY."

MR. PINERO, TO MR. ALEXANDER:—"I THINK I HAVE GIVEN YOU SOME-
THING HOT AND STRONG THIS TIME, GEORGE!"

Alfred Bryan, caricature (The Entr'Acte, *June 1893*)

were eventually cast included A. Vane Tempest as Orreyed, Ben
Webster as Ardale, Nutcombe Gould as Misquith, and Maude Millett
as Ellean.

One or two of the secondary roles, especially that of the sympathetic bystander Drummle, were harder to fill, but by far the greatest
problem was finding an actress to play Paula Tanqueray, perhaps the
most complex study of a female character attempted in British drama
for 200 years. Marion Terry, the current leading lady at the St James's,
was too mature (having, for example, just played Mrs Erlynne —
mother of a twenty-one-year-old — in *Lady Windermere's Fan*) and
moreover was generally associated with sympathetic roles. A series of
letters, written over several months, passed between Pinero and
Alexander considering and rejecting on various grounds one actress
after another until the manager was suggesting postponement and the
writer was threatening to look for another management.[15]

Just when frustration over casting had reached a peak, however,
Pinero's attention was momentarily distracted by the need to cast and
rehearse another play. He had written *The Amazons*, his fifth farce
for the old and new Court theatres, as light relief after *The Second
Mrs Tanqueray*, but it had gone straight into production. In an
interview for the *Sketch* Pinero described the piece as "a whimsicality,
a little unpretentious effort, a sort of digestive after dinner. In it I have
attempted to find the poetry of farce. As a comic play I hope it is
amusing, while I have endeavoured to import into it a suggestion of
daintiness."[16]

The plot is based on Pin's best comic idea since *The Magistrate*:
the decision of the sports-mad Marchioness of Castlejordan to bring
up her three daughters as the boys she had longed for is comparable
to Agatha Posket's concealment of her son's true age. Once again
nature has its way, but this time the effect is more whimsical than
farcical. Nevertheless, Ellaline Terriss, who played one of the "boys,"
later recorded in her autobiography that she and her two stage sisters
were so nervous about scandalising the audience with their male attire
(designed by Pinero himself) that they consumed half a bottle of flat
champagne to give themselves courage on the first night.[17]

This "farcical romance," as it was described, opened at the Court on 7 March 1893 and pleased most of the audience and reviewers but enjoyed only a modest run of 110 performances. A year later in New York, however, the novelty of the play — and in particular of the scene in the gymnasium where the young ladies exercise with weights and Indian clubs — attracted full houses to Daniel Frohman's Lyceum production for more than eighteen weeks.[18]

Immediately after he had rid himself of *The Amazons*, Pinero returned to the serious business of casting *The Second Mrs Tanqueray*. Alexander had bravely decided to put the play into the evening bill as soon as the current play, *Liberty Hall* (a sentimental comedy by Carton), had completed its run. By the end of March Carton's piece was fading, and with no Paula yet in sight, Alexander sent his wife and an artist friend, Graham Robertson, on a tour of the London theatres to find her. One night the pair visited the Adelphi Theatre to inspect Evelyn Millard, who was playing the heroine in a society melodrama entitled *The Black Domino*. Having decided Millard was "as much like Paula Tanqueray as a white mouse is like a wild cat," the pair had resigned themselves to another wasted evening when, as Robertson later recalled,

> the scene changed and the wicked woman of the play came on.
> She did not look wicked — a startling innovation. She was almost painfully thin, with great eyes and slow haunting utterance; she was not exactly beautiful, but strangely interesting and arresting. She played weakly, walking listlessly through the part, but in one scene she had to leave the stage laughing; the laugh was wonderful, low and sweet, yet utterly mocking and heartless.
> Florence Alexander and I both realised that there before our eyes was the ideal Paula Tanqueray. If she would only move, speak, look, above all laugh like that, the part would play itself. Neither of us knew the lady, who, as the programme stated, was a Mrs Patrick Campbell.[19]

A night or two later Pinero inspected Mrs Campbell's performance for himself and reported back cautious interest to Alexander (10 April 1893):

Mrs Patrick Campbell is playing in such a poor piece that it is difficult
to form an estimate of her powers. She is however a very interesting
actress, so much makes itself apparent. Whether in a theatre such as
yours, and under such good influences as we should hope to bring to
bear upon her, she could rid herself of a certain artificiality of style,
engendered doubtless by her present situation and surroundings, is
a riddle which I cannot pretend to solve. I should like you to see her;
if you have another attack of influenza you might lay up in a box at
the Adelphi![20]

Instead, deciding to see what she was like in person, they asked
her to call on them at the St James's. Though they were not aware of
it, Mrs Campbell was in a desperate situation. Obliged to support
herself and two young children while her husband sought in vain to
make his fortune in South Africa, she had been acting professionally
for several years and already had a following among the critics. Scott
had "discovered" her when she was playing in Colchester with a
touring company and subsequently praised her acting in an Adelphi
melodrama, *The Trumpet Call*, describing it as "a singularly unstagey
performance, well-considered, well-disciplined and effective
withal."[21] Recently though, she had nearly died from an attack of
typhoid fever and had been given two weeks' notice by the managers
of the Adelphi, the Gatti brothers, who blamed her enfeebled playing
for a poor public response to *The Black Domino*. Her unexpected
summons to the St James's suddenly offered the prospect of deliver-
ance from this crisis.

At the interview Mrs Campbell was asked a few questions about
her past career; then Pinero read the play to her, beginning with
Paula's entrance late in Act 1. She later confessed she did not gather
from this reading what Paula's previous life had been, but her lively
appreciation of the reality of the play after the melodrama she had
been struggling with at the Adelphi made Pinero eager to engage her.
When, however, she told the Gattis of the offer, they decided that what
was good enough for the St James's was good enough for them and
cancelled her dismissal.[22] Disappointed, Pinero told Alexander to
wrap the matter up by offering the part to Elizabeth Robins, an
American actress who had recently impressed as Hedda Gabler.

This was the situation when Pinero called at Alexander's home in Portland Place after lunch on Monday, 1 May, before driving to the St James's to read *The Second Mrs Tanqueray* to the cast. He had barely got out of his hansom when Alexander came rushing from the house crying, "We can get Mrs Campbell after all!" He had just heard that the Gatti brothers had been persuaded by George R. Sims, coauthor of *The Black Domino* and an admirer of Mrs Campbell, to release her. On reaching the theatre, Pinero told Alexander to go inside and sort out which of the two actresses waiting there would play Paula. He himself would go for a half-hour stroll in the park while the matter was being resolved. Alexander accordingly went to his office, summoned Robins, frankly explained the situation and asked her what he should do. She pointed to the book in her hand and replied that though the role was the chance of her life she knew what it meant to Mrs Campbell and would not take the opportunity away from her.[23] (As it turned out, Elizabeth Robins would spend the next month organising and playing in a thinly attended series of Ibsen matinees while Mrs Campbell rehearsed at the St James's.)

Pinero's reading of the play a few minutes later was almost as dramatic as Alexander's interview. According to Cyril Maude, who had been engaged at the last moment to play Drummle, Mrs Campbell sat nervously in a corner of the room while the company listened to "the wonderful play" and marvelled "at Alexander even having been able to get it past the Censor."[24] The next day Pinero began blocking the moves with the cast on a stage already set with the final scenery and props. Both he and his manager were fully aware that this production was crucial to their respective careers and were determined not to leave to chance anything that could be attended to beforehand.

iii. Rehearsals

From the first rehearsal Pinero concentrated on Mrs Campbell, sitting close to her and coaching her in every word and gesture. According to Cyril Maude, she bore this drilling "like a lamb," but she herself later frankly admitted she had been "wilful, self-opinionated, strangely sensitive, easily offended, with nerves stretched by illness. Both author and manager were worried and anxious at rehearsals. No doubt they hoped that I was teachable. A certain cold 'official' manner, which was the peculiarity of Mr Alexander's style, was very unsympathetic to me, whilst my unreasonable ways, wanting always to do instead of to listen — feeling their wishes hindered my own imagination — must have been tiresome beyond words."[25]

Remarks such as "Don't forget you are not playing at the Adelphi now, but at the St James's" gave her a wild desire to laugh and play the fool, and though she controlled herself as best she could, rehearsals went badly for the first week or so. Alexander told his wife and Graham Robertson they had made "a great mistake — they had seen a second-rate actress in a third-rate production and thought her good merely because she was not bad."[26] For her part, Mrs Campbell was later to remark about Alexander, "Acting with him was rather like acting with a walking-stick."[27] In fact the contrast of styles — Mrs Campbell's emotional and mercurial, Alexander's earnest and restrained — was to prove ideal for the ill-matched Tanquerays.

The turning point in rehearsals came when she was asked if she could play the piano, virtually the only refuge from misery Paula Tanqueray has after her marriage. It so happened that Mrs Campbell was an accomplished pianist, having earlier qualified for a scholarship at the Guildhall School of Music. In her memoirs she relates how she made the most of the opportunity:

> I sat down at the piano, hesitatingly, asking twice to be excused until I had prepared something suitable. A voice from the stalls: "We would like to hear whether you can play." This offended me. Holding my book in my right hand, with my left I played beautifully — and with impertinence — a piece written by a girl friend of mine. This moment quite changed the whole temper of rehearsals. Those who listened knew that my playing must be the outcome of serious study and some understanding of art; above all that my playing would invest the part of Paula with not a little glamour.[28]

After this, Pinero's attitude to her mellowed. Seeing how easily she became exhausted at rehearsals, he one day brought her a bottle of

Brand's Essence of Beef and a spoon and stood by her until she had swallowed down the contents. He even allowed her to put some touches of her own into her part. There was, for example, the difficult moment in Act 3 when Paula, after Tanqueray has made her look at her face in a mirror, breaks down, sobbing convulsively at the innocence she has lost. Mrs Campbell experimented with the scene at home and, feeling that her crying sounded false and silly, thought of breaking it up by a natural blowing of her nose. Pinero liked the touch, which in effect softened the potential melodrama of the scene.[29]

A more significant concession came at another rehearsal. In the climactic scene where Paula is confronted by her former lover, Pinero instructed Mrs Campbell to storm across the stage and angrily sweep everything off the top of the grand piano. There are two versions of what followed. According to Ben Webster, "she stormed on cue; she reached the grand piano; she picked up a very small ornament: 'Here', she said in tones of black ice, 'I knock something over', and dropped it delicately on to the carpet."[30] In her own account, though, Mrs Campbell states that she simply looked at Pinero in horror and told him she could not make Paula rough and ugly with her hands, however angry she was; to which he gently replied, "All right, my child, do as you like."[31] Whatever the means, she saved him from marring one of the most effective passages of the play with an excessively staged gesture.

For her part, Mrs Campbell profited greatly from Pinero's theatrical experience. He gave her particularly apt advice in coaching her in her final scene, as Paula describes to Tanqueray the hopeless prospect of their future life together. Years later she instructed the young John Gielgud, playing Oswald to her Mrs Alving in *Ghosts*, "Keep still, gaze at me. Empty your voice of meaning and speak as if you were going to be sick. Pinero told me this, I have never forgotten it."[32]

As Mrs Campbell's confidence grew, it gradually became apparent that she was capable of a memorable interpretation of her role. After seeing her rehearse one day, Myra Pinero told her husband and Alexander, "Well, I don't know what you're talking about; I think

Alfred Ellis, photograph, Mrs Patrick Campbell and Mr George Alexander in The Second Mrs Tanqueray (The Sketch, *December 1893)*

she's very good."[33] They were reassured by Myra's remark but knew that Mrs Campbell was still physically weak and acting on her nerves.

The first dress rehearsal was held on the afternoon of Thursday, 25 May. Armed with a lantern, a notebook, and a pencil, Pinero sat alone in the dress circle, having promised Mrs Campbell he would not interrupt her: "I implored him not to speak to me and I would play the part for him. I kept my word and to that dark silent house and that solitary man I poured out my 'secret' with all the fire and feeling of my temperament and imagination. I wanted to plead for Paula. I wanted her to be forgiven and remembered. Cyril Maude and Maude Millett implied by a furtive squeeze of my hand that I was doing well. Mr Alexander's official dignity was of priceless value to the play."[34]

That evening Pinero presided at the Royal General Theatrical Fund dinner; his elation no doubt contributed to his giving a speech that the *World* described as the finest "since the far-off brilliant days of Charles Dickens." Alexander had the task of replying and remarked he could do no better than encourage a habit he had lately formed — a very remunerative habit he hoped it would be — "of repeating Mr Pinero's words." Among the other speakers, Irving observed that "it was thoughtful of our friend Alexander to appoint his first night to follow so closely on the heels of this evening's entertainment. 'Eat, drink and be merry', for the day after tomorrow — well, what that may bring forth no man knoweth, though we hope — I hope we hope with all our hearts — it may bring to both author and actor, the most genuine and brilliant success."[35]

After Thursday's euphoria, however, the second dress rehearsal was a dismal occasion. Mrs Campbell was too nervously exhausted to act her part properly and just went through the motions while everyone grew more and more depressed. Pinero wisely did not go near her, realising she was worn out and that the fate of the opening night depended on whether or not she could regain her nerve and spirit.

iv. Performance

"I'm going to catch it tonight. I fear the house will not understand me," Pinero dejectedly told Salaman on the morning of Saturday, 27 May 1893.[36] But the audience that assembled that evening at the St James's was both large and sympathetic, though in the opinion of the *Westminster Gazette* not as "brilliant" as might have been expected had Parliament and the courts been in session.[37] The *Evening News*, though observing that "it was, of course, more a Pinero than a Carton or Oscar Wilde house (there are such distinctions and the experienced first-nighter notes them),"[38] was most impressed by the gathering and listed half a column of celebrities present, including prominent society figures, businessmen, artists, theatrical personalities, and writers. Among the last group were Henry James and Edmund Gosse, both of whom Pinero had personally invited. "It is not my practice to ask folks to witness my work," he had written to Gosse (2 May 1893), "but this is a play for grown-up people, and you are amongst the few grown-up people I care for."[39]

Further evidence of a general anticipation that this was to be an exceptional first night was the unusually large number of critics and columnists in the audience. All the regular metropolitan reviewers were present (except for Scott, who was honeymooning in the United States) as well as correspondents from the main provincial papers and even from as far afield as Australia.

Beyond a comment from Pinero that the play showed how "we are punished through the good that is in us, not the bad,"[40] virtually nothing about *The Second Mrs Tanqueray* had been leaked in advance to the press. Curiosity was therefore high. "Above all," noted the *Westminster Gazette*, "there was a very hearty pit. It interrupted the overture when a lady entered a private box, preceded by a gigantic bouquet, and it insisted on giving her an ovation."[41] The applause was so loud that those unable to see the box in question thought royalty must have arrived, but the lady was in fact the theatre's most popular actress Marion Terry, who had been passed over for this production.

By this time Pinero was outside the theatre, pacing the Embankment and chain-smoking even more rapidly than usual while Myra kept watch on the play from his stage box. Halfway through the first act, however, he slipped into the wings to give Cyril Maude an encouraging pat on the shoulder before the actor entered for what he later described as "an extraordinarily trying scene in which Drummle has to tell the whole story of Paula's life and describe things which up till then had rarely, if ever, been mentioned on the English stage."[42]

A few minutes later Ben Webster, who did not appear as Paula's lover until late in Act 3, arrived at the stage door and found Pinero standing nervously outside. "How is she doing?" Webster asked of Mrs Campbell, who had just made her first entrance. Pinero replied that Alexander thought she would be all right if she didn't crumble.[43] But when he slipped back into his box during the first-act applause and asked Myra, she shook her head and told him to go and boost Mrs Campbell's morale. Accordingly, he dashed up to the actress's dressing room to tell her she was doing splendidly and that the play was sure to be a great success. She hardly appeared to hear him but tucked a small picture of her young son into the top of her gown before going back on stage.[44]

From this moment there was a complete transformation in her performance. Over the next few weeks the critics were to struggle to convey some impression of the range of emotion she now encompassed. *Punch's* description of Paula, a tribute to both actress and author, was one of the more eloquent attempts:

> She has learnt the piano, that is evident; she has a refined taste, oddly enough, in music; she is loving, she is vulgar; she can purr, she can spit; she is gentle, she is violent; she has good impulses, and she is a fiend incarnate; she is affectionate, she is malicious; generous and trusting, selfish and suspicious; she is all heart and no soul, she is a Peri at the gates of Paradise; she is a *bête fauve* that should be under lock and key.
>
> And not Sarah Bernhardt herself, mistress of all the feminine feline arts as she is, could play this part better than Mrs Patrick Campbell. It is a wonderful performance, most striking, most convincing, from the utter absence in it of all apparent consciousness of the effects she is producing.[45]

As the curtain fell on the second act there was a tremendous outburst of applause, the curtain was raised again and again, and there were repeated loud cries of "Author!" — something quite without precedent before the final curtain at the St James's. Though Pinero did not appear, he knew the tide had turned and that Mrs Campbell's performance was sweeping all before it. She, however, was puzzled, even irritated, by what she regarded as the audience's unnecessary noise.[46]

The effect of the third act was even more marked. The audience, according to the *Era*, was stunned by the climactic moment when Paula discovers that her stepdaughter is engaged to her former lover: "As the full significance of the scene flashed upon the minds of the spectators, and quickened their pulses with horror and astonishment, the effect upon them was a study for any student of human nature. Some appeared to shrink, as if with pain, from the dreadful revelation; others, rigid with blank wonder, seemed hardly to comprehend it; fair faces became pale, and a visible shudder ran through the house and caused for a moment a breathless pause of silence and expectancy."[47]

It was past 10:30 when the third act ended, but there was still one more to follow. Several actors from other theatres who had finished their work for the night called in at the St James's to see the end of Pinero's play; Ellen Terry's arrival from the Lyceum during the final interval prompted an ovation that effectively silenced the entr'acte.[48] Meanwhile at the Avenue Theatre, where the Kendals were appearing in a drama called *The Silver Shell*, Mrs Kendal, thinking of Pinero and wondering whether she dare play Paula on a forthcoming American tour, whispered to her husband: "By now he will have made the success of his life, or been torn in pieces!"[49]

At the St James's the verdict was never in doubt. After the curtain fell on Ellean's shocked announcement of Paula's suicide, there was a long silence. Then, as the *Daily News* reported, "pent-up emotions found relief in a storm of applause which did not subside until the leading players had appeared again and again, and the author had responded to a call which shook the walls of the theatre."[50] Cyril Maude later recalled, "People stood up and waved their handkerchiefs — the enthusiasm was overwhelming. Alexander had a crowd of people rushing round to congratulate him and all of us."[51] Mrs Campbell was simply dazed by it all, later recording in her autobiography, "The tremendous applause stupified me, and I never for a moment thought that a share of it was mine. . . . I felt it was all for the author and his remarkable play. . . . Crowds of people flocked on to the stage; shy and terrified, I ran up to my dressing-room, picked up my dog, and went back to my lodgings worn out by fatigue."[52]

v. Verdicts

The newspaper coverage that greeted the opening of *The Second Mrs Tanqueray* was enormous, even by the generous standards of the time. It is doubtful whether any English play since has received overall a more rapturous press. The *Evening Standard* headed its review "A Great Play," as did the *Echo*, with the addition "and a Great Actress."[53] Two cartoons summed up the general consensus: one, in *Punch*, showed Pinero mopping his brow as Mrs Campbell triumphantly leapt a hurdle marked "Convention"[54] and the other, in the *Illustrated Sporting and Dramatic News*, depicted the debonair author telling a grumpy little Ibsen, "I think we have something now which will suit you!"[55]

There was less outrage at the play's theme than Pinero and his manager had expected. With Scott safely out of the way, the "old school" critics contented themselves with the view that if the play's subject matter was distasteful, its treatment was skilful and moral. Nisbet, for example, declared in the *Times*: "Nothing more essentially hideous and squalid has been set before the supporters of the *Théâtre Libre* or any of its offshoots. But let us do its author justice; it is written with a masterly hand and holds the spectator from first to last in the thrall of a horrible fascination."[56]

Among the many people who congratulated Pinero on his achievement was Gosse, who wrote that he considered the first night "a signal event in English dramatic literature" and believed Pinero was destined "as Ben Jonson put it, 'to raise the despised head of drama again, and strip her of those base and rotten rags wherewith the times have

adulterated her form.' "[57] Henry James stated he had found the play
"full of substance & full of art, and interesting from beginning to
end,"[58] and John Hare regretted having lacked "the good judgement
& the courage that Alexander [had] shown."[59] In a different vein, Mrs
Campbell wrote thanking Pinero for his "kind, encouraging words,"
which had "braced [her] heart up wonderfully" when she was trembling with fear.[60]

But it was Archer's good opinion Pinero craved most. The critic's
review in the *World* the following Wednesday contained not only high
praise for "an astonishing advance in philosophical insight and technical skill which places the new play in a new category" but also a
curious reservation:

> Frankly it is not a play I hanker after seeing again. I want to read it,
> to study it — but, with Mrs Patrick Campbell in the title part,
> though, or because, her performance is almost perfect in its realism,
> the sensation it gave one could not at any point be described as
> pleasure. It interests and absorbs one; it satisfies the intelligence
> more completely than any other modern English play; but it is not in
> the least moving. Not once during the whole evening were the tears
> anywhere near my eyes. Yes, once — when Mr Pinero came before
> the curtain, and the house rose at him. Then I felt a thrill of genuine
> emotion to think that here at last, in spite of all the depressing and
> stunting influences of our English theatrical world, was a man who
> had the will and the talent to emancipate himself and give the artist
> within him free play — to take care of his soul, and let his pocket,
> for the nonce, take care of itself.[61]

Archer felt that Pinero had written a painful case study rather than
presented "a fairly typical case." He was also concerned that, partly
owing to the limitations of the dramatic form, the audience was given
insufficient information fully to understand the motivation of Tanqueray and, to a lesser extent, Paula.

The first objection no longer seems significant. Marriages between
courtesans and respectable widowers may not have been typical of the
late Victorian period, but the misalliance between Paula and Tanqueray does present an effective test of late Victorian mores. Though
Pinero states the evidence circumspectly, he makes the nature of

Paula's previous career quite plain. Both Drummle and Tanqueray, for example, have been among her former sexual clients in the expensive half-world of Aldford Street, private supper parties, and Mediterranean cruises, the main difference between the two men being that Drummle is unconcerned about the gap between public and private morality in society whereas Tanqueray has a bad conscience about it. The latter, indeed, in proving to be the epitome of respectability, may be regarded as Paula's chief antagonist rather than Ellean. It is his fear that his daughter's virginal purity may be tainted by his second wife that Paula finds hardest to bear. In a crucial scene at the beginning of Act 2, she tells him that "there are two sorts of affection — the love for a woman you respect, and the love for a woman you — love. She gets the first from you: I never can."

The central feature of Paula's characterisation is her desperate craving for acceptance, both social and personal. Pinero does not, however, portray her as a calculating woman; if he had, there would have been no problem, as, she would, for example, have possessed the necessary self-control to be polite when Mrs Cortelyon, the representative of society, deigns to call. Instead, Paula is made to destroy her chance for social acceptance in one of the play's most effective scenes. The underlying cause of her vulnerability, incidentally, may be her inability to have children of her own — presumably a consequence of venereal infection, though this is left unsaid.

Paula is a creature of impulse, whether responding in anger or affection, as opposed to the well-bred restraint that typifies her husband. Once again in a Pinero play there is a clash between an impetuous young wife and a staid, middle-aged husband. Yet Paula's integrity is marred when Tanqueray tells her that a few years ago she was "like Ellean," and she breaks down crying, "O God! A few years ago!"[62] The collapse might be seen as an impulsive reaction to a scene of crisis, but it sits awkwardly with the angry scorn of a Paula who earlier dreads the prospect of becoming "stale and dry and withered from sheer solitary respectability" or who later responds to her former lover's protestation, "You don't know how I love Ellean," with the stinging rejoinder, "Yes, that's just what I *do* know." Nevertheless, her ultimate tragedy is that she is destroyed through her adoption of

Tanqueray's moral standards; in confessing the truth of her previous affair with Ellean's fiancé she does the decent and respectable thing at the cost, she believes, of final acceptance by the people whose respect she craves.

The sympathetic portrayal of such a character at the very centre of a drama that laid much of the responsibility for her rejection on the very people who viewed her fate from the stalls and boxes of theatres such as the St James's was an act of courage on the part of both Pinero and Alexander. The reverse side of Victorian respectability, merely flirted with in recent plays such as *Lady Windermere's Fan* and *A Woman of No Importance*, had been presented in a manner calculated to try the conscience of the audience. Many of the first-night critics acknowledged this.[63] "It is a vigorous painting of the lives men lead, and of the squalor and leprosy of our latter civilisation," stated the *Globe*'s reviewer, adding that "taking our pleasant and, as the world holds, pardonable vices, Mr Pinero makes of them whips to scourge us." The *Westminster Gazette* gave credit to Alexander and to the censor for permitting theatregoers to see "an earnest, truthful, horrible picture of the worm that ever gnaws at the heart of occidental society"; while the *Era* declared that "there was no getting away from the stern moral of the dramatist who had alarmed many, pained most, and shocked all of his auditors." As the reviewer from *Vanity Fair* observed, "Regarded as part of a movement, 'The Second Mrs Tanqueray' emphasises very sharply the parting of the ways. . . . Its influence on our modern playwriting will be very considerable." Though Ibsen had preceded him and other playwrights would go much further, Pinero had made a vital breakthrough for English drama by treating his respectable society audience as "guilty creatures sitting at a play."

There was one critic, however, who found this approach intolerable. Clement Scott returned to England in mid-June, three months after the premiere of *The Second Mrs Tanqueray*, determined to discredit what almost everyone else had been praising. His belated campaign began with a sarcastic little article in the *Illustrated London News* lamenting the "colour-blindness" that rendered him incapable of appreciating a great modern play in which "an Ibsenitish Hedda

Gabler shrew" caused every virtuous person in the piece to suffer horribly.[64] This was harmless enough, and Pin, on a working holiday in Suffolk, remarked to Archer (27 July 1893) that though he had heard about "Scott's Emulsion," was not sufficiently interested or curious to search for it in the *Illustrated London News*.[65] Scott's next assault, however, was far more devious and damaging. In a long article entitled "A Strange Coincidence, or, 'the Second Mrs Wife,' " publish- ed in the same journal on 19 August,[66] he suggested that the plot of *The Second Mrs Tanqueray* bore a distinct resemblance to that of a recent German play, *Der Schatten* (The Shadow) by Paul Lindau. He did not overtly charge Pinero with plagiarism, but the sneering innu- endo was unmistakable throughout the article and especially at the end:

> Perhaps Pinero's play was written long before Paul Lindau's. I am quite prepared to hear that. Why should not the same idea, scene for scene, occur to two dramatists? Possibly the plot was in the air and Blavatskied from England to Germany, or vice versa. There was an explanation to hand when some of us actually thought that *The Squire* reminded us of Thomas Hardy's *Far from the Madding Crowd*. Somebody blundered then, if I mistake not, but Hardy's influence still hangs about *The Squire*.
>
> It was foolish — was it not? — to mistake what seemed an innocent fact for a strange coincidence.

Though infuriated by Scott's tactics — especially his attempt to throw in some of the old *Squire* mud with this new smear — Pinero had no intention of being dragged into another public row in the papers. Instead, when the insinuations were repeated in the *Daily Telegraph*, he sent a brief formal note to the editor stating he had never heard of *Der Schatten* until a few days earlier and that the plot of *The Second Mrs Tanqueray* was entirely of his own invention.[67] Then he wrote (24 August 1893) to George Lewis, enclosing Scott's article and asking if the lawyer considered it actionable. Lewis was in Hamburg at the time but replied several days later that he thought that a libel had been committed and that he would pursue the matter with Scott and the *Illustrated London News* when he returned to London on 7 September.[68]

Archer had also been disgusted by Scott's insinuations and wrote to the playwright asking if he could help. Pinero replied (24 August 1893) that he did not think so but appreciated the "good word and good will of honest workers for the stage." Archer, however, did not let the matter rest there but with some difficulty acquired a copy of *Der Schatten* from Germany and published a lengthy article in the *World*, demonstrating that "no rational and candid critic, examining the two plays, could ever suppose that the one was borrowed from or suggested by the other." One by one he demolished the so-called similarities, concluding with the devastating point that though Scott had described the hero of Lindau's play (which the critic constantly referred to as "The Second Mrs Wife") as a widower, he was in fact a bachelor: "Thus the one 'coincidence' worthy of the name resolves itself into — shall we say a blunder? Yes, a blunder, for no one in his senses makes a deliberate misstatement of fact which is certain to be found out. But when a man is so eager to impugn another man's honour that he cannot be at the trouble of verifying the simplest facts, his case can scarcely be called one of mere stupidity."[69]

In the meantime Scott, alarmed at the hornets' nest he had raised, had tried to back off with a pathetic claim that his remarks, made "in a spirit of pure banter," had never suggested plagiarism. Writing to Lewis (10 September 1893), he stated he had not the slightest doubt "of Mr Pinero's personal honour" and then added plaintively, "But has it come to this that when some of the 'old school' do not like the dramatic tendency of the 'new school' we are to have a pistol placed at our heads & be threatened with actions for libel unless we bow low to the modern idea?"[70] Though he was putting the case the wrong way round — for the "old school" was the aggressor — a distaste for modern developments in playwriting was indeed the underlying cause of his attack.

The dispute ended on 30 September with a meeting in Lewis's office. Scott agreed to make a formal apology in the following issue of the *Illustrated London News*. Writing later that day to Archer, Pinero remarked that the ceremony had struck him as "supremely ludicrous" and that the office seemed to be flooded with Scott's tears, Archer having been "the King Charles's Head of his discourse."[71] But an old association had been damaged beyond repair. Pinero never communicated directly with Scott again. He had, for good or ill, broken irrevocably with the leading critic of the "old school."

The row did not have any effect on the success of *The Second Mrs Tanqueray*. At the end of July, Alexander had broken the run at the St James's to take the play (together with *Lady Windermere's Fan* and *Liberty Hall*) on a lengthy autumn tour of the main provincial centres. In Liverpool, despite a municipally inspired purity campaign in progress, the play's first night was attended by the Lord Mayor and his wife, and a Reverend T. W. Lund was inspired to preach and publish a sermon on Paula that rapidly sold out nine editions.[72] In Birmingham, however, the play sparked off a lively debate in the *Daily Post*, an anonymous correspondent attacking what he considered a betrayal of the theatre's conventional moral standards: "We have had to look for the triumph of virtue and innocence kept inviolate from the machinations of designing men and women. Here we have virtue and the graces turned upside down. . . . The moral tone of the piece tends to outrage all sense of propriety and makes one blush for our common humanity."[73] There was some support for this view from other correspondents, but most agreed with a reply from Alexander, which ended with the remark that "the playgoer who can assert that the chief attraction of *The Second Mrs Tanqueray* is its 'spiciness' is a marvel of inscrutable obtuseness."[74]

The play continued to arouse controversy — and to draw full houses — for the remainder of the tour, relegating Alexander's other two productions to matinees and Monday and Tuesday nights and netting the manager a profit of over £4,000.[75] After touring with Mrs Campbell and Marion Terry as rival leading ladies, however, he returned, as Graham Robertson observed, "with his brown locks becomingly but perceptibly silvered."[76] The London run of *The Second Mrs Tanqueray* resumed at the beginning of November and continued until the end of the following April, achieving a total (not counting the tour) of 228 performances and a profit of over £10,000.[77] The season could have continued longer, for the houses were still good, but Alexander did not enjoy long runs and wanted to move on to other things, the first of which was a new piece by Henry Arthur Jones.

The last nights of the run were noted in a number of newspapers and journals, writers hailing the play as a classic that would be revived again and again by actresses eager to reinterpret Paula in their own image. Already Charlotte Granville, who was understudying the part at the St James's, had won praise when Mrs Campbell had been unable to play because of illness. Mrs Kendal, too, had caused a sensation, but of a rather different kind, when she and her husband opened their U.S. tour with *The Second Mrs Tanqueray* the previous October.[78] In a letter to Archer (4 November 1893), Pinero noted that "they had played it three weeks out of four in New York to full houses. But, oh lord, the abuse!"[79] The spectacle of the Ideal British Matron playing a Lost Woman for all she was worth had been more than the New York critics could bear. But for many years Mrs Campbell was to remain incomparable in the role. It had made her famous, and she continued to revive it almost to the end of her stage career.

Among the many admirers she overwhelmed in the first year of her "Tanqueradiance" was the music critic of the *World*. In his column for 20 December 1893, he described how he had by chance wandered into the St James's Theatre one night, just in time to see the curtain rise on the second act. It had revealed

> a piano forte, at which the chief lady of the piece — a very attractive person — presently sat down and began to play . . . with such convincingly right expression and feeling and so sympathetic a hand that I immediately forgot all about the comedy, and prepared to enjoy Schubert. Will it be believed that the wretched people on stage interrupted her after a few bars? The same thing happened at a subsequent and equally promising attempt. After that she never succeeded in even sitting down to the piano, and at last, worn out by repeated interruptions, she left the stage abruptly, and we were presently given to understand she had committed suicide. No wonder![80]

Thus was launched a diabolical two-pronged attack on Pinero's standing as a serious dramatist and on the affections of Mrs Campbell by Bernard Shaw.

...11...
"At the Point of the Pen"

i. Enter G.B.S.

I again suggest that it is time for us to begin. As journalists we have had our turn; and if there is nothing higher before us — if the future, as Mrs Tank [Tanqueray] says, is only to be the past entered through another gate — why, then, the lethal chamber is the proper place for us.[1]

When on 20 August 1893 Shaw threw down this challenge for his colleague William Archer to stop criticising plays and start writing them, his own dramatic output consisted of *Widowers' Houses* (begun in collaboration with Archer in 1885 and completed alone seven years later for the Independent Theatre) and a second effort, *The Philanderer*, which even Grein had found intolerable. At thirty-eight (just a year and two months younger than Pinero), Shaw had little more to show for his literary endeavours than five rejected novels and a reputation as a lively reviewer of books, art, and music. With time and opportunity apparently running out for him it is hardly surprising that he decided his only chance was, in his own metaphor, to lay siege to the theatre, "cut his own way into it at the point of the pen, and throw some of its defenders into the moat."[2]

Foremost among the obstacles in his path was Arthur Wing Pinero's newly won standing as a brilliant writer of realistic problem plays. Although Shaw considered this reputation an illusion — the product of clever stage technique accompanied "by an air of novel,

"Bulbo" (Max Beerbohm), caricature of Pinero and Shaw (Vanity Fair, *January 1897; by permission of the Mary Evans Picture Library)*

profound and original thought"[3] — as long as it persisted there was little room for the kind of drama he wanted to write. It is understandable that he saw Pinero merely as the leading "society" dramatist, the chief purveyor of a drama that reinforced the prejudices of Victorian respectability, a code to which Shaw, with his Dublin background of "shabby genteel" poverty, pronounced himself implacably opposed. In a speech to the Fabian Society on "Socialism and Human Nature" (19 December 1890), for example, he denounced "our typical successful man" as

an odious person, vulgar, thick-skinned, pleased by the contrast between his own riches and the poverty of others, unable to see any reason why men should not be degraded into flunkeys in his kitchen or women poisoned by phosphorous and whitelead in his factory, as long as his pride and his purse are swelled. Need I add that he is religious, charitable, patriotic, and full to the neck of ideals — respectability, true womanliness, true manliness, duty, virtue, chastity, subdual of the lower nature by the higher, self-sacrifice, abstinence, the constitution, the family, law and order, punctuality, honesty, a good name: he has the whole rosary at his finger's ends. How do we contrive to make such a monster as this out of anything so innocent as a man?[4]

That Pinero, with his own youthful experience of shabby gentility, shared — if not so stridently — this distaste for hypocrisy masquerading as respectability does not appear to have occurred to Shaw at this time. Pinero after all was wealthy and successful, so it followed that the social criticism in plays such as *The Times* and *The Second Mrs Tanqueray* must be insincere as well as ineffectual. But this was not so. Pinero was of course no socialist, and his knowledge of the world had been limited by his preoccupation with the theatre. He did not shrink, however, from holding up his mirror to the society in which he moved, even though he was aware of the need for tact if he was to hold his audience.

Shaw had yet to learn discretion. He had responded to Pinero's recent triumph by writing the first act of a new play, *Mrs Warren's Profession*, which, he informed Archer (30 August 1893), "skilfully blended the plot of The Second Mrs Tanqueray with that of The Cenci" and would be "just the thing for the Independent Theatre."[5] The completed play effectively took Pinero's basic situations, made them even more shocking to conventional morality, and then ironically deflated them. Paula has been a courtesan, whereas Mrs Warren manages brothels; both women have unexpected encounters with former lovers — Paula's is now an army captain, Mrs Warren's a clergyman; and Paula confesses her past sins to her husband-to-be in a letter he burns unread, whereas Mrs Warren confesses the nature and details of her trade to her daughter in person at considerable length. As a counterpart to Pinero's daring third-act climax of (as Shaw later put it) "a step-daughter and step-mother finding themselves in the positions respectively of affianced wife and discarded mistress to the same man,"[6] Shaw's third-act climax has Mrs Warren's daughter and her daughter's lover discovering they might be children of the same father. But if Pinero's characters are trapped by their predicaments, Shaw's are unashamed. Mrs Warren is merely amused by the clergyman's tongue-tied embarrassment when they meet and vigorously defends her past when confronted by her daughter. In turn, the daughter rejects her young man not because he might be her half brother but because he is merely an amiable young rascal. In effect Shaw had it both ways: adapting the plot structure of the "Pinerotic" social drama enabled him to build strong climaxes, and deflating its typical situations emphasised his refusal to be circumscribed by conventional ideals and beliefs, though at a deeper level it may be that Shaw's habitual substitution of anticlimax for dramatic crisis reflects an aversion to strong emotion in life as well as on the stage.

In the short term *Mrs Warren's Profession* proved a disaster for its author. Even the Independent Theatre rejected it, Grein refusing so much as to show it to the censor, and the play remained unperformed, even privately, until 1902. Shaw, as he later confessed, could not have done anything more injurious to his prospects at the outset of his dramatic career. He was left with no option but to retire forthwith from the field of "unpleasant" drama and try something else.[7] Nevertheless, his little sally at Pinero's "comedy" in the *World* served notice that the real campaign against his rival was yet to come.

Shaw was not the only "new" playwright to dissent from the popular verdict on *The Second Mrs Tanqueray*. His compatriot, the novelist George Moore, nettled by the poor reception given his first stage effort, *The Strike at Arlingford*,[8] had written Archer two long letters[9] deriding the praise heaped on Pinero's play and pulling it to pieces scene by scene. Archer, however, had stood his ground, remarking in his final drama column for 1893:

> It is noteworthy that among the very severest critics of *The Second Mrs Tanqueray* we should find the authors of *The Strike at Arlingford* and *Widowers' Houses*, but I would not have Mr Pinero unduly abashed by their disesteem. There is a species of technical criticism which is in its essence unjust. The craftsman, especially if he is new to his craft . . . has an inclination to look at the work of other

craftsmen and think, "Now I would have done that differently — therefore it is bad." (Observe that the major premise of the syllogism is modestly suppressed.) Their approval of the mere brushwork of the picture blinds them to its more essential qualities. Thus, at any rate, I am fain to account for the absence from their judgements of all reasonable sense of proportion.[10]

ii. The Notorious Mrs Ebbsmith

Pinero had not concerned himself with this debate. He did not collect notices of his plays — even favourable ones[11] — and on principle never replied to his critics in public or even (with the sole exception of Archer) in private. Charges of plagiarism were another matter, but when his row with Scott was followed almost immediately by an accusation in a French magazine article that he had cribbed *The Profligate* from Sardou's *Denise*, his sense of the ridiculous overcame his indignation. "I am again with my back to the wall, hitting out wildly," he told Archer on 24 November 1893. "I have written to the *Gaulois* telling M. Duhamel that he has spoken untruths. *The Profligate* and *Denise* now! Methinks my detractors do protest too much."[12]

He had resumed work on a play for Mrs Campbell that Hare, in the hope of engaging her, had commissioned for the Garrick. Thinking and planning, begun in July during the Suffolk holiday, had been disrupted by the Scott affair, but now he was able to tell Archer he was getting along with the play, "sometimes thinking well of it, at others hating it."

As Pinero's letters over the next fifteen months reveal, the writing of the play eventually called *The Notorious Mrs Ebbsmith* was protracted and difficult. Whenever possible he tried to get away from town. "I have a craving to go down to Oxford to work: I must get away on Monday," he wrote to W. L. Courtney, editor of the *Fortnightly Review* (23 January 1894), adding wistfully, "Can you tell me of any quiet, cozy lodging? It would mean so much to me if the windows gave me a glimpse of a college with, perhaps, a peep at a bit of green."[13] Instead, he put up at the Granville Hotel, Ramsgate, from where three weeks later he informed Jones (14 February 1894) that he was "getting along fairly well" and would not be back in London for at least another fortnight.[14] But by early summer his confidence and inspiration had gone. Replying to a letter from Archer, who had been surprised to read a hint about the play's plot in a column by Scott, Pin denied (8 June 1894) he had been communicating with the enemy and confided the true state of affairs:

> C.S. can know nothing of my plans. As you suggest "under the same roof", or, as I intend to put it, "under one roof", is a common form of description of a certain form of relationship between husband and wife. I say "intended", because after doing an act and a half of the piece I had planned out I came to the conclusion that I was doing the thing badly. So I put it on the hob to simmer with some other half-empty pots; they will boil some day. Indeed I am now dealing with a five-year old scheme of mine — older, I believe, for I don't seem to remember the time, in late years, when it hasn't been worrying me. Perhaps you will come up here [London] to sup one night and let me tell you about it. Give me a few days' notice; it would be a great pleasure for me to have a talk with you.[15]

Three months later, refreshed by a vacation at Maloja in the Swiss Engadine, Pinero reported to Archer (5 October 1894) from Westgate-upon-Sea that he was currently working on both plays, the second promised to his old adversary Comyns Carr, who was now managing the Comedy Theatre:

> The play — the Garrick play — is still unfinished. But I am better in health than I have been for a long time and hope to really get the thing out by about Christmas. As a matter of fact, I have been very seedy for the last twelve months, though I haven't said anything about it. The Engadine has done me much good and I'm now in the highest spirits I can hope to attain. Carr's play is fully planned, and a bit of it written, so a great deal of work has been done — to bear creditable fruit, let us pray, by and by. I can't let anything go that is not at least up to my poor form — hence the delay. I want to talk to you, to gossip and ramble, it is an "age" since I last saw you. When I get back to town you must be kind enough to come and see me. I'm down here only to untie a knot in my work — alone, for at such times

I'm gloomy and depressing to those at home. Cibber [his dog] especially hates me when I'm like that; he and Mrs and Miss Myra shall
receive your friendly message. Were they here they would desire to
be mentioned kindly to Mrs Archer.

Several factors had contributed to Pinero's decision to persevere
with the "Garrick play." The most important had been his wife's
support — as noted by her son, Angus, in a gossipy but somewhat
inaccurate article about his stepfather published that October in a
New York magazine.[16] A second factor was his improved health, and
the third was news that Mrs Campbell would probably be available to
play the central role for Hare, though only for a limited run of several
months from the end of the year. She was under contract to Tree
(having by mutual — and heartfelt — consent parted company with
Alexander in July) but would not be accompanying her new manager
on a tour of the United States due to begin in December. That time was
pressing did not help to speed progress even when Pinero began
declining evening engagements, amongst them a party at the Gosse's
on 4 December. Two days later he turned down a request to contribute
an article to the *Theatre* about *The Second Mrs Tanqueray,* saying he
was beginning to loathe the very name of the new play and could not
write about it or anything else until he had acquitted himself of his
present task.[17] But Christmas came and went with the play still unfinished. His embarrassment became acute when Henry James invited
him to attend the first night of *Guy Domville* at the St James's Theatre
on 5 January 1895. Pin thanked James for the invitation (31 December
1894) which he described as "at once a compliment and the promise of
real enjoyment," but went on to say that he got "no pleasure from it,
only pain. For I can't come out on Saturday night. I am still behind-
hand with my work for the Garrick Theatre — it should have been
finished long ago, but it turned out a more perplexing job than I
reckoned for — and now, to my dismay, Hare's latest production, upon
which I depended for time to finish my difficult task leisurely, is, I
greatly fear, a failure." But, he added, his wife would be at the opening
and afterwards give him an account of what he sincerely hoped would
be the first of many dramatic triumphs for James.

But *Guy Domville* was no more successful at the St James's than Hare's latest production, Grundy's *Slaves of the Ring*, at the Garrick. Both pieces, however, acquired accidental immortality as the first Shaw covered in his capacity of drama critic for the *Saturday Review*. Although "G.B.S." dealt gently with James and even paid Grundy one or two backhanded compliments, he served notice of his iconoclastic policy by describing the acting of Hare's company as "on the whole, much worse than the play" and the expensive dresses and settings as "epitomising the whole history of plutocracy in England during the expiring century."[18] A week or two later he turned the point of his pen against Irving's "heartless waste" of Ellen Terry's genius on the "jobbing verses" of Carr's *King Arthur* while all the time there was "a stream of splendid women's parts pouring from the Ibsen volcano and minor craters."[19] A subsequent article committed a further act of lèse-majesté when he (accurately) described the lecture on "Acting, an Art" Irving delivered to the Royal Institution as a covert demand for the actor's own knighthood.[20]

It was soon Pinero's turn to suffer. The publication early in February of *The Second Mrs Tanqueray* gave G.B.S. the opportunity for some preliminary thrusts at the literary basis of his rival's reputation:

> The novels of Anthony Trollope, Charles Lever, Bulwer Lytton, Charles Reade, and many other novelists, whom nobody praised thirty years ago in the terms in which Mr Pinero is praised now, are full of feats of character-drawing in no way inferior — to say the least — to Mr Pinero's. The theatre was not ready for that class of work then: it is now; and accordingly Mr Pinero who in literature is a humble and somewhat belated follower of the novelists of the middle of the nineteenth century, and who has never written a line from which it could be guessed that he is a contemporary of Ibsen, Tolstoi, Meredith, or Sarah Grand, finds himself at the dawn of the twentieth hailed as a man of new ideas, of daring originality, of supreme literary distinction, and even — which is perhaps oddest — of consummate stage craft.[21]

Earlier in the same article Shaw had dismissed *The Importance of Being Earnest* (produced at the St James's on 14 February 1894) as having the general effect on him of a farcical comedy dating from the 1870s, exciting "miserable mechanical laughter" that left him "out of spirits before the end of the second act, and out of temper before the end of the third."[22] It is possible that his debunking of Pinero would have had as little long-term effect as his estimate of *Earnest* had not the staging of *The Notorious Mrs Ebbsmith* less than three weeks later presented him with a perfect opening for a really devastating attack.

The new play, genuinely ambitious in theme and, as Archer was to point out, in several respects "a great advance on *The Second Mrs Tanqueray*,"[23] proved seriously flawed in its portrayal of the central character. Agnes Ebbsmith is a former street-corner orator against the miseries of marriage who nurses and then lives with Lucas Cleeve, a young aristocrat and himself an escapee from an unhappy marriage, in a sexual relationship that she wishes to turn into one of purely intellectual companionship. He, however, is pressured by an emissary from his family, the Duke of St Olpherts, to return for appearance's sake and live under the same roof as his wife. Thus, having been forced to abandon all her ideals one by one, Agnes eventually finds that the only way she can retain her weak-willed partner is as his mistress, an arrangement to be connived at by his wife and family. As Sybil Cleeve tells Agnes near the end of the play: "When my husband left me, and I heard of his association with you, I felt sure that his vanity would soon make an openly irregular life intolerable to him. Vanity is the cause of a great deal of virtue in men; the vainest are those who like to be thought respectable" (208).

The central plot idea amounts to a savage denunciation of social hypocrisy, but in choosing a "platform woman" for his heroine, Pinero found himself out of his depth, lacking either knowledge or sympathetic understanding of such a person. Worse, having built Agnes Ebbsmith's moral struggle to a powerful climax, he was unable to resolve it except by having her fade into a feeble and unconvincing religiosity. Mrs Campbell herself later remarked, "The *rôle* of Agnes Ebbsmith and the first three acts of the play filled me with ecstasy. There was a touch of nobility that fired and inspired me, but the last act broke my heart. I knew that such an Agnes in life could not have drifted into the Bible-reading inertia of the woman she became in the last act; for her earlier vitality, with its mental and emotional activity, gave the lie to it — I felt she would have risen a phoenix from the ashes."

Her dislike of the last act did not prevent her from making an enormous success in the role when the play opened at the Garrick Theatre on Wednesday, 13 March 1895. Gosse expressed a consensual view a fortnight later as he told Mrs Campbell, "The play was — you. I tell you without exaggeration that I never saw on the English stage a piece of acting so brilliantly sustained, varied and vivified. . . . 'What did I think of the play?' I was thinking only of you."[24]

Mrs Campbell emerged from the production with her reputation enhanced — as to a lesser extent did Forbes-Robertson and Hare (respectively Agnes's lover, Lucas Cleeve, and her antagonist, the cynical Duke of St Olpherts) — but Pinero was not so fortunate. He had committed the cardinal dramatic sin of raising his audience's interest to fever pitch and then disappointing it. Although Archer did his best in the *World* to stress the play's positive features, only Scott among the leading critics commended it without reservation. This did not impress Pin, who privately remarked to Archer (16 March 1895) that "Scott's present praise" filled him "with as much disgust as his dishonesty and misrepresentation [had] done in the past." More typical were the *Sketch*'s description of the piece as "a powerful, painful, unsatisfactory play,"[25] and the *Pall Mall Gazette*'s opinion that its final act "amply justifies the verdict that Mr Pinero comes near to being, and yet beyond all question is *not*, a writer of great plays."[26]

But it was Shaw's trenchant ridicule in the *Saturday Review* that did the real damage.[27] After labelling the play as "bad" and remarking that Mrs Patrick Campbell had pulled her author through "by playing him off the stage," G.B.S. went on ironically to forgive "the mistakes into which Mr Pinero has been led by his want of practical acquaintance with the business of political agitation," yet added that his readers "would certainly not tolerate such nonsense from any intellectually responsible person." It was the play's climax, though, that aroused his deepest scorn. Noting that Agnes Ebbsmith's realisation that Cleeve's attachment to her was based on sex rather than respect for her ideas offered "a dramatic theme capable of interesting development," Shaw unleashed the full force of his contempt:

> Mr Pinero, unable to develop it, lets it slip through his fingers after one feeble clutch at it, and proceeds to degrade his drama below the ordinary level by making the woman declare that her discovery of the man's feelings puts within her reach "the only one hour in a woman's life," in pursuance of which detestable view she puts on an indecent dress and utterly abandons herself to him. A clergyman appears at this crisis and offers her a Bible. She promptly pitches it into the stove; and a thrill of horror runs through the audience as they see, in imagination, the whole Christian Church tottering before their eyes. Suddenly, with a wild scream, she plunges her hand into the glowing stove and pulls out the Bible again. The Church is saved; and the curtain descends amid thunders of applause. In that applause I hope I need not say I did not join. A less sensible and less courageous stage effect I have never witnessed. . . . this, I submit, is a piece of claptrap so gross that it absolves me from all obligation to treat Mr Pinero's art as anything higher than the barest art of theatrical sensation. As in The Profligate, as in The Second Mrs Tanqueray, he has no idea beyond that of doing something daring and bringing down the house by running away from the consequences.

At the end of the review, however, Shaw included three sentences that reveal his awareness that his temper had soured his judgement: "Many passages in the play, of course, have all the qualities which have gained Mr Pinero his reputation as a dramatist; but I shall not dwell on them, as, to tell the truth, I disliked the play so much that nothing would induce me to say anything good of it. And here let me warn the reader to carefully discount my opinion in view of the fact that I write plays myself, and that my school is in violent reaction against that of Mr Pinero. But my criticism has not, I hope, any other fault than the inevitable one of extreme unfairness." This last reservation did not prevent Archer from protesting at the vehemence of Shaw's attack on the writer Archer believed had done more than anyone to advance the cause of serious drama in England. He was alarmed that such unbridled criticism might drive its victim back to farce and light comedy. Shaw admitted (18 March 1895) he had been under severe work pressure when he wrote the review but affirmed he would "not at all mind seeing Pinero driven back into the comic line" as it was "in that line alone" he showed "the smallest fertility":

> It seems to me that it is only by the frankest abandonment of himself to his real tastes and capacities that he can do anything worth doing now on the stage. But he won't do that, because he is a Jew, with the Jew's passion for fame and effect and the Jew's indifference to the reality of the means by which they are produced. A man who, at Pinero's age and in his position and with his secure bank account, could bring himself to that Bible business, is hopelessly damned. You might as well try to fertilize a mule. We shall have to take these plays of his for exactly what they are, without trying to appeal for better to a will which he simply hasn't got in him. After all, I don't know what I could have done for him than what I did; and that was to alter the words "silly and cowardly" to "less sensible and less courageous."[28]

Shaw's unusually savage and racist outburst continued with a denial of Pinero's so-called pioneering, declaring him to have always been "a camp follower and not a leader." The letter ended with an even franker admission of Shavian self-interest: "Pinero is only cutting the grooves deeper that I wish to lift the drama out of. To the man who is touched and fascinated by Pinero, Shaw will be the merest sand and sawdust, all the more irritating because it would appear so very easy to give my subjects the Pinerotic effect. In the long run, of course, he can do me no harm; but in the meantime I am bound, not to be grateful to him as my John the Baptist, but to let him have his show goodhumouredly while it lasts." But the bitter prejudice of Shaw's remarks indicates the depth of resentment he bore towards his rival at this time. Until his own work achieved more success, good humour would not come easily for Shaw.

Mrs Ebbsmith continued to draw good houses until 11 May, when Mrs Campbell was forced to resign her role in order to honour her contract with Tree, now back from an unsatisfactory U.S. tour. Just before leaving the Garrick, she wrote Pinero a note thanking him for all he had done for her, to which he sportingly replied on 1 May with his "warmest wishes for a continuation, under Mr Tree's management, of the success which you have so worthily and so conspicuously won elsewhere."[29] Olga Nethersole took over on 15 May, but as Pin later remarked to Archer, "the vulgar public," after giving "Miss N. a fair chance of interesting them . . . came, and saw, and dwindled away."[30] The run ended after eighty-six performances, fifty-eight of them by Mrs Campbell.

iii. Public Occasions

On 3 May 1895 Pinero made a speech at a Royal Academy banquet in reply to a toast honouring "Music and the Drama." Referring to both art and drama, he argued against the adage "Good work rarely sells," claiming that "of all the affectations displayed by artists of any craft, the affectation of despising the approval and support of the great public is the most mischievous and misleading." He then outlined what amounted to his artistic credo:

> Speaking, at any rate, of dramatic art, I believe that its most substantial claim upon consideration rests in its power of legitimately interesting a great number of people; I believe this of any art, I believe it especially of the Drama. Whatever distinction the dramatist may attain in gaining the attention of the so-called select few, I believe that his finest task is that of giving back to the multitude their own thoughts and conceptions illuminated, enlarged, and, if needful, purged, perfected, transfigured. The making of a play that shall be closely observant in its portrayal of character, moral in purpose, dignified in expression, stirring in its development yet not beyond our possible experience of life, by thousands of men and women necessarily of diversified temperaments, aims and interests, men and women of all classes of society — surely the writing of that drama, the weaving of that complex fabric, is one of the most arduous of the tasks which Art has set us, surely its successful accomplishment is one of the highest achievements of which an artist is capable.

He went on to say that the thorough achievement of such a task was "a rare one in any country," let alone England, where reproaches had long been levelled that the theatre "possessed no drama at all." But, he asked, was this wholly the fault of the modern playwright? Might it not be attributable in part to a public that had been unwilling to accept "elements of seriousness in their theatrical entertainment?" However, he went on, "during recent years the temper of the times has been changing, it is now a period of analysis, of general restless enquiry, and as this spirit creates a demand for freer expression on the part of our writers of books, so it naturally permits our writers of plays a wider scope in the selection of subject and calls for an accompanying effort of thought, a larger freedom of utterance." Pinero ended the speech by rejoicing that to the dramatists of his day had fallen "the duty of striking from the limbs of English drama some of its shackles." He hoped that "the younger generation of dramatists, those upon whom the immediate future of our Drama depends," would accept this freedom "as a privilege to be jealously exercised," remembering always "that the real courage of the artist is in his capacity for restraint." These beliefs could hardly have been more at odds with the Shavian aim of writing "immoral and heretical plays" in order "to force the public to reconsider its morals."[31]

At the beginning of June, Pin, his wife, and stepdaughter, escaped from town to Whitstable in the Kentish countryside where he had leased "a small and inconvenient house" glorying in the name of Tankerton Tower. Writing to Archer on his arrival (2 June 1895), he remarked that though they only had room to entertain a bachelor (which he begged Archer to be for a night or two), they had much to offer him: "Terriss [one of Irving's principal supporting actors], Cricket and boating are at hand; Canterbury is only six miles away; the country is charming — hop gardens, cherry orchards, &c. &c. Mrs Pinero would drive you about — and *there is a bicycle on the premises.*"[32]

Pin returned to London briefly in mid-July for the celebrations marking Irving's knighthood. Though privately of the opinion that an actor should avoid wearing "the Court sword *off* the stage (When he is not spouting, let him sit with his fellow gypsies, watching the steaming pot),"[33] he knew (as, to be fair, Shaw did, too) that Irving had sought the honour for his profession, not himself. This was the keynote of an address to the new knight that Pinero wrote on behalf of the "Actors and Actresses of England," and that, signed by more than 4,000 of them and encased in a gold and silver casket Forbes-Robertson had designed, Bancroft presented to Sir Henry Irving on the stage of the Lyceum on 19 July 1895, the day after the Queen had conferred the title.[34] The document stated that the honour was "at once a formal recognition of [Irving's] supreme talent as an actor" and "a token that the barrier which has hitherto enclosed the stage and its followers is yielding to the forces of liberality and openmindedness. . . . From generation to generation, it will remind the English actor . . . that his position in the public regard is founded upon the pre-eminence of your career, and upon the nobility, dignity, and sweetness of your private character." Later that day Irving wrote a brief note to the playwright expressing his gratitude for the tribute: "I must . . . thank you for the most beautiful address today — which touched me to the heart," he wrote. "Thanks and thanks again old friend — I shall never forget it."[35]

On 27 July Irving concluded the Lyceum season with the announcement that on his return from a forthcoming American tour, he would produce *Coriolanus*, Sardou's *Madame sans Gêne* — and a new play by Mr Pinero.[36] The new play was not even begun, but Pinero stated in a letter to Irving's business manager, Bram Stoker, that it was to be set 100 years in the past and have fine character parts for Irving and Ellen Terry as a married couple with a grown-up daughter.[37] Eight months later the play was still unwritten, and Ellen Terry wrote despairingly to "Dear Mr Pinny" to ask why. Whenever she mentioned it to "the Governor," she reported,

> he wrinkles up the sides of his forehead, his eyes fly nearly to the top of his head, he sighs, he looks fearfully worried, & then of course one feels a coward to go on with the attack — Oh Lord, Oh Lord, *do* please let me have the enormous pleasure to see him act a play of yours there at the Lyceum. Why not? *Is it me?* Am *I* the too old woman who hinders? — But one can "specially engage anyone," you know — For pity's sake don't think you can hurt my feelings (except by not writing a lovely modern play for Henry) — I'll do anything you think I can do — I'll help in any way. I wonder & wonder — often and often why you just leave us out in the cold — Don't think for a moment that

Henry wd. be wanting to stage manage a play of yours if you wd. DO
IT FOR HIM — I think at times cd. that account for — But how silly.
You are both big men so no fear — But still *Why?* — *Why?*[38]

Despite this plea, the play was never written. Once again it seems Pin's
inhibitions about writing a part for his old Chief had stifled his
inspiration.

Poor health was another factor. Back in Kent and working on his
play for Carr, Pin caught a chill, tried to ignore it, and ended up "with
something like a collapse and the doctor ordering complete rest."[39]
After lying in a chair for a week gazing at the sea, he returned to his
desk only to find, as he told both Archer and Carton, that "a normal
temperature absolutely declined to ratify the labours of '101 point
five.' "[40]

iv. The Benefit of the Doubt

By early October Pin had recovered his health and finished Carr's
play, a three-act "comedy" about the aftermath of a divorce case. It
was, he informed Carton, "a very inconsiderable affair"[41] — though
he had not told Carr so. However, he reported, he was saving up his
money "to buy a new pair of waxen wings" for his next year's work.
In the meantime, the weather having broken at Whitstable and left
"everything there generally sad-looking and depressing,"[42] he would
be returning to town in time for the dress rehearsals.

The Benefit of the Doubt opened at the Comedy Theatre on 16
October 1895. Its fate was directly contrary to that of *Mrs Ebbsmith*:
the play was praised and the acting damned. Pinero had asked for
more than his two leading players were able to give in a long, dramatic
encounter in the second act, and his absence from most rehearsals
because of ill health had compounded their difficulties. The result was
a disappointing run of seventy-four performances. Still, the major
reviews were enthusiastic about the play.

Archer had expected a relaxation of standards after two serious
works but was delighted with the play, describing it as "the truest,

firmest, finest thing Mr Pinero has yet done" and its first two acts as
"masterly." (The third, though "essentially right," suffered in
Archer's view from some "technical errors, defects of manipulation.")
But the most notable feature of his review was an introductory polemic
against two classes of critics, "those for whom the drama died with
Congreve, and those for whom it only began to live with Ibsen," whom
he accused of venting "contemptuous and vindictive wrath" against
Pinero ever since he had produced *The Second Mrs Tanqueray* two
and a half years earlier. The attitude of the first class, "the nihilists,"
was, Archer claimed, at least rational, as they "hated the theatre" and
fiercely resented the suggestion that "anything worth a moment's
notice could come out of it." But the outlook of "our haughty idealists"
who had "nothing but sneers and disparagement for the man who was
gallantly fighting their own battles, though perhaps with other weap-
ons than theirs," showed "the densest ingratitude."[43]

This shaft, obviously aimed at Shaw, missed its mark. In his
Saturday Review notice, G.B.S., labelling the subject of the acting
"almost too painful to face," roundly declared his conviction that "The
Benefit of the Doubt is worth The Profligate, Mrs Tanqueray, and Mrs
Ebbsmith rolled into one and multiplied by ten." This time, he wrote,

> Mr Pinero has kept within the territory he has actually explored; and
> the result is at once apparent in the higher dramatic pressure, the
> closer-knit action, the substitution of a homogeneous slice of life for
> the old theatrical sandwich of sentiment and comic relief, and the
> comparative originality, naturalness, and free development of the
> characters. . . . Consciously or unconsciously, he has this time seen
> his world as it really is; that is, a world which never dreams of
> bothering its little head with large questions or general ideas. . . . His
> early weaknesses have disappeared along with his late affectations;
> and the happy issue is the best serious play he has yet produced.[44]

Shaw in fact was finally becoming aware that Pinero was no less
contemptuous than himself of the empty forms of society. Indeed, the
trenchant satire that informs the whole play may well have been as
significant a factor as the inadequate acting in the indifferent support
the public gave to *The Benefit of the Doubt*. Fashionable society

audiences must have felt some discomfort, for example, at the hypocritical compromise over clothing Theophila Fraser's mother and
sister display as they wait fearfully at home to hear whether her name
has been cleared by the court:

> MRS QUINTON TWELVES. Why these miserable looking gowns
> then? You are dressed more funereally today than you were
> yesterday!
> MRS EMPTAGE. [*Tearfully*] If you live to see a daughter of yours,
> however innocent she may be, dragged through the Divorce Court
> — !
> JUSTINA. We haven't been quite certain what we ought to put on.
> MRS EMPTAGE. I considered half-mourning a happy thought.
> MRS QUINTON TWELVES. To my mind it looks as if you had
> deliberately prepared for all emergencies.
> MRS EMPTAGE. [*Rising in a flutter.*] 'Tina, pin some flowers in
> your dress at once! I'll get Bristow to stick a bit of relief about me
> somewhere. And I'll wear some more rings — (7–8)

A similar preoccupation with appearances rather than truth is evident
in Theophila's plea to her estranged husband when he proposes to go
abroad for several years after she has been given "the benefit of the
doubt" in the case:

> THEOPHILA. Why don't you see? We've *got* to sit tight here in town;
> we've *got* to do it, to win back my good name. . . . Of course we
> shall be asked nowhere, but we must be seen about together, you
> and I, wherever it's possible for us to squeeze ourselves. [*Rapidly
> and excitedly*] There's the Opera; we can subscribe for a box on
> the ground tier — the stalls can't help picking you out there. And
> there we must sit, laughing and talking, Alec, and *convince* people
> that we're a happy couple and that you believe in me implicitly.
> (76)

Though her husband, unsure of her innocence, refuses the proposal,
the same solution is later offered to Theophila by the other wife in the
divorce case and is finally adopted by Theophila's aunt, wife of the
Bishop of St Olpherts. If we recall the unscrupulous character of the

Duke of St Olpherts in Pinero's previous play, the playwright's verdict on social morality becomes apparent.

Pin himself jokingly claimed to be above the vagaries of critical opinion, Shaw's in particular. In a "Prefatory Letter" to Archer's *Theatrical "World" of 1895*, he outlined his strategy of coping with criticisms of his work. Though "willing — nay anxious — to read, even commit to memory" criticism of his work that was *"distinctly flattering,"* because such praise was not always to be had, he considered it necessary for one of his humour diligently to "sharpen the instinct for detecting the presence of adverse criticism":

> I am, I congratulate myself, developing this instinct to a very fine degree. Indeed at certain times — during the week or fortnight following the production of a play of mine, for example — I am now able to stroll into my club and enjoy an hour's reading without opening a single journal containing a disagreeable estimate of my work. At such period I find the *Mining Journal* an invaluable resource. Sometimes I meet with a mishap, but as my scent grows keener accidents, I am pleased to say, become more rare. And there have been occasions — with bowed head I confess it — when I have yielded to temptation and have deliberately unclosed the pages of a review which I knew must — well, which I was *almost* sure would — and yet, I have reasoned, might not — no! there it was, the hateful thing! However, half a dozen words have been enough for me, and I have promptly hidden that review where it would be least likely to meet the eyes of members. Of recent years — thank heaven! — these temptations have shown a decided disposition to pass me by entirely.[45]

The sting of Pin's tale came at the end, when with tongue in cheek he confessed that his system had its drawbacks, one being that it robbed him "of the privilege of reading much brilliant writing," including articles on dramatic matters by Archer's friend "Mr Bernard Shaw — of whom I protest I am — in general — a warm admirer." To which G.B.S. replied, "Very well then, how does he know that my writing is brilliant?" before proceeding to claim with typical Shavian effrontery that his criticisms had been directly responsible for "the enormous improvement" in Pinero's work between *The Notorious Mrs*

Ebbsmith and *The Benefit of the Doubt*.[46] Pin, however, knew the real basis of Shaw's valuations, having earlier remarked to Archer, "As for Mr Shaw, he may always, I fancy, be entrusted to speak tolerantly of anything that doesn't encroach on what he is pleased to consider his preserve." All the same, he was taking care to keep off the Shavian grass.

v. On Turning Forty

During 1896 Pin was able to read theatrical criticism — even in the *Saturday Review* — with tolerable composure, as no new play of his was produced. He was, though, working on a comedy for Alexander that he described in some detail in a letter to Carton, knowing that his old friend was planning to write a piece on a similar theme for the Criterion once he had completed his current assignment, another light comedy for the St James's. Pin's letter dealing with these and other matters, including the death of Arthur Cecil, is worth citing in full:

> 63 Hamilton Terrace, N.W.
> 20 April 1896.

> My dear fellow,
>   Saturday, May 2nd, at the Criterion, one-thirty. Of course I won't tell Alec [Alexander] — whom I am not by way of seeing much of — but he is unwise, I think, to drive you hard. You have heaps of time — were I you I wouldn't be spurred. Here's treason! What I mean is that the longer I live, in the way I *do* live, the more I am assured that the brain will do your work for you, if you will but recognise that it is your master and not your servant. If you get in a muddle, throw your pen down *and don't think*.
>   I attend poor Arthur's funeral service tomorrow — just for a little relaxation. I haven't read much of what the papers say of him. But this I know — he was constantly trying to avoid hurting people's feelings, as often making himself believe that he *had* hurt them, and then devoting himself to repairing the imaginary injuries. My grammar strikes me as being — to put it charitably — involved; but my point is that Arthur was a gentleman. A fact that would, naturally, escape the average press-man in preparing a biographical record.

I have been reading through *my* poor stuff this afternoon. I hope
to God I am not in the smallest degree clashing with your idea for a
new Wyndham play — that of which you spoke to me. My piece deals
with a middle-aged man and woman — the woman forty, the man
forty-five — who discover that the tide of life within them is turning
and going down. To console each other they agree to marry, and then
fall in love — she with a young man of seven-and-twenty, he with a
girl of nineteen. I prepared the scheme some years ago for the
Kendals, and, the K's becoming uninteresting to me theatrically, put
the thing aside. I thought it required more romantic treatment than
they could give it, and now I am doing it for Alec and Miss Neilson.
My theme is, continually, Middle-age, Middle-age — that is the string
I harp on. If I remember your notion rightly, it is that of a society
jester who tires of his task of amusing people. My scheme in no way
crosses this. My man of forty-five is the simple society butterfly — of
the type, perhaps, of the recently-deceased Alfred Montgomery —
who suddenly finds that his wings are turning to dust. When we meet,
very likely you will let me give you an idea of some of the detail with
which I work out my story; and then I hope you will be able to assure
me that I am not, in any measure, on the same road as yourself. I
rather fear that *Rosemary* — the new piece that Wyndham is going
to do — will cut some of the ground from under my feet. I have about
five-and-twenty characters in my play — mostly of the snap-shot
order — but they lead me the devil of a dance.

Forgive me for inflicting this long screed upon you. But when,
looking through my work, it struck me that my character might clash
with yours, I turned hot and cold and have been wretched ever since.
I write this before going to bed, to give myself some little ease of mind.

Yours always, my dear chap,

A.W.P.

P.S. Don't tell Alec I have given the story of his play away.[47]

As this letter suggests, Pinero's new comedy was something of a
self-indulgence, with its five acts, five settings, cast of twenty-nine, and
continual harping on middle age. Detailed planning for *The Princess
and the Butterfly*, as it was to be called, had begun late the previous
year, only months after Pin had turned forty. The comedy was to
include echoes of private and family matters that the general public
was hardly likely to recognise, including the already-noted metamor-
phosis of Lucy Pinero into the Princess Pannonia, who in her son's

fantasy is offered the chance of marriage to a younger man (strangely resembling Pinero himself!) which she had been denied in real life. As for the comedy's parallel affair between the forty-five-year-old "butterfly," Sir George Lamorant, and the nineteen-year-old waif, Fay Zuliani, the age gap involved is minimal compared with the thirty-eight years between Pin's parents.

If the play had its origins in Pinero's mid-life reflections, the exotic settings he chose for his "Fantastics" required a great deal of research. Letters to contacts in the Foreign Office[48] in Paris, Rome, and elsewhere asked a stream of questions about matters relevant to the play: When exactly is a masked ball held at the Paris Opéra? Would it be possible for a big function at, say, the British embassy or the Elysée to be held on the same night? If an international convention for the disposal of Turkey were to meet in Paris, what nations would be likely to be represented? What are the names of some convent schools in Milan? Would it be contrary to custom to fight a duel in an orchard? Would Fontenay-sous-Bois on the outskirts of Paris be a suitable site? (Pinero made a special trip to Paris to check on it.)[49] And so on in almost obsessive detail.

On 18 February 1896 Pinero wrote to Alexander congratulating him on a successful production of *The Prisoner of Zenda* and fixing an appointment for the following week to discuss the outline of his comedy. Three weeks later he reported that the first act ("a lot of people of a light kind flitting in and out of a room. I think of it in my own mind as a Buzz of Bees") was finished. He was sending Alec a stage plan for it together with a "full written description of the scene and its properties," something he proposed to do with each succeeding act "so that you will always have some material by you to amuse yourself with at your leisure." The letter ended with the suggestion that Alec tell the young American actress Fay Davis that there *might* be a part for her in the play. If she were available the playwright felt he "could perhaps bend [the character] even more in her direction."[50]

Progress on the comedy continued at a leisurely rate through the year. Pin and Myra enjoyed their usual Engadine holiday (a distinctly wet one this time)[51] and on their return attended the first night of *Cymbeline* at the Lyceum on 22 September. The following day Pinero wrote to Irving (calling him "Sir Henry") suggesting some additional items of "business" for the character of Iachimo that Irving (calling the playwright his "Field Marshall") adopted.[52] But by October, with Alexander's comedy still not finished, Pin was once again refusing evening invitations.[53] A week before Christmas the play was finally dispatched to Alexander, who reacted with fulsome enthusiasm:

> It is wonderful — simply wonderful, and exceeds my highest hopes. Interesting — absorbingly interesting, especially in the last three acts. That fourth act — for direct humanity, perfection of workmanship, and sheer brilliancy of intellectuality and power equals anything you have ever done. The last act, too, is startling in its genius, with its manipulation of the "fairy-tale, happy ever after" ending — it fairly takes one's breath away, it is so delicate, so profound and so limitlessly human in its analysis.[54]

The following day Pinero acknowledged Alexander's "very warm expressions" about the play, remarking that there were "no pleasanter moments for the playwright than those in which he finds his manager in full sympathy and accord with him." Alexander was certainly determined to do his best. There were elaborate settings by William Telbin, H. P. Hall, and Walter Hann; the costuming (which included costly military and diplomatic uniforms as well as ball gowns and evening dress) was lavish; and the large cast featured leading players such as Fay Davis (about to make a great personal success as Fay Zuliani), Julia Neilson as the princess, Rose Leclerq, H. B. Irving (setting out on his stage career in spite of Pin's advice to study law),[55] H. V. Esmond, Vane Tempest, and Alexander himself as the middle-aged butterfly.

But the rehearsals did not go smoothly. The manager's concern to recoup his investment, combined with his anxiety over the play's length and the problems of managing such a large cast, led him to take a much greater hand in rehearsals than he had for *The Second Mrs Tanqueray*. Pinero watched with dismay and unspoken resentment as his usual absolute control was undermined. Immediately before the rehearsal period his strength had been sapped by a severe bout of flu, and this weakness, together with his concern for the subtleties of what was a more personal play than he cared to admit, added to his unhappiness. Four days before his first night he sent a deeply felt message to Jones, whose new play, *The Physician*, was opening that evening at the Criterion: "In my own hour of travail my heart goes out to you, old friend, and I wish you success."[56]

The Princess and the Butterfly opened on Monday, 29 March 1897; it was a lengthy evening. The notices were surprisingly respectful, though only Archer praised the comedy unreservedly. Not since Sheridan and Goldsmith had there been "work of anything like the calibre of Mr Pinero's," he declared in the *World*, and even Sheridan and Goldsmith had been followers of a tradition rather than an originator like Mr Pinero. Indeed, the last act of *The Princess and the Butterfly*, Archer felt, recalled in "its atmosphere of spring and sunshine" that of Alexander's previous production, *As You Like It*, and even that reminiscence did not rob it of its savour.[57]

Shaw's review was less indulgent.[58] A mix-up over tickets had forced him to upset arrangements with his future wife, Charlotte Payne-Townshend, and visit the play a night later than planned. He therefore went hoping, as he told Charlotte, that the performance would be "a bad one and the play worse, for then — THEN — THEN — *THEN* we shall see whose God is the Lord!"[59] He found the play not so much bad as excessively long, declaring in his review (which covered *The Physician* as well) that it was "no exaggeration to say that within two minutes Mr Jones has got tighter hold of his audience and further on with his play than Mr Pinero within two hours." G.B.S. also stated that he was appalled by the "fearful waste of power: out of twenty-nine performers, of whom half are accustomed to play important parts in London, hardly six have anything to do that could not be sufficiently well done by nobodies. Mr Pinero seems to assert his supremacy by being extravagant in his demands for the sake of extravagance; and Mr Alexander plays up to him with an equally high hand by being no less extravagant in his compliances."

Shaw could be forgiven his irritation with this aspect of the production: by now he had written six plays, of which one had been given two performances, one had run two months as a result of a subsidy from Annie Horniman (later the donor of the Abbey Theatre, Dublin), and four remained unperformed. He might have been consoled, however, to learn three months later, when *The Princess and the Butterfly* was taken off after ninety-seven performances, that Pinero's comedy had made a similar loss to *Arms and the Man* (nearly £2,000) despite running twice as long. But it was the play's theme of middle age, also featured in Jones's piece, that most irked G.B.S.:

> And now, as if it were not bad enough to have Mr Jones in this state of mind, we have Mr Pinero, who was born, as I learn from a recent biographic work of reference, in 1855, quite unable to get away from the same tragic preoccupation with the horrors of middle age. He has launched at us a play in five acts — two and a half of them hideously superfluous — all about being over forty. . . . During those [first] two hours, The Princess marks time complacently on the interest, the pathos, the suggestiveness, the awful significance of turning forty. The Princess has done it; Sir George Lamorant has done it; Mrs St Roche has done it; so has her husband. Lady Chichele, Lady Ringstead, and Mrs Sabiston have all done it. And they have to meditate on it like Hamlet meditating on suicide; only, since soliloquies are out of fashion, nearly twenty persons have to be introduced to listen to them. The resultant exhibition of High Life Above Stairs is no doubt delightful to the people who had rather read the fashionable intelligence than my articles. To me not even the delight of playing Peeping Tom whilst Princess Pannonia was getting out of bed and flattering me with a vain hope that the next item would be her bath could reconcile me to two hours of it.

Shaw himself had just turned forty and later confessed he had laughed at the play with the wrong side of his mouth.[60] But in his review he took a more optimistic stance: "Well, my own opinion is that sixty is the prime of life for a man. Cheer up, Mr Pinero. . . . 'What though the grey do something mingle with our younger brown" (excuse my quoting Shakespeare), the world is as young as ever."

He was right. Both Shaw and Pinero still had their best work to come.

...12...
The Autocrat

i. The Made Man

By mid-life Pinero had developed a formidable presence, capable of arousing awe — and sometimes even terror — in actors and managers alike. One actress, soon to become his favourite and create more leading roles for him than any other, later remembered him as "a figure nearly six feet tall, rather thickset, with a highly-coloured complexion, [and a] dome-like bald head."[1] Another actress, fascinated by his "penetrating keen clear eyes," was sure when she came under his scrutiny at rehearsals that he was carrying out "a brain vivisection" on her.[2] But for those close enough to see, behind this eaglelike gaze there was still a stagestruck boy more than a little surprised at the position he now enjoyed.

He had, of course, been lucky, having set out to succeed as a playwright when British drama was at a particularly low ebb. His gifts of industry, commitment, and a sharply observant eye, combined with a well-developed sense of theatrical effect and — perhaps most important of all — a basic sympathy with the fundamental values of his audience, were precisely the qualities needed to achieve his goal. Nor had his success yet been seriously challenged by any rival. Henry Arthur Jones was equally committed to raising the standard of British drama — and was indeed a good deal more vocal about it — but lacked Pinero's naturalistic touch and dramatic range; Oscar Wilde had shone brilliantly but briefly in the Victorian twilight before his career

228

had been snuffed out savagely by the forces of respectability he had gaily mocked; and Shaw had yet to find a paying audience for his plays. Over the next few years this situation would change, but for the majority of theatregoers, Pinero remained England's premier contemporary dramatist well into the Edwardian era.

All things considered, he enjoyed his success without being unduly deceived by it. He had ceased to strive (as, for example, with *Mrs Ebbsmith*) for dramatic territory beyond his reach but could afford to please — even indulge — himself (as he had done with *The Princess and the Butterfly*) when the mood took him. Nevertheless, he remained committed to doing the best work in his power and to ensuring its exact transmission in the theatre. In this respect he was acquiring the reputation of an autocrat. An American admirer and later editor, Clayton Hamilton, provided a lively and typical description of the playwright in his prime:

> He is a man of extraordinarily attractive personality, a man of astonishing brilliancy and charm, a very magnetic person. . . . The main reason he is so charming is that he is tremendously alive. He radiates energy. He is not very tall; and he is plump without being stout for his height. His figure reminds you of that of Napoleon. He has a very wonderful face and head, with extraordinarily brilliant beady black eyes, overshadowed by the thickest and bushiest eyebrows I have ever seen. He has a very fine profile of the Jewish type. He is extremely dapper in appearance. He dresses very well, but somewhat obviously well; he is the sort of person who always has a flower in his buttonhole. He paces the room very rapidly, his hands flickering with a Latin nimbleness of gesture. He is very quick and snappy in conversation; exceedingly brilliant, witty and clever; and tremendously young. . . . Everybody who knows him at all adores him.[3]

Even to those who did not know Pinero well, his profile and taste in dress caused him to stand out in any crowd. Lytton Strachey, observing him at a private showing at an art gallery, penned another memorable, if less flattering, portrait: "That astounding creature Pinero was there. . . . Large red face, immense black eyebrows, rolling eyes, vast nose, theatrical manner, bandana handkerchief, trousers creased *à la rigeur*, and patent leather boots with brown fronts."[4] The costume may be taken as emblematic of Pin's unique blend of flamboyance and respectability at the height of his career.

ii. Trelawny of the "Wells"

During the months following the production of *The Princess and the Butterfly*, Pinero was preoccupied with two matters: the possibility that the great Italian actress Eleonora Duse might produce *The Second Mrs Tanqueray* in Paris and the writing of a new comedy celebrating the theatre of his boyhood. The first was to prove a vain hope, the second his most charming and enduring success.

Duse had been playing in London when Mrs Campbell's Paula had swept her and every other actress from the theatrical headlines. She had been piqued, of course, but also intrigued by the role and tempted to add it to her repertoire as soon as she could acquire a suitable translation. In May 1894 Pinero had remarked to Archer that "Il [*sic*] Seconda Signora Tanqueray" was unlikely to see the light for a while, as it was rumoured that Duse feared having the acting of her company compared with that of the St James's; he added she was probably right, as "at the Italian Tanqueray's dinner party the waiters might appear to be in excess of the guests."[5] Three years later, however, in spring 1897, he was delighted at an announcement that Duse would present *La Seconda Moglie* (with *La Dame aux Camélias* and *Magda*) during a forthcoming season at the Théâtre de la Renaissance in Paris. This would be the first serious play by a contemporary English dramatist to be staged in the French capital.

The production was announced for 19 June, but ten days earlier Pinero heard that the actress was having second thoughts. It seemed, he told Archer, she had been advised by her manager and Sarah Bernhardt not "to present herself in a play, the story and substance of which [were] unfamiliar to Parisians." "So," Pin continued, "unless Madame Duse — who is a beautiful but irresolute creature — alters her mind, I do not go to Paris on the 18th." She was talking about playing Paula in London at some future date, but this was hardly a satisfactory alternative:

> London is not Paris, and it seems to me that city is, as regards any serious English work, quite impregnable. This is the third time I have been beaten back over *Tanqueray*. The first time was over my negotiations with Sarah Bernhardt; the second in dealing with Mm. Porel and Carré; and now comes this last blow. I have carried this play into every theatrical centre in Europe except Paris, and I am very much nettled by the influence which has evidently been brought to bear upon Eleonora Duse to induce her to withhold my work after announcing its production. She is, like all great artists, a very modest woman, and talks little about her acting, but she pays me the compliment of admiring *Tanqueray*, and says she finds great pleasure in acting "Paula."[6]

Duse did not play the role in Paris. Three years later, however, she played a tender and poignant Paula in London, though the *Stage* was more diverted by her leading man, Carlo Rosapina, who rendered the normally "grave and self-contained" Tanqueray "with Southern effusiveness, with tears, sobs, profound sighs and clasping of hands."[7]

With *Mrs Tanqueray* so much on Pinero's mind, it is not surprising that *Trelawny of the "Wells,"* completed in September 1897, contains elements of the earlier plot, especially in that exposure to more refined manners makes the heroine dissatisfied with her former mode of life. This time, however, the context was theatrical and the mood nostalgic. The piece was both an acknowledgement of the inspiration Pinero had received on that "red-letter" night of his youth when he saw the Prince of Wales's company play *Caste* at the Standard Theatre in Shoreditch and a remembrance of earlier, less sophisticated performances at the old Sadler's Wells Theatre. Indeed, *Trelawny*'s theme was the superseding of the latter by the former: the supplanting of theatrical "gypsies" by a new breed of players whose principal qualifications were gentility and respectability.

If the old troupers in Pinero's play owe something to Dickens's Crummles company,[8] they were also drawn from memory.[9] Telfer, the onetime manager of the Wells, and his wife, Miss Violet Sylvester, probably correspond to Robert Edgar and Miss Marriott, and Tom Wrench, the "general utility" turned playwright, is Pinero's portrait of Tom Robertson. Spanning the old and the new styles of theatre are the actresses Rose Trelawny and Imogen Parrott, both inspired by Marie Wilton. Rose, unfitted for the old style of drama because of her genteel background, becomes the perfect exponent of the new comedy when Imogen takes over the derelict Pantheon Theatre to present Wrench's innovative play. Among the minor characters, Mortimer and Denzil, two of the new socially superior actors who displace the old ones, were probably modelled on Bancroft and (more obviously) Hare. Indeed, the social polish imparted to theatre by such well-bred players had just received the ultimate seal of approval with the conferral of a knighthood on Bancroft on the occasion of Queen Victoria's Diamond Jubilee.

The play's "nontheatrical" folk — especially the peevish little vice-chancellor, Sir William Gower, and his spinster sister Trafalgar — had real-life counterparts, too. The Gowers' wealthy but oppressive residence is located in Cavendish Square, as was that of Pinero's grandfather (whose wife was proud of her brother's service on the *Victory* with Nelson). And it is likely that the Act 4 scene when Sir William appears heavily muffled at Imogen's theatre and distantly presents two fingers for Wrench to shake also owes something to Pinero's last meeting with Charles Mathews twenty years earlier at the Liverpool Alexandra.

Both the role of Sir William and the play were intended for Hare. With his usual impulsive bad judgement as far as Pinero's plays were concerned, though, he decided that the piece was a satire on the theatrical profession and rejected it.[10] He soon repented and commissioned another play from the playwright but lost the chance of producing Pinero's best comedy and of creating what might have become his most famous role. Both were instead snapped up by the younger Dion Boucicault (generally known as "Dot"), who had recently returned to England after a long spell of theatre management in Australia. Boucicault was now in partnership at the Court with Arthur Chudleigh ("Chuddles" to his friends at the Garrick), who had earlier produced *The Amazons*. They agreed to stage *Trelawny* the following

January and to give its author as free a hand with casting as limited funds would permit.

iii. Pinero and Sullivan — Overture

Pinero now moved on to something completely different: writing the book for a light opera. In 1896 Gilbert and Sullivan had finally parted company after the failure of their last collaboration, *The Grand Duke*. Sullivan had already worked with other partners — including Burnand and Grundy — without much success. He had also recently composed some more serious dramatic scores, including the incidental music and choruses for the 1895 Lyceum production of *King Arthur*. The author of that play, Comyns Carr, now conceived the idea of a three-way collaboration on an opera, combining Pinero's skill as a theatrical storyteller, his own facility as a writer of lyrics, and Sullivan's musical genius. The three men met in January 1897 and decided to work together on the project later in the year, though they did not then have a suitable story or theme. By 17 September, however, the writers had a provisional plot idea to suggest to Sullivan, who noted in his diary: "Joe Carr and his wife lunched. . . . Long talk about opera. He stated he and Pinero were going away on the 28th to work for me."[11]

What the pair had in mind was not another Gilbertian piece but something more serious. Sullivan was no longer interested in composing comic operas, only grand — or at least grandish — ones. He had already made one attempt with *Ivanhoe* (1891), and his success with the music for *King Arthur* had tempted him to expand this, too, into an opera. When Pinero (through Carr) suggested a serious fairy tale, set in medieval Flanders, about a magic stone that confers beauty on its possessor, Sullivan was enchanted. The precise source of the story is unclear, but it is probably not coincidental that Pin's stepdaughter, Myra Hamilton, was by this time contributing original fairy tales to journals such as *Cassell's Magazine*, the *Sketch*, the *Lady*, and the *Court Journal*.[12]

At the end of September Pinero and Carr journeyed to Brussels to spend a fortnight soaking up local lore and atmosphere. By the time

MR. D'OYLY CARTE, TO SIR ARTHUR SULLIVAN AND MR. PINERO: "NOW, I HOPE YOU
TWO FELLOWS WILL PUT ON THE STEAM AND NOT KEEP ME WAITING."

Alfred Bryan, caricature (The Entr'Acte, *January 1898*)

they returned to London (12 October), they had worked out a scenario. Four days later Carr read it to Sullivan, who noted warm approval in his diary but also a lingering doubt that it might be too serious.[13] Progress on the book was rapid, with Carr tactfully playing a supporting role in the work, as the holograph manuscript and following extracts from undated letters from Carr to Pinero reveal:[14]

My dear Pinero,

I challenge nothing: looking at it as critically as I can I don't see how our story could be better laid out. You have told a lot in little, and in the telling it you have never been forced to cry a halt in the action. I think a brave beginning has been made: it is now for me to follow worthily.

* * * * * * * * * * *

I pray you never to be burdened or worried by any points that you may feel it necessary to raise and discuss with me over my share of the work. Of course it is not to be expect[ed] that two men can always be in agreement over every little detail but I have felt from the beginning that as with you lay the initiation in the writing and conduct of our story it was fit and proper that you should control with a final judgement the harmony of the work as a whole and that with your sense of this harmony my share should always conform.

* * * * * * * * * * *

My dear Pinero,

I see The Yeomen of the Guard [revived at the Savoy Theatre on 20 November 1897] is described on the title as

Written by
W.S.G.
Composed by
A.S.

Perhaps we had better adopt that form and I think it would be well to send the suggested title to Arthur — As to the other point, I mean your generous desire that I should stand in the place of honour, it is very gratifying to me and will count as one more pleasant memory of an association that has throughout been wholly delightful as far as I am concerned. As between ourselves I know that any such questions count for little for I think we have been conscious of only one desire and that has been by our joint labours to make of the work the best we could. But in the public eye it may not be so, and from the public point of view I feel no manner of doubt that your name should stand first. Therefore, my dear Pinero, so it shall be.

It is unfortunate that a similar harmony did not prevail between the writers and their composer. Sullivan's initial enthusiasm for the project cooled following a dispute with the manager of the Savoy Theatre, Mrs Helen D'Oyly Carte, over the casting of the lead soprano for the new opera.[15] Pinero soon learnt of the friction through letters from Mrs Carte. Carr, alarmed at Sullivan's bitterness against the Carte family and their company, observed that the composer was "unstable and unsettled" and in his opinion "a sick man."[16] Sullivan's dissatisfaction soon spread to the script. After a working dinner on 16 December to discuss the first act, he wrote in his diary: "Dined at Joe Carr's with Pinero — long talk after dinner. First signs of difficulty likely to arise. Both Pinero and Carr, gifted and brilliant men, with *no* experience in writing for music, and yet obstinately declining to accept any suggestions from me as to form and construction. Told them that the musical construction of the piece is capable of great improvement, but they decline to alter. 'Quod scripsi, scripsi,' they both say."

By 21 December strained relations had reached a point where Mrs Carte felt compelled to intervene. Writing to Pinero about a meeting with Sullivan that afternoon, she stated that though, surprisingly, all difficulties over casting seemed to have disappeared, the composer's concern over the script had deepened:

His trouble seems to be that he has not been consulted as to the places where the story had better be told in music (lyrics) and where in dialogue — and (as I understand him) that there is not sufficient room for music. I reminded him that you had from the first said you must write the piece as a *drama* — and it must move on as you would wish for it to do *as* a drama and that no person could be brought on, not required otherwise, for musical effect. He acknowledged we had told him this — but said he had not wished to alter the drama or the persons on the stage — but asked to be consulted as to *when* the story should be told in music and when in dialogue.

At Sullivan's insistence a formal meeting to discuss the script was arranged for the following day, despite Mrs Carte's warning that such a confrontation was not the best way to resolve the problem. She was right. Afterwards the composer indignantly recorded in his diary that he had been "amazed at the position taken up by P. and C. Stubborn refusal to alter anything or act upon any suggestion made to them. My explanation as to musical requirements not listened to! We are at a deadlock and I cannot accept the position of a cipher. Finally I said I should send them my requirements in 1st Act for them to accept or reject."

Christmas and Mrs Carte intervened, after which the three men, agreeing to forget "principles" and stick to "practicalities," reached a compromise involving the conversion of only one long dialogue scene to a quartet. As Sullivan (via Mrs Carte) explained to Pinero, "opera artists — even when very fair actors — cannot be expected to be as good actors as those selected *only* for acting — and . . . there is always a risk of making a *long* dialogue go slowly"[17] — a principle Pinero would have done well to consider more deeply.

iv. *Producing* Trelawny

After Christmas Pinero had to suspend work on the opera to rehearse *Trelawny of the "Wells"* at the Court. Impressions of his work with the cast were later published by the actresses who played the lead roles of Rose Trelawny and Imogen Parrott: Irene Vanbrugh and Hilda Spong.

Vanbrugh was to become even more important to Pinero's mature drama than Mrs Campbell. As it happened, Rose Trelawny was not her first important part in a Pinero play. The daughter of a clergyman, she had served a useful apprenticeship with Sarah Thorne's stock company at Margate before making her London debut as the White Queen in a Globe Theatre presentation of *Alice in Wonderland*. She had then joined Toole's Theatre and, among other parts, played the title role in *Hester's Mystery* before moving on to work with Tree at the Haymarket. From there she had gone to the St James's, where in addition to creating Gwendoline Fairfax in *Earnest*, she had played Ellean to Evelyn Millard's Paula. Two years later she was acting in Jones's *The Liars* at Wyndham's when Pinero approached her about the title role in *Trelawny*. Wyndham generously agreed to release her if (as proved the case) Pinero's new comedy opened before Jones's had finished its run.

Vanbrugh was now exposed to the full force of Pinero's keen scrutiny and attention. It was to become a familiar experience, and in her autobiography she gave a vivid impression of the playwright as director:

> He would walk back and forth along the stalls, the front row being removed for this purpose. Hands clasped behind his back, concentration personified, each step taken in complete measure with what he was thinking, each word carrying its full weight so that everything he said seemed to pierce through to your brain.
>
> His clothes were well-cut and orthodox — pepper and salt trousers, a black morning-coat, tie very carefully tied. His overcoat was unusual; it was short, boxy and rather full and gave him a horsy appearance. A hard bowler hat, bigger than the ordinary, and always a pair of immaculate wash-leather gloves.
>
> In manner he was not genial but he was alertly sympathetic and would devote himself completely to your interest during the time he talked or listened to you. I have seen and known him angry, sarcastic and relentless, but I have never imagined him snubbing anyone. His deep appreciation of human nature would have led him sooner to say something which would sting the other person into a betrayal of a natural reaction rather than snub them and make them withdraw into themselves.[18]

To this account may be added Spong's:

> It is his custom to take the actress he has chosen for a part on a promenade of confidential advice. . . . He takes you by the arm and while he strolls back and forth across the apron of the stage, he explains. He gives you the voice, the style, the walk, the gesture, the heart and brain of the character. After that he devotes three days to you exclusively, squeezes your inmost soul into the mould he wants. Then he takes the next character in the same way. . . . He wants all

the colours at rehearsal. He insists upon scenery, properties and costumes being ready before he directs the play. In *Trelawny of the "Wells"* the women wore their hooped skirts at all rehearsals. Not a word is ever altered, not a word is ever added, the breath of life is in the manuscript and woe be he who alters a sigh, a smile, a tear in it.[19]

Pinero had by now established a unique authority for himself as an author-director. Actors inevitably responded in different ways to his dictatorial rehearsal methods. Some — probably most — respected his efficiency, experience, and total dedication to the work and, at a time when formal training in acting was virtually nonexistent, valued what he taught them. Others, such as Lena Ashwell, considered that he (and later Shaw) "turned the artist into a mere machine" and by imprisoning the actor in a preconceived mould "began the most vicious of the changes that have affected the [modern] theatre."[20] But for Pinero, the securing of a precise enactment of his play was as much part of his work as writing the script:

All that we call "business" is in the printed matter which I carry into the theatre. Why should it be altered when it has all been carefully and even laboriously thought out, every detail of it, during the process of construction? The movements of a man and what he has to say are inseparable. Expression is multiform and simultaneous; to alter one phrase is to weaken all. I try to think of these things beforehand. Rehearsal is not — or certainly should not be — a time for experiment. It is to prepare for the acting together of the players, not for the making of the play.[21]

The cast that had been assembled for *Trelawny* varied in ability, the lead women being better than the men. "Dot" Boucicault could only give Pinero a competent stock old man for Sir William Gower[22] compared with what Hare would have created, and several of the other actors (including a young and inexperienced Gerald du Maurier as the Wells juvenile lead, Ferdinand Gadd) were less than adequate in their parts. It was fitting, though, that in a play that evoked the theatre of Pin's youth, there were faces from his past: Mrs Saker, widow of the former manager of the Liverpool Alexandra, albeit not a former tragedy queen, brought a pathos and dignity to the role of Mrs Telfer;

and Isabel Bateman, once Irving's leading lady and vainly in love with him, played the aging spinster Miss Trafalgar Gower, her last stage part before retiring to a convent. Two of the other actresses had played in earlier Pinero plays: Patti Browne, back from Australia with Boucicault, had been one of the three "boys" in *The Amazons*; old Rose le Thière, formerly a dowager duchess in *The Cabinet Minister*, to make her presence felt despite the smallness of her part in *Trelawny*, would waddle down to the footlights several minutes after the start of her rehearsals and call out, "I hope I'm not late. How are you, Pin, and how is dear Myra?" before retiring to an upstage chair and taking out her embroidery.[23]

If these actresses worthily represented the old stock company players who are replaced in the action of Pinero's comedy by "society" actors, the only effective example of the latter in the cast was a real-life peer, Lord Rosslyn, making his stage debut under the name of James Erskine. He had been given the appropriate role of Arthur Gower, the well-bred young man who abandons his family and turns actor out of love for Rose Trelawny. Highly conscientious, he was altogether ideal for his role according to Vanbrugh, who described him as being "to the manner born in the clothes of the period" and possessing natural breeding that "enabled him to strike just the right note in his association with the bohemian circle" in the play.[24]

Trelawny of the "Wells" opened at the Court Theatre on 20 January 1898 to the applause of the audience but the confusion of many critics; as Pinero noted, they seemed "divided as to whether the piece is a weak farce or an imperfect realistic drama."[25] Only Archer appreciated Pinero's reasons for writing the play: "One of the most delightful works of a great and original humorist — that is *Trelawny of the 'Wells'*. A memorable chapter in our theatrical history delicately and ingeniously dramatized — that is *Trelawny of the 'Wells'*. A graceful homage from the captain of today to the pioneer of yesterday, the man who paved the way for all his effort and achievement — that is *Trelawny of the 'Wells.'* "[26] Although labelling the comedy "a Robertsonian tribute to Robertson," Archer was at pains to point out that it was far above anything written by the earlier playwright, containing as it did "enough intellectual power . . . to furnish forth half a dozen cup and saucer comedies" and demonstrating "a pressure of thought to the square inch" as high "as in Mr Pinero's most serious work." But the review carried a sting in its tail as far as the acting was concerned:

> And now mark the retribution which has overtaken Mr Pinero! He has celebrated, he has chuckled over, the displacement of the old school of acting by the new; he has invited us to smile, instead of dropping a tear, when Mr James Telfer, the tragedian of "the Wells", is reduced to accepting, in a "new-fangled" comedy, the trumpery part of "an old, stagy, out-of-date actor.". . . He has satirised in a hundred touches the frowzy old stock-company with its hard-and-fast "lines of business"; and now, behold! the new school, whose advent he acclaims, altogether fails to back him up and justify his complacency. I do not mean the performance was altogether bad; three or four of the actors, who fortunately held the leading parts, were adequate without being specially brilliant; but most of the subordinate characters, on whom the effect of the comedy so largely depends, were either feebly presented or fatally mis-presented. In every revolution there is loss as well as gain; and we shall have to undo, in a certain measure, the work of the revolution which Mr Pinero celebrates — that which substituted for the James Telfers of yesterday the Arthur Gowers of today.

Years later du Maurier, knighted and famous, was dining with Pin and other theatrical friends when the conversation turned to the topics of critics in general and William Archer in particular. Pin having remarked that he considered Archer the most honest and kindly critic he had ever met, du Maurier recalled a comment from Archer's review of *Trelawny* to the effect that "not even the acting of Mr Gerald du Maurier could entirely ruin this brilliant play" and plaintively asked the playwright, "That was not very kindly, was it?" "No, Gerald," came Pin's gentle reply, "it wasn't. And not true either."[27]

An unexpected admirer of the play was Shaw, who noted a "delicacy of . . . mood [inspiring] the whole play which has touched me more than anything else Mr Pinero has ever written." Critical of the costumes, accents, and acting, Shaw was nonetheless so charmed by the play that he pronounced himself "loath to lay [his] critical fingers on it." If Mr Pinero, he sighed, would only keep to the period to which he was spiritually attuned instead of venturing into modern territory that had "virtually no real existence for him," he need never fear censure from G.B.S.:

> When [Pinero] plays me the tunes of 1860, I appreciate and sympathise. Every stroke touches me: I dwell on the dainty workmanship shewn in the third and fourth acts: I rejoice in being old enough to know the world of his dreams. But when he comes to 1890, then I thank my stars that he does not read the Saturday Review. Please remember that it is the spirit and not the letter of the date that I insist on. The Benefit of the Doubt is dressed in the fashions of today; but it might have been written by Trollope. Trelawny of the Wells confessedly belongs to the days of Lily Dale. And whenever Lily Dale and not Mrs Ebbsmith is in question, Mr Pinero may face with complete equanimity the risk of picking up the Saturday Review in mistake for the Mining Journal.[28]

This was not, as it turned out, an accurate statement. G.B.S.'s review of *Trelawny* was the last he was to write on a Pinero play. Three months later, following an operation on a poisoned foot, Shaw followed the advice of his doctor and his own inclination and swore a solemn oath to renounce dramatic criticism, declaring that "the subject is exhausted; and so am I."[29] But the departure of G.B.S. from the *Saturday Review* did not signal the end of hostilities from that quarter as far as Pinero was concerned. Shaw's swashbuckling penmanship was replaced by the precise and deadly pinpricks of Max Beerbohm.

v. Pinero and Sullivan — Finale

Immediately after producing *Trelawny*, Pin, instead of taking his usual holiday, resumed work on the opera. He did so with resentment, having just learnt that though he and Carr had agreed to a share of the profits (if any), Sullivan had insisted that Mrs Carte agree to pay him a percentage of the gross receipts. Pinero and Carr were not merely aggrieved at the more secure financial terms negotiated by the composer but suspicious that he had little confidence in, or commitment to, their script. By this time Sullivan had escaped from London to work on the music in seclusion at a villa he had hired at Beaulieu on the Riviera. He had no sooner reached it when he heard from Mrs Carte of his authors'' annoyance over his percentage contract. Believing (wrongly, as it happened) that he had told them all about it a year earlier, he wrote on 31 January 1898 a long letter to Pinero insisting on his right to make his own terms and rejecting the charge that he had lost interest in the joint work: *"Dismiss this idea entirely from your mind.* In the first place, I could hardly have lost interest in the piece when I hadn't seen it a year ago — the time I told you of my decision; and 2[nd]ly, I have been, and am working with the keenest interest, and the greatest industry. Moreover, I am working with if possible greater zest than usual from the fact that I am working for a certainty — not on speculation entirely."

Having asserted his rights, Sullivan typically relented and two days later sent telegrams to Pinero and Mrs Carte stating his willingness to accept the same profit-sharing arrangement as his collaborators and "stand or fall" with them "as the result may be." This was to prove a costly gesture, but it restored friendly relations between the two sides. Mrs Carte, in a private note to Pinero after learning of this change of heart, remarked on the "slight mist" that had affected the composer's memory before adding, "But, after all, what does it all matter — so long as it ends well? A long course of comic opera has brought me to that amiable view of things."[30]

There were further difficulties over the opera but no more disputes amongst the collaborators. Sullivan struggled with the text privately. "Heart-breaking to have to try and make a musical piece out of such a badly constructed (for music) mass of involved sentences," he noted in his diary on 25 February. But he kept such feelings to himself, cooperated generously over further casting problems, and finally posted off the last musical numbers on 7 April before returning to London to work on the orchestral score and rehearse the chorus.

Pinero took charge of directing the stage rehearsals, which began in the second week of April and proved heavy going. Not only did he

have to direct singers (including a pair of overpriced and underexper-
ienced American "stars") for the first time but he had to manage larger
forces than ever before. Mrs Carte noted with alarm in a letter written
on 30 March that the opera's dress plot called for ninety-three people
on stage, including principals, chorus, and supers. Not only was this
thirty more than used by any previous Savoy opera, but the theatre
did not have dressing space for them all! Under this pressure Pin
suffered another bout of influenza but battled on regardless.

After all this effort *The Beauty Stone*, as the "New and Original
ROMANTIC MUSICAL DRAMA" was finally called,[31] failed dismally when
it opened at the Savoy on Saturday, 28 May 1898. The basic trouble
was not Sullivan's music, which was as charming as ever, nor even the
barely adequate lead singers, but the script's (un-Gilbertian) lack of
humour and its stilted pseudomedieval dialogue. This last fatal flaw
was wickedly parodied by Max Beerbohm in a mock reenactment of
the origin of the opera:

THE BEAUTY STONE

Scene: Wardour Street
Time: The Immediate Past

Enter R., Mr A. W. Pinero; *L.*, Mr J. Comyns Carr

Mr C: Give thee good morrow, gossip!
Mr P: Heaven save thee, merry gentleman! What do'st?
Mr C: Nay, but I gad me to no special quest.
Mr P: Art not here in the servicement of that good knight, Sir Henry?
For well I know he hath much trust of thee, and that 'twas e'en
here thou didst disinter for him King Arthur's hallowed bones.
Mr C: 'Twas e'en here! But th'art in misprision, natheless, of my
immediate presence. Fared I hither but for my own pleasuring,
having ta'en for many yearn delightment i' the spot.
Mr P: By Saint Carolo, a right goodly reason! For myself —
Mr C: Aye, tell me of thyself! Art still in thrall to that accursèd knave,
Henrik of Norway?
Mr P: I'sooth, I ha' somewhat totter'd in my fealty o' late. My
thought hath stray'd back to old Thomas de Robertson, my first
dear liege. Hast seen my fair mummer-maiden, my last-begot?

Mr C: Aye, I did clap eyes on her at the Court, not many eves agone. Beshrew me, a personable wench! And hast cast off those naughty drabs — on whom a malison! — *The Second Dame Tanqueray* and *Dame Ebbsmith Of Whom All Men Wot?*

Mr P: That have I, gossip — 't least for a space.

Mr C: Then by the finger-nails of St Luke, art thou so much the more blessèd!

Mr P: Methinks that I misdoubt me not of thy good wisdom.

Mr C: Methinks that he who would fain doubt the wisdom of a sage is not sage himself!

Mr P: Ha, ha, ho! Ho, ho, ho! A right shrewd jest!

Mr C: But in all graveness, gossip, sith we have thus encounter'd one the other here in the very abodement of Romance herself, and sith we have naught better to do, wherefore should not we make some joint emprise?

Mr P: Why, by the arrows of Saint Sebastian, that will we!

Mr C: Thy hand on't!

Mr P: Let us to pen!

Exeunt arm in arm[32]

As Max went on to remark, the difficulty with this style was not writing but listening to it. Even set to Sullivan's music and enacted on elaborate sets by Telbin, the archaic diction wearied audiences. Thus while Pin recuperated in the Engadine and Sullivan lamented his lost percentage, Mrs Carte dropped *The Beauty Stone* after a mere seven weeks and brought back a revival of *The Gondoliers* that rapidly restored the Savoy to profitability.

vi. The Gay Lord Quex

After his holiday Pinero, shrugging off his failure as a librettist, began work on a new comedy for Hare, who was now managing the Globe Theatre, having relinquished the Garrick two years earlier. Hare wanted the play to open his autumn season, but the writing did not go according to plan. Having sketched out a plot and written a first act, Pinero told Hare to be ready to start rehearsals in October and to engage Irene Vanbrugh for the leading woman's role. Then deciding that his script was hopeless, the playwright tore it up and began a new one, working long hours behind his locked study door and at home to no one. *The Gay Lord Quex* was eventually completed in late February 1899, and the opening night set down for early April.

Vanbrugh now found herself confronted with the most unusual and demanding role of her career: the scheming manicurist Sophy Full-garney, who risks her prospects and respectability in order to compromise a supposedly wicked lord engaged to marry her foster sister:

> Little did I think when I walked on to the stage for the first rehearsal what an immense influence on my life that play would have. I had read the privately printed copy but had not been able to grasp the immense possibilities of this masterpiece. . . . I had a task far bigger than anything I had ever attempted. Pinero had shown his faith in me, in spite of some opinions to the contrary, and I longed to justify it.
>
> How he toiled with us and how hard I tried to do what he wanted. His method was very exacting to the artist, but there was always an uneasy feeling at the back of one's mind that he was right, and that if you could get what he wanted you would be right too. But would you ever get it? The agony of going to rehearsal feeling like nothing, leaving rehearsal with large blocks of knowledge in your mind refusing to be used. The gradual sifting out, the wonder of finding, when you were shivering down your spine, that he said, "Now you are feeling cold down your back!" The building of the character of Sophy Fullgarney; getting the commonness underneath, then putting on the polish and the veneer on the top and the natural bit of her when she is in love. The goal had to be reached, the curtain had to go up.[33]

The role was as important for her as Paula Tanqueray had been for Mrs Campbell, and the first night of *The Gay Lord Quex* at the Globe on Saturday, 8 April 1899, remained the most memorable she experienced in her long and distinguished career. In her autobiography Vanbrugh records a brief conversation with the playwright following a knock on her dressing room door as the orchestra began playing the opening selection:

> "Are you there, Irene?"
> "Yes. Who is it?"

"Pin."

"Oh, Pin, come in."

"Well, my dear, are you all right? I can do nothing now, but I can trust to you. Don't let it upset you if you find the audience is against you. You see, Sophy is a liar and a sneak, and though she is doing it for her foster-sister, they may still resent her attitude."

"All right, Pin. Oh, my goodness, I am nervous."

"That's right, my dear, but remember I am trusting to you and I have every confidence. Good luck!"[34]

Her account continues with a moment-by-moment description of her feelings in minute detail until the rising of the curtain and her first entrance. Then, significantly, to the remainder of the performance she gives just three paragraphs, as she admits being "in a trance" from which she emerged only for the "deafening applause" at the end of the bedroom scene and again at the final curtain, when she took the last call "alone with Pinero . . . the proudest moment of my life."[35]

The play, coming almost at the dawn of the Edwardian era, perfectly suited the taste of the time and played to crowded houses at the Globe for most of the 300 performances of its first run. There was hardly a trace of the old Victorian morality in it, which angered the Bishop of Wakefield, who publicly condemned it,[36] but disturbed few of the regular critics. Scott, dismissed from the *Daily Telegraph* three months earlier for stating in another journal that it was "nearly impossible for a woman to remain pure who adopts the stage as a profession,"[37] was no longer around, and even the surviving conservatives accepted the new licence as a fact of life. Commenting that "Pinero seems to aim at being the Congreve of the new birth," Knight conceded that the modern dramatists were "saucy rather than obscene" compared with those of the Restoration but hardly less frank in their depiction of society.[38] Nisbet confined his moral disapproval to the observation that Pinero had "written nothing cleverer than *The Gay Lord Quex*," and yet a world which spends its mornings in manicure shops and palmists' apartments — a world which keeps French novels which are "rather — you know — rather" in its bedroom and pretends to admire them for their "exquisitely polished style"; a world of midnight appointments in women's boudoirs — is not a pleasant or an edifying spectacle."[39]

Most of the critics admired the play's stagecraft and ignored its morality. Some indeed felt the author had struck a new lode of comedy equivalent to his Court farces, and hoped he would continue to exploit it rather than strain himself and his audiences with painfully serious problem plays. Max, for example, remarked that "when Mr Pinero was trying to be strenuous, he was always being tripped up by his own genius for stagecraft" but that in *Quex* he had "set out to tell an amusing story for the stage, and . . . not troubled about anything else," with the result that the new play was "a very delightful entertainment." This view was emphatically endorsed by Gosse, who wrote Pinero:

> I have just seen *The Gay Lord Quex*. May I bore you by expressing my enthusiastic admiration? That third act is one of the most magnificent pieces of stagecraft in our literature. I look upon this play as the finest specimen of pure comedy that you (and therefore anyone in our time) has produced. I could say many things, but I should only weary you. But I am still a little under the dazzlement of your great play — so vigorous and beneficent and gay.
>
> Do stick to COMEDY now you have come safe to it — no more melodrama or farce or Ibsen, or anything else but the pure heroic comedy which is the very child of the gods — the laughing child, the child of *April*. I feel very strongly about this; *Comedy* is what we want.[40]

Pin's reply, though warmly appreciative of Gosse's kindly "pat on the back,"[41] made no mention of the exhortation that he should stick to comedy in future: he wanted public approval, but he could do without it if necessary. *Quex*'s third act is indeed a virtuoso feat of stagecraft, comparable with the "Screen Scene" in Sheridan's *The School for Scandal*, yet the play as a whole has more to offer than humour and technical dexterity. It presents a sharply observed portrait of the manners and morals of English society at the turn of the century. Sophy's seductive patter as she manicures Lord Quex provides a typical sample:

SOPHY. Seven-and-thirty, *you* look — not a day older; that's what
we say. There, dip your fingers in that, do.
QUEX. Into this?
SOPHY. [*Thrusting his fingers into the bowl*] Baby! [*The water
splashes over her dress and his coat*] Oh!
QUEX. I beg your pardon.
SOPHY. Now what have you done? [*Wiping the water from his coat*]
You clumsy boy!
QUEX. Thanks, thanks.
[*She commences operations on his left hand. He is now thor-
oughly entertained by her freedom and audacity.*]
SOPHY. Ha, ha, ha! do you know what *I* maintain?
QUEX. [*Laughing*] Upon my word I dread to think.
SOPHY. Why, that every man who looks younger than his years
should be watched by the police.
QUEX. Good heavens, Sophy — Miss Fullgarney!
SOPHY. Yes — as a dangerous person.
QUEX. Dangerous! Ho, come!
SOPHY. [*With the suggestion of a wink*] Dangerous. The man who
is younger than he ought to be is always no better than he should
be.
QUEX. Ha, ha, ha!
SOPHY. Am I right? Am I right, eh? [*Putting her cheek near his lips
— speaking in a low voice, breathlessly, her eyes averted*] Tell me
whether I'm right, my lord. (81–82)

Pinero in affluent middle age appears to have been writing from
firsthand knowledge of such girls and, if not deceived by their wiles,
seems not to have been indifferent to them either. His discretion was
such that the assertion cannot now be proved, but even apart from
suggestive indications in *Quex* and his later plays, there is some
circumstantial evidence to support it. In his will, for example, he left
a bequest of £1,000 to a hostess at the Sesame Club in Grosvenor Street
as a mark of his "gratitude and affection"[42] — a late echo, perhaps,
of Quex's creed that mistresses be suitably provided for. And his fellow
playwright Alfred Sutro records in his memoirs a visit he and Pin made
to a revue at "one of the more frivolous halls" in Paris, where an
English dancing girl, on seeing Pin in the audience, called out to him

and turned three somersaults in his honour. "That," Sutro enviously remarked, "is fame."[43]

vii. Conflicts

Pinero's resolve to write purely for his own satisfaction was force-fully demonstrated several months after the production of *Quex*. On 9 August George Alexander asked him to write a play for the opening of "the new St James's" (the theatre was being extensively remodeled) at the start of the 1900 autumn season. The reply the manager received next day began amiably enough with a paragraph in which Pin outlined his holiday plans for the following two months — Maloja, then Turin for an Italian production of *Quex*, and finally Venice to amuse his step-daughter. Then he dropped his bombshell:

> Coming to the dry bones of your proposal, I consider it best to be quite open and candid with you. . . . Frankly, dear Alec, I don't think you and I go well together in harness; or, rather, I do not feel happy at running in tandem with you, myself as wheeler to your lead. I know you take a pride in being an autocrat in your theatre; it is a natural pride in a position you have worthily won for yourself. But I also have won — or have chosen to usurp — a similarly autocratic position in all that relates to my work. I hope I do not use my power unfairly or overbearingly, but I do exercise it — and any other condition of things is intolerable to me. In my association with you on the stage I have always felt that you resented my authority. In the case of our last joint venture the circumstances that led up to it were of so unhappy a character that I resolved to abrogate this authority — to reduce it, at any rate, to a shadow. But, at the same time, I did not relish my position and determined — even before I started upon a campaign I foresaw could not be otherwise than full of discomfort and constraint — that I would not again occupy it. To put the case shortly, there is not room for two autocrats in one small kingdom; and in every detail, however slight, that pertains to my work — though I avail myself gratefully of any assistance that is afforded me — I take to myself the right of dictation and veto.[45]

In his reply (11 August 1899) Alexander stated that he appreciated all Pinero had said and would be happy to work with him on that basis in future if he would but say the word.[46] Six years would pass, however, before they again joined forces at the St James's.

For the moment there were more serious matters to think about than writing plays. Tension between the British government and Paul Kruger's South African republic had risen to such a pitch that the colonial secretary, Joseph Chamberlain, convinced that war with the Boers was inevitable, dispatched 10,000 additional troops to augment the meagre British forces already in South Africa. In early September Pin's stepson, Angus, now a war correspondent with the *Times*, departed by steamer for Capetown. By the end of the month Angus was at Kimberley, where he reported that a single shot would set the border aflame, and on 11 October he reached Mafeking just as war was declared and the town came under siege.

In what must have been a desperately worrying time for his mother, he remained holed up in Mafeking until the relief force eventually arrived to raise the siege on 17 May 1900. His reactions ranged from initial jingoistic enthusiasm ("there will be no holding back on the part of our men once the fun begins") to eventual exhaustion ("Our nerves are altogether raw, our tempers soured, our digestions failing. We were young men six months ago, but we have aged considerably since then").[47] No mere bystander, he had taken part in every major sortie against the enemy, having had his horse shot from under him during the Boers' last desperate attack on 13 May and been held prisoner with thirty-one others in a tiny, stifling room until the surrender. That last experience increased his respect for the Boers, who, he reported, "treated the prisoners humanely and behaved throughout a situation almost maddening in the strain it must have imposed on them with a conspicuous gallantry, coolness and consideration."[48] His stepfather shared this view and proposed the American war correspondent, novelist, and playwright Richard Harding Davis for the Garrick Club even though he knew Davis would be blackballed for his pro-Boer sympathies.[49]

Soon after the raising of the siege, Angus reworked his notes and dispatches into a book, *The Siege of Mafeking*, which was published immediately in London. Pin must have been amused to read, for example, the following description of the Mafeking commander: "Colonel Baden-Powell is young, as men go in the army, with a keen appreciation of the possibilities of his career, swayed by ambition, indifferent to sentimental emotion. . . . His reserve is unbending, and one would say, quoting Mr Pinero, that fever would be the only heat that would permeate his body."[50]

Perhaps the book's most provocative passage for the playwright was Angus's description of the white women's behaviour in Mafeking during the siege. Unlike the pioneer women of Australia, New Zealand, Canada, and the western United States, white women in Africa, wrote Angus, were curiously incapable, delegating most of their duties to native servants. Their view of life was "petty and impressed with prejudices and absurd jealousies," they were "abnormally lazy," and during the siege they were responsible "for a great deal of the discontent, the unwillingness to make the best of an exceedingly trying situation."[51]

Though no memorandum survives to prove the point, it is likely that these remarks provoked Pinero to embark on his longest and most detailed dramatic portrait. When completed, *Iris* would dramatize (over five acts and nine scenes) the decline and fall of a pampered, weak-willed society woman who, unable to face the hardships of a life in the Canadian outback with the young man she loves, becomes instead the mistress of a wealthy Jewish financier who finally, in disgust at her fecklessness, throws her out into the street.

This long play occupied Pinero for more than a year, much of which was spent abroad supposedly holidaying in Maloja, Lake Como (the setting for the Italian scenes of *Iris*), the Riviera, and Paris. During brief intervals back in London, Pin made time for a number of smaller matters. These included a successful appeal to the Prime Minister, Arthur Balfour, for a Civil List pension to be granted to Herman Merivale,[52] congratulating Edward Carson (the prosecutor in Oscar Wilde's case) on his appointment as Solicitor General,[53] writing to the *Daily Mail* on the subject of dramatic critics ("amongst whom I have found some of my best friends and worst enemies"),[54] and contributing a preface to W. L. Courtney's *The Idea of Tragedy in Ancient and Modern Drama* — in which several of his own plays were warmly praised. On 11 December he responded to a request from the *Daily Express* for his thoughts on what the twentieth century might bring, remarking: "With your permission I will restrict myself to the mere expression of the wish that in the coming century there may be less rancour in political life; in artistic life less self-advertisement; in the pulpit, and in all places where judgement is pronounced, less hypocrisy; and in private life a little privacy."[55]

Six weeks later, on 22 January 1901, all the London theatres closed their doors for the death of Queen Victoria. Just over a fortnight later their curtains rose on a new and exciting, if short-lived, era of British drama that would see Pinero, though challenged by younger playwrights, reach the peak of his career.

...13...
Respectability in Danger

i. Iris *and* Letty

Pinero's first contributions to the drama of the Edwardian era were two substantial plays, each depicting a woman who is forced to choose between luxury and respectability. Whereas in *Iris* (1901) the title character is a pampered beauty who takes the line of least resistance at every crisis in her affairs, in *Letty* (1903) she is a working-class girl whose innate respectability finally enables her to resist temptation. Together the plays amount to a rejection of the corrupt manners of society and an endorsement of the solid virtues of suburbia. As the former group were the more significant theatregoers, it is perhaps not surprising that neither play achieved the popularity of the comparatively amoral *Quex*.

Iris Bellamy may be regarded as Pinero's full-length portrait of a "lady" in similar vein to Anton Chekhov's Madame Ranyevskaia or Harley Granville-Barker's later study of Jessica Madras. Of Iris, too, the question might be asked, "Is not the perfect lady perhaps the most wonderful achievement of civilisation, and worth the cost of her breeding, worth the toil and the helotage of — all the others?"[1] Pinero grants his heroine beauty, charm, and good intentions but remorselessly shows her fatal lack of character. The demonstration is set up by a typical Pinero device: a will that forbids the youthfully widowed Iris to remarry on pain of losing her deceased husband's fortune. She

254

is thus presented with the dilemma of marrying either Laurence Tren-with, an attractive but poor young man with whom she plays at being in love, or Frederick Maldonado, a wealthy Jewish financier who is passionately attracted to her. She vacillates between the two men even after she has been deprived of her fortune by an embezzling solicitor and trapped into becoming Maldonado's mistress.

The trouble with Iris as a dramatic heroine — especially for modern audiences — is that she is not endowed with the courage of her lack of convictions. Despite her apparently aristocratic languor (her family background is never filled in), she manifests a middle-class bad conscience every time she fails to act. For example, speaking early on of her reluctance to marry the almost penniless Trenwith, she says "wistfully," "Only I should like to think that I don't shrink from it out of sheer worldliness and cowardice," and near the end of the play, confessing to him that she is a kept woman, she "bursts into tears" and cries, "Oh I meant to be poor! I meant to be poor!" Like the caged birds she carries around with her, she is afraid of freedom and resentful of captivity, her only possible value being decorative.

Though Iris might have been a suitable match for the pallid Trenwith, it is hard to imagine the source of Maldonado's fervent desire for her, apart from the perverse stimulation of her indifference. Nevertheless, his passion drives the play and gives it dramatic force. When in the first act she agrees to marry but not to love him, he is prepared, despite his pride, to accept the humiliating offer:

MALDONADO. [*Grimly*] It's a bargain, then? You are to be mine;
    as much mine as the Velasquez, the Raphael hanging on my walls
    —mine, at least, to gaze at, mine to keep from others?
[*Her head droops in acquiescence.*] (46)

When Iris subsequently breaks her promise, he exacts revenge by trapping her into economic dependence and physical submission but is still willing to marry her on her original terms until she again betrays him by making a final assignation with Trenwith. At this point, according to Archer,[2] Pinero had planned to have Maldonado strangle her, but in the event rejected this melodramatic ending in favour of having

255

him turn her out of her (or rather *his*) Park Lane flat before furiously wrecking it.

To a modern audience this reaction would seem amply justified and long overdue, but for most of the play's first-nighters at the Garrick Theatre on 21 September 1901, Pinero's demonstration of Iris's slide into oblivion possessed an almost tragic intensity. The *Globe* described their reaction thus:

> From the beginning "Iris" took a strong hold on the public. The first three acts were a little nebulous, through no fault of the author, but simply because a considerable section of the audience hesitated to believe that a heroine so sweet and fascinating as Mr Pinero depicted was capable of conduct such as assigned to her. . . . During the last two acts, when the pall of tragedy begins to enshroud the characters, the public sat spellbound, gazing with rapt attention at scenes the like of which have not often, if ever, been put upon the stage. Not a sound was heard except the words spoken. None dared even to cough, scarcely even to stir, until the close when, the full significance of the action being realized, the public indulged in a storm of applause amid which signs of discontent and disapproval were distinctly audible. Comprehensible enough were both applause and censure. Artistically the work is great, far greater than we are used to see. But it is strong meat and weak stomachs may turn. Nothing so terrible is often encountered in literature. . . . "Iris" stands in relation to the stage much as "Tess of the D'Urbervilles" stands to prose fiction.[3]

If *Iris* had achieved nothing else, it had at last removed the shadow of *The Squire* controversy.

To win sympathy for his irresponsible heroine Pinero had cast Fay Davis in the title role. Archer, who was otherwise lost in admiration at "the consummate art of the story-telling," felt that Davis's "porcelain personality" made the character's "total and really facile lapse from self-respect" difficult to accept and therefore judged that the author had "not produced an actor-proof character."[4] Perhaps because audiences could not stand seeing a sympathetic Iris thrown into the street, the play's first London run totalled a mere 115 performances. In New York a year later at the Criterion Theatre, a less sympathetic portrayal by Virginia Harned won respect but no greater popularity. But Oscar

Asche, repeating his impressive London portrayal of Maldonado, was greeted by "round after round of applause at the final curtain." According to the *New York World*, the audience left the theatre silently, having just witnessed "one of the most crudely and audaciously brutal scenes ever placed on the English-speaking stage — a scene, logical, true to nature, and yet so antagonistic to the conventions, so cynical in its unmasking of society that it fairly awed a public certainly hardened to the realities of life."[5]

Though not a commercial success at its original productions, *Iris* achieved at least an honorable *succès d'estime*. By 1925, however, when it was revived in London at the Adelphi Theatre with Gladys Cooper in the title role, the play was generally considered by the critics to be rather ponderous and old-fashioned. The *Illustrated London News* remarked, "Had Miss Cooper persuaded her playwright to make wholesale cuts she would have won thanks from modern audiences, and a good play would have gained in strength."[6] It has not been given a professional revival since, and it is unlikely to get one despite the view of some commentators that it is Pinero's best serious play. As a historical document, however, it remains an impressively candid portrait of an Edwardian lady.

Letty, though lacking the intense drama of *Iris*, presents a much more varied and crowded canvas. Two of its four acts are set in a luxurious apartment in the vicinity of New Bond Street, but the others take place on the rooftop of a lodging house and in a restaurant, and the play ends with an epilogue in a photographer's studio in Baker Street. The heroine on this occasion is not a lady but a typist, and most of the supporting characters — a far more lively, if at times caricatured, collection than Iris's vapid circle — belong to the lower middle class. Though Pinero classified this play, as he did *Iris*, as a drama because of its serious scenes, it features a significant amount of broad comedy, sometimes bordering on farce, and the outcome for the heroine is positive rather than pessimistic. As Pinero's American editor Clayton Hamilton somewhat portentously remarks in *The Social Plays*, "*Iris* told the life-story of a woman doomed to ruin, though launched in luxury and ease; and *Letty* tells the life-story of a woman destined to salvation, though launched in poverty and danger. In this respect, the second story may be regarded as a reversal of the first; and Pinero can scarcely have remained unconscious of the element of irony in the comparison."[7]

At least two critics appear to have influenced the playwright in his choice of environment and theme for *Letty*. Archer, in what he described as a "real conversation" with Pinero (published January 1901), charged him (and his colleagues) with having "of late years concentrated [his] attention rather too exclusively on one corner of life: the Hyde Park Corner, so to speak."[8] When shown the page proofs of this imaginary interview, the playwright mildly protested at being set up as a "Nine-pinero" but sought in a letter (19 January 1901), subsequently incorporated into the published "conversation," to justify his use of upper-class characters in serious drama:

> I have been brooding over the point you raise about the tendency of modern drama to gravitate towards *high life*, and cannot help believing that the cause goes deeper than mere imitation of French models — that it is to be found, in fact, in the very root of drama. From the Greeks onward the dramatist has always drawn his inspiration, at any rate borrowed his method of expression, from the lives of people of exalted station. Nothing of considerable merit but low comedy has ever come from the study of low life. As for tragedy, there is none that can be properly so esteemed in low life, because there is no height from which a common person can fall — consequently no irony of circumstance nor refinement of suffering. One is not greatly stirred by the sorrows, appropriate as one thinks, of those of humble condition; one is rather surprised and amused by the prosperity of the lowly —and then you get comedy, but not even then high comedy.

Despite this justification, the charge that the social range of his drama had become too narrow seems to have contributed to his decision to depict a broader spectrum of life in *Letty* and his subsequent plays.

The second critic who appears to have influenced, if indirectly, the writing of *Letty* was Sir Edward Russell, editor of the *Liverpool Daily Post*, who attacked *The Gay Lord Quex* (revived the previous May at the Duke of York's) in a public address at Stratford-upon-Avon at the beginning of September 1902. In a letter to the *Times* (4 September 1902) Pinero indignantly rejected Russell's charge that the play was "deserving of the severest censure" for containing "no suggestion of any feeling for the right side in life and conduct," and he counter-charged Russell with possessing outdated prejudices that prevented him from appreciating a comedy that did "not belong to the school of composition which labels each of its characters wolf or 'lamb.' " Russell replied in the *Times* on 9 September:

> Plays in which the characters are labelled "good" and "bad" are indeed undesirable, and beneath the level of critical consideration. By all means let us have men and women as they are — or as nearly as our best dramatists can with decorum come to the truth. But if a play is non-moral, while the tone of character of its main persons is licentious, it ought to be condemned. It is a cool dialectical expedient for Mr Pinero to write as if *The Gay Lord Quex* were typical of the drama of the day. This is not so. Happily the comedy is not typical even of its author. It is an exception. But it might have plunged us into a second Restoration.[9]

The debate continued with Russell praising the morality of *The Profligate* compared with *Quex* and Pinero replying that much water had flowed into the Mersey since 1889: during that time English drama had "taken strength, drawn closer to life, advanced," whereas his critic remained "among those who have stood still."[10] The argument ended inconclusively, but Russell's protest, although Pinero officially discounted it, appears to have had some effect on the moral line he took in *Letty*, then still in the planning stage.

Like *Quex*, *Letty* (to quote Hamilton), deals with "a personal struggle between a virtuous working-girl and a libidinous aristocrat."[11] On this occasion the "aristocrat" is an untitled but wealthy twenty-nine-year-old philanderer with the appropriate name of Nevill Letchmere, and the girl, Letty Schell, works in the typing pool of Dugdales, a stockbroking firm "thriving mainly upon the shamefaced gambling propensities of the respectable classes," as Letchmere puts it. The conflict, however, is far different from Sophy's battle of wits with *Quex*; in the later play the question is simply whether, despite her foolishness, the poor but respectable heroine will manage to preserve her virtue and reject the temptations of luxury. The basic plot is as moral as Sir Edward Russell could have desired, relating more to early Victorian melodrama than a second Restoration; the play's Edwardian elements lie instead in the range and treatment of the characters and in the attitudes Pinero expressed about the milieu.

Though the story of *Letty*, like that of *Iris*, occupies a time span of more than two years, the key scenes take place in the space of the single afternoon and evening covered by the four acts; some two and a half years are then supposed to have elapsed between these and the epilogue. The effect is of a rapid succession of events that hardly gives Letty a moment's pause for reflection before she almost compromises herself. (*Iris* creates the opposite effect — of a slow drift into sin — by placing a two-year time lapse between the third and fourth acts.) Letty's weakness is temporary whereas Iris's had been ingrained. The child of an unsuccessful solicitor (like her author), Letty is at heart a respectable girl despite her wistful longing for glamour and excitement. During her time of trial, her strength is at a low ebb because she has gone without food so that she can dress herself prettily for Letchmere, whom she imagines to be a bachelor. Indeed, she is essentially so moral that she has never allowed a man even to kiss her, thereby setting up telling dramatic moments when two rival suitors subsequently do so in the space of a couple of hours.

Throughout the play Letty is accompanied by two contrasting girlfriends who offer conflicting advice, like the good and evil angels in Christopher Marlowe's *Dr Faustus*. Marion Allardyce, another typist-clerk at Dugdales, is a prim moralist who takes on herself the role of guardian of Letty's virtue; in contrast Hilda Gunning, a languid and worldly-wise assistant in a fashionable dressmaker's shop, has no scruples other than advising Letty not to sell herself cheap. Though the plot (and especially the epilogue) proves Marion's advice sound, even Pinero considered her a preacher, "unrolling thoughts that are crammed away in her brain, polished and complete."[12] Despite his best efforts, Hilda (as the playwright confessed to his Letty, Irene Vanbrugh) "ran away" with the script.[13] When the play opened at the Duke of York's Theatre on 8 October 1903, a comparatively unknown actress called Nancy Price made a great hit in the part, quite eclipsing Irene's Letty. Hilda is a marvelous character, whether flaunting her secondhand finery ("not in the least *magasang*"), stuffing free food into her mouth at every opportunity, or telling off Marion ("There you go! One would imagine the world's nothing but Sunday-school, to hear you. My world isn't, at all events. [*Loftily*] I don't belong to that *mongde*'). Like Sophy Fullgarney, she seems drawn from life.

The male characters, too, are more entertaining than usual in Pinero's social dramas. Letchmere is an unorthodox libertine in his concern for his unhappily married sister's reputation, though prone to verbose irony and unlikely self-criticism ("that blithe mercurial spirit — your husband — was reminding me a few minutes ago that we Letchmeres are a vicious crew. Ha! the utterance may have lacked something of urbanity; [*Shrugging his shoulders*] but — "). Letchmere's chief rival for Letty's affections, a vulgar Jewish stockbroker called Bernard Mandeville, offers an interesting contrast with Frederick Maldonado. Although neither portrait is flattering, Maldonado at least wants to be loved for himself, not his money, whereas Mandeville boorishly parades his "generosity" in order to inflate his ego. As long as Letty's options appear restricted to marriage with Mandeville or sinful luxury with Letchmere, the latter seems the better bargain.

But a third option is planted in the action without drawing attention to itself: to marry within her own circle. In the first three acts she is also courted by an apparently comic trio of suitors — a commercial traveller, an insurance salesman, and a photographer — who simultaneously pursue whatever business opportunities come their way. It is their propensity to mix their amorous and entrepreneurial concerns that prevents either Letty or the audience from taking any of them seriously. They then disappear in the fourth act, where Letty escapes Letchmere's clutches only at the last moment, when he learns that his married sister has run off with a lover.

In this fourth act geographical allusions subtly point up the contrast between the temptations of pleasure and the merits of respectability. Where Letchmere tempts Letty with the prospect of escape to luxurious European settings ("We shall hear this [music] when we are in Venice, you and I — at night, upon the Grand Canal"), Marion wants her to move to one of the new suburbs rapidly springing up on the northern outskirts of Edwardian London ("The suburbs. She's been at me constantly to live in the suburbs with her. That's where simple happiness is to be found, she always contends. . . . Simple happiness — fresh air — and — and fewer temptations").

This emphasis on the new suburban respectability is the reason for the epilogue, which many critics have condemned as "an unnecessary anti-climax"[14] superfluous to the dramatic interest of the play. It does, however, set up a key speech by the heroine, now happily married to the photographer and enjoying domestic bliss in a modest little suburban cottage (The Laurels) in Neasden. The listener is Letchmere, who, with alarming poetic justice, is wasting away from a fatal (no doubt venereal) disease. Letty endeavours to console the dying philanderer by reminding him of his one good deed — sparing her virtue:

> LETTY. I should like you to carry with you, then, as almost the last word you ever heard me utter — this word —
> NEVILL. What word, my dear?
> LETTY. *Thanks.* I was very foolish when — when you knew me, worse than foolish; and now I find myself, as it were, in harbour — through no desert of my own. I have married, in my proper rank, an honest man who is devoted to me; we have a child; we are tolerably prosperous. We shall live, God willing, the humdrum lives of "respectable people"; and if old age is granted to us, we shall nod over our winter fire, and doze in our garden in summer, as meek and humble a white-haired couple as could be met with out of an alms house. As true as I stand here, instead of scoffing at these things as I would have scoffed at them two and a half years ago, I believe in them as being the richest gifts this world can bestow. [*Drawing herself to her full height and offering him her hand*] Thanks. (244–245)

The worthy inhabitants of the new suburbia — whether in humble Neasden or the more prosperous reaches of Hampstead or Golder's Green — could hardly have been offered a more moving endorsement of their respectability.

ii. Max

In his review of *Iris* for the *World*, Archer predicted that the play would have to endure "the deliverances of the little knot of critics whose chief glory and accomplishment it is to despise Mr Pinero," a group he labelled "the anti-Pineroites."[15] Despite their predictable assaults, Archer claimed that *Iris* was "not a play which criticism can make or mar" and that therefore their verdict would not be "of any real importance." It was only natural that a number of the leading theatre critics objected to these remarks. "H.A.K" in the *Sunday Times*, for example, responded with the rhetorical question, "Should a critic, however eminent, endeavour to influence by the mere weight of his authority his fellow scribes, however modestly gifted they may happen to be?" Max Beerbohm, wearing a cloak of sympathy, was even more scathing in the *Saturday Review*:

> During the off-season, it seems, Mr William Archer has not been idle. He has been practising the delicious functions of a private detective and, with the luck of the novice, has made a most sensational discovery. Scotland Yard looks silly, and the myrmidons of State hide their diminished heads, while the novice, flushed with triumph, tells us of a dastardly plot against the art of Mr Pinero. . . . I applaud Mr Archer's enterprise. I am touched by his anxiety to save, with these preliminary cracks of the whip, his darling from the dogs. But where are the dogs? . . . Mr George Moore, it is true, did not like Mr Pinero's work. Nor did Mr Shaw. But neither of these delightful Irishmen is engaged now in dramatic criticism. To the best of my belief, Mr Walkley, Mr Symons and I are the only current dramatic critics who have shown any reluctance to acclaim Mr Pinero as a builder of masterpieces. . . . According to Mr Archer, anyone who denies to Mr Pinero "the quality of genius" must be "the victim of a paralyzing prejudice". If that is true, mine is a clear case of paralysis.[16]

Though Archer in a private letter to Max claimed he had been thinking of other critics,[17] Max *was* the leading "anti-Pineroite" amongst the London reviewers. Since his reluctant accession to the drama critic's chair at the *Saturday Review* in May 1898, he had lost no opportunity to puncture what he regarded as Pinero's overinflated reputation. Unlike his victim, he was not in the least stagestruck, though he was a younger half brother of Beerbohm Tree. "Frankly," he confessed in his first notice, "I have none of that instinctive love for the theatre which is the first step towards good criticism of drama." Instead, he admitted to having "the satiric temperament: when I am laughing at any one I am generally rather amusing, but when I am praising anyone, I am always deadly dull."[18] With his fastidious sense of style and detached view of life, both nourished by his time at Oxford, Max could hardly have been less sympathetic to Pinero's efforts to elevate British drama, a mission the young critic found both pretentious and ridiculous — especially as pursued by a former "mime," as Max was wont to label actors.

Unlike Shaw, Max did not consider Pinero an obstacle to his dramatic ambitions — he had none. Their mutual dislike seems to be traceable to a biographical note Max wrote to accompany a pencil drawing of the playwright by William Rothenstein, intended for publication in a portfolio entitled *English Portraits*. Rothenstein, uneasy about the tone of the note, showed it to Pinero, who objected to the text and suggested that Archer be asked to draft another one on the grounds that "he, at least, writes like a gentleman."[19] In the end Rothenstein rewrote the passage himself, and Max, professing not to mind the change, remarked that the playwright lived "in deadly fear of being seen through."[20]

Whatever the cause, Max was to find Pinero an ideal butt for his merciless wit — so much so that he could hardly resist loosing off the odd shaft even when reviewing other writers' work. The following is a representative sample of Max's pinpricks:

> If only the serio-propagandist critics had encouraged the public in believing Mr Pinero to be a wicked man, instead of showing them how good he was, the realistic drama might still be flourishing in London. (22 October 1898)
>
> In *The Gay Lord Quex* he has returned to his stage-craft. And I am glad that he has done so. For his ideas were never half so good, nor his observation of life half so sure, as his stage-craft. (15 April 1899)

Mr Courtney [in his series of lectures on "The Idea of Tragedy"] has carried his playfulness too far. . . . To begin with Aeschylus, then to work through Sophocles and Euripides to Shakespeare, and from him to Maeterlinck and Ibsen, and to finish up with *Pinero, Mr., profound significance of* — ! — that, I admit, was a quite happy thought. To trumpet Mr Pinero among the Immortals, in the rarefied air of the Royal Institution, without a smile — that was a well-deserved hit at the kind of illiterate folk who, having no standards of taste, shriek "masterpiece!" over anything that comes along. (7 July 1900)

"The Notorious Mrs Ebbsmith" . . . belongs to that period when Mr Pinero was respectfully begging to call your attention to his latest assortment of Spring Problemings (Scandinavian Gents' own materials made up, West End style and fit guaranteed). (9 March 1901)

Despite his reluctance to praise him, Max did occasionally qualify his criticisms before burying Pinero. For example, though branding *Iris* as stylistically "the worst-written of all Mr Pinero's plays," he did concede that the characters had been made to "feel and act more convincingly than in any other."[21] *Letty* inspired Max to write two reviews, one of which offered equivocal praise, and the other outright condemnation. In the first ("A Magnificent Dis — Play") he argued that

Mr Pinero would write better plays if he were a less richly endowed playwright . . . . there would be not such a general bowing-down to "our premier dramatist," if Mr Pinero were less eager to dazzle us with a generous display of his perfectly-appointed technique, and more eager to illustrate simply a philosophic idea, or to develop simply a human theme. . . . His skill is such that he can handle a whole mass of extraneous things with masterly ease, making them seem, at first glance, quite necessary. And that is the reason why he handles them. He must needs exercise and display his skill, perform feats of which all other men are incapable. Behold how many characters he can manipulate! Behold in how many exciting scenes he can place them without loss of verisimilitude![22]

In a second long article on *Letty*, published a week later, Max turned his attention to "Mr Pinero's literary style," claiming it to be "nothing but the lowest and most piteous kind of journalese" and backing this opinion by quoting several of Letchmere's more ponderous witticisms. Archer, who had himself noted without further comment "some oddities of diction in the play,"[23] again sprang to the playwright's defence:

> Ah! if it were as easy and as effective to demonstrate beauties as to suggest defects, what an article one might write on *Letty*! But it is one of the fatalities of dramatic criticism that one must praise in generalities, while for blame one can often give chapter and verse. There is nothing easier than to tear a phrase from its context and hold it up to ridicule; but as the merit of any given speech entirely depends on its relevance to the situation and to the character uttering it, one would have to quote the whole scene, and almost the whole play, in order to justify one's admiration for it. . . . And the writing, as a rule, is not merely good, but excellent — terse, nervous, sometimes touched with real pathos and beauty. I do not pretend that the criticisms levelled against certain individual expressions employed by Mr Pinero are entirely groundless; but I do most emphatically aver that the critic who fails to recognise a very rare literary quality in the dialogue of *Letty* does not know the meaning of literary quality as exemplified in drama.[24]

Archer had recently received a long, amiably abusive letter from Shaw on the topic, claiming that the critic's championship of "the dreadful leading-article clichés which serve for literary dialogue in *Iris*" was "a crime for which [Archer] ought to be condemned to sit out a Pinero Festival."[25] But if Pinero sometimes made his characters speak too rhetorically, he could also allow them to express themselves at moments of crisis with affecting simplicity. In her autobiography, Irene Vanbrugh mentions one such moment in *Letty*:

> This took place in an unusual setting — the roof of a house with the spire of All Souls, Langham Place, showing in the background. Happily dreaming and waltzing round to the strains of a barrel organ in the distance, Letty eagerly awaited her Prince Charming. Then his arrival and telling her he was a married man. All the author asked of Letty was to get up from her little chair and move very quietly away and say, "You might have told me."

Irene Vanbrugh and H. B. Irving in Letty (Illustrated Sporting and Dramatic News, *November 1903*)

This method of his repeats itself constantly in his writing — the sudden absence of all words and apparently almost trivial movements in the tensest and most shattering moments of feeling. It comes again in *The Notorious Mrs Ebbsmith* when Mrs Ebbsmith realises that all her sacrifices for Lucas Cleeve have been in vain and that he is leaving her. In simple words she encourages him to go, looks at her wrist and says, "Oh, I haven't got my watch."

These are the moments which must inevitably live with an actress more than any amount of long speeches; they are opportunities which you get in plays written by a master-hand and which never occur in those of lesser writers.[26]

iii. *"The One Great Function of Theatre"*

Pinero was prepared to defend himself vigourously when a critic such as Russell attacked his work on moral grounds, yet he continued to refrain from public comment about the quality of his work. This, of course, did not mean that he lacked opinions about his craft or reasons for the manner in which he wrote his plays. For example, to a private query from Archer about the dialogue in *Letty*, he responded with a long letter (13 October 1903) explaining exactly what he had been attempting. Neither the pedantry of Letchmere's diction when he "is on his verbal stilts" nor the simplicity of lines such as Letty's when she discovers that Letchmere is married were accidental. "The note may be a false one but it is not struck by me carelessly," Pinero insisted. "And here I want you to notice this — that I have attempted throughout (not only in this play but in others) to make the difference between the spontaneous utterance and the utterance which is the outcome of deliberate thought."

His most detailed public statement about his craft came, characteristically, in an address not about his own plays but about those of another writer and his collaborator. As the writer was no longer alive and no one considered his plays of great merit compared with his fiction, Pinero had no reason to expect that his address on "Robert Louis Stevenson as a Dramatist," delivered to the Philosophical Institution of Edinburgh on 24 February 1903,[27] would cause any offence. His preparation had been thorough, involving not merely a detailed study of Stevenson's four plays — three of which had been written in collaboration with W. E. Henley — but a close search of Stevenson's letters and essays for significant comments about drama and theatre. Throughout this investigation Archer, also a Stevenson enthusiast, had been a willing and helpful consultant.

Pinero's basic argument was that Stevenson had failed with his plays because he taken neither the theatre nor the task of writing for it seriously. Though abundantly gifted with "dramatic" talent, which Pinero defined as "the power to project characters and to cause them to tell an interesting story through the medium of dialogue," Stevenson had not been able to develop this into "theatrical" talent "by hard study and long practice. For theatrical talent consists in the power of making your characters not only tell a story by means of dialogue, but tell it in such skilfully devised form and order as shall, within the limits of an ordinary theatrical presentation, give rise to the greatest amount of that peculiar kind of emotional effect, the production of which is the one great function of theatre."

Though Pinero considered the cultivation of theatrical talent essential for a play's success, he acknowledged the further and higher aim of the drama, that "of showing the age and body of the time his form and pressure." To to do that, however, a modern playwright had to study and solve "the problem of how to tell a dramatic story truly, convincingly, and effectively on the modern stage — the problem of disclosing the workings of the human heart by methods which shall not destroy the illusion which a modern audience expects to enjoy in the modern theatre." That illusion, of course, was the realistic illusion. To create it, a playwright needed to pay close attention to realistic detail without losing sight of the overall design of an effective plot. The Victorian melodramatists Stevenson admired had been good at the latter but poor at the former:

> In strategy — in the general laying out of a play — these transpontine dramatists were often . . . more than tolerably skilful; but in tactics, in the art of getting their characters on and off the stage, of conveying information to the audience and so forth, they were almost incredibly careless and conventional. They would make a man, as in the Chinese theatre, tell the whole story of his life in a soliloquy; or they would expound their plot to the audience in pages of conversation between characters who acquaint each other with nothing that is not already well-known to them both.

Stevenson had "never either unlearned their tactics or learned their strategy" with the result that he had failed as a playwright. He had expected the stage to be a gold mine and the work easy. Once he knew this wasn't so, he, like many other nineteenth-century writers, had turned from the theatre in disgust, claiming "that the work of *falsification* which a play demands is of all tasks the most ungrateful." Pinero, for his part, saw the task as a challenge: "The art — the great and fascinating and most difficult art — of the modern dramatist is nothing else than to achieve the *compression* of life which the stage undoubtedly demands — without falsification."

Although the speech had something useful to say about Stevenson's small output of plays, it is much more interesting as an exposition of Pinero's own views on playwriting. Essentially, it amounts to a justification and a defence of the realistic "well-made play," a form developed by leading French dramatists such as Sardou and the younger Dumas from a formula pioneered by Eugene Scribe. The well-made play was concentrated around a single action, with the basic problem stated clearly in the first act, a slow and detailed exposition preparing for increasingly suspenseful conflict between the principal antagonists, a cause-and-effect chain of events leading to a major climax at the end of the penultimate act, and the resolution coming in the last one. Pinero had experimented with the form in *The Profligate* and refined it in *The Second Mrs Tanqueray* and his subsequent social dramas by taking extreme pains with his "tactics," ensuring not only that each detail followed in its most effective order but that it was convincingly motivated in terms of character, situation, and setting.

In his speech on Stevenson, Pinero emphasised the difficulty of successfully accomplishing this task:

> When you take up a play-book (if you ever *do* take one up) it strikes you as being a very trifling thing — a mere insubstantial pamphlet beside the imposing bulk of the latest six-shilling novel. Little do you guess that every page of the play has cost more care, severer mental tension, if not more actual manual labour, than any chapter of a novel though it be fifty pages long. It is the height of the author's art, according to the old maxim, that the ordinary spectator should never be clearly conscious of the skill and travail that has gone into the

making of the finished product. But the artist who would achieve a
like feat must realise its difficulties, or what are his chances of
success?

It was perhaps inevitable that the speech, which was widely reported, would provoke some unfavourable comment. The most critical
response appeared in the Edinburgh-based literary weekly *Blackwood's Magazine*. Noting Pinero's remarks about the failure of many
distinguished nineteenth-century authors to write successful plays, the
Blackwood's columnist (a friend of Henley's) asked derisively, "In
what, then, have they failed? Not in art, for the terms 'success' and
'prosperity' put that out of the discussion. They have failed to arouse
to enthusiasm an after-dinner, idle audience, which detests poetry, and
has no ear for fine English." Nor was the columnist impressed by
Pinero's insistence on the demands of realism, claiming that the style
was "as remote from the stage as from fiction. So long as you have
footlights and flies and backcloths, the drama will remain, and should
remain, a mere mass of conventions."[28]

This opinion was also strongly endorsed by Shaw, who derided the
elaborate preparations of the realistic well-made play as "superfluous
attempts to persuade the audience to accept, as reasonably brought
about, situations which it is perfectly ready to accept without any
bringing about whatever."[29] Despite the vehement objections of critics
such as Archer, Shaw was to oppose the form throughout his long
career, maintaining that

> no writer of the first order needs the formula of the well-made play
> any more than a sound man needs a crutch. In his simplest mood
> when he is only seeking to amuse, he does not manufacture a plot: he
> tells a story. He finds no difficulty in setting people on the stage to
> talk and act in an amusing, exciting and touching way. His characters
> have adventures and ideas which are interesting in themselves, and
> need not be fitted into the Chinese puzzle of a plot. . . . Now if the
> critics are wrong in supposing that the formula of the well-made play
> is not only indispensable in good playwriting but is actually the
> essence of the play itself — if their delusion is rebuked and confuted
> by the practice of every great dramatist even when he is only amusing
> himself by story-telling — what must happen to their poor formula

when it impertinently offers its services to a playwright who has taken on his supreme function as the Interpreter of Life? Not only has he no use for it; but he must attack and destroy it; for one of the first lessons he has to teach a play-ridden public is that the romantic conventions on which the formula proceeds are all false.[30]

If Pinero had ever debated the issue publicly, he would no doubt have argued that such a statement begs the question, as a non-Shavian "Interpreter of Life" may well view life as determined or repetitive and therefore express that view theatrically by means of tightly patterned, cause-and-effect plot structures. Indeed, ultimately the difference might be simply between seeing life as tragic rather than comic.

In any case, as the author of *Trelawny of the "Wells"* was aware, theatrical fashions come and go, and the public's idol of today may be its scapegoat tomorrow. He was about to receive a salutary reminder of just how fickle its favour could be.

iv. The Dancing Doll

Pinero's next comedy, *A Wife Without a Smile*, staged at Wyndham's Theatre on 12 October 1904, was an odd piece in a number of respects. Subtitled "A Comedy in Disguise," it combined farce and satire, the tone being generally sardonic. That the playwright felt edgy and defensive about the play even before its production is suggested by a curious announcement that appeared in the papers and the programme: "As it is quite uncertain at what point, if any, the interest of this piece commences, the audience is respectfully requested to be seated at the rise of the curtain."[31]

The "request" appears to relate to a minor newspaper controversy a year earlier on the most suitable timing for evening theatre performances. To avoid the familiar nuisance of late arrivals, Archer had proposed 4:30 to 7:30 p.m. — play first, dinner later — but Pin considered this a half measure that would leave "the 'confounded British Aristocrat' upon whom . . . the existence of our theatres in a large measure depends . . . freer to devote himself to 'musical comedy.' " In any case Myra Pinero was positive "that no lady over 18 years of age, escaping from a theatre at 7.30, could make herself presentable for the dinner table by 8.30 or anything like it."[32] So evening performances continued to begin at 8:00 or 8:15, and late diners continued to arrive during the first act.

There is some internal evidence in *A Wife Without a Smile* to support the idea that it was intended as a satire on the questionable taste of Edwardian audiences. The protagonist is an ex–civil servant and habitual practical joker called Seymour Rippingill, who at the age of forty-four has come into a small fortune, divorced his first wife, and married a younger and prettier one. His problem is that the second Mrs Rippingill never smiles, appearing to be totally without a sense of humour. The plot, like the old fairy tale, centres on Rippingill's strenuous and ill-conceived attempts to make her laugh. His most outrageous attempt is at the expense of a newlywed couple, the Webbmarshes, who are amongst the houseguests at his luxuriously appointed villa and boathouse at Taplow. He ties a cord to the springs of a sofa in the Webbmarshes' room, pushes the free end through a hole bored in the floor, and attaches it to a doll that is left dangling a couple of feet from the ceiling of the living room below. Any amorous activity on the sofa is thus immediately registered by the doll's jigging up and down.

The joke of course backfires. Rippingill is hoist with his own device when his wife, on learning to her great relief and amusement that a flaw in his divorce proceedings has made their marriage null and void, rushes off to besport herself on the sofa with a young artist. The practical joker is left at the end of the second act gaping in horror and embarrassment at the vigorously dancing doll. In the final act Rippingill's discomfiture is completed by a series of ironic reversals. The young artist's fervour for the wife cools when he finds that most of her tresses are false; she with Gilbertian ruthlessness then decides that remarriage to a wealthy bore is preferable to poverty with the artist; and Webbmarsh, the intended butt of Rippingill's joke, determines to turn the whole sordid episode into a play that will "hurl, as it were, chunks of raw, bleeding humanity upon the boards" and expose the "shallow and soulless" morality of middle-class society.

But if Pinero was intending to satirise contemporary theatrical tastes (including perhaps even the "raw meat" served up by avant-garde groups such as the Stage Society and the new Vedrenne-Barker management at the Court Theatre), he got more than he bargained for. Most of the first-night audience, though relatively indifferent to the play's rather ponderous verbal wit, guffawed uproariously at the doll, which was jiggled more and more vigorously by a laughter-intoxicated stagehand as the play continued. At the final curtain, boos from the gallery were drowned by cheers from the stalls, but the calls for the author were answered instead by "Dot" Boucicault, the play's lead actor, who announced that "Mr Pinero is not in the house" — at which a voice from the gallery cried out, "And a bloody good job, too!"[33]

Next day the doll — which A. B. Walkley in his *Times* review labelled an "Erotometer"[34] — had become more notorious than *Mrs Ebbsmith*. It was the subject of sternly disapproving leading articles, ambiguous remarks in gossip columns, caricatures in the picture papers, and coy comic verses, such as the following stanza from a ditty called "Naughty Dolly" about a man "in sad disgrace for giving his little girl a doll":

> "Sir," she said in accents hard,
> (That's Mamma) "I'd have you know
> Dolls within this house are barred,
> Since that Mr Pinero
> Tied that horrid jigging thing
> To a sofa by a string."[35]

Though Pinero insisted that the doll be manipulated in a less unseemly manner at subsequent performances, and gave a press interview in which he stated that the significance of its movements had been misinterpreted by some critics and members of the audience, the scandal dominated the news for a week or so. One magazine even claimed to have interviewed the doll, which, while admitting its French origin, protested its innocence and censured the audience, quoting in its defence the royal motto *Honi soit qui mal y pense.*[36] George Redford, the Lord Chamberlain's reader of plays, seemed to second this rebuke; he stated that he had licensed the comedy for public performance without the least suspicion that it might be thought indecent. "For my part," he told the *Evening News,* "it would seem to be sheer insolence to seek for a vile suggestion in the work of our greatest dramatist."[37]

But many people did. For a while they flocked to Wyndham's to savour or investigate the scandal. After attending the second night, the reforming editor and guardian of public morals, C. T. Stead, proclaimed that both the play and the doll should be publicly burned by the common hangman. King Edward himself (despite having tested the springs of many a sofa himself) was rumoured to have declared that the doll was indecent and should be removed from the play — which, of course, he had not been to see. And Max had a field day "defending" the playwright's respectability:

> Appearances would look black against anybody but Mr Pinero. Anyone but he would stand convicted of impropriety. In his case it is felt there must be some unfortunate mistake. And so, indeed, there is. Mr Pinero has received in audience the representative of a daily newspaper and spurned the factitious doubts of his rectitude. He does not, he declares, envy the minds of those who have read an indelicate meaning into his doll. The declaration is as final as it is superfluous. It leaves us nothing to say but that we, whose state Mr Pinero does not envy, cannot but envy him his — cannot but envy a man whose mind is so untainted that he never, in repeated rehearsals, foresaw that we might find an indelicate meaning which was bound to be staring all of us in the face. . . . And so I conjure Mr Pinero not to be angry. No man should judge others by himself, if he himself be on a pinnacle.[38]

Whatever he had meant to imply by the doll business (presumably merely hugging and kissing on the sofa, not full sexual intercourse), Pinero found himself severely compromised by its reception. Writing to Archer (2 November 1904), he stated that he was "not angry but exceedingly indignant" at the "insult and opprobrium" that had been poured on him. As for the play itself, he reported that there had been

MRS. GRUNDY WANTS TO SPEAK A WORD WITH THE GENTLEMAN
WHO PULLS THE DOLL STRINGS.

"Limelight" caricature on the "dancing doll" controversy (The Entr'Acte,
October 1904)

276

packed houses for a fortnight "composed mainly of people who have come to search for the indecent suggestions discovered by certain gentlemen of the press. And in many instances people have left the theatre expressing dissatisfaction at not finding evidence of indelicacy. The middle-class playgoer — i.e. the dress circle man and his wife and daughter has never been near us at all and shews no sign of coming. . . . In these circumstances I cannot see a very long career for the little piece."

The comedy did indeed prove a commercial failure, lasting just seventy-seven performances in London and a pitiful sixteen when Charles Frohman produced it (with an immobile doll!) in New York a month or two later. There one critic described the play as "an abortion . . . centred about a filthy idea" and the people who had ventured to see it, knowing of its ill repute in London, as "so stewed in the stench of their own vulgarity [that] nothing but something more vulgar could thrill through their filth-saturated brains."[39] Although such extreme vituperation was no doubt motivated as much by the desire to sell newspapers as to protect morality, the fact remained that Pinero's standing as a serious playwright had been dangerously undermined.

At this low ebb in his fortunes, help suddenly came from an unexpected quarter.

...14...
England's Premier Dramatist

i. His House in Order

At the height of the outrage over Pinero's latest comedy, London's most respectable theatre manager came forward (like the redeeming clergymen in *Mrs Ebbsmith* and *The Benefit of the Doubt*) to protect his reputation. Ignoring their seven-year rift, George Alexander approached Pinero with an urgent request for a new piece for the St James's, to be written on a subject of the playwright's own choosing and produced under his direction and conditions. According to A.E.W. Mason, Alexander's friend and biographer, the manager

> was convinced . . . that if Pinero lost his high status amongst the dramatists the status of the stage would be inevitably lowered. He discoursed earnestly to me as we walked our horses along the rails. Pinero brought to his work not only a supreme knowledge of the conditions under which a dramatist must work, but intellectual equipment and a courage which few others possessed. The joke and clever twist which falsified all the characters in order to bring down the curtain upon a comfortable conclusion, were devices foreign to Pinero, impossible to him. He might have perpetrated a vagary. But you must not forget on that account the work which had gone before. It had an integrity and aim which were not to be denied. Alexander had therefore put his theatre at Pinero's disposal.[1]

278

England's Premier Dramatist

The "Entr'acte Annual," 1905.

33rd Year.   Now in Preparation.

MR. GEORGE ALEXANDER TO MR. PINERO:—" NOW, LOOK HERE, I HAVE THE
FIRST CLAIM ON YOU, MIND!"

Pinero and Alexander (The Entr'Acte, *November 1904*)

279

The offer was gratefully accepted, and the old firm were soon back in business with a new play, appropriately titled *His House in Order*, that proved their greatest success.

Some two and a half years earlier, Pin had moved from Hamilton Terrace to a fine house at 14 Hanover Square. There he had a new workshop where, as he poetically told Archer (6 June 1902), "my aery buildeth in the cedar's top, and dallies with the wind and scorns the sun, and affords a fine view of the old square."[2] However, in early 1905 he acquired a second property, a country "cottage" at Northchapel on the Sussex-Surrey border. "Stillands," as it was called, was over two centuries old when the Pineros purchased it: an attractive, two-storey, red brick house with a walled garden, adjoining a farm of the same name. When working on a new play, Pin had long been in the habit of secluding himself in a rented house by the sea or in the country to be free from interruptions. Now Stillands became the Pineros' real home. Henceforth they came to town only when necessary, which in Myra's case was hardly at all.

His House in Order contains suggestions of the countryside where it was written. It is set in a country mansion owned by a wealthy member of Parliament, Filmer Jesson, who as the play begins is about to give a park to the nearby town as a memorial to his first wife, Annabel, killed three years before in a carriage accident. The gift is faintly reminiscent of the orphanage that Mrs Alving in Ibsen's *Ghosts* erects in the name of her dead husband, except that Filmer believes his former spouse to have been the epitome of virtue and order, whereas Mrs Alving's "tribute" is hypocritical. He has since married Nina, his son's governess, whose best efforts at household management fall far short of Annabel's. The second Mrs Jesson is therefore subjected to invidious comparisons by her husband and by Annabel's relations, one of whom, Geraldine Ridgeley, has taken over the running of Filmer's house. Poor Nina cannot even romp on the lawn with her dogs (one of Myra Pinero's favourite pastimes) without being censured collectively by the Ridgeley clan.

Two details of the plot have particular biographical interest: Filmer's obsession with order and Nina's reaction to persecution. Obsession with order was a trait that Pinero shared, having acquired it in his father's law office in reaction to John Daniel's careless ways. The pens, ink, and blotter on Pin's desk were always kept exactly in place, as were the books on his study shelves. Even the corrections on the neatly written manuscripts of his plays are clear and precise, so that no printer could have a moment's doubt as to the author's intention. He paid bills by return of post, and he or his secretary immediately answered all correspondence, whether important or not, precisely dating every letter. Even on holiday Pin could not relax his standards. In his autobiography Sutro recalls accompanying him for a fortnight in Paris, where they got on splendidly — except for Sutro's habit of littering their hotel suite with opened envelopes and Pin's compulsion to pick them up and put them in the wastepaper basket. In *Filmer Jesson* the playwright simply magnified this trait to the point of caricature:

> FILMER. . . . When I ask that my house shall be in order, I am asking not only that my luncheon, my dinner, shall be decently and punctually served; not only that this inkstand, this paperknife, may be found invariably in the same place; but that every wheel in the mechanism of my private affairs, however minute, shall be duly oiled and preserved from grit. I am asking that the impressions of home and its surroundings formed by my son in boyhood shall be such as will influence him in after years to his mental and moral advantage; in short that I may be permitted to pursue my public career in complete confidence that nothing — nothing — outside that career is liable to the slightest confusion and derangement. [*Sitting upon the settee on the right*] That is what I intended to convey by "my house in order."
>
> HILARY.[*Bringing himself to a sitting posture*] By Jove, Filmer, and a precious tall order, too, upon my soul!

Pinero would also have identified with the hapless Nina, reviled on all sides despite her best efforts to please her persecutors. The constant sniping at his plays by certain reviewers, after the months and even years of effort he put into them, must have tempted him at times to round on his critics. Instead, he tended to bury such feelings in his work — which may indeed help to account for the chorus of hostility that his last "comedy in disguise" had provoked. In *His House in Order*, however, he adopted the strategy of imaginatively heaping "coals of fire" on his persecutors by having his ill-used heroine abstain from revenge when she is given the perfect opportunity to exact it.

Nina comes into possession of a packet of letters that reveal that Annabel had a lover who is the real father of the son Filmer imagines to be his. Then, as Clayton Hamilton puts it, "instead of using this weapon to establish her own superiority, she decides, after due consideration, to wear the pale halo of 'the people who have renounced.' "[3] In fact, she is talked out of using the letters by Hilary Jesson, Filmer's sympathetic elder brother, in the play's climactic scene. Some critics have regarded this as a flaw, but whether Nina would have behaved as nobly in real life as she does in the play is beside the point. The secret of the comedy's effectiveness is that it is brilliantly designed to make every member of the audience sympathise with Nina, thrill to her renunciation of revenge, and, finally, when Filmer learns the truth from Hilary and sends the Ridgeleys packing, bask in the glow of seeing her reinstated in her rightful place. No fairy tale could offer greater satisfaction, for to secretly demonstrate moral superiority over your persecutors and then be richly rewarded for virtue is the sweetest form of revenge.

The writing of *His House in Order* took most of 1905. During this period both manager and playwright behaved, as A.E.W. Mason puts it, with "watchful cordiality." By July Pinero was ready to discuss casting. Whereas he wanted the eight-year-old Derek Jesson played by an actress ("I doubt whether you could find a real boy to look it and do it. A girl is, as a rule, so much the more graceful, charming and receptive"[4]), he required a real Frenchwoman for the boy's governess, Mlle Thomé. ("No one can give you natural broken English but a foreigner. Forgive me if I have inconvenienced you in this matter."[5]) By 22 September Alexander was gently pushing him for production dates, and Pinero replied with good-natured anguish:

> The dates you give me in you letter are most attractive. But can it be managed? You ask me if I have finished. Cruel! Heartless! Have I ever finished till about ten minutes before the first rehearsal? The position of affairs is this. Acts I and II go to the printers on Monday.

Act III I am now engaged upon; and then there is Act IV to follow. I can't *hurry*; that paralyses me. But the piece *may get itself done* by the date you mention — or earlier — and I will spare no natural effort to that end.

I have taken enormous pains over the thing, as I know you will believe; and when it is complete it will appear — I hope — as if it were a week's work. Which is what I understand by technique.[6]

A fortnight later the manager received the page proofs for the first two acts, together with a confident note from the playwright wishing that he could also have sent Act 3, "which is progressing famously . . . so that you could have seen at the first glance how every hint and every clue contained in the earlier acts are followed up and rounded off."[7] Pin also remarked that he hoped Alexander would not be "very seriously disappointed" in his own part, that of Hilary Jesson, who had necessarily "to play somewhat of a waiting game." Alexander replied he had found the first two acts "lifelike and interesting from beginning to end" and that "Hilary could not be better or different in the earlier part of the play."[8]

Although both author and manager had hoped to begin rehearsals in December, casting problems delayed the start of rehearsals for a month. But Alexander nevertheless secured precisely the actors Pinero had asked for. These included Iris Hawkins, an expert player of boy's parts, and a real Frenchwoman for Mlle Thomé. The leads included Herbert Waring as a precise and pedantic Filmer, Irene Vanbrugh as Nina, and, of course, the manager himself as Hilary, the play's ironic but sympathetic *raisonneur* upon whom the success of the play's argumentative climax depends. Pinero, as agreed, had sole charge of rehearsals and was, as Vanbrugh later recalled, "very inspiring, but very exacting":

> The great scene in the third act, with Nina's disclosure to Hilary Jesson (a part so suited to George Alexander), we went through for the first time without our books, rather breathless but not altogether dissatisfied with the attack we had made on it.
>
> Pinero, walking slowly up and down the stalls, his hands behind his back, his hawk-like eyes keen under the heavy, black eyebrows, came up on the stage by the steps which had been specially placed for

him and said, "Not a bad run-through; now we will get to work on it." Taking it sentence by sentence, I may almost say word by word, he guided us both through that scene like a true master knowing every intonation, every movement, every feeling, every reaction to those feelings from both the characters. He had no script in his hand, knowing every word of the whole play by heart. Not one syllable could you alter without his immediate correction.[9]

At rehearsal Alexander accepted this intense supervision "as meek as a lamb,"[10] though the following note suggests that he privately felt a little aggrieved:

> My Dear Pin,
>   Thank you for your kind words today. I know I am a disappointment at rehearsal and that you are very patient and sympathetic. I think you will find that I shall serve you better than you imagine. Talk to me quite freely, and I will do my best to be worthy of your trust. Only don't lose confidence in me.
>   Yours ever,
>   Alec.[11]

Pinero replied (20 January 1906) that he had "*every* confidence" in Alexander's ability "to deal successfully and brilliantly with [his] very difficult task" and apologised if his anxiety that the manager should do himself "the fullest justice" in a part which was "a little foreign to [his] usual methods" had showed itself too strongly. "Once more, Alec — I look to you to pull us through, and I feel sure that I shall not be disappointed." Nor was he, even though at a press preview the night before the official first night (1 February 1906), Alexander nervously cut out Vanbrugh's climactic speech![12]

The reviews for the London production of *His House in Order* were almost universally enthusiastic, triumphantly justifying Alexander's support of Pinero. The playwright was now not only forgiven his previous transgression but reestablished as England's premier dramatist. "Take it all in all," said Walkley in the *Times*, "the play is a very choice specimen of Pinero's work; in other words a play yielding the highest possible measure of delight." Archer in the *Morning Leader* was equally complimentary: "A play with bright and witty lines and with situations which showed that our leading dramatist's skill has not failed him." In the popular papers the reviews were unreservedly ecstatic, the *Daily Mail* describing the piece as "the finest, noblest play that stands to the record of even so brilliant a dramatist," and the *Daily Express* calling it "the most important achievement in comedy contributed to the English stage for a very long time." Alexander, too, reaped a rich harvest of praise for a part that in other hands might have appeared tedious and verbose. According to the *Daily Telegraph* he had played Hilary Jesson "with a breadth and sobriety which was of incalculable service to the play. Through the third and fourth acts he is the life and soul of the piece, bearing with ease the burden of the plot upon his shoulders, and carrying it to its triumphant conclusion." What especially pleased the *Telegraph* was that for once Pinero had put virtue rather than vice at the centre of his plot: "It has been conceived, thought out and written on the loftiest plane. It deals, not with the mean liaisons of gaudy, disfigured fragments of humanity, but with a broad, grand theme that must appeal to the spark of nobility that lurks in each of us — the attainment of real happiness by virtue of self-renunciation."[13]

Only the unblinking Max perceived exactly how cleverly Pinero had flattered his audience and manipulated its emotions. Remarking that "what does not, on reflection, commend itself highly to one's 'best self' may, at the moment, have pleased one's inferior self very much indeed," he proceeded ruthlessly to expose the machinery of the plot, concluding his review with the following "apology":

> Remember, it is my "best self" that is speaking to you. As a critic, retrospective and cerebrative, I cannot ignore the play's fundamental weaknesses. But do not forget that my inferior self enjoyed the play immensely. Figments though the Ridgeleys are, I was really anxious that Nina should put them to rout. I really was touched by her magnanimity in handing the letters to Hilary, and really annoyed by it. I was really delighted when, in the fourth act, Hilary, provoked beyond bounds by the continued insolence of the Ridgeleys, and by his brother's continued acquiescence in it, drew the letters from his breast-pocket and thrust them into his brother's hands. Judged on a low plane, "His House in Order" takes very high rank indeed.[14]

Time seems to have confirmed this judgement. *His House in Order* was perfectly designed to arouse "the greatest amount . . . of emotional effect" in its original Edwardian audience, but it has not greatly interested later generations. The St James's production ran continuously for fifty-seven weeks, a total of 427 performances, and took over £78,000 at the box office — to say nothing of the further profits reaped by the two touring companies Alexander organised to stage the play throughout Great Britain. Daniel Frohman's New York production, however, opened at the Empire Theatre on 3 September 1906 to mixed reviews and achieved a respectable, but not impressive, run of 127 performances. There were only two subsequent London revivals: the first at the St James's Theatre in late 1914 featured most of the original principals and ran for 73 performances, the second in 1951 at the New Theatre achieved 114. Nevertheless, a well-acted and presented period revival would probably demonstrate that the play's skilful plotting can still grip an audience.

ii. Private Business

On 19 May 1905 a young man named Edwin Stephens responded to an advertisement in the *Times* requesting applications for the position of private secretary to Mr A. W. Pinero. Three days later Stephens received a reply, sent from Stillands, arranging an interview at Hanover Square the following evening. After another interview a fortnight later, Stephens was appointed to the post, which he held for two and a half years. Except on rare occasions, he worked at Hanover Square, often receiving instructions by post from his employer at Stillands. Stephens accumulated some 200 of these letters. Although most are brief and functional, they do provide glimpses of Pin's private life that are all the more interesting because of the lack of intimate family correspondence.

Soon after Stephens took up his position, evidence came to light that the previous secretary, a Mr Rice, had been intercepting and pocketing small royalty payments sent to his employer and using his headed notepaper for various unauthorised transactions. The sums involved were not large, but Rice, aware that he could not hope to deceive his precise and methodical employer for long, had resigned his position to reduce the risk of detection. Pin was annoyed when he found what had been going on, but apart from informing people that Rice had left his service took no action against him, despite his fear that "this wretched fellow is on the road to the police-court." The playwright ignored a letter from Rice regretting that his former employer had been troubled by his "paltry affairs," but when Rice's father-in-law, a Mr Croft, wrote asking if Pinero would consider giving Rice a reference if he repaid his "debt," Pin was quite nonplused. "Mr Croft, I am sure, knows only a part of the fellow's misdeeds. My position is a difficult one. How on earth can I say anything favourable of the man?" Stephens was called upon to explain everything to Mr Croft "clearly and frankly and, of course, without exaggeration." The reason for Rice's petty thefts was finally revealed when a young unmarried woman, pregnant with his child and in great distress, came looking for him at Hanover Street. Pin wrote to Stephens, "I am much concerned at Mrs Pinero's account of the unfortunate young woman's visit. It seems to me she is much to be pitied and I would willingly help her, to the extent of a few pounds, in her sad strait. Perhaps Mr Croft would do the same."

After this upsetting start, Stephens's work took a more orthodox course. Much of his time was spent politely refusing a never-ending stream of requests and demands from various people, including minor managements ("Tell the Bexhill-on-Sea gentleman that I am giving *The Second Mrs Tanqueray* a rest at present"), actors and actresses Pin liked ("Write a nice letter to Mrs Saker and tell her that I regret my new play does not give me the opportunity of serving her") and others that he didn't ("Tell the persistent Miss Molesworth that I am in the country till the winter"), newspapers ("Tell the *Tit-Bit* gentleman that, to my regret, I am too busy to forward the contribution he is kind enough to ask for"), and would-be playwrights ("Send back the rubbish sent me by a Mr Andreas Maciel. Say I am travelling — anything!"). On one occasion (17 July 1907) Pin's instructions show him responding rather testily to a request for special terms from Mrs Patrick Campbell: "You may tell Mr Wilde, on the point of reducing the fees, that if the play were *not* an old one, the fees would hardly be so low as seven per cent. You may add that this particular piece, though played constantly in *second* and *third* class towns, is always reserved for Mrs Campbell in the *first*-class towns. But whatever is done or suggested, this lady will always haggle." Then, with weary generosity, the note ends by giving Mrs Campbell what she wanted: "As it is, she may play a [free] matinee provided she gives two night performances [a week]."

Much of Pinero's mail had to be answered personally, and some idea of the volume of this private correspondence can be inferred from the playwright's frequent orders for additional stocks of his headed notepaper and letter cards. On 21 August 1905, for example, he wrote to Stephens, "Please let me have 2000 cards *exactly similar* to the enclosed. Get Stockley to do them as soon as possible. I find to my horror —for I use them in preference to note-paper — that I am out of them." The death of his mother on 2 October 1905 created another stationery supply emergency. Eight days later Stephens bore the brunt of his employer's annoyance over the printer's failure to provide the mourning cards:

> Stockley must be a slow person. I have no use for people about me who are not alive and active and cannot put on steam in an emergency.
>
> Of course, both addresses must be on my, and Mrs Pinero's, mourning cards. Have you delayed putting them in hand to make this enquiry? . . .
>
> The packet of stationery you handed me on Friday contained five quires of notepaper and envelopes for less than half the quantity.

Two days later he acknowledged the arrival at last of a small packet of stationery, adding that in the meantime his "letters of condolence — which I must acknowledge with my own hand — have got into such arrears that the task before me is a terrible one." These difficulties were compounded on 15 October when Pin learned of the sudden death of his old chief, Sir Henry Irving. In a note requesting Stephens to attend to the sending of a wreath, he also asked him to "hurry up

Stockley over the stationery," explaining that "poor Sir Henry's death is taxing my present little stock still further."

Apart from normal secretarial duties, Stephens was also required to assist with a variety of matters relating to the Pineros' life in the country. One of his first tasks was to find suitably framed maps of Sussex and Surrey to hang in the hall at Stillands as a guide for walks and outings. On Stephens's suggestion Pin agreed to a composite map of the two counties but insisted on having the best available one, properly varnished, backed, and stretched. After much correspondence on its nature, size, and frame, the map finally arrived. "It is a capital map," Pin acknowledged but could not say as much for the framing. "Instead of being stretched tightly upon stout canvas, the thing flaps and bellies like a sail in a dead calm. . . . However I must put up with it at present, for I need the map." Stephens was more successful in other matters: acquiring a new pet for his employer ("The dog arrived safely yesterday. A *nice* dog"); ensuring a continual supply of cigarettes, cigars, tobacco, and pipe cleaners; and purchasing sports gear such as "a dozen best golf-balls and two or three artificial tees" and "a set of bowls — not a very costly set, but sufficiently good not to split or otherwise go wrong."

Other wants to which Stephens attended included buying new and secondhand books and exchanging selections from Mudie's circulating library. Most of the bought books were on the theatre — for example, Aristotle's *Poetics*, the *Memoirs of Mathews*, Bram Stoker's recollections of Sir Henry Irving (which Pin wanted as soon as it was issued), and Henry Saxe Wyndham's *Annals of Covent Garden Theatre*. Others were more down-to-earth, such as garden guides ("I think there is a little book called *Mrs Beeton's Shilling Book of Gardening*. If so — and if it deals with the Kitchen-garden — buy it and post it to me") and an illustrated catalogue of glasshouses and conservatories. As far as general reading was concerned, Myra liked biographies of royalty and society figures (*Confessions of a Princess*, *A Story of the Late King and Queen of Serbia*, and *Recollections of Lady Dorothy Nevill*), whereas Pin enjoyed adventure fiction (*The Lost Leader* by E. Phillips Oppenheim and *Ithuriel's Spear*), short stories by W. W. Jacobs ("if these are new stories, buy the book"), and spicy literary biography (*George Sand and Her Lovers*).

Riding, walking, and especially bicycling were all regular activities at Stillands. Even Stephens was expected at first to cycle some 15 miles from the nearest railway station (with tins of tobacco tied to his handlebars!) when his employer required his services in the country. In summer 1906, however, Pin bought a car and hired a chauffeur, though subsequent breakdowns of the one and illnesses of the other made him wonder whether they were worth the trouble and expense. A second chauffeur supplied by a London agency a year later proved even less satisfactory, as the following (rather self-revelatory) letter indicates:

Stillands,
North Chapel, Sussex.
24th June 1907

Dear Stephens,

The "relief" car has arrived and the Daimler Limousine has started for London. The object of my writing is to say that I am a little doubtful as to whether Spellar will suit me. His driving is all right. He is rather inclined to take risks; of that, however, he can be cured perhaps by warnings. But his manners are bad, if they can be said to be called manners at all. I want a smart, bright man who will occasionally condescend to touch his cap to his "lady and gentleman", not a heavy, loutish fellow who looks and behaves as if he had come out of a cab-yard. In short, I must have a chauffeur who is fit to be a gentleman's servant; and this Spellar, at present, is not. You had better go into the matter thoroughly with Mr Eggleston's secretary. Read this letter to him.

I am also in doubt as to whether Spellar is up to the work of cleaning his car. On arriving here, the first thing he did was to instruct one of my gardeners to wash the car for him! I don't think he is over-strong. He walks in a shambling fashion, like a weak person. The German who is driving the other car is a far more likely looking chauffeur.

Faithfully yours,
Arthur W. Pinero.

If he was unhappy with Spellar, Pin was generally pleased with the efforts of his young secretary and took an almost avuncular interest in him that lasted long after Stephens left his service in early 1908. Shortly after taking up his next position, Stephens wrote a gloomy letter to his former employer, who characteristically advised him to stick it out: "The fact is, *all* work is dull, whether in Monmouthshire or Hanover Square; and the only way of counteracting the dullness is to provide yourself with plenty of mental recreation. I advise you to turn your leisure to good account by reading the best stuff you can get hold of assiduously." Before many years had passed, however, Stephens, along with hundreds of thousands of his generation, was experiencing more excitement than he could ever have thought possible. Writing to him (23 October 1918), care of the 120th Heavy Brigade of the Royal Ground Artillery, British Expeditionary Force, France, Pin exclaimed

> What an interesting time you are having! A little different from the days when you wrote innumerable letters to pertinacious actresses, telling them there was nothing for them in the next play.
>
> Splendid as your present job is, however, I hope it will not be long before it is over and you return to civil life. But, mind, you are not to come back till you have imposed "unconditional surrender" upon the enemy and have accompanied your battery in a triumphant march through a German city.

It is pleasant to be able to record that these wishes came true.

iii. National Affairs

Pin would have liked nothing more at this stage of his career than to be able to live quietly in the country, free not only from the demands of playwriting but also from the obligations that his eminence in the theatre entailed. After the triumph of *His House in Order*, he had taken a "well-earned vacation" from writing, explaining to an interviewer for the New York publication the *Theatre Magazine*, "I have been working steadily for twenty-five years. . . . I believe that if ever a man deserved and needed a vacation I did. Perhaps work, literary work, is harder for me than for some people. At any rate I have almost exhausted myself in my unceasing effort to give the best there was in me to the theatre. Now I am tired out."[15]

Though his vacation from writing was to last more than a year, other claims on his time could not be avoided. He had, for example, been an honorary examiner in elocution for his alma mater, Birkbeck College, from 1893 to 1904 and from 1899 was vice-president of the College Council. In 1906 he was appointed to the council of the newly formed Royal Academy of Dramatic Arts, a body he was to serve for the next twenty years, in addition to the voluntary help he gave its students from time to time by means of private coaching and rehearsals.

He was also called on to help with the organisation of special theatrical occasions, of which the most notable was the Ellen Terry jubilee in June 1906. When Irving had died the previous October, Pin had been to the fore in petitioning the Dean of Westminster for the burial to take place in the abbey, though Alexander had been the principal organiser on this occasion. But with the jubilee, Pinero's long-standing friendship with Ellen Terry, his eminence in the profession, his conscientious attention to detail, and — perhaps above all — his no longer being an actor made him the logical choice for chairman of the executive committee.

Ideally, the jubilee would have been held at the Lyceum, where Ellen Terry had been Irving's leading lady for nearly a quarter of a century, but the former "temple of art" had declined into a music hall, and moreover the vast auditorium of Drury Lane was needed to accommodate the huge audience expected. The programme posed all sorts of problems as to who should be invited to perform and what each person might be asked to do. Sir Charles Wyndham, for example, wanting to be seen to advantage in suitably dignified material, rejected the idea of appearing in a farce and agreed to play in a scene from *The School for Scandal* only after he was satisfied about the rest of the casting.[16]

The worst blunder Pinero and his committee made was their initial failure to ensure that actresses were adequately represented in the programme. In a curious oversight, not even one woman had been invited to serve on either the general or executive committee, with the result that apart from Ellen and other female Terrys, and Lady Bancroft as mistress of ceremonies, no leading actresses were featured in the programme as first drafted. When Ellen Terry saw this, she told the committee that it was such a good joke to have "an actress-less programme in honour of an actress" that she didn't want to spoil it by appearing herself! The committee then endeavoured to solve the problem by the last-minute inclusion of a series of *tableaux vivants* featuring Lillie Langtry, Violet and Irene Vanbrugh, Kate Rorke, Julia Neilson, and other leading actresses, whereupon Ellen, still not mollified, wrote a letter to the chairman:

> Dear Pinny,
>   An amusing notion this, of women of talent appearing in *tableaux* only, but if that has been decided upon by the Committee, I elect if you please, to appear only in a tableau myself. I couldn't, I couldn't, I *couldn't* do anything else![17]

Poor "Pinny," who had merely wanted to ensure that she was centre stage at her jubilee, was by now at his wits' end. "More Ellen Terry today, and every day. My brain is giving out," he exclaimed to Archer a month before the performance.[18] But Ellen finally relented, and the great jubilee performance on 12 June 1906 — a theatrical marathon lasting over six hours — ended up a triumphant success.

This, however, was just one of Pinero's public concerns at the time. As "England's premier dramatist," he found himself called on to support a variety of theatrical campaigns: for the rights of dramatists, for the abolition of censorship, for the erection of a Shakespeare memorial in London, and for the establishment of a national theatre. Advocates of these causes soon realised that Pinero's respected, moderate, and sensible voice was of the utmost value to them, even though he was now generally identified with the "old gang" of dramatists rather than the "progressives."

Though the idea of a national theatre had been promulgated by a number of writers, critics, and players during the nineteenth century, its principal Edwardian advocates were William Archer and Harley Granville-Barker. Their parliamentary-style blue book, *A National Theatre: Scheme and Estimates,* was printed and privately circulated in 1904 but not published until October 1907, after the completion of the Vedrenne-Barker management of the Court Theatre, in many respects a pilot project for a national repertory theatre. Pinero supported their campaign but for reasons of his own. In a lecture to an Edinburgh literary society in February 1903, he noted that the playwright Edward Fitzball had asked in 1858, as others were asking fifty years later, for a national theatre to remedy the decline of English drama. In Pinero's opinion, however, a national theatre could do no such thing; its job would be to celebrate achievement:

> A fine play is the rarest product of any country. But where other countries are ahead of us — at least I hold so — is that when a fine play is produced, they do something for it. They preserve it; they take a reasonable amount of pride in it; they do not allow it, when it has once been seen and admired, to lie neglected, forgotten; they take good care that from time to time it shall be displayed as evidence of what they can do in that particular department of art and literature. And there you have, in a nutshell, one of the great uses — I do not say the only use — of a theatre which, whether established by the State, or by a municipal corporation, or by private munificence, shall be independent of the purely commercial conditions which too frequently govern the drama in Great Britain. Yes, but you will ask, have we existing in Great Britain sufficient material to stock such a shop? I think we have.[19]

A misleading summary of this speech, implying he had claimed that English drama had declined so far there was no point in having a national theatre to preserve it, led to a brief exchange and clarification of views between Pinero and Archer in the *Morning Leader,* though the latter, aware of Pin's real position, was simply using the report for further publicity. Several months later, in April 1904, Pin read the proofs of Archer and Barker's book, which he told the critic was "the crowning point of your work for the theatre,"[20] but in a subsequent letter (16 June 1904) he expressed doubts about the project's chances in the existing political climate:

I met Mr Balfour at dinner a few weeks ago . . . and managed to turn the talk towards the subject of a National Theatre with a school attached to it. Mr Balfour airily observed "Englishmen can never be *taught* anything". That was, of course, applied to the school rather than to the theatre, but it shewed the attitude that such men take with regard to matters outside the political game. Balfour left the room after this weighty pronouncement — over which I had a wrangle with him — having to return to the House; and I remarked to Sir Edward Grey, who sat on the other side of the table, that we evidently had nothing to look forward to from the present Government and that we must pin our hopes on the next one. Grey gave us one of his wan smiles and said nothing.

Following the publication in October 1907 of Archer and Barker's blue book, the idea of a national theatre gained impetus, and on 10 June 1908 a public meeting was held at the Lyceum Theatre in support of its establishment. Pinero was called on to move the resolution in favour of appointing a committee to draft a suitable scheme. His speech was controversial in its scathing rejection of arguments for a national theatre based on the disparagement of contemporary Shakespearian productions, contemporary English drama, or the work of the leading actor-managers. He, on the contrary, held that such a theatre "can only serve as a natural stimulant for a drama that is already vigorously alive and healthy. It will never create a new drama, nor restore an old drama that is moribund." The reasons for establishing a national repertory theatre, he went on to say, were to provide the opportunity for good plays to be revived, to establish a practical "court of appeal" for cases "where the dramatist's work has miscarried through a failure in the acting, or through the impatient temper of the time," and to offer the dramatist "his ideal representation" from a company of actors "accustomed to play together with unity of method and point of view — all familiar with each other's temperaments and personalities, trained to the habit of contributing to the general harmony of effect, and inspired by the desire to subordinate personal interest."

As for the financial side of the venture, he asked his audience not to be dismayed by "the prohibitive estimates" that his "old friend Mr Bram Stoker" had given in a recently published article, estimates derived "from memoranda made during his long and honourable association with the late Henry Irving." A national theatre needed a different model:

> No man admired Irving more than I; no man loved him more deeply. Standing upon this ground I rejoice in the opportunity given me of acclaiming him a fine actor, a great man, a noble, generous gentleman; but I do say that a more recklessly extravagant manager never signed cheques in the office of a theatre. We all gloried in Henry Irving's management and — perhaps rather thoughtlessly — in its magnificence; but nobody in his senses would commend a policy such as Irving's, if policy it could be called, as the policy to be pursued in the conduct of a National Theatre.[21]

Nine months later an *Era* editorial, noting that the executive committee of the Shakespeare memorial scheme — including the Lord Mayor of London, Bulwer-Lytton, Hare, Forbes-Robertson, Tree, and Pinero — had reported in favour of the establishment of a national theatre, announced, "We may now consider the theatre a *fait accompli*."[22] The total cost of building, equipping, and endowing it was estimated at a modest £500,000 — just one-fifth of the annual subsidy granted to the National Theatre that was finally built sixty-seven years and two world wars later at a cost of £17 million.

iv. The Thunderbolt *and* Mid-Channel

Despite his long vacation from playwriting, Pinero had never intended to retire from his real work. A severe bout of influenza in autumn 1906 dragged on into the new year, but by February 1907 he was able to get up from his sickbed in Hanover Square and venture outside for brief strolls, encouraged by the gift of a walking stick from the cast of *His House in Order,* which had completed a full year at the St James's. Accompanying the stick was this note: "The only [blot] on this happy anniversary is your Absence — we are all so delighted to know you are better and we hope that when you leave your House in

Order to take your walks abroad you will use this stick less as a support than as a mark of our Affection and Gratitude."[23]

After a brief convalescence in Paris, Pin set off for a working holiday in Wiesbaden, Germany, where he began writing a new serious play for the St James's. "My theme interests me very much," he informed Alexander (20 April 1907), "and, if I am capable of realising my intentions, the treatment should be moving and, I think, novel."

The novelty of *The Thunderbolt*, as the new play was called, was threefold in relation to Pinero's other social dramas: it was set not in London but in a provincial city; it did not focus on a central female character but on a family group; and its theme was not sexual double standards but greed. As several commentators were to point out, the play may have been influenced by Granville-Barker's *The Voysey Inheritance* (1905), in which the moral basis of a family's respectability is tested by the revelation of a tainted inheritance. If Barker's play is more challenging in its thematic treatment and subtler in its characterisation, Pinero's not only has the more exciting plot but is expertly crafted in every respect.

Subtitled "An episode in the history of a provincial family, in four acts," *The Thunderbolt* portrays the limitations of "respectable people" when given the opportunity of acquiring a fortune to which they are legally but not morally entitled. From the play's opening sequences, it is obvious that in the normal course of events Edward Mortimore, a wealthy brewer who has died the previous day, would have left his fortune to his illegitimate daughter, Helen Thornhill, rather than to his surviving brothers and sister, from whom he has been estranged for many years. In the absence of a will, however, the official next of kin appear to be the legal heirs. Pinero's strategy is to demonstrate how the surviving Mortimores and their spouses behave individually and collectively in this situation and how they then react to the "thunderbolt" that a will leaving everything to Helen has been deliberately destroyed by one of the Mortimore wives. The main scenes are ensemble ones, the climax coming in the third act as the family catches out the husband of the offending woman when he tries to take the blame on himself. The rest of the clan in turn are shown to be a cause of the wife's crime, having continually persecuted her because of her father's inferior trade.

Though the unsympathetic Mortimores hunt together in a pack like the Ridgeleys, the characterisation of the family in *The Thunderbolt* is generally more rounded. For example, the hypocrisy of the two senior brothers, James and Stephen, becomes evident when they determine to resign from their leading positions in the local temperance league rather than give up their shares of the dead brewer's fortune. James is aware of the irony, whereas Stephen remains oblivious to it; no doubt Pin was quite deliberate in making the former a building contractor and the latter a newspaper editor. Their sister Rose attempts to cut a figure in London society even though her husband, Colonel Ponting, has little money and fewer manners. The couple regard themselves as members of the "smart set" and therefore above the conventional conduct of their provincial relations ("In London, my friends, reg'lar mournin' is confined to the suburbs nowadays. May I have an ash-tray?").

The only sympathetic Mortimores are the youngest brother, Thaddeus, a forty-two-year-old music teacher, and his wife, who is looked down on by her brother-in-laws' wives and their circle for being a mere grocer's daughter. Snobbery, as rife in "Singlehampton" as in London, has punished Thaddeus for "marrying beneath himself" by denying him "the choral societies, and the High School, and the organ at All Saints" that the Mortimore family connections and his own talent would otherwise have secured him. Phyllis's destruction of Edward Mortimore's will, then, was motivated by her love for Thaddeus and her desperate wish to make up for these disappointments, but the act only brings her deeper misery when she meets the decent young woman she has effectively disinherited.

Albeit one of Pinero's most impressive dramas, *The Thunderbolt* had a disappointing run of less than two months after it opened at the St James's on 9 May 1908. The reviews were generally respectful but not of the kind likely to attract the fashionable audience that usually patronised Alexander's theatre. The *Daily Telegraph*, for example, commented that

"The Thunderbolt" is not a play which attracts, but it is a play which stimulates the mind. It is at once powerful and depressing. It is mainly satirical, and yet here and there reveals tender touches, as though goodness were struggling painfully in the midst of super incumbent gloom. But the one fact which emerges triumphantly and which no well-equipped critic could possibly miss in the performance of Saturday night was the admirable dramatic workmanship, whereby a theme, somewhat thin and painful, was made to hold an audience through the whole of its four acts, and become more impressive as it proceeded.[24]

George Rowell, in his edition of *Plays by A. W. Pinero*, suggests that Pinero may have been stimulated to write *The Thunderbolt* by the beginnings of the new repertory movement in Manchester and elsewhere, and he speculates that it "might have earned a very different response played by Manchester's skilled ensemble with authentic accents."[25] As it was, George Alexander's attempt to resemble an impoverished provincial music teacher consisted of wearing a new corduroy jacket with his usual immaculately pressed trousers. But Pin blamed no one but himself. In a letter to Archer (17 June 1908), who had been on holiday when *The Thunderbolt* was produced, he remarked: "I cannot flatter myself that it has failed from any other cause than that it is composed of material for which the public has no fancy. The drab in literature and drama is not for our climate. . . . I have now snapped my fingers, and am at work again."

The idea for his next play had come while he was still struggling with the final act of *The Thunderbolt*. Writing to Archer on 2 December 1907, Pin indicated that he was having trouble finishing his present job because his head was "buzzing with a scheme for its successor." *Mid-Channel* effectively represented his last look at his most familiar serious theme: the hypocrisy of sexual double standards, exemplified in this case by a wife's discovery that though she is prepared to forgive her husband's infidelity, he is not prepared to condone hers. Linked with this idea are two others: the difficult period of adjustment married couples often face in middle age and the spiritual barrenness that results from forgoing children in favour of social climbing.

Neither the pleasure-seeking Zoe Blundell with her circle of male admirers (whom she calls "tame birds") nor her coarse-grained stockbroker husband, Theodore, is an appealing theatrical character, but Pinero had outgrown the conventional lovers of sentimental comedy. He informed Clayton Hamilton that "he had come to a point in his development where the only characters who acutely interested him were mature people whose lives had 'somehow gone awry.' He liked to speculate "upon the difference between what they were and what they might have been."[26] This the play does convincingly but at a cost. Because Zoe and Theo have no credible purpose in life, their story is dramatic but constricted, and the total effect depressing rather than tragic. But once again the plot is expertly organised, and as a remorseless indictment of the moral bankruptcy of middle-class society, the play has a grim integrity.

Mid-Channel proved as unpopular with the St James's audience when it opened there on 2 September 1909 as had *The Thunderbolt*. It ran less than two months, despite a moving portrayal of Zoe Blundell by Irene Vanbrugh. She attributed the failure to the lack of a part in the play for Alexander, claiming that "the public at that time was so accustomed to connect the actor-manager with his theatre that anything produced there without him lost prestige."[27] Alexander had indeed felt hurt that the playwright did not want him to play Blundell and wrote him a note immediately before the production saying that the part afforded "a great acting opportunity, and would have greatly added to my reputation as an actor."[28] But the main reason for the production's failure was probably neither Alexander's absence from the cast nor the shock of Zoe's suicide at the end of the play (which on the opening night sent "an audible shudder . . . through the house")[29] but the unflattering mirror the playwright had again held up to his audience. Writing to Pin after the end of the run, Shaw accurately summed up the situation:

> Between ourselves, I greatly dislike the audience at the St James's Theatre. . . . They are the very people you are getting at in the play. They do not enjoy that scene where the young man has to put up with familiarities from the maid. The women do not want to be told that

they are not wives in any real sense, but only kept women. The
husbands, who have brought their wives to the theatre because they
are afraid of quarreling if they stay at home, do not want to have the
quarrel thrown in their faces across the footlights. And as you have
no sort of mercy on them and no sort of hope for them, and simply
rub their own misery and disgrace into them with the skill and
ruthlessness of a scientific torturer, they stay away, and give Alick
thereby a broad hint that they are not taking it kindly.[30]

v. G.B.S. Bestows a Knighthood

Pinero and Shaw had become much better acquainted in recent
years, and, though they had hardly become close friends, they had
developed a mutual respect sometimes tinged with irritation but more
often with amused tolerance. Success had perhaps mellowed them
both, but Pin had never resented G.B.S.'s attacks on him in the
Saturday Review the way he resented Max's. For one thing, Shaw had
always admitted his prejudiced point of view as a rival dramatist,
whereas Max's jibes had often seemed gratuitous. Moreover, Shaw,
like Pinero, cared about the theatre, though his caring generally took
the form of strenuous campaigns against what he saw as its weaknesses
and defects. Pinero, because of his much greater success within the
existing theatrical establishment, was less committed to theatrical
reform than his rival, but, as the acknowledged leader of the commercial dramatists, his support was necessary to the "progressives" for
whom Shaw had constituted himself spokesman if their various campaigns were to get anywhere.

An important bridge between the two playwrights was Archer,
though the basis of their friendships with him was dissimilar. The
consistent support and encouragement Archer gave to Pinero's work
contrasted strongly with his equally consistent disparagement of
Shaw's dramaturgy. It is not surprising that this was a continuing cause
of friendly contention between Shaw and Archer, the former claiming
his criticisms had done Pinero less damage than the latter's praise. In
September 1903, for example, Shaw told Archer:

In your letter to me you say the absolute truth about Pinero; but when you write about him for the public, and for *himself* (which is the main thing) you will lie like a trooper about him & lure him down to further Iris abysses with a horrible childish ignorance of the fact — which can only be learned in public life, not defined by wit or talent — that flattery will ruin a man more surely and swiftly than any extremity of abuse. Walkley has done Jones no harm. I have encouraged Jones, but if you read my notice of Michael [*Michael and His Lost Angel*] you will see that I dealt faithfully with him. You have almost destroyed AWP; another Iris and, with Barrie already far outrunning him, he is lost.[31]

It was Archer who became the separate confidant of both playwrights when five years later a split threatened between the "old" dramatists and the "new." Some forty members of the Society of Authors, unhappy with the existing membership of its Dramatic Subcommittee, announced their intention at the society's annual general meeting on 20 March 1908 to form (or, rather, revive) the Dramatic Authors' Society. Shaw, who had been elected to the society's committee of management in 1906 and more recently to the Dramatic Subcommittee, was the driving force behind an attempt to turn the subcommittee into an effective pressure group for playwrights against anyone or anything that threatened their professional interests. Pinero, though also on the subcommittee, had agreed to become acting chairman of the organising committee for the proposed Dramatic Authors' Society, which he envisaged not as a political body but as "a little, exclusive society for our amusement and, perhaps, benefit."[32] To forestall a split between dramatists, the management committee of the Society of Authors (effectively Shaw and the society's secretary, G. Herbert Thring) ordered a reorganization of the Dramatic Sub-committee so that both factions of playwrights would be adequately represented. Pinero, irritated at what he saw as an attempt to cut the ground from under the new society, nevertheless stayed on, becoming chairman of the Dramatic Sub-committee in early 1909 — and first president of the Dramatists' Club that was inaugurated soon afterwards. Shaw continued to attempt to work behind the scenes.

In the midst of these political maneuverings, and considerable activity over issues such as the national theatre and censorship campaigns, Shaw conceived the notion of seeking a knighthood for Pinero. It is impossible to be certain quite what his motives were, but in a letter to Archer (3 July 1908) he announced, "I have made up my mind to make Pinero a knight. In this National Theatre scheme we have a lot of knight-actors; but we have no knight-dramatist except Gilbert who is too old and not really representative. Pinero is the man. His position, like Irving's, is strong enough to save him from any suspicion of wanting a knighthood on personal grounds; and the accolade would undoubtedly strengthen the theatre movement."[33] But this seems specious. Apart from exaggerating the number of available knight-actors (at the time Bancroft, Hare, and Wyndham) and ignoring the possible candidacy of James Barrie (who was to hold out for a baronetcy), the political influence of a knight-dramatist, appointed by the very government the campaigners were seeking to persuade, could hardly have been expected to make any significant difference to their cause. It seems more probable that the notion of knighting Pin appealed strongly to Shaw's sense of humour and that he set about pulling the appropriate wires largely for the sheer fun of manipulating the establishment.

Having first obtained Pin's reluctant consent "to suffer knighthood on public grounds," Shaw attended a garden party given by Prime Minister H. H. Asquith's wife on 2 July 1908. According to his report to Archer,[34] he bluntly put the proposal to her in front of "a whole assembly of duchesses," whereupon Mrs Asquith replied that "she could not do it until next November." Although Shaw kept up the campaign through the rest of 1908, November proved too soon, and as late as 4 May 1909 Shaw, having heard no news, wrote to another ally, Lord Esher: "What about Pinero's knighthood? Barrie wouldn't dress it; Jones wouldn't look it; Pin would do both to perfection; and the national aspiration towards a higher drama would receive a thrilling impulse. Could it be managed for June?"[35] In fact, it had been already arranged for the birthday honours list, but if the establishment had indeed responded to Shaw's wire-pulling, it had no intention of telling him of his success in advance. The belief that Pinero would receive a knighthood had been in the air at least as far back as June 1907, when the newly honoured Sir W. S. Gilbert, replying to Pin's letter of congratulations, predicted it would come to him at a much younger age.

Shaw and Archer were amongst the many friends and colleagues who wrote congratulating Sir Arthur Pinero when his honour was announced on 25 June 1909. Thanking the first for "his brotherly pat-on-the-back," Pin remarked that Shaw, busy as he was, found time for many kindnesses. But replying to Archer, Pin wrote, "Of all the kind letters I have received today yours is the one that gives me most pleasure. You will know why." Shaw may have been responsible for the initiative that had resulted in Pinero's knighthood, but Archer had encouraged the work that earned it.

If the new knight felt at all inclined to vanity, however, another letter he received at this time helped to keep things in proportion. Beerbohm Tree having been knighted in the same honours list as Pin, a friend of both sent each a congratulatory note, mixing up the envelopes. The letter Pin received read, "My dear Tree, hearty congratulations. You ought to have had it long ago. But why Pinero?" Pin sent the note to Tree and in exchange received the one meant for himself: "My dear Pinero, hearty congratulations. You ought to have had it years ago. But why Tree?"[36]

.. Act 4 ..
Resolution
(1909—1934)

...15...
Shaw and Pinero

i. The Dramatists' Club

If Shaw had been playing Mephistopheles to Pinero's Faust by tempting him with a knighthood, the latter had no intention of selling his soul for it. He continued to maintain his independence from radicals and socialites alike, although he remained attached to his clubs (which at least respected his privacy). Despite his distaste for self-advertisement, Pin had felt obliged to accept the honour on behalf of his craft in much the same spirit as Henry Irving had before him. Waiting outside the throne room at Buckingham Palace for the investiture, he is said to have nervously wondered aloud to Tree whether he could be dubbed under gas![1] Thereafter he ignored the title except for shortening his signature from "Arthur W." to "Arthur" Pinero. Nevertheless, the honour that affirmed Sir Arthur's standing as the most successful dramatist of the time also marked the fading of his success. For more than a decade he had been wealthy enough to write for himself, but now he expressed his distaste for well-to-do society even more abrasively than before, and the unflattering portrait he painted of its vanities and hypocrisies was one few of his audience cared to regard.

He did still enjoy the company of colleagues, especially of old friends such as Jones and Carton; this was his main reason for founding the Dramatists' Club, which he saw as filling a need not quite served by the Garrick. But while plans for this "little, exclusive group" went

Sir Frank Lockwood, caricature in anticipation of Pinero's knighthood (Cassell's Magazine, *1899*)

ahead, Shaw exerted all his powers of charm and persuasion to keep Pinero on the Dramatic Sub-committee of the Society of Authors. "*You are absolutely indispensable*: don't give way to anybody," Shaw told him. "You are the only man whose presence or absence makes a serious difference in the authority with which we can act."[2] The two debated the merits of the various possible candidates for the reconstituted committee, Shaw agreeing to most of Pin's suggestions but expressing strong reservations about several, including Sutro, whom he described as "too thickskinned for the give and take of democracy."[3] Despite outbursts and misunderstandings from several of their supporters — notably Sutro on the one hand and Thring on the other — a mutually acceptable list was gradually worked out. "It is certainly a blessing to have you to deal with in the matter," Shaw flattered Pin in a letter outlining his vision for the future of the society:

> Remember, there is no such thing as the Society of Authors really. There is an office, and an office staff, and a capital fund, and an income, and an agency for collecting debts and bullying dishonest publishers and managers, all of which we can use for our own purposes as a professional organisation of playwrights. But that organisation doesn't exist yet: we have got to make it. . . . You know yourself what it used to be — nothing for the Sub-committee to do, and nobody there to do it. And your chaps are just as bad: they haven't a notion of what to do or how to do it. We'll have to create an organisation capable of dealing with the managerial combinations which are now being forced into existence by economic pressure.[4]

By the beginning of February 1909 the composition of a reformed Dramatic Sub-committee had been settled between Shaw and Pinero, the list favouring the "old guard" by the inclusion of Carton, Jones, Sutro, and several others, the "new" playwrights represented only by Shaw, Barker, and Cicely Hamilton, an actress-playwright. In addition Shaw ensured that Pinero was elected chairman of the new subcommittee. On 11 February Pin wrote thanking him for his "good offices in this matter," without which he was sure "the present *rapprochement* could never have been brought about." The letter was headed with a new and impressive London address, 115A Harley Street (in fact, situated around the corner in Devonshire Street), which was to be Pin's London home until his death. Drawing Shaw's attention to the change, Pin disarmingly added that he hoped at his new premises "to merit a continuance of that patronage and support which have

hitherto been accorded me. The gentry waited on at their own residences. Plumbing in all its branches."

Although Pin was prepared to give attention to trade concerns
through the Dramatic Sub-committee, he was more interested in fostering convivial relations among his colleagues. The Dramatists' Club
was launched at a foundation luncheon at the Criterion Restaurant on
17 March 1909, its initial members including Barrie (who failed to
attend the lunch, having mistaken the week), Carton, Somerset
Maugham, Sutro, and H. M. Paull, a retired civil servant turned minor
playwright who became the club's honorary secretary. Pinero of
course was the unanimous choice for president. Shaw, who had departed on a trip to Algiers the day before, was offered membership a
month or so later in the expectation he would refuse, but he instead
accepted immediately and sent Paull an unsolicited donation to make
sure of his place.[5]

Shaw had little liking for exclusive male clubs, his private intention
being to convert this one into a trade union of dramatists or at least
into a professional body that would act collectively in its own self-interest. His basic tactic was to propose new members he hoped would
stir up the "old guard" and make the club a more outward-looking
affair, but he soon realised his folly. He later informed his biographer,
Hesketh Pearson, that the club had begun "as a clique of old stagers
who insisted on excluding everyone who was not 'a dramatist of
established reputation' which was their definition of one of themselves."[6] Each of his nominees was vetoed by the existing members.
The first reject was St John Hankin, blackballed on the grounds that
he had been publicly contemptuous of Pinero's work. (Soon afterwards Hankin committed suicide, not because of his rejection, of
which he was probably unaware, but because he believed he had
contracted a fatal disease.) When subsequent attempts to nominate
Hall Caine and Gilbert Murray were similarly vetoed, Shaw wrote
Pinero an indignant letter (17 March 1910) charging that the club's
members were deliberately affronting him.[7]

Pin's reply the following day attempted to humour Shaw while
educating him in club manners:

No member of the club is more beloved than you are — indeed, is so much beloved; but the fellows like to attack you because they know you are clever, don't mind really, and can defend yourself. And two thirds of your candidates are, you will yourself admit (in the privacy of your chamber) rotten. Poor Mr Hankin! It is a cowardly objection to wage against him now that he is dead; but when he was alive, he used consistently to attack men who were more successful than himself, and that was not considered quite good form — men, I mean, practising the same calling as himself. The big 'uns never do this; nor the nice little ones. As to Caine — that able, preposterous creature — you cannot, and do not I am sure, wonder that he is regarded as unclubbable. He is, from a reasonable point of view, uneverything-able. Murray is, however, in my view, entirely eligible. I told the members so months ago, in your absence, said all I could for him, and was, like yourself, crushed. We shall get him in, in time.

Shaw was not reassured, arguing that in his view the most serious case had been Hankin's, because "if we boycott the young chaps who attack us, we shall find that we have boycotted the choice and master-spirits of the age; for they all begin like that."[8] Later that year (Murray having been at last elected at Pin's insistence) Shaw wrote that he was considering putting up Arnold Bennett for membership. Pin replied (15 October 1910) that he not only doubted if Bennett had "done enough dramatically" to qualify but thought that "some of the fellows" would object to him "on the score of his having written rude things about myself." However — no doubt bearing in mind Shaw's remarks about Hankin — Pin went on to say that if they did so he "would put it to them that they would be paying me a very poor compliment by black-balling Mr Bennet [*sic*] on that account." The letter then concluded with a wickedly pointed postscript: "Besides, if *that* were a sufficient reason for excluding a man, how came they to elect — ? But I won't pursue the subject."

ii. The Censorship Debate

One of Shaw's principal reasons for trying to ginger up the Drama-tists' Club had been to persuade — or shame — its members into presenting a united front against the absolute censorship powers of the Lord Chamberlain and his examiner of plays. The playwrights had mixed attitudes on this matter, the newer writers being far more concerned and indignant than the older ones, who had learned to work within the censor's guidelines — which effectively banned any frank dealing with sexual, political, or religious matters. To the "new," noncommercial dramatists, such prohibitions struck at the very purpose of their work ("to force the public to reconsider its morals," as Shaw would later put it).[9] To the established commercial playwrights, in contrast, these restraints actually provided a significant aid to dramatic tension: the kind of theatrical frisson implied by titles such as *The Notorious Mrs Ebbsmith* or *The Benefit of the Doubt*.

Shaw's objections to the censorship were the result of both philosophical conviction and personal harassment. If the theatre was to be a force for social change, then what he termed "immoral and heretical plays" were necessary to challenge the existing order. But, as he had discovered with *Mrs Warren's Profession*, writing such works was professionally hazardous under the existing system. More recently, with pieces such as *The Shewing-up of Blanco Posnet* and *Press Cuttings*, Shaw had deliberately flouted the censor's rules in order to make a fool of him.

Pinero had adopted a totally different strategy to extend the limits of what was permissible in the theatre. Rather than question accepted moral standards, he had kept (just) within the rules in plays such as *The Second Mrs Tanqueray* by showing apparently respectable people falling short of those standards. He had thus acquired such a stern reputation as a moralist that (as mentioned in Chapter 13) the examiner of plays had not even thought of questioning the blatantly suggestive effect of the dancing doll in *A Wife Without a Smile*. Pinero's real objection to the censorship, which eventually led to his willingness to campaign for its abolition, was that it subjected drama to demeaning controls imposed on no other branch of art or literature. It was, in effect, a slur on his profession.

On 29 October 1907 he had been amongst the signatories of a letter to the *Times* protesting against dramatic censorship and calling for its abolition. Early the following year Sir Henry Campbell-Bannerman, the Prime Minister, agreed to receive a deputation of authors and playwrights at Downing Street, but when he fell ill the deputation instead met the Home Secretary, Herbert Gladstone, on 25 February 1908. After a brief introduction by Barrie, Pinero, working closely from a draft by Archer, outlined the historical background to the censorship and argued that it was "manifestly repugnant to the whole spirit of the Constitution that the property and reputations of any class of citizens should lie at the mercy of a man, empowered to sit in secret judgement, and — without hearing any pleadings or giving any reasons — to issue edicts from which there is no appeal."[10] The dramatists were, though, prepared to accept as "a transitional expedient" the establishment of a court of appeal to consider disputed rulings.

Shaw had agreed not to join the deputation because as a censored playwright he would have appeared prejudiced. (Archer and Barrie privately feared he would annoy the politicians if he attended.)[11] But when a joint committee of both houses of Parliament was set up in 1909 to consider submissions on the censorship of stage plays, Shaw was determined to control the dramatists' performance. As Michael Holroyd observes, he "assigned to himself the job of voice-trainer," coaching the playwrights appearing before the committee, "tirelessly, showing where one or the other had gone off-key during a performance, and expounding the general effect their chorus should produce on its select audience."[12] As a climax to the show, he had prepared and printed at his own expense an 11,000-word statement he distributed in advance to the committee in the expectation that they would debate it with him. He was devastated when they ruled it inadmissible as evidence.

Pinero had kept aloof from these proceedings during the early hearings of the parliamentary committee, as he was more concerned about the completion and production of his latest play, *Mid-Channel*. On 7 July 1909 he replied with some irritation to a call to action from Shaw, insisting that he was so far behind with his work he had to put his foot down and refuse to be disturbed on any account whatever. Reacting to the news that Barker, despite illness, was busying himself over the hearings instead of getting on with his latest play, Pin commented grimly that he was beginning to think "that the preservation of the drama is engaging so much of the dramatists' time that soon there will be no drama to preserve." For him (unlike Shaw), work came first, propaganda last.

Once *Mid-Channel* had been produced, however, he prepared himself conscientiously to give evidence to the committee, duly appearing before it on 24 September 1909, the final day of sitting. Admitting that he had never been asked by the censor to modify any of his plays, he told the committee, "I want to take my stand with the great majority of my fellow dramatists in urging . . . the view that the autocratic power of the Lord Chamberlain over the drama is opposed to the best interests of our art. In my opinion it degrades the dramatist by placing him under a summary jurisdiction otherwise unknown to English law, and it operates as a depressing influence on a body of artists as fully alive to their responsibilities as any in the country."[13] Though he did not claim that the censorship had yet seriously retarded the growth of the drama, he believed that it was "entering on a period of new fertility and power, and that this development must be seriously impeded by the continuance of an irresponsible Censorship." Nevertheless, he was prepared to accept the continuance of censorship provided dramatists could at least have the right of appeal to a board of arbitrators appointed jointly by the Lord Chamberlain and the dramatists.

Reporting to Archer the following day, Pin revealed his relaxed attitude about the campaign by remarking that he really thought that his "performance of the role of The Reasonable Man" had done "the comedy no disservice." Although he was happy to chat informally about the proceedings with Archer and Barker, he was against summoning a special meeting of the Dramatic Sub-committee of the Society of Authors as "it would mean discussion, dissension, and — G.B.S.!"

In due course the censorship committee reported to Parliament endorsing most of the recommendations and compromises that Pin and others had advocated, but nothing was done beyond setting up an advisory committee that in practice proved ineffectual. Shaw was bitterly disappointed and disillusioned, but Pin, wiser in the ways of the world, had not expected any real reform from the politicians. The final irony came in November 1911 when the Lord Chamberlain appointed as co-censor, with George Redford, the actor Charles

Brookfield, author of a smutty little farce called *Dear Old Charlie* that mocked Barker's banned drama *Waste* as "*Sewage*" by "Mr Bleater." Archer was furious, writing in the *Morning Leader* that the appointment was "nothing less than a blow in the face to all who have any care for the past, or hope for the future of English drama."[14] Pin, who quite liked Brookfield and had even helped him out with a small loan two years earlier,[15] was inclined to be more tolerant. Writing to Shaw on 27 November, he remarked that he did not think Brookfield was "at all a bad man for the post which has been offered him" and that it would be "time enough to attack him . . . when he really does misbehave himself." When Shaw in response proposed that the playwrights draft their own bill to remove the censorship, Pin ironically suggested (5 December 1911) that as Shaw would need to abolish the monarchy first, he should perhaps begin by drafting a bill to that effect. Two weeks later Redford, exhausted by the controversy, resigned, leaving Brookfield in sole charge. This slap in the face was ultimately the only change achieved by the entire debate and the expenditure of so much time and effort. The Lord Chamberlain's powers to license and censor plays remained intact for another fifty years.

iii. Pinero and the "New" Drama

Though Pinero and Shaw maintained their philosophical differences, their personal relationship had become quite close, to the surprise of observers such as Barker, who had once told Archer that "nothing would ever put those two in double harness."[16] Pin often thought Shaw's idealism wrongheaded but could not resist his kindness. When, for example, the *Saturday Review* published a savage and woundingly personal attack on the Bancrofts under the guise of reviewing their joint autobiography, Shaw immediately wrote to Pinero (24 May 1909) pointing out "how it could be answered in such a way as to put the Bs right again with the readers of the paper and take the sympathy from the slater." Pin thanked him for his "extreme good nature" in the matter — especially as Shaw himself had once written "slashing articles" in the same journal — and passed on the suggestion to Bancroft.[17]

A month earlier in a speech at a Royal General Theatrical Fund dinner, Pin, in paying tribute to the leading younger dramatists — including Barrie, John Galsworthy, Barker, and Maugham — had made special mention of "the brilliant Mr Shaw," despite the risk of "his being annoyed at my bringing upon him a little extra publicity." Noting that Shaw had come into the world not long after himself, Pin remarked that as a playwright Shaw was "still young and shows no sign of growing up. He is the elfish Peter Pan among dramatists."[18] This indeed was how Pin tended to regard his former rival these days: as an enfant terrible whose outbursts and enthusiasms he regarded with an indulgent and almost avuncular eye.

For his part, Shaw tried with youthful missionary zeal to persuade Pinero to support a new repertory scheme that in effect was an attempt to transplant the Vedrenne-Barker Royal Court regime to the West End. The American impressario Charles Frohman (Daniel's brother) had agreed not only to make the Duke of York's Theatre available for the experiment but to underwrite the venture for a whole season. Hearing that Pinero had refused to write a play for the enterprise, Shaw asked him to reconsider on the grounds that

> this new game will involve a sorting out of authors that has not hitherto been effected. At present you cannot compromise yourself by a success, as you have so often done, without being thrown into the same category with the Charley's Aunters & Knights-Were-Bold-ers. . . . The repertory plan will draw a line nearer the top; and I shall take care to ticket myself for the top compartment. I think Frohman has succeeded in persuading the public that the present address of that compartment is the Duke of York's Theatre; and though of course your accession would help this pretension more than it could help you at present, yet in the long run his batches of authors will be stronger than any of us can be individually; and the repertory men will get classed as the intellectuals as against the fashionable long-runners.[19]

Acknowledging the force of Shaw's "wicked and Jesuitical arguments," Pin nevertheless replied (6 May 1909) that rather than "cling

desperately to the coat-tails of the intellectuals," he would have to let
his work take its chance with the critics, though somehow he had at
the back of his mind "a notion that in the long — or the short — run
it is only the quality of the work that tells; and that when a man does
his best, his best will be no better in St Martin's Lane, and no worse,
let us say, in King Street." In response to further requests, however,
he did agree to allow Frohman to include a revival of *Trelawny of the*
"Wells" in his repertory programme, though he warned Shaw (16
March 1910) that the system was "a cut-throat business" because the
public would "make one play its favourite, and then to hell with the
rest of the pieces."

And this was exactly what happened. *Trelawny* proved so popular
that it outperformed all the new plays with the solitary exception of
Galsworthy's *Justice*. Both Barker's *The Madras House* and Shaw's
Misalliance, with their preponderance of talk over plot, failed to
please the West End audience and, to the discomfiture of their authors,
were speedily removed from the repertory. Even with *Trelawny* playing most nights, Frohman suffered a heavy financial loss from the
experiment, which he thankfully brought to an end when a temporary
closure of the theatres because of the death of King Edward gave him
a suitable excuse. In tribute to the manager's philanthropy, Pin and
others treated him to a special dinner at the Garrick.

An interesting aftermath of the repertory debacle occurred three
months later when a debate on playwriting appeared in the correspondence columns of the *Times*. The controversy was prompted by an
article entitled "Leaving Aristotle Out," in which the paper's dramatic
critic, Walkley, gently chided Shaw and Barker for writing plays "on
the go-as-you-please principle, with total disregard of such trifles as
unity of impression, continuity and cumulative force of interest."[20] As
was inevitable, both men replied to the charge, Shaw claiming that he
was totally in favour of Aristotle and personally took "the greatest
pains" to secure "unity of impression, continuity, and cumulative force
of interest" and had thus been "led finally to the Greek form of drama
in which the unities of time and place are strictly observed."[21] Granville-Barker went further, claiming that in Europe the previous fifty
years had been marked by "a great re-testing of method both in the

writing of plays and the acting of them," adding that "in England our native development has but newly begun; and this go-as-you-please method, so far as I know it, is rather an earnest, if a little too consciously an earnest, endeavour to — no, not to be clever and original, but simply to find the most appropriate way of saying just what dramatically one has to say."[22]

Barker's letter annoyed Pinero, who wrote to the *Times* on 27 June sarcastically observing that his "friend Mr Granville-Barker" had complimented "the elder brethren of his craft by telling us that the development of our native drama is an event of quite recent date."[23] Barker then added insult to injury by rejoining that though "foreign criticism at least is apt to date the claim of our modern drama from the production of *The Second Mrs Tanqueray* in 1893," he himself was of the opinion that "our present development of native drama is not much more than ten years old." It had come, he claimed, from an "extraordinary development during that time of the playwright in embryo," whose work, if produced at all, had been staged "mostly . . . on a Sunday evening or a Monday morning or a Tuesday at teatime — to quote a phrase of Sir Arthur's that he will have forgotten."[24] This was too much for the knight; he replied with the deadly thrust that "if Mr Frohman were to publish figures in connection with his recent spirited enterprise in St Martin's Lane they would be an eye-opener as to the precise value" of public support for "the go-as-you-please drama in its latest aspect."[25] This implied reference to the recent triumph of *Trelawny* over *The Madras House* and *Misalliance* ended the argument.

iv. *"Fine Souls" and "Big White Teeth"*

Before long Sir Arthur would regret his unchivalrous allusion to his own success and the failure of others. As a follower of Aristotle, he should have been aware of the penalty for hubris, for he, too, was writing to please himself regardless of the taste of his audience. After the grim drama of *Mid-Channel*, he had decided to return to farce, perhaps in response to Shaw, who had told him, "There is not enough fun in Mid-Channel: you bit hard; but you do not let yourself wag your tail. The fun is in you: it is the divine secret of the light hand and the merry and charitable heart; but you seem to me to have begun to mistrust it in these later times: I miss Baron Croodle among all these dull, scared, vulgar people who are so fiercely true to their own life, and so very false to yours."[26] It cannot be said, however, that Pinero's next piece demonstrated either a "light hand" or a "charitable heart." The unpleasantness of most of the characters in *Preserving Mr Panmure* undermines the comedy and leaves such a bitter aftertaste that even its author admitted that it was "a grimy little satire at best."[27]

The action takes place at the country house of an apparently reformed middle-aged roué, St John Panmure, recently married to an excessively pious young widow (the leading light of her vicar's "Guild of Fine Souls") who insists on his giving a ten-minute sermon twice a week at family prayers, a task in which his incompetence is exceeded only by his embarrassment. When, however, he is helped out of his misery by Josepha Quarendon, his stepdaughter's pretty but impoverished governess, he impulsively kisses her, provoking a hysterical reaction from Josepha that leads the women of the household to band together in a hunt for the culprit. But out of gratitude to Mrs Panmure, whom she regards as her benefactress, Josepha not only refuses to name her assailant but states that he was not Panmure. He is thereupon deputed by the women to interrogate the various male guests in the house in order to force a confession from the guilty party.

The idea is suitably farcical, but compared with the ease and good nature of the Court farces, the plot is ponderous and the tone mordant. Josepha's distress and hysteria are of an order that suggest rape rather than a kiss, and Panmure's pathetic eagerness to blame and castigate others (including Josepha) to prevent the discovery of his own guilt passes beyond the comic to the contemptible. One need only compare Panmure's moral cowardice with the mental paralysis that causes Posket to sentence his own wife in *The Magistrate*, to appreciate the vital difference in outlook between the earlier farces and this one. Suitably cut, however, *Preserving Mr Panmure* might stand revival as a sardonic black comedy of Edwardian middle-class hypocrisy, with its spineless protagonist; its vengeful, sanctimonious women;

its pompous, self-serving men; and its quixotic heroine, who ultimately decides to marry for money.

Indeed, such an interpretation would appear to have been what Pinero intended, judging from the reviews of the original production (which opened at the Comedy Theatre on Thursday, 19 January 1911, with Arthur Playfair in the title role and Marie Löhr as Josepha). The *Stage*, for example, remarked that

> *Preserving Mr Panmure* is sardonically and pitilessly funny. . . . The author will plead that his Panmure is merely satiric. Unfortunately this country gentleman is bred not of the light heart of the farces, but of the pessimism of the later social dramas. He is not satiric but satyric; and we do not need an old classical reference to point the difference. Panmure does not stand alone. He is the head of a country house of which the combined inmates do not number a single pleasant person, if we except Josepha Quarendon, who is pleasant to a degree that endangers her good name.

The reviewer went on to note that Pinero as his own director had clearly "rendered the play as he desired," especially in regard to the portrayal of the title character: "The part is a most arduous one to act. Bully, coward, sneak, hypocrite, sensualist, imbecile, Panmure must be all without realising that he is any one of them. That is the supreme cleverness of the part. It is also the artistic difficulty of the actor. Mr Playfair overcomes it with rare ability. Panmure with his shaking hands, unwholesome face, and furtive and unclean wits, is a repulsive figure. And yet he compels laughter."[28]

Yet the laughter was too uncomfortable for contemporary audiences: the original London production closed after ninety-nine performances, and — despite alterations made to please Charles Frohman, who produced the play in both cities — the subsequent New York production folded within a month.

Soon after staging *Panmure*, Pinero was approached by Alexander (who still regretted not having played Blundell in *Mid-Channel*) for a new play with major roles for himself and his current leading lady, Ethel Irving. The playwright had begun work on a new piece about the world of musical comedy but felt it was unsuitable for the St

James's. Unable for the moment to devise an alternative, he wrote regretfully to Alec on 31 May 1911 that he would have to carry on with the current project, placing it where he could, and hope that in the meantime his brain would "evolve naturally something which . . . will shape in the direction of King Street." This he thought was "a much better plan . . . than to go on squeezing my powers of invention and produce, perhaps, something which is in the result dry and mechanical." The following month he was at least able to congratulate the manager for receiving a knighthood in George V's coronation honours list. Alexander replied (26 June 1911) that he found it difficult to say to Pin what his heart dictated: "I am deeply sensible of how much gratitude I owe to your 'written words'. You have enabled me to win distinction and money, and these two things mean a lot in our short lives. That my good luck is pleasant to you is a *delight* to me and my wife."

In the meantime Pinero continued work on The *"Mind the Paint" Girl*, which he intended as a more satisfactory vehicle for Löhr than was his previous play. When *Panmure* failed, he had told her he would not be satisfied until he had written her another part that would carry her talents "further than they have yet been allowed to travel."[29] Lily Parredell, the musical comedy star known as the "Mind the Paint" Girl because of her hit song, was his attempt to fulfil this promise. The character, according to Dunkel, subsequently became the playwright's personal favourite out of all his creations.

When, however, Löhr appeared in the part on the play's opening night at the Duke of York's Theatre on Saturday, 17 February 1912, she found herself greeted with unprecedented hostility. The gallery had apparently been infiltrated by a claque that according to the *Times* review disconcerted the players with angry cries of "Speak up!", groaned loudly after every act, and at the final curtain "peremptorily shouted down the faint cries of 'Author!' in the rest of the house."[30] Writing to Archer the following Monday, Pin reported that the opposition "which manifested itself before the rising of the curtain, was inspired by some gentlemen in the City who are 'protecting' — an odd word in such a connection — certain ladies of the musical comedy world!" Löhr had been the prime target, he added. "The bullies treated her brutally, evidently being under orders to 'go' for the heroine of the play." As a result, her courage had been shaken and her performance suffered accordingly, though the production did make a partial recovery from the disastrous opening to achieve a moderate run of 126 performances.

That some of the regular patrons of George Edwardes's "Gaiety Girls" were responsible for the disruption seems probable, for the portraits Pinero painted of their kind, and of their protégées (Lily alone excepted), are distinctly unflattering. Unlike *Trelawny of the "Wells,"* Pinero's latter-day theatrical comedy is contemptuous rather than affectionate in tone. In place of the "gypsies" of the Wells, with their mutual camaraderie and support, the "girls" of the significantly named Pandora company, with their "healthy pink gums and big white teeth," are revealed in lengthy display scenes (notably the second act's after-show supper party) as blatantly manipulative of the mostly middle-aged "boys" who flock vapidly about them. Even Lily, whom Pinero would later claim "redeemed them all," is castigated with some justification in the third-act climax by an impoverished and embittered suitor for having been too "in love with herself, and her success, and what it was bringing her" to realise that she was sapping "all the spunk, all the energy" out of him.

Although the reviews were generally unfavourable, Pin did receive some consolation and encouragement from his friends. Lord Esher wrote that he considered the play "faultless," judged by the test of whether it had succeeded in doing what it had been meant to do, and Gosse declared that the satire was "severe and just, without passing into caricature" and prophesied (inaccurately) that when the play had "the patina of a generation on it," it would "be seen by successive crowds with constantly increasing emotion and interest. You will be to the reign of Edward VII what Farquhar is to Queen Anne, and more too."[31] Shaw, in contrast, could not help asking (18 May 1912) what had impelled Pinero to torture his audience so unforgivingly:

Mind the Paint is an awful play. That ghastly vacuum where nobody does anything — those inorganic bits of human society — that tragic Colonel and all the young men who haven't even a sense of rolling

down into his abyss of despair — those dishonest vulgar girls who
carry on a spurious prostitution trade with promissory temptation
notes which they don't meet when due: all this makes one especially
uneasy on the English stage, where it comes so closely home. How can
you bring yourself to do it? There was the same horror in Mid-Channel: another merciless thing. People howl at them like tormented
fiends: they crave for people who *are* something, who *do* something,
however ridiculous and mean it may be — something organic. But
you don't let them off for a moment: you say (truly) "*You* don't
matter, my good people: in fact that is half the comedy." Do you really
feel this; or are you like Thackeray, driven daimonically to expose
with apparently savage truth a condition of things which nevertheless
does not revolt you particularly? It makes me a revolutionary — a
tub thumper.[32]

Six weeks earlier (28 March 1912) Shaw had labelled Pinero "an
Enigma" because of his refusal to comment on his work and suggested
it was about time he started giving himself away as "the only point in
being an Enigma is that you should finally provide the solution. To die
an Enigma is in a manner to die a virgin: it is an unfulfilled destiny."
Pin had replied (29 March 1912) that Shaw himself was an enigma
("not to me, unless I misread you, but to many others; only you are a
voluble one") and that Shakespeare had been another ("and he made
a jolly good thing of it"), so felt himself to be "in excellent company."
Now, however, Shaw's comments on what was to remain his favourite
play[33] provoked Pin to speak his mind. To a letter (18 May 1912) firmly
disagreeing with a pet Shavian proposal that playwrights should seek
to impose a treaty of conduct on the West End theatre managers, he
added an unusually frank postscript:

> Sir, I thank you for your criticism of *The "Mind the Paint" Girl*. Yes,
> I know it's unpleasant in parts; but not in others. And I thought the
> others would make amends. And so they would, with stronger, more
> human and less theatrical, handling. And isn't *Othello* unpleasant;
> and some of the plays of Ibsen — as George Moore used to call him;
> and a few of those of Shaw? As to what impels me to write such things,
> if it isn't a desire to speak the truth I dun'no what it is. Yet I read
> only yesterday that I've depicted a phase of life which a serious

dramatist should disdain to handle. Pouah! That's rot, at any rate, and while I preserve *your* letter, I kick that stuff into the grate.

v. The Triple Bill

In June 1912 Charles Frohman conceived the notion of staging a triple bill of one-act plays that would be a showcase for his three favourite British dramatists: Barrie, Shaw, and Pinero. The playwrights readily agreed to the scheme at a meeting of the four of them, with Pin rashly announcing that he had already thought of an idea for his piece. The effect on Barrie and Shaw, as the latter noted in a letter to Pin on 25 June, was "to relieve us of all sense of responsibility, and to make us resolve to shove you into the middle of the bill for the grand situation, and plunder you of two thirds of the fees under cover of a curtain-raiser and an after-piece."[34] Difficulties did indeed arise over terms, with Frohman's business manager playing the dramatists off against each other; Pin, though concerned to support his colleagues, did not take the matter of fees for "the forthcoming trilogy very seriously, regarding the affair as rather a spree."[35]

By mid-July the playwrights were hard at work, though Shaw had confessed at the start that he had "written himself clean out in a recent burst of activity," and had not "the faintest ghost of an idea" for his contribution — apart from idly wondering whether he might be allowed to do "The Third Mrs Tanqueray"! Writing to him on 23 July 1912, Pin expressed satisfaction with the schemes Shaw and Barrie had in hand:

> Both ideas sound first chop. For my part I have tried to get away as far as possible from you and J.M.B. — which is prudent of me, for I could ill afford to risk direct competition with either of you. I concluded too, in less selfish moments, that as you were likely to be purely — or impurely — Shavian and immoral, and Barrie to be whimsical and tender, it would be better for the programme if I contributed something rather romantic and picturesque. So I am doing a little "costume" drama wherein the men say "Egad" and "Zounds" and the lady is continually dropping courtesies.

As to the method of announcing the pieces, etc., I will share in any feat you may devise; and, though I also have given up taking calls — don't always get 'em to take — I will be the Nijinsky to you and Barrie's Karsavina and Pavlova with the greatest pleasure.

On 2 September Pin was able to tell Shaw that his play would be ready to go to the printer in a week's time, though he considered it "such a be-ew-tiful work" that he was reluctant to part with the manuscript. He was, however, convinced his drama would be "an admirable set off to Barrie's puling production and [Shaw's] vicious farce." A few days later Shaw sent a copy of his play, then entitled *Trespassers*, which Pin read with keen enjoyment. The only criticism he ventured to offer was that "a short Act of Parliament should be passed making it a criminal offence to include such work in a programme not composed wholly by yourself," the piece being "disillusionizing to the furthest degree, and destructive of any item of ordinary character that may precede or follow it." But while soaking in his bath Pin had been struck by the thought that there was an excellent reason for calling the forthcoming entertainment "a triple Bill" — it was being "written by three Shakespeares."[36] For his part, Shaw reported (13 September 1912) that he had read the Pinero play, *The Widow of Wasdale Head*, to his wife with the greatest success, the ghost's part being especially lively. "If only Barrie does his duty," Shaw added, "we shall pull this triple William off."[37]

But two obstacles arose: Shaw discovered his title had been used already, and Pin discovered that Barrie had ended up writing a play with *six* ghosts in it! In true cooperative spirit Pin offered Shaw a list of alternative titles — all of which he rejected, finally calling the piece *Overruled*. The second problem was more serious, as Pin had no other short play he could substitute for *The Widow*. Frohman eventually agreed to release another unperformed Barrie play for which he held the rights; this piece, called *Rosalind*, centred on the role of an aging but still magical star actress, a part given to Irene Vanbrugh, with (as it would prove) dire consequences for the other two bards in the bill.

Despite these and other difficulties, rehearsals went ahead for the opening of the triple bill at the Duke of York's Theatre on 14 October.

*Thomas Downey, caricature of Shaw and Pinero being cut out of "The
Triple Bill," leaving Barrie triumphant.* (Illustrated Sporting and Dramatic
News, *November 1912*)

Public interest in the event was high, and the theatrical columnists
eagerly printed every scrap of information and rumour they could
glean about it. Frohman had tried to make a mystery of the authorship
of the pieces, a futile ploy, for (as Pin had pointed out two months
before),[38] the hallmark of each author was bound to be on the plays,
and theatrical gossip would do the rest. Indeed, by 1 October the beans
had been well and truly spilt, despite an attempt by Shaw to imply that
the one-ghost play was Barrie's and the discarded six-ghost play his.
Nevertheless, the opening night was widely billed as a major theatrical
event, almost a gladiatorial contest among the three outstanding playwrights of the age.

There was not the slightest doubt about the victor: Barrie, power-
fully aided by the charm of Vanbrugh, totally eclipsed his rivals, both

of whom had made the basic mistake of stretching out weak plots past the limit of the audience's tolerance. The following morning Shaw wrote a lively but heartfelt letter of commiseration to Pin, who as usual had been nervously pacing up and down outside the theatre during the performance:

10 Adelphi Terrace, WC.
15th October 1912.

My dear Pinero,
There is nothing for it but assassination (of Barrie) and suicide. They simply loathed us. They weren't indifferent: we didn't fall flat: they were angrily disgusted: we were trampled on, kicked and hurled downstairs and into the street.

God! if you had heard the shriek of delight with which they welcomed Irene. Until then I had hardly realized the intensity of their annoyance and discomfort. What has become of our respective judgements? *Did* you think my play SO very bloody when you read it? How did I miss the horror of yours? I thought it quite nice — to say no more.

However, there can be no doubt about the result. Barrie's piece will never be so delightful again as it was after our ghastly attempts; but that it is popular to infatuation there can be no doubt. Boucicault wants to consult me about cuts: I have replied that only two cuts are necessary, my piece and yours. When one has to jump overboard to save the ship it is a great comfort to seize a friend round the waist and jump with him.

They began the Widow at the pitch of the discovery of Duncan's murder in Macbeth, and were heard. *My* people began half a shade softer and weren't heard — the Telegraph actually quotes "Don't be horrid" as "Don't be hot". There was rather less poetry in both performances than in a tube lift. The atmosphere was impropitious; the charm didn't work; and the miss was as bad as a mile.

I am looking forward confidently to another failure tonight with that silly old Brassbound. You and I have mistaken our professions: Let's go into market gardening. — G.B.S.[39]

In reply Shaw received a note from Pin who was "throwing things into a trunk furiously" prior to leaving for Paris early the following morning. He was, he claimed, flying the country. But though the whole affair had been "one of muddle and miscalculation," Pin had really enjoyed the disaster — possibly because his old rival had suffered the same fate.

Real tragedy, however, was waiting just around the corner.

...16...
Public Ordeals, Private Griefs

i. Angus

On Friday, 13 June 1913, Lady Pinero's son, Angus Hamilton, committed suicide, penniless and alone in a small apartment hotel in New York. Writing for various London and American newspapers, he had covered virtually every significant theatre of conflict from the Boer War onward, having been at the relief of Peking after the Boxer rising, in Somaliland in 1902–1904, at the Russo-Japanese War of 1904–1905 and at subsequent smaller uprisings in Persia and Central Asia. In October 1911, as a correspondent for the London Central News Agency, he had gone to the Balkans and had been captured by Bulgarians who took him for a Turkish spy, bound him to a cartwheel, and were about to shoot him when he was recognised by an officer and released. During his brief adult life he had endured incredible hardships and dangers in almost every corner of the globe but had proved unequal to the stresses and strains of everyday life.

Like his stepfather, he was reticent about his private affairs and feelings. The half dozen books he wrote about the various campaigns and countries he experienced after the siege of Mafeking say little about himself, instead presenting solid information in an often ponderous manner. One exception, however, comes at the end of *Korea* (1904), as he describes how, after a peaceful stay of five weeks at a monastery and despite a touch of fever, he prepared to undertake a journey of 800 miles of wild, largely unexplored territory between

Seoul and Vladivostok. All his effects, his guns and campbed, tent and stores, were packed and roped, when his servants and bearers suddenly went on strike for higher pay, led by the head groom. After a brief attempt at negotiation, Angus lost his patience:

> I refused the thirty dollars and struck him with my whip. The end of my journey had come with a vengeance! The head groom stormed and cursed and ran raving in and out of the crowd. He then came for me with a huge boulder, and, as I let out upon his temple, the riot began. My baggage was thrown off the horses, and stones flew through the air. I hit and slashed at my assailants and for a few minutes became the centre of a very nasty situation. . . . In the end Mr Emberley [the hotel owner] cleared his courtyard and recovered my kit; but I was cut a little upon the head and my right hand suffered a compound fracture — native heads are hard things to hammer. . . . By nightfall upon the day of this outbreak signs of sickness had developed; the pain had increased in my head and arm; my head was aching; my throat was inflamed.[1]

As a result of this experience, he suffered a bout of enteric fever that nearly killed him on the voyage back to England. There, however, he gradually recovered his health and completed the book that he dedicated to his mother.

His account of the dispute suggests not only his reckless disregard of personal safety but a violent temper — especially when crossed by members of what he, with the typical British arrogance of the period, regarded as lesser races. But in the company of his own countrymen, Angus suffered dreadfully from a nervous stammer. When, for example, King Edward sent for him on his return from the front in Manchuria, he was so overcome that he was unable to speak for several minutes until the king had put him at his ease by handing him a cigar and getting him to smoke it. In 1906 Angus had married the daughter of an official at the War Office, but they had had no children, and he appears to have spent little time with his wife. After the Balkan campaign he had foolishly undertaken a lecture tour of Canada and the eastern United States, the failure of which left him destitute in the cheap New York hotel where he took his life.

Why he had not in this crisis asked for help from his friends and colleagues in New York or from his ducal relations in England or above all from his mother and wealthy stepfather, is impossible to tell. He attended to his death with calm deliberation — leaving his clothes neatly folded, his shoes and boots (with a shoe tree in each) in a neat row, and his campaign medals in a jewel case to be returned to his wife — before standing in front of the bathroom mirror and cutting his throat.

The suicide made headlines in the New York papers; the *New York Tribune*, for example, proclaiming on its front page: BALKAN LEC-TURER, PENNILESS, SUICIDE and, in smaller letters, Angus Hamilton, F.R.G.S., Stepson of Sir Arthur Pinero, Ends Life Because of Reverses. In London coverage of the event was less detailed and more circumspect, but the obituary in the *Pall Mall Gazette* (for which he had worked) conveyed a note of personal regret: "The tragic death of Mr Angus Hamilton in New York is a sad ending to an adventurous life. The fit of despondency can be well understood. Mr Hamilton had few of the attributes of the popular lecturer, for he stammered badly and was both nervous and shy. . . . But . . . his courage shone forth in the wilds. . . . Though he never quite found himself, those who knew him best will only recall at this moment an innate kindliness and modesty which carried him through many difficulties."[2]

The funeral, a week later in New York, was, according to the *Times*, "attended by representatives of the Royal Geographic Society, London daily newspapers, the London Press Club and other bodies. The wreaths included one from Lady Pinero (Mr Hamilton's mother)."[3]

There is only indirect evidence of the effect of Angus's death on his mother and stepfather. Pinero never made public mention of it, and (as already noted) virtually no family correspondence survives. Only the heavy black edging on the playwright's letters at this time and one or two comments to Henry Arthur Jones (for example, on 17 June 1913, "I am quite unable to help just now. You will know why," and on 21 June, "We are deeply grateful to you, old friend, and to your dear wife, for your kind sympathy") make any reference to what must have been a traumatic ordeal. As far as biographical accounts of Pinero are concerned, the very existence of a stepson was ignored or overlooked until nearly forty years after the playwright's death. But the consequences of the suicide were severe and lasting for both Pinero and his wife.

Despite her love of horses and driving, Lady Pinero had not enjoyed good health for many years, her main reason for living in the country rather than London. The shock of her son's death appears to have destroyed her remaining vitality and almost the will to live. For the next two years she remained bedridden, constantly referred to in her husband's letters as "my poor dear invalid." Her daughter had married Claude Neville Hughes, a stockbroker, some five years earlier, so most of the responsibility of looking after her fell on Pin, who did so without uncomplaining but in the realisation that she was unlikely ever to fully recover.

ii. The Big Drum

At the time of Angus's death, Pinero had just begun a new full-length comedy for Alexander, after a busy spell of other work at the St James's Theatre during the first half of 1913. On 31 March an entertaining one-act skit called *Playgoers* had been introduced into the bill, the first Pinero curtain raiser since his far-off Lyceum days. The piece focusses on a young wife who resolves to reward her servants for staying with her a whole week by treating them to a night at the theatre — only to have them resign on the spot when they learn they are to see "a play of ideas." Slight, but deftly told, this "domestic episode" was disparaged by critics such as E. F. Spence, who remarked in the *Sketch*: "It is a penalty of greatness that it may not do very little things, and 'Playgoers' is a very little thing."

A month or so later Pin was again at the St James's, conducting rehearsals for a revival of *The Second Mrs Tanqueray* with Alexander and Mrs Campbell in their old parts. Alec had decided to stage the play as a kindness to Mrs Pat, who needed the work, but he soon regretted his generosity, as she proved more difficult to act with than ever. Even Pin had come in for the sharp edge of her tongue when she turned on

H. E. Bateman, caricature of Mrs Patrick Campbell and George Alexander "In Their Old Parts" in the 1913 St James's Theatre revival of The Second Mrs Tanqueray (The Sketch, *June 1913)*

him for interrupting her at rehearsal and darkly declared that if he
did it again she would lose all respect for him and call him — "AR-
THUR"! After again receiving enthusiastic reviews for her Paula,
however, she sent him a peace offering of books, to which he replied
with affectionate humour that if she ever needed a testimonial at any
time to her "sweet reasonableness and pretty behaviour at rehearsals," she should not fail to apply to him![4] But Alexander had had
enough and swore that he would rather die than work with her again,
thereby losing a few months later the opportunity to play Professor
Higgins to her Eliza Doolittle, the thoroughly besotted author of
Pygmalion refusing to consider any other actress for his "pretty slut."[5]

In fact the new comedy Pinero was writing for the St James's may
have originated from his feelings about Shaw's talent for self-advertisement. Several years earlier the latter had written to him expressing
an intention of beating "the big drum" for a national theatre;[6] now
(whether by accident or design) Pin had adopted the same phrase for
the title of his play. The plot of *The Big Drum* centres on a serious-
minded novelist, Philip Mackworth, who adamantly refuses to seek or
allow personal publicity to promote the sale of his books. Arguing with
a middle-aged friend near the beginning of Act 1, Philip expresses an
attitude to fame that may be taken as Pinero's:

> ROOPE. Oh! I've no patience with you! [*Spluttering*] Upon my
> word, your hatred of publicity is — is — is — is morbid. It's worse
> than morbid — it's Victorian. [*Sitting in the chair by the small
> table*] There! I can't say anything severer.
> PHILIP. [*Advancing*] Yes, but wait a moment, Robbie. Who says I
> have a hatred of publicity? I haven't said anything so absurd.
> Don't I write for the public?
> ROOPE. Exactly!
> PHILIP. [*Standing near Roope*] I have no dislike for publicity —
> for fame. By George, sir, I covet it, if I can win it honestly and
> decently!
> ROOPE. [*Shrugging his shoulders*] Ah — !
> PHILIP. And I humble myself before the men and women of my craft
> — and they are many — who succeed in winning it in that fashion,
> or who are content to remain obscure. But for the rest — the
> hustlers of the pen, the seekers after mere blatant applause, the

> pickers-up of cheap popularity — I've a profound contempt for
> them and their methods.
> ROOPE. You can't deny the ability of some of 'em.
> PHILIP. Deny it! Of course I don't deny it. But no amount of ability,
> of genius if you will, absolves the follower of any art from the
> obligation of conducting himself as a modest gentleman —
> ROOPE. Ah, that's where you're so hopelessly Victorian and out o'
> date!
> PHILIP. Well, that's my creed; and whether I've talent or not, I'd
> rather snuff out, when my time comes, neglected and a pauper
> than go back on it. (12–13)

Philip's statement may explain why some of Pinero's letters to Shaw
are said to have been signed "with admiration and detestation";[7] more
significantly, its final lines may also be Pin's personal tribute to his
dead stepson.

The key plot twist Pinero had devised for *The Big Drum* comes
after Philip stakes his desire to marry a former love, the Comtesse
Ottoline de Chaumié, against the success of his next novel; to ensure
that he wins his bet the lady secretly buys up thousands of copies so
that the book appears to be a best-seller. As usual the playwright called
on expert advice to make certain the details of his story were as
plausible and authentic as possible. His adviser in this case was a
publisher friend, Sidney S. Pawling, who wrote him a long and detailed
letter on 9 June 1913 outlining how the deception might be accomplished:

> Placing myself in the position of the lady, I should follow this course:
> Go to the Publisher before (3 weeks say) the date of publication
> of the book. Offer to buy 5000 copies and to provide £200 or £250
> for extra advertising — all under the seal of secrecy. Urge publisher
> in view of his being safe from loss to push the book by every form of
> publicity he can. Arrange that instead of, say, 100 copies going out
> to the Press for review — every paper in Gt Britain and the colonies
> was to have a review copy — and offer to pay for these & to pay the
> postage on such copies: this would mean 450 or 500 more copies. The
> publisher being a party to the conspiracy, as it is to be assumed that
> he naturally would as he has accepted the book, would try and

convince the author that his own belief in the high quality of the book caused him to make this obvious extra splash.

The finding out of the conspiracy could be effected either by incautious talk of the publisher or by the indiscretion of one of his clerks.[8]

A few days after this letter was received, progress on the play came to a halt with the news of Angus's death. As soon as Alexander heard of the tragedy, he suggested postponement of *The Big Drum* and hinted that instead one or two earlier Pinero plays might be revived at the St James's. Pin agreed (21 June 1913), remarking that Maldonado and the Duke of St Olpherts would furnish Alec with two good parts and that he had always "seen" Alec in the latter role.[9] Nothing came of this idea, but in October *His House in Order* was revived at the St James's Theatre for seventy-three performances. This production ended up delaying the new play still further, as Pin had a severe bout of influenza at the final rehearsals, but six months later (22 April 1914) he was at last able to report some progress:

> I am, I think, after many set-backs, now getting on well. My invalid is stronger, and I am freer from anxiety than I have been for several months past; but I still have much to do on my job — one of the most difficult and delicate I have ever undertaken — and I should like you, if you can possibly manage it, to make my new play the second production, instead of the first, of your new season. Let me know if you *can* contrive this rearrangement, which would be, I believe, to the advantage of all parties.

But disasters and delays now followed one after another, despite the playwright's best intentions. On 29 May Laurence Irving and his wife were drowned on a ship that sank in fog in the St Lawrence river in Canada. To Pin, it was almost like losing another son. With a heavy heart he wrote to H. B. Irving, who replied (3 June 1914) that Pin's letter had "brought more comfort" and given him "greater heart and encouragement to bear my sorrow than any other. . . . To know at such a time that we two boys to whom you were so kind and good in those far-off days have not disappointed in our lives the hopes of so true and affectionate a friend is something to be happy about in the midst of so much that is dark and sorrowful."[10] Even after this unhappy event, Pin sent off the first two acts of the new play to Alexander, who wrote back (11 June 1914) expressing his delight with it and the character of Philip. The following week Pin wrote to Irene Vanbrugh, who had been cast as Ottoline, offering to take her for a walk in which he would tell her "the history of the girl up to the time of the opening of the story, so that you shall live that part of her life in your imagination." Six weeks later Great Britain was at war with Germany.

On 9 August 1914 Pin sent a depressed note to Alexander: "I can't help feeling that the stroke of circumstance has thrown the piece thoroughly out of touch and tone with the times, and that I might as well fling the manuscript into a drawer and endeavour to forget its existence and all the thought and labour it has given me." With other drums beating throughout Europe, completing his now misleadingly titled comedy became a burden that Pin several times sought to relinquish, aware that the public was interested only in jingoistic music hall shows. At Alexander's insistence he grimly carried on with the job, but it was not until the beginning of August 1915 that he was ready to start rehearsals — and even then the last act was not quite finished. It is hardly surprising that though the first half of the play is effective and entertaining, indeed almost Sheridan-like in places, the second half is laboured and unconvincing. This was also the general impression created by the opening performance at the St James's Theatre on Wednesday, 1 September; according to the *Telegraph*, "the reception was favourable, but of rather diminished warmth at the close."[11]

The main interest aroused by the production of *The Big Drum* came after the first night, when, in response to a plea by Alexander, Pinero modified the ending so that Philip and Ottoline, instead of going their separate ways after the exposure of Ottoline's deception, agree to marry. On 4 September the *Times*, along with the other dailies, informed its readers that Sir Arthur Pinero's play had been altered to provide a happy ending as a "concession to popular taste," and referred to the similar change made many years earlier to the ending of *The Profligate*. The revision helped the comedy to run for 111 performances, but when it was published the original ending was restored, a special preface by the playwright explaining why:

Caricature of Alfred Sutro, William Archer, Sir George Frampton, and Pinero watching a wartime musical (Illustrated Sporting and Dramatic News, *September 1915*)

Thomas Downey, caricature of Irene Vanbrugh and George Alexander
(**Illustrated Sporting and Dramatic News,** *September 1915*)

I made the alteration against my principles and against my con-science, and yet not altogether unwillingly. For we live in depressing times; and perhaps in such times it is the first duty of a writer for the stage to make concessions to his audiences and, above everything, to try to afford them a complete, if brief, distraction from the gloom which awaits them outside the theatre. . . . Luckily . . . certain matters are less painful, because less actual, in print than on the stage. The "wicked publisher," therefore, even when bombs are dropping around him, can afford to be more independent than the theatrical manager; and for this reason I have not hesitated to ask my friend Mr Heinemann to publish *The Big Drum* in its original form.[12]

iii. Pin "Does His Bit"

Only Pinero's sense of obligation to Alexander kept him working on *The Big Drum* after the declaration of war; as he told the manager (21 September 1914), had the play been designed for anybody else, he would have "put it aside promptly." To an American friend and colleague, Louis Evan Shipman, he confided (6 December 1914) that even though the play was two-thirds done, he could not remember what he had written. "With me," he explained, "it is as if an iron door had suddenly banged and shut out the operations of one's brain before the war." What interested him far more than playwriting was the forma-tion of volunteer corps in Britain for home defence, and, he proudly told Shipman, he was now chairman of one of these groups, the United Arts' Force. "We are about 1,700 strong — art workers of all grades. There are more than a million of such volunteers in England, drilling hard and ready to shoulder a rifle if need be."

The United Arts' Force (later renamed the United Arts' Rifles) had been formed in early September and consisted of men associated with one or other of the arts who had been prevented from joining the regular army. Their headquarters, by the permission of the president and council of the Royal Academy of Arts, was at Burlington House, and they drilled each day in the quadrangle and in nearby public parks. But their efforts appear not to have been taken seriously by the

authorities, for a year later (3 September 1915) Pinero wrote to the
Times protesting at the way in which the national volunteer force,
300,000 to 400,000 strong, was "absolutely neglected and ignored"
even though it had proved "the finest recruiting ground that the Army
has got." One of the principal objections to the employment of volunteers, he noted, was that they were not subject to military authority,
but in his opinion the difficulty could easily be removed: "Every
volunteer, having expressed his willingness to undertake duty, and
having had his liabilities explained to him, can be detailed for guard
or patrol and be under military discipline from the hour when he is
ordered to the hour when he is dismissed at the conclusion of his duties.
Legislation is hardly necessary for this. An order from the Army
Council, through the Central Association Volunteer Training Corps is
sufficient." One observer who was not impressed with this proposal
was Shaw, who suggested that instead of treating the civil status of the
volunteers as a disadvantage, Pin should "make a tremendous merit
of it" with recruiting slogans such as: "Britons, Defend Your Country
as Free Men, Not as Slaves. Join the Volunteers, Where You Can
Punch Your Colonel's Head For Fourteen Days or Forty Shillings.
Down With Prussianism and Viva Pinero!"[13]

Pinero, however, like most of his compatriots, was not inclined to
joke about the war. He had been so appalled at the German sinking of
the *Lusitania* (in which Charles Frohman lost his life gallantly trying
to save other passengers) that he wrote to the *Times* (10 May 1915)
suggesting that the distinguished Germans then resident in England
"in their own interests, if for no higher reason, should break silence
and individually or collectively raise their voices against the infamous
deeds which are being perpetrated by Germany." This word of warning, he went on to say, was "neither gratuitous or unfriendly. The
temper of this country, slow to rouse, is becoming an ugly one."

At the end of October an incident occurred that illustrated just
how ugly the mood had become. Shaw's published comments about the
war had provoked bitter resentment in many quarters. Amongst those
who considered him a near traitor were a number of fellow playwrights, who expressed their disapproval by demanding he be expelled
from the Dramatists' Club. It is ironic that the prime mover was the

man whom Shaw had gone out of his way to support and encourage during his years as a theatre critic: Henry Arthur Jones. When tackled directly by Shaw, Jones accused him of being, whether he knew it or not, "one of our country's worst enemies" and of being "generally regarded as a man who for the sake of showing his agility kicked and defamed his mother when she was on a sickbed." In the face of such hysteria, nothing could be done to remedy the situation. Pin had not been a party to the demand (having been at Stillands at the time) but when Shaw appealed to him could only write regretfully, "I am very sorry, but the facts are as stated by Paull" and offer to talk with him when he was next in London.[14] Refusing to accept the validity of the expulsion, Shaw then resigned from both the Dramatists' Club and the Dramatic Sub-committee of the Society of Authors. In a letter to Pin on 13 November 1915, he tried to put a brave face on the matter, but his upset and disillusionment were apparent:

> I have no further use for the club. When it started, the profession was broken up with two main cliques, with you at the centre of one, and Barker and myself at the centre of the other. This was in my opinion very unhealthy and unsocial and morbid and intellectually snobbish, besides being a source of weakness in business. Also, I wanted to know you better personally; and wanted you to know me better, as the legendary G.B.S. is rather a nuisance occasionally. Well, all that is done now as effectually as it will ever be done. . . .
>
> Then there was the Trade Union side. Well, I have drudged at that job for ten years; and I have come to Grundy's conclusion that playwrights are unorganizable beyond the point of forming a reasonably efficient debt-collecting and contract-enforcing Society. As I have done my share of that, and it can be done just as well without me, I am now giving it up. . . .
>
> To me therefore, this now is a bit of a godsend as a pretext for a dramatic exit. I shall never turn up at the club again. If I did, I should not keep it up; and there would be no reason for my absence but the real reason, which is, that as you and I and Carton and one or two others can't decently get into a corner together every time, I don't want to meet men who don't want to meet me.[15]

Shaw's break with the Dramatists' Club did not mark the end of his relationship with Pin, but the genial insults they had exchanged in recent years — with, for example, G.B.S. tweaking Pin's "Wellington nose" and Pin offering to serve him "stewed geranium leaves" for lunch — became a thing of the past and their letters and meetings less frequent. However, Pinero's regret over the xenophobic abuse Shaw suffered during the war is apparent in a little fable he later contributed to one of the tiny volumes in the library of Queen Mary's dolls' house:

The Redeeming Quality

Two oxen browsing in a field, both conscious at the back of their horns that they were soon to be slaughtered, were conversing sadly on current topics. They talked of Bernard Shaw, and one condemned him for his lack of patriotism. "I hear Mr Shaw is a vegetarian," remarked the other. "Ah," said the first ox quickly, "I dare say the man is very much maligned."[16]

Learning from bitter experience that "truth-telling was incompatible with the defence of the realm," Shaw was to decide that his major play of this period, *Heartbreak House*, would have to be held back until the end of the war, but Pinero put his pen at the service of the war effort. The results, although mildly experimental in form, did little to advance his standing as a dramatist. First came a little burlesque melodrama, *The Bulkley Peerage*, which Pin contributed to the 1914 Christmas issue of *Pearson's Magazine*, and offered to stage in aid of the British Red Cross Society at the Active Service Exhibition in March 1916 "if some five or six convalescent men with histrionic ability" could be obtained.[17] On 15 January 1917 a one-act piece called *Mr Livermore's Dream* and subtitled "A Lesson in Thrift" received a single performance during a concert at the Coliseum. In this little propaganda piece a wealthy merchant is persuaded to practise war economies as the result of having a dream. The Lord Chamberlain's examiner of plays summed it up in a note accompanying his recommendation for a licence: "It is a very naive play to be written by Sir Arthur Pinero, but needless to say it is very neatly written. I trust it will do good."[18] More unusual was a "musical playlet without words" called *Monica's Blue Boy*, which Pinero scripted for music by Sir Frederick Cowen and which enjoyed a run of thirty-eight performances in April and May 1918 at the New Theatre. The ballet tells a Cinderella-like story of a girl who is ridiculed by her sisters for falling in love with a wounded private soldier until he is finally revealed to be a peer.

The only new full-length Pinero play apart from *The Big Drum* to be staged during the war was a curious piece entitled *The Freaks*, "an idyll of suburbia in three acts," which Boucicault produced at the New Theatre on 14 February 1918. Set, according to a programme note, "before the war, in those far-off days when, in our ignorance, small troubles seemed great, and minor matters important," this inconsequential comedy concerns a small troupe of so-called freaks from a disbanded circus (a "living skeleton," a lady contortionist, a giant, and two dwarfs) who come to stay at a well-to-do suburban household. A special feature of the production was a "Wonderful Drop-Scene of the Freaks,"[19] used instead of a curtain between the acts, from a painting by Claude Shepperson portraying the troupe entertaining an audience that was made to appear more freakish than the performers at whom they were gawking. But if Pinero might once have treated such a theme in a strongly satirical vein, here, he told an inquirer, "the little piece has no higher aim than to amuse — which I take to be the function of the theatre at the present moment."[20] It ran for fifty-one performances.

Another three-act comedy written during 1918, *Quick Work: A Story of a War Marriage*, was never staged in England, though it received a production in November 1919 at the Court Square Theatre in Springfield, Massachusetts.[21] It is a feeble little piece in which the two principal characters after six months of marriage agree to divorce each other on a whim in the first act and take a further two acts to swallow their pride and get back together again. But as Pin confessed to Shipman (while apologising for an unanswered letter) on 21 October 1918, his mind had not been on the job:

Forgive me. I have been busy. That is, I have been trying to be busy — hardest thing of all; but really and truly I do little else than think about the war, and read about it, and dream of it, and watch and wait. The awful bloodiness of the thing is always present. Struggle as one may to get a grip of other matters, the gory spectre *will* come and seat himself in the best chair in one's room, and cross his bony legs comfortably, and say, "Look here! Put the lid on that ink-pot of yours, and throw that stupid pen down; you've got to have a talk with *me*!" And so one falls into a condition of drifting, and duties are unperformed, and letters from kind friends left unanswered.

It was fortunate for Pinero's bank balance, however, that a musical called *The Boy*, based on *The Magistrate*, had been an enormous success when it was staged at the Adelphi on 14 September 1917. The *Times* reviewer observed that the show preserved "more of the famous farce over which many of us laughed in the old days than one might have expected to find," including some of the original dialogue, though "much of it that was new proved — well, of a different quality." But Lionel Monckton and Howard Talbot's music contained many good tunes, the presentation was suitably lively and boisterous, and the whole production so fitted the taste of the war (and the postwar) audience that it enjoyed an enormous run of 804 performances. It was succeeded two years later by *Who's Hooper?* — a freely adapted version of *In Chancery*, which, with music by Talbot and Ivor Novello, ran a further 350 performances. Pin would have noted the irony that these highly profitable runs occurred at the very theatre from which he and Alexander had once rescued Mrs Patrick Campbell.

iv. Early Films

On 10 November 1914 Mrs Campbell, who still included *The Second Mrs Tanqueray* in her touring repertoire, cabled Pinero from New York to ask if he had sold the film rights for the play. A company called Warner Features was advertising all over New York a "powerful film production of Sir Arthur Wing Pinero's famous drama" starring a pair of obscure actors, Arthur Maude and Constance Crawley. Pinero, who had not even been approached about the film, immediately handed the matter over to Herbert Thring, the Society of Authors' secretary, to seek legal redress from the pirates. The attempt proved something of a fiasco because of the difficulty of identifying and locating the principal culprits. Warner Features, the distribution company, claimed to have purchased the rights from the Evans Film Manufacturing Company of New York, which had in turn secured the original print from the film's producers, Maude and Crawley, who simply failed to respond to all enquiries. The upshot of the proceedings, which lasted more than six months, was that the original pirates escaped scot-free, whereas the company that manufactured the prints ended up paying costs and a grand total of $250 damages. Pin passed this sum on to the Society of Authors (together with a small cheque of his own) to ensure the society did not lose money over the affair. His only practical gains were the confiscation of the prints and the warning served to the processing and distribution companies.

He had been concerned that the pirated film production of *The Second Mrs Tanqueray* would destroy its value to other film companies, but it appears to have excited interest in his work rather than quelled it. During the next few years silent film versions were made of a number of Pinero plays, including *Sweet Lavender*, *The Profligate*, *The Gay Lord Quex*, *Trelawny of the "Wells,"* *Iris*, *Mid-Channel*, and *The Second Mrs Tanqueray*. Pinero had direct involvement with only the last of these, produced by a British group, the Ideal Film Renting Company, with his own choice of cast. He had regretfully passed over Mrs Campbell for Paula, having been sternly advised by an agent that she would be unacceptable for a variety of reasons, including her temperamental behaviour and her age. "The stage," he was told, "takes off ten years and the film puts on ten years." Mrs Campbell was by this time over fifty. So Paula was offered to Hilda Moore, a niece of Myra Pinero, and George Alexander, in his first cinema role, again played Aubrey. Pin and Myra watched the final result at a private showing on Monday, 13 March 1916, after which they each wrote to congratulate Alexander on a performance Pin found "full of grace, tenderness, and, where it is called for, power."[23] Myra had been "amazed and wonderfully impressed" by the scenery and effects, finding it all "so strange and new . . . and such a gigantic affair." But though she thought all was *"wonderful,"* she felt it was impossible to depict "real sentiment, feeling and pathos" without the words.

The cinema journals did not share Myra's reservation. Reviewing the premiere of the film at the West End Cinema, the *Kinematograph*

Monthly Film Record declared that "from the point of view of human interest, dramatic force, and lifelike veracity, no finer production than 'The Second Mrs Tanqueray' has ever been screened," and the presentation would "probably long be remembered in the history of the film."[24] The *Bioscope* described it as "a masterpiece of cinematography." Though no print of this "epoch-making" film now survives, the *Bioscope* review gives a useful account of the changes that Fred Paul, the film's producer, had made to the play's action:

> The adaptation to the screen has been accomplished in a masterly fashion. It has been necessary to introduce scenes in the earlier lives of Aubrey Tanqueray and Paula Ray, and these have been most adroitly interwoven, showing no ragged edges, and rather tending to increase the sympathy for the unfortunate heroine and accentuate the problem of her social regeneration. The glimpse we get of Tanqueray's first wife fully accounts for the narrow and somewhat selfish views imbibed by her daughter, and also explains Tanqueray's susceptibility to the attractions of a woman of Paula's temperament.
>
> Tanqueray's first meeting with Paula takes place in a well-staged scene at the Opera House, while she is living under the "protection" of Peter Jarman, and a strong scene shows the indignities to which she is subjected. The gathering intimacy is sketched with convincing effect, and gradually leads up to Tanqueray's announcement to his friends of his forthcoming marriage, the scene with which the play itself begins. From this point the story is very closely followed with certain amplifications such as the first meeting of Ellean and Captain Ardale, which takes place in Paris.[25]

According to the *Kinematograph Monthly*, the acting was "totally natural," with Alexander as restrained on screen as he had been on stage:

> Never at any time is he betrayed into an excess of gesture or violence of emotion which would be foreign to the good-humoured, somewhat phlegmatic, temperament of the man he represents. It is, therefore, the more remarkable that the absence of the spoken word should hardly be noticed, and that the meaning of every happening in the story is absolutely clear, in spite of very sparing use of subtitles. . . . When Paula finally commits suicide one feels that is the only possible

solution of an impossible situation. So much is this the case, indeed, that one scarcely realises the unhappy ending. The last scene of all showed Aubrey Tanqueray bending over his wife's dead body, motionless, his eyes fixed straight in front of him, but with a tragic intensity of gaze, more impressive than any amount of gesture.[26]

From these accounts it is clear that Paul, though taking advantage of film's capacity to use a greater variety of locations than the stage, had kept faithfully to the essence of the play. Other early film versions of Pinero plays were less scrupulous, as Shaw had noted several months earlier after viewing a film of *Iris*: "The happy ending was perfectly crushing. Iris left the Maldonado flat; walked down a miserable alley-like approach to the graveyard in Bleak House; and found at the end of it the beachéd margent of the sea. She was walking into it — probably thinking it was a mirage — when Trenwith rushed to the rescue and the band played Tristan and Isolde. You might have knocked me down with a feather."[27]

It is hardly surprising that Pin soon came to the conclusion (which would be echoed by countless other writers over the years) that "in the case of serious work, these Cinema pictures will never be quite satisfactory until actor, author and film 'producer' are brought into a closer relation."[28]

In early 1917 Pin himself appeared on screen as, in an epilogue to a film of *Masks and Faces* in aid of the Royal Academy of Dramatic Art, members of the academy council were shown discussing the need for their fund-raising venture. The epilogue had been the idea of Irene Vanbrugh, the only woman on the council, who had employed all of her considerable charm to get the other members to travel by train to the Elstree Studios on a bitterly cold winter's morning. In her autobiography she describes how "in varying stages of controlled fury" the men made their way through snow and ice to the film studio but finally rebelled when they were ordered to have their faces painted yellow for the filming. In despair Irene begged the film producer to carry on filming despite the men's lack of makeup but submitted to the full treatment herself: "The scene was the Council Chamber and round the table were sitting Sir James Barrie, Sir George Alexander, Sir Arthur

Pinero, Sir Squire Bancroft, Bernard Shaw, Sir Johnston Forbes-Robertson, and C. M. Lowne. The scene was started and was finished and, believe me or not, when we saw the 'rushes' of that particular scene, there they all were looking perfectly right, dignified and natural, and I the only one looking unnatural, in fact rather like a painted doll!"[29]

The sequence has been preserved in the archives of the British Film Institute, where it may still be viewed: ghostly giants of a bygone age of theatre debating animatedly amongst themselves with silent eloquence.

v. A Blow Falls

Though Myra Pinero had very gradually regained some strength and mobility in the years following Angus's death, her recovery had been very fragile. The few letters of hers that survive from this time indicate that she was suffering from strained nerves and fits of depression. Notes, for example, congratulating Alexander on his film performance as Aubrey Tanqueray and on his twenty-five years of management at the St James's Theatre contain seemingly irrelevant references to her being "worried to death and bothered," having "no heart for anything," and being "horridly pinched for money" because every shilling she could do without was going to "some war fund which it distresses me to read about at the moment."[30] In October 1917 she suffered a bad accident in the country, which required surgery in London and resulted in another relapse.

Then in a cruel irony — the war having ended a month earlier — an aircraft crash-landed at Stillands while she was convalescing there. Writing to Shipman (24 December 1918), Pin described the incident and its effect: "I . . . am working under a burden of grave anxiety. Lady Pinero, who suffers from a weak heart, was terribly frightened the other day by an aeroplane which came down in a meadow adjoining my garden. After nearly removing my chimney pots, it hovered over her and her dogs for some time, and she thought she would never escape from it. She has been seriously ill ever since, as a consequence of this upset."

The episode proved the last straw for Lady Pinero, though she lingered on for another six months. In April and May 1919 Pin contributed to a debate in the correspondence columns of the *Times Literary Supplement* on the identity of the shadowy Mr Datchery in Dickens's unfinished novel, *The Mystery of Edwin Drood.* But as he informed Shipman (9 June 1916), this was merely "a form of 'doping' " to cope with his stress and worry: "my poor wife is very, very ill, and I am borne down by trouble and anxiety. I can't write about it."

On 29 June, at the age of sixty-seven, Myra Emily Pinero died at Stillands in the presence of her husband, daughter, and son-in-law. Obituary notices outlining her stage career duly appeared in the *Times* and other papers such as the *Era* and the *Stage,* but only family members and a few close friends attended the private funeral at Godalming. Writing to Henry Arthur Jones and his wife a day or so later (4 July 1919), Pin remarked that although the blow had been hanging over him for many years, it was no less severe now that it had fallen. Their flowers, he added, lay on Myra's grave "in the pretty churchyard" at the nearby village of Northchapel, where he had seen them that morning "still fresh and pretty."

He was left helpless and bereft, but with the assistance of his stepdaughter, he distributed various articles that had belonged to his wife, including gifts he had given her, among the many friends she had made in the district. One of these, the wife of the vicar of Northchapel, felt quite heartbroken and overwhelmed to receive such "costly and sacred things . . . gifts fit for a Queen" and promised to treasure them always in memory of Lady Pinero's "sweet love and generosity."[31] It seems, however, that Pin could not bear to go on living in the midst of objects and places that reminded him of his loss. Finally, at the end of August, he sold Stillands itself and from this time lived year-round at his Harley Street residence in London. There, according to Dunkel's record of conversations with Myra Hughes, Pin's stepdaughter did her best to keep him occupied, especially during the mornings, which had been his usual time for relaxation and companionship. "Sometimes they talked; more often he sat in his favourite chair by the fireside and dozed, indicating his happiness that she was with him by smiling and then, as if realising that she must be bored, suggesting a drive through nearby Regent's Park or through the Oxford shopping district."[32]

For months Pin sat at his desk in the evenings without completing a line of dialogue. Writing to Archer on 25 April 1920, he hoped his old friend and mentor was well, or at least better than he. "I don't mean that I am in bad physical case; but I suffer terribly these days from lowness of spirits. Next week I go away, with Myra, for a time. But one has to come back." Then he slowly resumed work, only to find that the brave new world of the present bore little resemblance to the old one he had known.

...17...
A Voice from the Past

i. Remembering

The Great War, linked with the personal tragedies he suffered immediately before and after it, marked a final turning point in Pinero's life and work. Once he had (with the exception of *Trelawny*) chronicled the present; now he mostly wrote and thought about the past. Time and recent suffering had mellowed him or, rather, had put the "small troubles" and "minor matters" of everyday life into a wider perspective. The brash commercialism, frenetic gaiety, and smart cynicism of the 1920s not merely failed to interest him but were positively distasteful to him, so for the most part he gave up writing about the contemporary social world. His main concerns were to do what he could for the war wounded and, while it was still possible, to enjoy the company of his rapidly dwindling band of friends and contemporaries.

Amongst much else, the war had effectively seen the end of the great actor-managers who had dominated the London stage since the 1860s. It was ironic that the youngest had died first: Sir Herbert Tree's death in 1917 had been followed on 16 March 1918 by the grievous loss of Sir George Alexander through tuberculosis and overwork. Of the older men who had retired before 1914, Kendal had died in 1917 and Sir Charles Wyndham in 1919. In 1921 they would be followed by two of the originals, the "impetuous, often irascible, but always lovable"[1] Sir John Hare in December and, seven months earlier, Lady Bancroft.

Only her husband, Pin's closest crony and an indefatigable attender of the funerals of others, would defy death a few more years. In place of the actor-managers there was now a new breed of commercial managers — people whom (according to Pin in one of his less charitable moments) "one would not touch with the end of a twenty-foot scaffold-pole."[2]

Many of his fellow playwrights, however, were still living, as were senior actors such as Boucicault and du Maurier, so as his health and spirits improved, Pin resumed going to the Garrick Club and attending the weekly lunches of the Dramatists' Club at the Hotel Metropole. There was important work to be done, the chief task being the organisation of a nationwide tribute by the entire entertainment industry of Great Britain to all who had fought in the war. The scheme (originally suggested by Lady Tree) was that on 31 March 1921, a day to be known as Warrior's Day, "every house of entertainment in the United Kingdom" would "give a matinée performance . . . on behalf of Lord Haig's Fund for the help of all ex-servicemen in distress."[3] Pinero became chairman of the general organising committee and threw the full weight of his influence and prestige behind the scheme, which was launched at a great meeting at the Drury Lane Theatre on 18 January 1921 in the presence of the Prince of Wales and the chiefs of the armed services. The idea was enthusiastically taken up by professional theatre companies, musicians, cinema owners, and over a thousand amateur societies throughout the land. In addition to the special matinees, all manner of associated fund-raising devices were employed; Irene Vanbrugh, for example, auctioned off a theatre programme signed by both crews of the annual Oxford-Cambridge boat race. The final amount raised was £115,140, Pinero handing a cheque for the first £100,000 to Lord Haig at a meeting of the general committee held in the foyer of His Majesty's Theatre on 27 May 1921. The money, he said, was not a matter of charity but an attempt "to pay one-millionth part of the debt due to those who served us in the Great War."[4]

Another, if much smaller, contribution to the cause of peace was a little one-act play Pinero provided for a matinee in aid of the League of Nations, held at the Winter Garden Theatre on 22 February 1922. The sketch, entitled *A Seat in the Park*, featured Boucicault as a well-dressed gentleman and Vanbrugh as a lady with whom he flirts when they meet by accident in a park. The encounter comes to a rapid and embarrassed end, however, when the gentleman discovers that his wife has engaged the lady as her parlourmaid. The piece was "well-received," but as the *Times* reviewer remarked, "What did the drama matter when everybody had an opportunity to meet their friends and wear new frocks in a good cause?"[5] Three months later the sketch was repeated before the King and Queen at a charity matinee at Drury Lane, where it helped raise £3,500 for disabled war correspondents.

Most of Pinero's limited creative energy during this period, however, had gone into a full-length play, "a little fantastic thing" he had begun before Lady Pinero's death but then laid aside for nearly a year.[6] Even after he resumed work on it, the writing had gone slowly and with little spirit. "For a time at any rate," he told Shipman (14 July 1920), "the 'snap' has gone out of me." Six months later (26 December 1920) he reported without enthusiasm that he was still forcing himself to work and supposed, despite the theatres' being "in a parlous state," that something would come of the effort. Finally, after another year, he was able to tell Shipman (29 December 1921) that in a fortnight he would start rehearsals for the play — "a fanciful thing which may amuse or (more likely) fail miserably. . . . But, oh, the altered feeling with which one enters a theatre nowadays! With rare exceptions, nothing but commercialism of the vulgarest kind."

His forebodings proved only too justified when *The Enchanted Cottage* was presented under the management of Owen Nares and B. A. Meyer at the Duke of York's Theatre on 1 March 1922. Despite a strong cast of over twenty actors and dancers, original music by Sir Frederick Cowen, and special lighting and effects, this "Fable in Three Acts" lasted only sixty-four performances. The critics found the play a disappointing attempt by Pinero to compete in the realm of Barriesque fantasy, and they strongly criticised an extraneous ballet in which various "extra-natural personages glide in and out or dance or wildly gambol, the witches even quoting *Macbeth* around an improvised cauldron." The reaction of the first-night audience, however, which had begun "with warm applause" but had "cooled towards the end,"[7] suggests a major factor was disappointment with the play's sad, anticlimactic ending.

The plot concerns a love affair between Oliver, a maimed and embittered war casualty, and Laura, a plain young woman who takes pity on him. He proposes marriage in an offhand manner, explaining that as a poor wreck he cannot hope for a pretty bride so must settle for a kind one, to which she replies that even plain women have their dreams in which they are beautiful and are loved for themselves. In the second act a magical transformation appears to have taken place, whereby Oliver's twisted limbs have straightened and Laura has become beautiful, but in the third act, when they attempt to show their transformed selves to others, they have relapsed back to their original state — though there remains the propect of a baby that may possess the beauty they had momentarily seen in each other.

In fact the "fable" was probably a private fantasy Pinero attempted to dress up for public exhibition. A number of key details suggest the likely sources of the play's hidden allegory. The scene was "laid in a cottage on the edge of Fittlehurst Park, Lord Wisborough's seat in Sussex" — in reality the Pinero's own cottage, Stillands, on the edge of the great Petworth estate. The owner of the cottage in the play is Oliver's stepfather, "a gaunt, black-haired man of fifty five," who finds it difficult to communicate with the embittered youth ("The position of a step-father is difficult at all times"); Oliver's mother attempts to jolly him out of his lethargy ("What I have urged upon Oliver till my throat has ached is that he should make an *effort*. . . . But I seem to have lost every vestige of influence over him, let alone authority"). Though this pair are treated comically, their relationship with Oliver appears to parallel the Pineros' with Angus (who one obituary suggests never recovered mentally from his torture and near-execution at the hands of the Bulgarians.)[8] The fantasy that underlies the play wherein Oliver is healed, in mind at least, by love and the prospect of fatherhood, appears an attempt to rewrite a personal tragedy that had been infused with the wider suffering of the Great War. *The Enchanted Cottage*, written so slowly and painfully, may thus be seen in relation to Pinero's war work: both, in all probability, were ways of coping with personal grief and failure.

ii. Revivals

Whatever ghosts the playwright may have been trying to exorcise in *The Enchanted Cottage*, it remains such a dramatic hodgepodge that its failure on stage was almost inevitable. Pinero, however, blamed the times, telling an interviewer for the New York magazine *Theatre*: "The theatre in England is in a bad way. The war has brutalised audiences. The people who go to be entertained do not wish to think. I doubt if we shall get a different type of audience this generation. We must wait for the children of today to form the audiences of tomorrow before we can hope for change. It is a discouraging thing for the playwright to face."[9] But if by this he meant that the new audiences were incapable of appreciating his work, the facts do not bear out such an assertion. The record shows that a number of his established plays were still popular with London audiences in the early 1920s.

If we leave aside a musical based on *The Schoolmistress*, there were six significant revivals of Pinero plays in the first five years of the decade. Judged by length of run, the most successful were the revivals of *The Second Mrs Tanqueray*, which opened at the Playhouse on 3 June 1922 (220 performances) and of *Iris*, which began on 23 March 1925 at the Adelphi (150 performances). Both productions featured Gladys Cooper in controversial reinterpretations of the title roles. As Paula, according to the *Evening News*,

> Her conception of the part demanded a make-up that included a complexion of extreme pallor — great staring eyes and brown hair parted severely in the middle and drawn back without the vestige of a curl. Her gowns were of the shimmering, clinging, sheathlike sort, and stockings she had discarded, or so it seemed from the stalls. She never smiled, even when taking her calls. . . . She showed us a vain, absurdly sensitive woman, neurotic and hysterical, subject to flaming outbursts of temper — a woman, cold, dissatisfied, wrecking men's lives, with a deep and justifiable self-scorn, and a sneering grievance against the world and the people in it. One longed to shake her at times.[10]

The interpretation appears to have been perfectly fitted to a 1920s context but did not please the first Mrs Tanqueray. Mrs Patrick Campbell, conceding that her latest rival had given a "splendidly consistent, human, sincere performance," asserted that Miss Cooper was not the "Paula of her dreams," having missed "the *child*" in the role."[11] However, this, according to the *Times* reviewer, was precisely the new quality that two years later Cooper gave to Iris: "So sweet, so child-like, so tender is the Iris presented by this actress that the spectacle of her torture and destruction by an untoward fate and human vileness revolts you; it seems a piece of wanton cruelty."[12] Emphasising the child in Iris instead of her lack of will and fortitude may with hindsight be seen as anticipating Elyot Chase's exhortation in Noël Coward's *Private Lives* "to enjoy the party as much as we can, like very small, quite idiotic school-children."

Although these productions suggested that at least some of Pinero's plays could be made to fit the temper of the new age, two out of three revivals in which Pinero again acted as his own director showed there was also an appreciative market for old-fashioned sentimentality. *Sweet Lavender* at the Ambassadors Theatre enjoyed a popular run of ninety performances beginning on 14 December 1922, and on 1 June 1925 *Trelawny of the "Wells"* was revived for fourteen special perform-ances at the Old Vic in aid of the fund for rebuilding the Sadler's Wells Theatre. The *Times* reported that the first-night audiences at both revivals responded to the plays as to much-loved old friends. During *Sweet Lavender* they had laughed "to the verge of exhaustion" at Holman Clarke's Dick Phenyl and cried, too, "a little bit, when nobody was looking, at some of the sentiment."[13] At *Trelawny* they delighted in the reminders of old times:

> The smell of oranges and the savour of the 'sixties: Sir William Gower with his snuff and his great rolling collar and his memories of Edmund Kean; Miss Trafalgar, born in the year of victory; James Telfer, who strode the stage with Napoleonic gesture and triumphed in parts he could "get his teeth into"; and Rose Trelawny herself, perched on a chair, speaking through tears to the party that has come to bid her good-bye from Sadler's Wells — how good it is to encounter them all again. . . .

> The smell of oranges did we suggest? Let us say rather the fragrance.[14]

Only two of the Pinero revivals staged in the first half of the decade failed to impress: *Mid-Channel* played just forty performances at the Royalty in late 1922, probably because it was "not old enough to be history, and yet not absolutely contemporary";[15] and *Quex* ran a mere fifty-six performances at His Majesty's in the middle of 1923 owing to a weak performance in the title role by George Grossmith the younger. However, the success achieved by the other London revivals encouraged the formation toward the end of 1924 of a "Pinero Repertory Company" for an extended tour of the provinces with a repertoire consisting of *The Magistrate, Dandy Dick, Trelawny*, and *The Notorious Mrs Ebbsmith*.

The Old Vic revival of *Trelawny* in June 1925 proved to be the climax of the postwar interest in the older Pinero plays. After this what had been a steady flow of revivals declined into a mere trickle. An inferior production of *Trelawny* was staged at the Globe in late 1926 and had a moderate run of seventy performances. "Perhaps we cannot get 'back to the Wells' at all by now," the *Times* reviewer lamented; "We dream, and dream fondly, because the secret is lost."[16] After this there were only two London revivals of his old pieces during the remainder of the playwright's lifetime: *Dandy Dick* and *Sweet Lavender*, both staged at the city's oldest "fringe" theatre, the Lyric at Hammersmith. A slight, one-act piece called *A Private Room* lasted twenty-three performances in a programme of five short plays at the Little Theatre in May 1928. Pinero's reputation was gradually fading away, like the two elderly lovers in this little play. "For 40 years they had dined together in the same restaurant on one evening of the year. He was another woman's husband, she another man's wife. Who knows whether, at their time of life, they would dine again next year. Who knows? The question echoes faintly in the sentimental air."[17]

iii. Retrospects

On 27 December 1924 William Archer, the critic who had encouraged and championed Pinero's work from the outset of his career, died at the age of sixty-eight after undergoing surgery. Some eighteen months earlier he had published his last book *The Old Drama and the New*, a personal survey and re-evaluation of British drama from the Elizabethans to the early 1920s. In this study he expressed his conviction that the previous thirty years had "witnessed a greater efflorescence of English drama than any similar period since the thirty years from 1590 to 1620, which include the whole life-work of Shakespeare," and that, "in so far as any one man can be called the re-generator of the English drama, that man is Arthur Pinero."[18] This high praise was tempered with the criticism that Pinero had "never quite shaken off certain limitations of thought and style" until he wrote the two plays the critic considered "perfect of their kind," *The Thunderbolt* and *Mid-Channel*. But having reread Pinero's plays "with renewed and increased admiration," he had felt "more and more strongly" the need "to redress a very grave critical injustice which has been done to a man to whom we all owe so much. I have admitted that he has intellectual limitations; I have admitted that he sometimes (by no means always) writes in a somewhat stilted style; but how insignificant are these blemishes upon the splendid series of comedies and dramas with which, undiscouraged by the most glacial criticism, he has enriched our literature! . . . When history views things in their just proportions, he will stand out as a great master of the essentials of drama."[19] Pinero had expressed his gratitude in a private letter to the critic (20 May 1923) after receiving a copy of his book, saying that Archer's appreciation was "in itself no small reward for the labour and the striving of so many years. But for you, I honestly believe I couldn't have managed to keep my end up. I think I have told you this before, and I am glad of the opportunity of repeating it."

Another sad loss for Pin — though not so unexpected — was the passing of Sir Squire Bancroft on 19 April 1926 in his eighty-fifth year. Since the deaths of their wives, their friendship of many years had become even closer. The previous year, at the old actor's request, Pin had written him a long letter recalling the "red-letter" night of his youth when he had first seen Marie Wilton as Polly Eccles in Tom Robertson's *Caste*. Bancroft had been so pleased and touched with the account that he published it in full in his last volume of reminiscences, *Empty Chairs*. Just before the onset of Bancroft's brief final illness, Pin, noticing that his old friend was not looking his usual robust self, had taken him for a medicinal holiday at Bath but after only a few days had to summon Bancroft's son urgently from London. When George arrived, his father begged to be driven back to his chambers in the Albany and, declining to be removed from his room in a wheelchair, like "Guy Fawkes" insisted on walking without assistance to the lift and out to the waiting car.[20]

On the day of Bancroft's funeral nearly all the shops around Piccadilly, where the upright old man with the monocle had been a familiar sight for many years, put up black shutters over their windows as a mark of respect; while "a great wreath of brass and silver gilt, its brightness blasted by a big, black bow" was placed in the foyer of the Garrick Club, where it was observed with scant respect by a new arrival in London, the Irish playwright Sean O'Casey:

> Sean noticed that most of the members, when they passed the silver and brass, gave a grin, ornamented with no reverential nod; and it seemed plain that the thing failed to reverently link the day of radium of speed, of the golden bough, with the day of Dickens' mute and Mr Mold. Bancroft? Who was he? Sean asked one or two of the members, but neither was eager to talk of the dead man, one of them murmuring that he had been a great actor in the days that were past. A dead actor down under the dusts of years ago. Sean had never heard of him before, and had never heard of him since.[21]

Perhaps if he had not sensed O'Casey's indifference, Pin, who had been one of the members addressed, might have told him a great deal more about the old actor who had been buried that day. Instead, the older playwright did his best to be hospitable to the surly Irishman who in return etched Pin's portrait in acid as a symbol of a privileged but moribund theatrical establishment: "So this was Pinero who was standing before Sean? How old-fashioned the little figure looked in its cut-away coat and dark grey trousers; the expansive collar and the padded tie; the gleam of a watch-chain caressing as it crossed the neatly-buttoned waistcoat; all setting off the timid face offering a look of pertness to the public gaze, looking like something too long bedded in lavender, now sharing the scent of its withering with the figure it had tried to preserve. Another fossil, still above ground, and faintly visible in the light of the withering moon."[22] A less prejudiced observer might simply have seen an elderly gentleman grieving for the loss of an old and dear friend. Writing to Boucicault some two months later (24 June 1926), Pin confessed that after Bancroft's death the coffee room at the Garrick, however crowded it might be, now seemed strangely empty to him. "Our little group is dwindling," he added, "which draws us closer together."

In September of the following year, while on holiday in Brussels, Pin himself came near death as the result of catching "the worst cold and chill" his stepdaughter had ever seen. By the time she had got him back to England, he was so desperately ill that he required complete bedrest in a nursing home for two and a half months. Writing to Shipman (early November 1927), Myra Hughes reported that her stepfather had "had a *very* bad time and suffered a great deal" and that, though she did not think he would "slip back any more," the greatest care would have to be taken of him for a while.[23] By 14 November, however, a notice in the Court Circular column of the *Times* reported that Sir Arthur Pinero was much better and had gone to Bath for some weeks, but was "most grateful for the kind messages he had received during his recent illness and for the enquiries made about him."

One of those "kind messages" had been a note from Sir Anthony Hope Hawkins, author of *The Prisoner of Zenda*, to say that he felt privileged to be invited to chair a special dinner in Pinero's honour at the Garrick Club.[24] By the time it was held, on Sunday, 12 February 1928, Pin had recovered and was able to mark the occasion with an engaging speech in which he outlined a chapter in the story of his life. It was, he said, a romantic chapter, for every man's life, no matter how insignificant it might be, was a romance to himself. And then, announcing the title of the chapter as "The Garrick Club," he reviewed his association with the club from the days when as a stagestruck lawyer's clerk he had spent his lunch hours gazing at its windows; to the year 1887, when, after a thirteen-year apprenticeship as actor and playwright, he had been elected to membership; to 1899, when he "was regarded as a person of sufficient mental and moral responsibility to be entitled to sit on the General Committee; to 1926, when he had been chosen to be one of the club's three trustees"; and finally to the present gathering, which he would always recall with pride and gratitude even if he had as many years before him as he had left behind.[25]

In July 1928 Pinero was invited to lecture to a meeting of the Royal Society of Literature on "The Theatre of the 'Seventies" as part of a series on the literature of the period. Though a fellow of the society since 1910, he endeavoured to excuse himself on the grounds of convalescence and unfinished work, but he was gently but firmly bullied into accepting the assignment by Granville-Barker, who had been appointed editor of the volume in which the texts of all the lectures would be preserved. "I don't mind if you curse me," wrote Barker. "I know my duty, which is to make you set down the 'Theatre as you found it'. I shall follow up later with the Theatre as *I* found it, which was the theatre *you* made."[26]

The lecture, delivered on 27 March 1929, could almost have been titled "The Theatre of the 'Sixties," as much of it was a tribute to Tom Robertson, whom Pinero credited with creating "a renewal of interest in purely native-born comedy" that had prepared the way for the playwrights who followed: Gilbert, Albery, W. G. Wills, and Byron. Admitting that he took perhaps too romantic a view of Robertson's work, the lecturer pleaded that "in dealing with the stage you must judge an author's work in relation to the age in which he wrote, the obstacles he had to grapple with in the shape of ancient prejudices and seemingly impassable barriers, and so judged it can scarcely be denied that Robertson was a man of vision and courage."[27] No doubt he secretly hoped for a similar verdict about himself one day. Having said something about each of the principal playwrights of the period, he had little time left to discuss its leading actors. One, however, called for special tribute: his old chief, Henry Irving, whom he described as always "the most dignified figure in any assembly, no matter how eminent," but, despite his "somewhat awe-inspiring personality," the possessor of a smile that almost brought "tears to one's eyes in the recollection."[28]

Pinero's own eminence was given special recognition a few weeks later when his colleagues of the Dramatists' Club held a special dinner on his seventy-fourth birthday, 24 May 1929, at which he was declared life president of the club. Amongst the guests were several distinguished actors who had appeared in his plays, such as Sir Gerald du Maurier, Charles Lowne, and Herbert Waring, and the members included most of the established playwrights of the day. At Pin's request there were no speeches, but Barrie, in toasting Sir Arthur's health, declared, "Pinero was our leader when we started writing; he is our leader still."[29]

Nearly three years later the aging playwright wrote an article for the *Times* surveying the entire period during which he had been actively involved with the stage. Entitled "Fifty Years: The Theatre in Transition," it spanned the time, as the subheading announced, "From Irving to the Films."[30] In the 1880s, Pinero recalled, playgoing had been the chief form of evening amusement, as there were few restaurants, and no other rival except for the music hall, "a place at which women of the upper and middle class did not care to be seen." It had been the age of the actor. "Thus they [the public] flocked to the Lyceum to see Irving and Ellen Terry, to the Haymarket to see the Bancrofts; to the St James's to see Hare and the Kendals, to the Criterion to see Charles Wyndham; and the play in which this or the other of such artists appeared, even if it were one of Shakespeare's or a classic comedy, was a secondary consideration." Later in the decade, however, the public had begun to show a concern for "the subject and quality of the play apart from its interpretation," and "some young men started writing plays that were at least original to the extent that they were not adapted from the French." The close of the decade had been "full of promise, and the nineties brought fulfilment," with the actor no longer completely dominant and the author achieving "a decided importance," despite having to cope with the timidity of managers and the petty strictures and interference of the censor.

Since those difficult days the drama had made "great progress," the article continued, advancing without interruption "from the nineties to the War." But with the war had come "the further development of the films" with which the theatre was "now engaged in a struggle for existence." What, Pinero asked, were "the chances of preserving the regular theatre," given that the "pictures" had, "for the moment at any rate, captured the masses who formerly were the faithful supporters of the regular theatre, and are now content with the thrills and humour furnished by the mechanical process"? His answer showed how his opinion had gradually changed over the years from a reliance on the verdict of the "great public" to an acceptance of the need for subsidy and protection for theatres he would once have called sideshows:

> A ray of hope comes from the "little" theatres and the repertory theatres which are being established pretty widely throughout the land. They are doing good work, and in due course may help to put our stage on its feet again. Meanwhile they have their own special war to wage, and we are told that many of them have no easy job in keeping their trenches unshattered. They deserve a loud hurrah. But the chief hope of those who demand a living drama — the drama which is a true and vivid reflection of the age that has given birth to it — lies in the foundation of a National Theatre. By that we should brush the cobwebs from our classic dramatic literature, preserve what is excellent of our own day, encourage the writer, and breed and train players equal to their responsibility.

iv. Remnants of Respectability

During these years Pinero had not stopped writing plays, though he had great difficulty finding backers for them after the failure of *The Enchanted Cottage*. Old friends like Sir Gerald du Maurier were said to have gone to work in the morning "in fear and trembling . . . lest a new play had arrived from Sir Arthur Pinero,"[31] whereas the new commercial managers, interested only in "crook plays and revues," ignored him.[32] But the work habits of a lifetime were too strong to break, even though the playwright privately admitted that the public did not want his plays anymore.[33]

His final plays display an attempt to adapt the drama of respectability to the postwar context by re-examining attitudes, using new techniques, and, in two cases, portraying characters and settings from a lower strata of society than previously depicted in his drama. *Dr Harmer's Holidays*, written in 1923–1924, demonstrates all of these features. The starting point for the plot was a criminal trial the playwright had witnessed at the Old Bailey in November 1892 in which three men were accused of murdering a young doctor in a back alley of a London slum:

> What interested me at the moment, and continued to interest me thirty years later, was the problem of a respectable young doctor — the trusted assistant of an older practitioner in the City, if I remember aright — apparently living a sober, honest and cleanly life, who met his end in such an ignoble fashion; and I set myself to the task of forging a chain of circumstances, intensifying rather than diminishing the tragedy of his death, which would, granting the premises, account naturally for that desperate, and final, fight for breath in those lone and noisome surroundings.[34]

In Pinero's version of the story, Dr Harmer suffers from what Victorian critics would have called *nostalgie de la boue* (literally, attraction to filth). In the opening scene he half admits his obsession to his elderly locum, attributing it to a patient: "At intervals — once a year perhaps — he'll slink away from his wholesome surroundings — where he's regarded as a model of rectitude — and abandon himself to a course of utter depravity." Yet Harmer is not a sinner on the scale of Mr Hyde or Dorian Gray; he merely wanders in a daze through the slums (where his worst excesses are drinking heavily and living with a prostitute) until he comes to his senses and feels bitterly ashamed of himself. After a futile attempt to escape from his compulsion by "winning the love of a good, pure girl," he returns, only to be murdered for his money by some louts. However, apart from a kindly landlady, the play's "respectable" characters (the elderly doctor, the landlady's empty-headed niece, and her clergyman fiancé) are so shallow and self-serving that Harmer's desire for the company of the prostitute (who at least shows some concern for his welfare) appears less reprehensible than its author probably intended.

The slum scenes, a novelty in Pinero's drama, are the liveliest in the play and appear to have been closely researched. The cockney dialogue is convincing, and the description of the setting, the prostitute's room, occupies more than three pages. These scenes are juxtaposed against others in Harmer's sitting room (another detailed, realistic set) and three brief transitional scenes without dialogue outside Harmer's house at night. The scenic juxtaposition would require either a composite set or some device for rapid changes such as a revolving stage, although the text does not suggest how continuity is to be achieved. The technical difficulties, together with the shortness of the piece, appear to have been factors in the play's failure to secure production in England, according to a letter (1 August 1927) to an American manager, George C. Tyler, in which the playwright stated that he would have no objection to "an experimental performance . . . provided it were given under circumstances as favourable as possible."[35] In 1931 it received such a production at the Shubert-Belasco Theatre in Washington, D.C.

In a postscript to his letter to Tyler, Pinero mentioned that he had written his next piece, *A Private Room*, "with the idea that it should be billed with *Harmer*, to enable the actor of Dr Harmer to give a *"tour de force.*" However, as already noted, this little play about a pair of elderly lovers who have sacrificed love to respectability was staged instead in a programme of five short plays at the Little Theatre in 1928. The following year the playwright tried his hand at something completely different, a "sedate farce" called *Child Man* that satirised a current fashion for books idealising children. The title character is an unsuccessful writer who is persuaded by his wife and an artist friend to write such a book using his own children as models, even though he dislikes children in general and his own in particular. The book is wildly successful, as are others that follow, but the writer finds himself trapped by publicity in the role of the "Child Man" and at the mercy of his thoroughly spoilt and obnoxious offspring. He eventually rebels and throws his family out of the house until they agree to submit to old-fashioned discipline and authority.

Much of the satire is so heavy-handed and, at times, queasy in tone that if the farce (which appears to have remained unproduced) were ever staged, audiences would probably be more embarrassed than amused. Its third act, however, contains one character conceived in Pinero's best farcical vein: Mrs Lumb, the artist's housekeeper, who on learning that the writer's wife has left her husband and intends to spend the night in the artist's studio, rejoices in the prospect of abetting a scandalous affair:

> MRS LUMB. 'Ush, now; no 'oneyed words. I was born plain, and I've acted accordingly. Being born plain means that you're doomed to respectability, and I've accepted my doom with Christian resignation. My late husband was verger at St Simon's, Notting'ill, and I had the cleaning of the vestry and the organ loft and one o' the aisles. There's respectability for you! You should hear how I'm spoken of in church circles to this day; in hushed whispers they speak of me. But, as I say, for choice give me vice. Outwardly I'm an icicle; inwardly I'm all for ardent love, and marriage bonds may go hang.[36]

But her enthusiasm is sadly deflated when the wife arrives with her children expecting the artist to spend the night in a hotel while she and her daughter take over his apartment! Making the best of a bad job, the artist asks the housekeeper to open a bottle of champagne provided for the anticipated night of sin, but when the cork is withdrawn *"there is no explosion, merely the faintest plop"*; whereupon Mrs Lumb, *"regarding the bottle with a glassy eye,"* gloomily remarks, "Flat as ditchwater. Like life. Like life."

In early 1930 Pinero published *Dr Harmer's Holidays* and *Child Man* in a volume entitled *Two Plays*. Although he had refrained throughout his career from commenting on his own work, he took the opportunity to write a foreword defending his practice of including detailed stage directions in the text and disputing the notion that a playwright should leave the staging of his work to "that modern excrescence of the theatre . . . the 'producer.' " Instead, the dramatist, he declared,

> should in a practical way stage-manage his play as he goes along, describing fully in his manuscript, in simple decent English . . . his scenes, his characters and the action of his drama, and so prevent a "producer" from coming betwixt the wind and his nobility and pushing him to the wall. If, in addition, he can subsequently get upon the stage and expound his views, so much the better; if he lacks the necessary assurance, the aplomb, to do this, a "producer" may be called in to act as interpreter, which is that functionary's real job. But I venture positively to assert that the dramatist who does not stage-manage his play, at least with his pen, performs only part of his task, and that to suffer another to clothe the bare bones of his work in garments not of his own choosing is tantamount to an admission of incapacity.[37]

He was to have one last chance to do the whole job himself.

On 13 June 1931 an item in the theatre column of the *Times* announced that "a new comedy in three acts, as yet untitled" had "just been completed by Sir Arthur Pinero, . . . now in his seventy-seventh year." Some months later *A Cold June* was accepted for production by Nancy Price, who nearly thirty years earlier had made a hit as Hilda Gunning in *Letty*, and now was managing a company somewhat grandiosely called "the People's National Theatre." Rehearsals began at the start of May 1932 and were conducted not merely behind closed doors but behind the lowered stage curtain until three days before opening night. This device not only ensured privacy for the elderly writer-director and his cast but aroused intense curiosity in papers such as the *Evening News*, which headlined a report from its theatre correspondent, "Sir Arthur Pinero — Secret Rehearsals of New Comedy." The correspondent, who had finally been permitted to watch a dress rehearsal, was able to inform his readers that the title of the play was a pun, "June" being the name "Sir Arthur has given to the principal character — a calculating blond, who takes advantage of two elderly men's respective belief that each is her father to get all she can out of them."[38]

It is unfortunate that the reception of Pinero's first full-length play for ten years proved even colder than his heroine when the comedy opened at the Duchess Theatre on Friday, 20 June 1932. Despite an announced month's run, *A Cold June* was withdrawn after only nineteen performances. James Agate, the most influential London critic of the day, noted in his *Sunday Times* review that it was a pity that Price had staged the play, "since it can give our bright and unreflecting young things no notion of the greatness of Pinero. I have read that this is "a play for Edwardians," which implies that this is the kind of play Pinero used to give the Edwardians. It isn't. . . . Miss Price has done a disservice to the greatest master of stagecraft of her generation. In addition, the play is badly cast, poorly acted, and mounted in a way to make Edwardians weep."[39] Agate noted privately in his diary, "Distinguished old men should be protected from themselves."[40]

Despite the weaknesses in the production, the principal reason for the play's failure was almost certainly the playwright's depiction of the heroine, who appeared too cynical to audiences and critics. W. A. Darlington in the *Telegraph* summed up their objection with the comment that Sir Arthur "shows the girl no mercy, allows her no humanity," with the result "that she has no individual existence at all," being merely the author's "idea of the Modern Girl."[41] Although June may indeed appear, from a sentimentalist's point of view, "a rapacious and soulless gold-digger," it is possible to regard her behaviour (like Josepha Quarendon's) as a sensible adaptation to her circumstances, for the main butts of Pinero's satire are her foolish, elderly "protectors." At any rate the playwright saw no reason to punish his heroine at the end of the play for ignoring the conventions of respectable conduct.

Pinero's last play, *Late of Mockford's* was completed in 1934, the year of his death, but has remained unpublished and unperformed. It exists in two manuscripts: one in the playwright's handwriting held in the British Library; and the other a typewritten copy, with a significant alteration on the title page, now in the Garrick Club library. The play is a comedy in three acts and nine scenes set, except for the opening scene, in a two-bedroom, lodging-house apartment. The main plot concerns a shopgirl who is dismissed from Mockford's department store and loses her "character" when she confesses to the theft of some small items from the shop. Eventually, after being reduced to working as a serving maid, she is restored to her former position by the son of the store's founder after his stern old father's death.

Audrey, the shopgirl, is an essentially moral and respectable young woman, quite unlike her irresponsible sister, Hazel, who on the strength of two brief engagements regards herself as an actress. The play's best scenes concern Hazel's affair with a bookie called Stanley Capper, who, after nearly succeeding in seducing her, finally proposes marriage instead. Though Audrey, like Letty, is somewhat colourless, Hazel and Capper are a thoroughly convincing, if obnoxious, pair, especially in the seduction scene, which is more explicit than any other in Pinero's drama. There are some excellent minor characters, notably Brenda, a serving maid who leaves her employment to become the mistress of "an elderly gentleman — bald as your knee — but . . . none the worse for that, nor for being on the fat side."

The play ends with a hilarious wedding reception at which the newlywed Mrs Capper (who has earlier grudgingly agreed, at Stanley's insistence, to "give up her art" for marriage) announces her retirement from the stage:

> HAZEL. Stanley agrees with me that the tone of the drama in this country has fallen into a shockingly low state, and he's willing that I should shake the dust of the theatre from my feet. The public'll have to look elsewhere for an intelligent actress who doesn't mind stooping to such dreadful things as are required of an artist in these days; they won't get them from Hazel Hemming, to give myself my professional name.

Hazel's swan song to her art (which impresses no one but herself) points to a final irony about this neglected play. The original manuscript, in Pin's beautifully firm and clear handwriting, announces the comedy on its title page as "A Play in Three Acts, by Arthur Pinero,"[42] but the title page of the typescript copy in the Garrick Club library describes the piece as "A Play in Three Acts by ELLIS AND KATHERINE REARDON." It would appear that just as young Arthur, the stagestruck law clerk, had endeavoured to impress theatre managers with his early plays by writing covering letters on his employer's letterhead, old Sir Arthur, the famous dramatist, had decided that his best chance of securing a production for his last play lay in anonymity.

v. Reticence

Pin's final years were punctuated with intermittent bouts of ill health arising from the chronic bronchitis to which he had been prone since his youth. These did not prevent him from helping old friends and colleagues in need. Whenever, for example, Mrs Campbell requested yet another reduction in fees on yet another tour with his old plays, the request would be granted in a friendly note. In one of these (14 May 1928) Pin apologised that as he was going away for a bit he would not be able to stand her "a drink (of tea) yet awhile," but promised on his return to meet with her and listen to all her hopes and aspirations. "As long as those survive," he added, " we are in the spring of life. I kiss your hand."

He was equally appreciative of the kindness and goodwill of others. In January 1932 a mutual friend passed on a quotation from a letter written to him by the American playwright, Louis Napoleon Parker: "Do you ever see Pinero? I feel a very real & deep reverence and affection for him, although he & I have, I suppose, not exchanged a dozen sentences. I admire not only his work, but his life, his silence, his dignity, and his self-respect."[43]

Nine months later, learning that Parker was about to turn eighty, Pin wrote to a number of playwrights and critics (including Shaw, John Drinkwater, St John Ervine, and even his former bête noir, Max Beerbohm) asking them to send the old author a letter or telegram congratulating him on his birthday in remembrance of "the fine work he did for the theatre in his active days."[44] They all did so, including Shaw, who sent Pin a postcard note: "Fancy congratulating a man on being eighty! They will be congratulating *us* presently. Yes: I remember, God forgive him! I will condole, at your command. — G.B.S."

Pinero had indeed reached an age where few of his old friends survived. Henry Arthur Jones and "Dot" Boucicault had died in 1929, and in July 1933 news came from Mrs Shipman that her husband was gravely ill. Full of concern, Pin requested her to keep him informed of Shipman's condition; on 3 August a telegram announcing the American's death arrived at the Garrick Club. Perhaps it was for Shipman's sake that Pin, despite his dislike of any form of self-advertising, agreed the following February to meet a young American academic, Wilbur Dwight Dunkel, who was eager to write a biography of him. Dunkel recorded his first meeting with Pinero in an appendix to his brief biography:

> The enormous vitality which had spurred him on to write over fifty full-length plays impressed itself upon me. He spoke rapidly and without the slightest diffidence. "I'm glad to see you. You know I've been ill. I'm just a wreck of a man now. My secretary thought I shouldn't see anyone, but I wanted to see you. A young man who would bring a year-old baby across the Atlantic in mid-winter interests me. I'm glad you've come. What may I do to help you? Are you well located? Are Mrs Dunkel and the children all right? They stood the trip? Now, just where is it you are living?"
>
> These questions cascaded into my mind. But before I could reply, he was asking, "Why do you want to write a book about me, about my plays?" And I replied, "Because you wrote *The Second Mrs Tanqueray*, and I can find out so little about you."[45]

Somehow Dunkel did not find out a great deal more. The playwright did show him a number of letters he allowed him to copy and painstakingly read through the notes on first-night reviews Dunkel made over the next four months at the British Museum's Newspaper Library. But with the greatest appearance of goodwill and cooperation, he told the young man almost nothing he did not already know.

In June 1934 a severe bout of influenza left Pinero so exhausted that he felt the need for "a long rest from work of any description."[46] Late that September he undertook to mention to the Garrick Club committee an old actor's bequest of some theatrical relics to the club, though he feared there were "few there now who knew the poor fellow. Our losses from death have been considerable lately."[47]

Less than seven weeks afterwards he was admitted to a nursing home for an operation on a strangulated hernia, even though his heart had been seriously weakened by his bronchial condition. He did not recover from the operation and died on 23 November 1934. A memorial service was held at the St Marylebone Parish Church on 28 November, and in accordance with his request, Sir Arthur Pinero's ashes were deposited with his wife's remains in the little churchyard at Northchapel. The stone over their obscure grave bears a somewhat ironic inscription:

> FORGET NOT ME AMONG YOU
> WHAT I DID IN MY GOOD TIME

Epilogue: Legacies

The day after Pinero died, Shaw suffered a heart attack. Had he succumbed to it, instead of assuming an almost legendary eminence by living until the middle of the century, his name might have been linked with Pinero's in theatrical history, instead of Pinero's being paired with the lesser figure of Henry Arthur Jones. For Pinero and Shaw, each possessing the virtues of the other's defects, were the founders of two contrasting schools of modern British drama — as G.B.S. himself recognised. Shaw's style of drama, coming as a reaction against Pinero's, proved more spectacular and intellectually stimulating, with its open, freewheeling approach and lively subversion of theatrical and social conventions. Pinero's work, by comparison, appeared more conventional, but his development of a realistic, closely observed, tightly structured drama, based on generally accepted standards of behaviour, probably had a more widespread and enduring influence on later British drama.

But the world took little notice of Pinero's death. The *Times* and the *Telegraph* duly published lengthy but lukewarm obituaries relegating the playwright's work to a bygone era, whereas some of the other leading papers did not even bother to note his passing. The world, after all, had more to worry about, including the Great Depression, though other authors would have noted with envy that Pinero's estate had amounted to over £60,000. In May 1935 forty of the manuscripts of his plays, together with letters and books, were sold by auction at Sotheby's, with most of the lots going at bargain prices. The top price of £70 was paid for the signed holograph manuscript of *The Second Mrs Tanqueray*, from whence there was a steep drop to *Trelawny* at £17 and *The Magistrate* at £14, after which the manuscripts of major

374

plays such as *Mid-Channel* could be picked up for several pounds and the early one-acts for a few shillings.

For the next twenty years, Pinero's reputation remained in a state of near eclipse, and his plays virtually disappeared from the London stage, though playwrights as diverse as Coward, Terence Rattigan, Ben Travers, and even T. S. Eliot carried on in their own fashions the forms he had developed. After World War II, however, a steadily increasing flow of revivals, beginning with the chief Court farces, appeared on the London stage and at leading provincial theatres, such as the Bristol Old Vic and the Liverpool Playhouse.

In 1950 a major revival of *Mrs Tanqueray*, with designs by Cecil Beaton, ran 206 performances at the Haymarket and began a sequence of more than two dozen professional productions of the play, culminating in the National Theatre's 1981 revival. Though it had taken more than a generation since Pinero's death to come into being, the National vindicated his hopes and helped restore his theatrical reputation. It is fitting that one of its first productions was a highly successful, star-studded revival of *Trelawny of the "Wells"* in 1965, staged both at Chichester and the Old Vic. Its third Pinero revival, *The Magistrate* in 1986, also proved popular with audiences and continued in the repertoire well into the following year. And though the National has yet to venture outside the small core of Pinero classics, other major British theatres (such as the Manchester Royal Exchange with its 1988 production of *The Cabinet Minister* — its first major revival in ninety years) have begun to rediscover more of his extensive and varied canon.

In his will, along with a share in the residue of his literary estate, Pinero bequeathed to the Garrick Club a marble bust of himself by Emil Fuchs. Today it stands on its pedestal by the entrance to the reading room where Pin once took refuge in the pages of the *Mining Journal* from the barbs of "G.B.S." Behind it is a Max Beerbohm caricature depicting the playwright reflected in a succession of diminishing mirrors, but the dignified marble head ignores this and instead gazes silently at the eminent playwrights and players who still climb and descend the great portrait-lined staircase.

*Emil Fuchs, marble bust of Pinero (E. T. Archive photograph, by permission
of the Garrick Club)*

Notes

References to Pinero's plays, unless otherwise stated, are from the uniform Heinemann edition, published between 1891 and 1922. The following abbreviations are used for frequently cited sources:

Pinero's Letters

CL — *The Collected Letters of Sir Arthur Pinero*, ed. J. P. Wearing (Minneapolis: University of Minnesota Press, 1974).

Where no footnote reference is given for a dated letter, it will be found in *CL* in its natural chronological position. Frequently cited sources of previously unpublished letters, typescripts, and manuscripts are abbreviated as follows:

BL — British Library
Leeds — Brotherton Collection, University of Leeds Library
Garrick — Pinero Boxes, Library of the Garrick Club, London
Harvard — Harvard College Library
NYPL — New York Public Libraries
Rochester — Special Collections and Rare Books Department, University of Rochester Library, N.Y.
Texas — Harry Ransom Humanities Research Centre, University of Texas at Austin
TM — Theatre Museum, London

Other References

BSCL — *Bernard Shaw Collected Letters*, ed. Dan H. Laurence (London: Reinhardt, 1965, 1972)
Dunkel — Wilbur Dwight Dunkel, *Sir Arthur Pinero: A Critical Biography with Letters* (Chicago: University of Chicago Press, 1941)
ILN — *Illustrated London News*
ISDN — *Illustrated Sporting and Dramatic News*

OTN — Bernard Shaw, *Our Theatres in the Nineties*, 3 vols. (London: Constable, 1932)
POLD — *Post Office London Directories*
TW — William Archer, *The Theatrical "World,"* 5 vols. (London: Walter Scott, 1894–1899)

Prologue: The Drama of Respectability

1. Clayton Hamilton, ed., *The Social Plays of Pinero*, vol. 1 (New York: AMS, 1967 reprint), 3.
2. "Fifty Years: The Theatre in Transition," *Times*, 20 February 1932, 11.

Act 1: Preparation

Chapter 1: Outside the Garrick Club

1. Dunkel, 95–96.
2. Tom Girton, *The Abominable Clubman* (London: Hutchinson, 1964), 52.
3. Malcolm C. Salaman, "Arthur Wing Pinero," *Cassell's Magazine* (London, 1899), 52.
4. *CL*, 196.
5. *CL*, 259–260.
6. Salaman, op. cit.
7. *CL*, 133. *Law Lists* for 1851–1865 (except 1855, 1857–1859, and 1862) have entries for J. D. Pinero.
8. Deaths Register, September 1851, General Register Office, London.
9. *POLD 1855.*
10. *CL*, 286.
11. *POLD 1856.*
12. *Law List 1859.*
13. *POLD 1860.*
14. This passage of dialogue is jotted down in pencil in Pinero's working notebook for the play. Garrick.
15. Chance Newton ("Carados"), *Cues and Curtain Calls* (London: Bodley Head, 1927), 30. The full address is recorded on Mary Ross Pinero's birth certificate, 14 March 1865.

16. *POLD 1861.*
17. Newton, op. cit.
18. Seymour Hicks, *Hail Fellow, Well Met* (London: Staples Press, 1949), 208–209.
19. "Magic Nights at Old Sadler's Wells," *Evening News*, 19 June 1925, 6.
20. Ibid.
21. Garrick.
22. Letter to the *Times*, 2 December 1931, 10.
23. Dunkel, 10. The Spafields Chapel Charity School was the only school in Exmouth Street, Clerkenwell, according to *POLD 1865.*
24. *CL*, 133.
25. "Mr Arthur Wing Pinero," *Era*, 3 September 1881, 6.
26. *Era*, 10 May 1868, 8.
27. Genevieve Ward, *Both Sides of the Curtain* (London: Cassell & Co., 1918), 230.
28. "Magic Nights," op. cit.
29. "Mr Arthur Wing Pinero," op. cit.
30. Salaman, op. cit.
31. *POLD 1870.*
32. Will proven 7 October 1871, Somerset House, London.
33. Dunkel, 11.
34. "Royal General Theatrical Fund Dinner," *Era*, 25 July 1885, 14.
35. Dunkel, 11.
36. *POLD 1872.*
37. J. P. Wearing, "Pinero the Actor," *Theatre Notebook*, 26 (Summer 1972), 133–134.
38. Sotheby & Co, *Catalogue of Valuable Printed Books, etc.* (London: Sotheby & Co., 1935), 29–30.
39. Unpublished letter, Texas.
40. Handlist, Garrick.
41. Dunkel, 95.
42. Ibid.
43. Previously unpublished letter, Texas.
44. Cited in Squire Bancroft, *Empty Chairs* (London: John Murray, 1925), 228–232.
45. Ibid., 232.

46. "The Theatre in the 'Seventies," in *The Eighteen-Seventies*, ed. H. Granville-Barker (Cambridge: Cambridge University Press, 1929), 141.

47. Ibid., 139–140.

48. *CL*, 29–30.

49. Unpublished letter, Texas.

50. Unpublished letter, Texas.

51. Unpublished letter, Pinero to Mrs Schneider (12 March 1874), Texas.

52. Introduction to *The Position of Peggy Harper* by Leonard Merrick (London: Hodder & Stoughton, 1918), v–vi.

Chapter 2: "General Utility"

1. Texas.

2. J. P. Wearing, "Pinero the Actor," *Theatre Notebook*, 26 (Summer 1972), 134.

3. "Prefatory Letter," *TW 1895*, xix.

4. Ibid., xvi–xvii.

5. Ibid., xvii–xviii.

6. Ibid.

7. *Scotsman*, 5 February 1875, 4.

8. *TW 1895*, xxi.

9. Ibid., xxiii.

10. "Mr Arthur Wing Pinero," *Era*, 3 September 1881, 6.

11. Letter to Eliza Schneider (2 August 1874), *CL*, 36.

12. "Mathews and Sothern," *The Era Almanac and Annual 1884* (London: *Era*, 1884), 87.

13. Ibid.

14. Letter to Eliza Schneider, 22 November 1874, *CL*, 43.

15. "Mathews and Sothern," 86.

16. Ibid., 87.

17. Ibid.

18. *TW 1895*, xxix.

19. *Era*, 3 January 1875, 4.

20. "General Theatrical Fund Dinner," *Era*, 25 July 1885, 14.

21. *Scotsman*, op. cit., 4–5.

22. Ibid.

23. *TW 1895*, xii.

Chapter 3: A "Walking Gentleman"

1. *The Era Almanac and Annual 1879* (London: Era, 1879), 54.

2. *The Era Almanac and Annual 1880* (London: Era, 1880), 105–110.

3. Previously unpublished letter, Texas.

4. Previously unpublished letters to Tom Tolman cited in this chapter are held at the University of Rochester.

5. *TW 1895*, xxii–xxiii.

6. *Era*, 7 March 1875, 4.

7. *Era*, 14 March 1875, 5.

8. Letter to Eliza Schneider (20 September 1874), *CL*, 40.

9. Letter to Eliza Schneider (4 April 1875), *CL*, 47.

10. *Daily Post* (Liverpool), 30 March 1875, 5.

11. *Daily Post*, 27 April 1874, 5; *Era*, 9 May 1875, 6.

12. *Era*, 26 September 1875, 4.

13. Ibid.

14. *Era*, 31 October 1875, 4; letter to Eliza Schneider (30 October 1875), *CL*, 53.

15. Cited by Walter de la Mare, "The Early Novels of Wilkie Collins," *The Eighteen-Sixties*, ed. John Drinkwater (Cambridge: Cambridge University Press, 1932), 68–69.

16. *Era*, 12 December 1875, 4.

17. "Mathews and Sothern," *The Era Almanac and Annual 1884* (London: Era, 1884), 87.

Chapter 4: Irving and Authorship

1. *Globe*, 17 April 1876, 4.

2. *Era*, 23 April 1876, 13; *Daily Telegraph*, 18 April 1876, 2.

3. Dunkel, 17.

4. Austin Brereton, *The Life of Sir Henry Irving*, vol. 1 (London: Longmans, 1908), 213–214.

5. Alfred Sutro, *Celebrities and Simple Souls* (London: Duckworth, 1933), 61.

6. *Era*, 22 September 1877, 12.

7. "At the Beginning," *The Era Almanac and Annual 1903* (London: Era, 1903), 25–26.

8. *Era*, op. cit.

9. "At the Beginning," op. cit.

10. *ISDN*, 27 October 1877.

11. BL Add. Ms. 53238.

12. *Era*, 28 April 1878, 8.

13. *Croydon Guardian*, 27 April 1878; cited in *Era* advertisement, 5 May 1878, 7.

14. "At the Beginning," op. cit.

15. BL Add. Ms. 53202.

16. Texas.

17. "Fifty Years: The Theatre in Transition," *Times*, 20 February 1932, 11.

18. "Mr Arthur Wing Pinero," *Era*, 3 September 1881, 6.

19. Ellen Terry, *The Story of My Life* (London: Hutchinson, 1933), 158.

20. Ibid.

21. Hamilton Fyfe, *Sir Arthur Pinero's Plays and Players* (London: Ernest Benn, 1930), 12.

22. Laurence Irving, *Henry Irving* (London: Faber, 1951), 319.

23. Fyfe, op. cit., 15.

24. "At the Beginning," op. cit.

25. BL Add. Ms. 53222.

26. *Era*, 28 September 1879, 5.

27. Previously unpublished letter, Rochester.

28. *ISDN*, 30 September 1879.

Chapter 5: A Difficult Courtship

1. *Harte's Army List*, October 1868, 300.

2. *Burke's Peerage*, 99th ed. (London: Burke's Peerage Ltd, 1949), 923.

3. I am indebted to Major Philip Daniel, the son of Lady Pinero's half brother, Oscar Wood Moore, for information about the family that he assembled in the document "The Wood-Moore Connection" (1985).

4. "Our Omnibus Box," *Theatre*, 1 December 1884, 319.

5. "Deaths," *Times*, 25 December 1879, 1.

6. BL Add. Ms. 53238.

7. Dunkel, 19.

8. *The Era Almanac and Annual 1881* (London: *Era*, 1881), 119–124.

9. *The Era Almanac and Annual 1882* (London: *Era*, 1882), 102–105.

10. *The Era Almanac and Annual 1886* (London: *Era*, 1886), 20–21.

11. "J. L. Toole: A Great Comic Actor," *Times*, 12 March 1932, 13.

12. Garrick.

13. Previously unpublished letters by Pinero to Loveday, Rochester.

14. Sotheby & Co, *Catalogue of Valuable Printed Books, etc.* (London: Sotheby & Co, May 1935), 45.

15. *Daily Telegraph*, 20 September 1880, 5.

16. Laurence Irving, *Henry Irving* (London: Faber, 1951), 360–361.

17. Ibid., 200–201.

18. Austin Brereton, *"H.B." and Laurence Irving* (London: Grant Richards, 1922), 24–25.

19. Ibid., 91.

20. *ILN*, 15 January 1881, 113.

21. *Theatre*, 1 February 1881, 113.

22. George Rowell, *Theatre in the Age of Irving* (Oxford: Basil Blackwell, 1981), 66–67.

23. *Era*, 15 January 1881, 14.

24. T. Edgar Pemberton, *John Hare, Comedian* (London: Routledge, 1895), 89–90.

25. *ILN*, 19 March 1881.

26. Letter from Pinero to Mrs Foreman (Alma Murray) (29 March 1881), Rochester.

27. M. E. Bancroft and S. Bancroft, *Mr and Mrs Bancroft on and off the Stage* (London: Richard Bentley & Son, 1891), 309–312.

28. Ellen Terry, *The Story of My Life* (London: Hutchinson, 1933), 207.

Act 2: Development

Chapter 6: The Madding Crowd

1. Dunkel, 120.

2. Ibid., 121.

3. Ibid.

4. Carlton Miles, "Jaunts into Brightest England: Sir Arthur Wing Pinero," *Theatre*, April 1923, 25.

5. Unpublished manuscript, Garrick.

6. The memorandum no longer exists but was quoted by Pinero in a letter to the *Daily News*, 31 December 1881; *CL*, 59. The principal modern discussions of the

ensuing controversy over the relationship between Hardy's *Far from the Mad-
ding Crowd* and Pinero's *The Squire* are: James F. Stottlar, "Hardy v. Pinero,"
Theatre Survey 18 (November 1977), 22–43; and R. L. Purdy, *Thomas Hardy:
A Bibliographical Study* (Oxford: Oxford University Press, 1954) 28–30. That
Mrs Kendal — despite her later claim in her autobiography, *Dame Madge
Kendal, by Herself* (London: John Murray, 1933), that she had never seen Carr
and Hardy's script — had passed ideas from it to Pinero, was common gossip at
the time (see R. L. Purdy and M. Millgate, eds., *The Collected Letters of Thomas
Hardy, 1840–1892* [Oxford: Clarendon Press, 1978], 101), and Pinero later
confessed as much to Carr (see Purdy, op. cit., 30).

7. Promptbook, Garrick.

8. *Era*, 30 July 1881, 6.

9. *Theatre*, 1 September 1881, 174.

10. *ISDN*, 27 July 1881, 6.

11. *Weekly Dispatch*, 31 July 1881, 6.

12. *Stage*, 29 July 1881, 9.

13. Reprinted in *Era*, 3 September 1881, 6.

14. Letter to the *Daily News*, 4 January 1882; *CL*, 61.

15. M. E. Bancroft and S. Bancroft, *Mr and Mrs Bancroft on and off the Stage*
    (London: Richard Bentley & Son, 1891), 330.

16. Unpublished letter, Rochester.

17. *Era*, 31 September 1881, 9.

18. *Daily News*, 30 December 1881, 3.

19. Letter by J. Comyns Carr to the *Times*, 2 January 1882. This and ensuing
    correspondence on *The Squire* reprinted in *Era*, 7 January 1882, 10. Pinero's
    letters to the *Daily News* are reprinted in *CL*, 58–66.

20. See *Era*, op. cit.

21. See Stottlar, op. cit.

22. *CL*, 59.

23. *Era*, op. cit.

24. Ibid.

25. *CL*, 60–61.

26. *Era*, op. cit.

27. Purdy and Millgate, op. cit., 101.

28. Michael Millgate, *Thomas Hardy* (Oxford: Oxford University Press, 1982), 227.

29. *Era*, op. cit.

30. *Daily News*, 10 January 1882, 2.

31. *CL*, 65.

32. BL Add. Ms. 45291.

33. *Punch*, 14 January 1882.

34. William Archer, *English Dramatists of Today* (London: Sampson Low & Co., 1882), 286.

35. *Times*, 6 March 1882, 6.

36. *CL*, 66.

37. Hesketh Pearson, *Beerbohm Tree* (London: Methuen, 1956), 30.

38. Programme, TM.

39. Bancrofts, op. cit., 340.

Chapter 7: Low Water

1. William Archer, *English Dramatists of Today* (London: Sampson, Low & Co., 1882), 3.

2. Ibid., 11.

3. Ibid., 16.

4. Ibid., 270–271.

5. Cited by Hamilton Fyfe, *Sir Arthur Pinero's Plays and Players* (London: Ernest Benn, 1930), 247.

6. Austin Brereton, *The Life of Sir Henry Irving*, vol. 1 (London: Longmans, 1908), 337.

7. *ILN*, 4 November 1882, 467.

8. *CL*, 69.

9. *Era*, 31 March 1883, 6.

10. *Atheneum*, 31 March 1883, 419.

11. Dunkel, 25.

12. Cited by Walter de la Mare, "The Early Novels of Wilkie Collins," *The Eighteen-Sixties*, ed. John Drinkwater (Cambridge: Cambridge University Press, 1932), 69.

13. *Theatre*, 1 September 1883, 168.

14. Fyfe, op. cit., 250.

15. Myra Hamilton, *Fancy-Far Land* (London: Chapman and Hall, 1901).

16. The disability would affect Angus throughout his life, as a Harley Street specialist, Morrell MacKenzie, writing to Mrs Pinero on 11 April 1891, warned. Letter in Myra Hamilton's Autograph Album, Pierpont Morgan Library, New York.

17. *Times*, 26 March 1883, 6.

18. *CL*, 68.

19. Malcolm C. Salaman, "Arthur Wing Pinero," *Cassell's Magazine* (London, 1899), 358.

20. *Times*, 26 November 1883, 7.

21. M. E. Bancroft and S. Bancroft, *Mr and Mrs Bancroft on and off the Stage* (London: Richard Bentley & Son, 1891), 366.

22. *Truth*, 29 November 1883, 7.

23. Percy Allen, *The Stage Life of Mrs Stirling* (London: T. Fisher Unwin, 1922), 213.

24. *Daily News*, 26 November 1883, 6.

25. *Sportsman*, 29 November 1883, 3.

26. *Daily Telegraph*, 26 November 1883, 3.

27. *ILN*, 1 December 1883, 527.

28. *Referee*, 19 January 1884, 6.

29. Cited in *ILN*, 19 January 1884, 481.

30. *Referee*, op. cit.

31. *Punch*, 26 April 1884, 197.

32. *Stage*, 9 May 1894, 14.

33. Unidentified newspaper review, TM.

34. *Era*, 11 May 1884, 6.

35. *Stage*, op. cit.

36. Johnston Forbes-Robertson, *A Player Under Three Reigns* (London: T. Fisher Unwin, 1925), 124–125.

37. "Prefatory Letter," *TW 1895*, xxvii.

38. *Era*, 29 September 1884, 10.

39. *CL*, 77.

40. Cited by Margaret Scott, *Old Days in Bohemian London* (London: Hutchinson, 1919), 189.

Chapter 8: The Court Farces

1. *Referee*, 22 March 1885, 3.

2. *ILN*, 28 March 1885, 317.

3. *Referee*, op. cit.

4. *New York Times*, 28 March 1885, 5.

5. *ILN*, op. cit.

6. Malcolm Salaman, "Introductory Note" to A. W. Pinero, *The Magistrate* (London: Heinemann, 1892), ix–x.

7. *CL*, 79–80.

8. *The Era Almanac and Annual 1886* (London: Era, 1886), 86–87.

9. M. E. Bancroft and S. Bancroft, *Mr and Mrs Bancroft on and off the Stage* (London: Richard Bentley & Son, 1891), 398.

10. *CL*, 83.

11. *Era*, 23 July 1885, 14.

12. TM.

13. Seymour Hicks, *Between Ourselves* (London: Cassell & Co., 1930), 153–154.

14. *New York Times*, op. cit.

15. Unpublished and undated letter to H. A. Jones, Leeds.

16. John Drew, *My Years on the Stage* (New York: E. P. Dutton, 1922), 111.

17. *New York Times*, 8 October 1885, 5.

18. *Graphic*, 17 October 1885, 3.

19. *Punch*, 1 November 1885, 232.

20. *CL*, 85.

21. H. G. Hibbert, *A Playgoer's Memory* (London: Grant Richards, 1920), 91.

22. *Referee*, 28 March 1886, 3.

23. Membership records, Garrick.

24. George Pleydell Bancroft, *Stage and Bar* (London: Faber, 1939), 99.

25. *CL*, 88.

26. *Daily Telegraph*, 25 October 1886, 3.

27. *CL*, 88.

28. Malcolm Salaman, "Introductory Note" to A. W. Pinero, *Dandy Dick* (London: Heinemann, 1893), vi.

29. Previously unpublished letter, Rochester.

30. *Era*, 29 January 1887, 9.

31. *Graphic*, 5 February 1887, 131; *Times*, 31 January 1887, 3; *Era*, 29 January 1887, 12.

32. *ILN*, 5 February 1887, 149.

33. *Era*, 30 July 1887, 12.

34. Alexander Leggatt, "Pinero: From Farce to Social Drama," *Modern Drama*, September 1974, 333.

Notes

Chapter 9: New Directions

1. Programme, TM.

2. Cited by H. G. Hibbert, *A Playgoer's Memory* (London: Grant Richards, 1920), 90.

3. Unpublished letter to W. Moy Thomas (2 February 1888), University of Chicago library.

4. The location of the pub, and Dick Phenyl's description of it as "a very old-established inn . . . Doc'or Johnson and all that sor' o' thing"(13), indicate that Pinero was really referring to "Ye Olde Cheshire Cheese," the pub that had belonged to his wife's father, Beaufoy Moore.

5. Hibbert, op. cit.

6. *CL*, 99.

7. *Daily Telegraph*, 22 March 1888, 5.

8. Hibbert, op. cit.

9. Daniel Frohman, *Memories of a Manager* (London: Heinemann, 1911), 54–55.

10. *World*, 28 March 1888, 9–10.

11. BL Add. Ms. 45294.

12. William Archer, *The Old Drama and the New* (London: Heinemann, 1923), 288.

13. Previously unpublished letter, Rochester.

14. *Pall Mall Gazette*, 25 April 1889, 1.

15. Cited in *Theatre*, 1 June 1889, 317.

16. *ILN*, 2 May 1889, 551.

17. *CL*, 106–107.

18. *World*, 1 May 1889, 8.

19. *Stage*, 14 June 1889, 9.

20. Unpublished letter from Sidney Grundy to William Archer (16 May 1889), BL Add. Ms. 45291.

21. *World*, 22 May 1889, 9.

22. *CL*, 109.

23. *CL*, 118, 123.

24. Michael Orme (Mrs Grein), *J. T. Grein* (London: John Murray, 1934), 68.

25. Unpublished letter to H. A. Jones (29 January 1890), Leeds.

26. Full article reprinted in James Woodfield, *English Theatre in Transition 1881–1914* (London: Croom Helm, 1984), 175–177.

27. Ibid., 40–41.

28. *CL*, 115.

29. *Entr'Acte*, 16 November 1889, 9.

30. *CL*, 115.

31. Johnston Forbes-Robertson, *A Player Under Three Reigns* (London: T. Fisher Unwin, 1925), 126.

32. Malcolm C. Salaman, "Introductory Note" to Arthur Pinero, *The Cabinet Minister* (London: Heinemann, 1892), x.

33. Unpublished letter (21 April 1890), Rochester.

34. *Theatre*, 1 June 1890, 327.

35. Malcolm C. Salaman, "Arthur Wing Pinero," *Cassell's Magazine* (London, 1899), 362.

36. *Era*, 29 November 1890, 10.

37. Unpublished letter to Clement Scott (1 December 1890), Rochester.

38. Unpublished letter to J. T. Grein (9 December 1890), Rochester.

39. Forbes-Robertson, op. cit., 125.

40. William Archer, *The Old Drama and the New* (London: Heinemann, 1923), 189.

41. *Times*, 9 March 1891, 8.

Act 3: Climax

Chapter 10: The Second Mrs Tanqueray

1. Malcolm C. Salaman, "Arthur Wing Pinero," *Cassell's Magazine* (London, 1899), 355.

2. "Ibsen and English Drama," *Herald* (London edition), 7 June 1891, 3.

3. *CL*, 135.

4. *CL*, 112.

5. Clayton Hamilton, ed., *The Social Plays of Pinero*, vol. 1 (New York: AMS, 1967 reprint), 20.

6. Preface, A. W. Pinero, *The Times* (London: Heinemann, 1892), vi.

7. *CL*, 132.

8. *CL*, 129.

9. Salaman, *Cassell's Magazine*, op. cit., 356.

10. "Fifty Years: The Theatre in Transition," *Times*, 20 February 1932, 11.

11. Ibid.

12. George Pleydell Bancroft, *Stage and Bar* (London: Faber, 1939), 89.

13. "Fifty Years," op. cit.

14. Graham Robertson, *Time Was* (London: Quartet Books, 1981 reprint), 244.

15. A.E.W. Mason, *Sir George Alexander and the St James's Theatre* (London: Macmillan, 1935), 45–53; *CL*, 137–143.

16. *Sketch*, 15 March 1893, 412.

17. Ellaline Terriss, *Just a Little Bit of String* (London: Hutchinson, 1955), 79.

18. Daniel Frohman, *Memories of a Manager* (London: Heinemann, 1911), 64–65.

19. Robertson, op. cit., 248.

20. *CL*, 142.

21. *ILN*, 8 August 1891, 172.

22. Mrs Patrick Campbell, *My Life and Some Letters* (London: Hutchinson, 1923), 64.

23. Squire Bancroft, *Empty Chairs* (London: John Murray, 1925), 205–207.

24. Cyril Maude, *Behind the Scenes* (London: John Murray, 1927), 86.

25. Campbell, op. cit., 66.

26. Robertson, op. cit., 249.

27. Alan Dent, *Mrs Patrick Campbell* (London: Museum Press, 1961), 179.

28. Campbell, op. cit., 68.

29. Ibid.

30. Margaret Webster, *The Same, Only Different* (London: Gollanz, 1969), 160.

31. Campbell, op. cit., 66.

32. Dent, op. cit., 286.

33. Robertson, op. cit., 249.

34. Campbell, op. cit., 70.

35. *Era*, 29 May 1893, 11.

36. Salaman, *Cassell's Magazine*, op. cit., 356.

37. *Westminster Gazette*, 29 May 1893, 1.

38. *Evening News*, 29 May, 1893, 2.

39. *CL*, 144.

40. *Daily News*, 8 May 1893, 3.

41. *Westminster Gazette*, op. cit.

42. Maude, op. cit., 87.

43. Webster, op. cit., 160.

44. Campbell, op. cit., 73.

45. *Punch*, 10 June 1893, 273.

46. Campbell, op. cit., 72.

47. *Era*, 29 May 1893, 9.

48. *Westminster Gazette*, op. cit.

49. Robertson, op. cit., 247.

50. *Daily News*, 29 May 1893, 3.

51. Maude, op. cit., 87.

52. Campbell, op. cit., 73.

53. *Evening Standard*, 29 May 1893, 2; *Echo*, 29 May 1893, 2.

54. *Punch*, op. cit.

55. *ISDN*, 10 June 1893, 522.

56. *Times*, 29 May 1893, 8.

57. E. B. Charteris, *The Life and Letters of Sir Edmund Gosse* (London: Heinemann, 1931), 228.

58. *CL*, 146.

59. Unpublished letter (28 May 1893), Harvard.

60. Unpublished letter (29 May 1893), Harvard.

61. *TW 1893*, 131–132.

62. This point was later strongly criticised by Shaw. See *OTN*, vol. 1, 61.

63. *Globe*, 29 May 1893, 2; *Westminster Gazette*, 29 May 1893, 3; *Era*, 3 June 1893, 9; *Vanity Fair*, 1 June 1893, 361.

64. *ILN*, 19 August 1893, 212.

65. BL Add. Ms. 45294.

66. *ILN*, 19 August 1893, 212.

67. *Daily Telegraph*, 26 August 1893, 5.

68. Unpublished letter, Lewis and Lewis to Pinero (25 August 1893), Boston Public Library.

69. *World*, 13 September 1893. Archer omits the last two sentences of this passage in *TW 1893*.

70. BL Add Ms. 45294.

71. *CL*, 153.

72. T.M.W. Lund, *The Second Mrs Tanqueray: What? and Why?*, 9th ed. (Liverpool, 1894), BL.

73. *Birmingham Daily Post*, 16 September 1893, 3.

74. *Birmingham Daily Post*, 21 September 1893, 5.

75. Mason, op. cit., 63.

76. Robertson, op. cit., 271.

77. Mason, op. cit.

78. See "Mrs Kendal v. the Public," *Harper's Weekly*, 28 October 1893, 1024.

79. BL Add. Ms. 44294.

80. *World*, 20 December 1893, 15.

Chapter 11: "At the Point of the Pen"

1. *BSCL 1874–1897*, 402.

2. *OTN*, vol. 1, v.

3. *OTN*, vol. 1, 60.

4. Cited by Allan Chapelow, *Shaw: The Chucker-Out* (New York: AMS Press, 1968), 234.

5. *BSCL 1874–1897*, 403.

6. *OTN*, vol. 1, 45.

7. Preface to *Mrs Warren's Profession*, in G. B. Shaw, *Plays Pleasant and Unpleasant* (London: Constable, 1931), 147.

8. Staged by the Independent Theatre on 21 January 1893 at the Opera Comique.

9. BL Add. Ms. 45293.

10. *TW 1893*, 296.

11. See letter to Archer (8 February 1894), *CL*, 156.

12. BL Add. Ms. 45294.

13. Unpublished letter, Berg Collection, NYPL.

14. Unpublished letter, Leeds.

15. BL Add. Ms. 45294.

16. J. Angus Hamilton, "Arthur Wing Pinero," *Munsey's Magazine*, New York, 8 October 1894, 247–251.

17. Unpublished letter to Frederick Hawkins (6 December 1894), New York University libraries.

18. *OTN*, vol. 1, 5.

19. Ibid., 17.

20. Ibid., 30–36.

21. Ibid., 45.

22. Ibid.

23. *TW 1895*, 77.

24. Mrs Patrick Campbell, *My Life and Some Letters* (London: Hutchinson, 1923), 128.

25. E. B. Charteris, *The Life and Letters of Sir Edmund Gosse* (London: Heinemann, 1931), 247.

26. *Sketch*, 20 March 1895, 390; *Pall Mall Gazette*, 14 March 1895, 4.

27. *OTN*, vol. 1, 59–66.

28. *BSCL 1874–1897*, 500–501.

29. BL Add. Ms. 45982.

30. 18 March 1895; *CL*, 172.

31. A typescript of Pinero's speech is held by BL Add. Ms. 45294. Shaw's statement is cited by C. B. Purdom, *A Guide to the Plays of Bernard Shaw* (London: Methuen, 1963), 98.

32. BL Add. Ms. 45294.

33. Unpublished letter to Frederick Hawkins (6 January 1895), New York University libraries.

34. Austin Brereton, *The Life of Sir Henry Irving*, vol. 2 (London: Longmans, 1908), 221–223.

35. Ibid.

36. Ibid.

37. Unpublished letter to Bram Stoker (21 November 1895), Ifan Kyrle Fletcher Catalogue 231, London 1968.

38. Dunkel, 63.

39. Letter to Archer (12 October 1895), *CL*, 166–167.

40. Unpublished letter to R. C. Carton (20 September 1895), Rochester.

41. Ibid.

42. Unpublished letter to Archer (17 January 1896), BL Add. Ms. 45294.

43. *TW 1895*, 313–321.

44. *OTN*, vol. 1, 217.

45. *TW 1895*, xxxii–iii.

46. *OTN*, vol. 2, 56.

47. Previously unpublished letter, Rochester.

48. Garrick.

49. Unpublished letter to Archer (17 January 1896), BL Add. Ms. 45294.

50. *CL*, 172–173.

51. Dunkel, 60.

52. Unpublished letter to Sir Henry Irving (23 September 1896), TM.

53. Unpublished letters to Edmund Gosse (9, 16, 20 November 1896), Leeds.

54. A.E.W. Mason, *Sir George Alexander and the St James's Theatre* (London: Macmillan, 1935),120.

55. Austin Brereton, *"H. B." and Laurence Irving* (London: Grant Richards, 1922), 41.

56. Unpublished letter to H. A. Jones (25 March 1897), Leeds.

57. *TW 1897*, 103.

58. *OTN*, vol. 3, 90–97.

59. *BSCL 1874–1897*, 739.

60. Preface, G. B. Shaw, *Plays Pleasant and Unpleasant* (London: Constable, 1931), viii.

Chapter 12: The Autocrat

1. Irene Vanbrugh, *To Tell My Story* (London: Hutchinson, 1948), 53.

2. Hilda Spong, "Working with Pinero, Barrie and Shaw," *Theatre*, July/August 1920, 32.

3. Clayton Hamilton, *Conversations on Contemporary Drama* (New York: Macmillan, 1924), 116.

4. Cited by Michael Holroyd, *Lytton Strachey: The Unknown Years, 1880–1910* (London: Heinemann, 1967), 315.

5. *CL*, 159.

6. Unpublished letter to William Archer (9 June 1897), BL Add. Ms. 45294.

7. *Stage*, 17 May 1900, 15.

8. See Joel H. Kaplan, " "Have We No Chairs?': Pinero's *Trelawny* and the Myth of Tom Robertson," *Essays in Theatre*, May 1986, 119–133.

9. Dennis Arundel, *The Story of Sadler's Wells* (London: Hamish Hamilton, 1965), 177.

10. Vanbrugh, op. cit., 47.

11. Cited by George Rowell, "Sullivan, Pinero and 'The Beauty Stone,' " *Sir Arthur Sullivan Society Magazine*, 21 (Autumn 1985), 4–14.

12. Myra Hamilton, *Fancy-Far Land* (London: Chapman and Hall, 1901); Myra Hamilton, *Kingdoms Curious* (London: Heinemann, 1903).

13. Cited by Caryl Brahms, *Gilbert and Sullivan* (Boston: Little, Brown, 1975), 238. Other citations from Sullivan's diary taken from Rowell, op. cit.

14. Unpublished letters to Pinero from J. Comyns Carr and Mrs Helen D'Oyly Carte cited in this chapter are held by Garrick.

15. Rowell, op. cit.

16. Undated (c. 30 November 1897).

17. Unpublished letter from Mrs Carte (21 December 1897), Garrick.

18. Vanbrugh, op. cit., 53.

19. Spong, op. cit.

20. Lena Ashwell, *Myself a Player* (London: Michael Joseph, 1936), 256.

21. Cited by Hamilton Fyfe, *Sir Arthur Pinero's Plays and Players* (London: Ernest Benn, 1930), 255.

22. See, for example, William Archer, *Study and Stage* (London: Grant Richards, 1899), 140–141; *OTN*, vol. 3, 307–308.

23. Vanbrugh, op. cit., 48–49.

24. Ibid.

25. *CL*, 179.

26. Archer, op. cit.

27. George Arliss, *On the Stage* (London: John Murray, 1928), 320.

28. *OTN*, vol. 3, 304–310.

29. Ibid., 386.

30. (2 February 1898), Garrick.

31. Brahms, op. cit., 139–140.

32. Max Beerbohm, *More Theatres* (London: Hart-Davis, 1969), 27–28.

33. Vanbrugh, op. cit., 53.

34. Ibid., 54–55.

35. Ibid., 56.

36. *Atheneum*, 15 April 1899, 476.

37. Madge Kendal, *Dame Madge Kendal, by Herself* (London: John Murray, 1933), 53.

38. *Atheneum*, op. cit.

39. *Times*, 10 April 1899, 3.

40. E. B. Charteris, *The Life and Letters of Sir Edmund Gosse* (London: Heinemann, 1931), 260.

41. Unpublished letter to Gosse (15 April 1899), Leeds.

42. Will dated 22 October 1934, Somerset House, London.

43. Alfred Sutro, *Celebrities and Simple Souls* (London: Duckworth 1933), 175.

44. A.E.W. Mason, *Sir George Alexander and the St James's Theatre* (London: Macmillan, 1935), 121.

45. Ibid., 122–123; *CL*, 180–182.

46. Mason, op. cit., 124.

47. J. Angus Hamilton, *The Siege of Mafeking* (London: Methuen, 1900), 44, 282.

48. Ibid., 305.

49. Unpublished letters to Davis (8 August 1899, 3 April 1901), University of Virginia library.

50. Hamilton, op. cit., 193.

51. Ibid., 230.

52. Unpublished letter from Balfour (16 March 1900), Rochester.

53. Unpublished letter from Carson (11 May 1900), Rochester.

54. Letter to the *Daily Mail* (11 September 1900), Texas.

55. *Daily Express*, 1 January 1901, 4.

Chapter 13: Respectability in Danger

1. Harley Granville-Barker, *The Madras House* (London: Methuen, 1977), 58.

2. William Archer, *Playmaking* (London: Chapman & Hall, 1912), 48.

3. *Globe*, 23 September 1901, 4.

4. *World*, 25 September 1901, 29.

5. *New York World*, 24 September 1902, 7.

6. *ILN*, 26 March 1935, 560.

7. Clayton Hamilton, "Critical Preface to *Letty*," in *the Social Plays of Pinero*, vol. 3, ed. Clayton Hamilton (New York: AMS Press, 1967 reprint), 11.

8. William Archer, *Real Conversations* (London: Heinemann, 1904), 20–21.

9. *Times*, 9 September 1902, 8.

10. *Times*, 12 September 1902, 5; 13 September 1902, 14.

11. Hamilton, op. cit., 12.

12. *CL*, 193.

13. Irene Vanbrugh, *To Tell My Story* (London: Hutchinson, 1948), 69.

14. Hamilton, op. cit., 15.

15. *World*, 25 September 1901, 29–30.

16. *Saturday Review*, 28 September 1901, 396.

17. Unpublished letter from Beerbohm to Archer (14 May 1902), BL Add. Ms. 45290.

18. Max Beerbohm, *Around Theatres* (London: Hart-Davis, 1924), 3.

19. William Rothenstein, *Men and Memories* (London: Faber, 1931), 301.

20. David Cecil, *Max* (London: Constable, 1964), 130.

21. Beerbohm, op. cit., 164.

22. Ibid., 282; 289.

23. *World*, 13 October 1903, 607.

24. *World*, 27 October 1903, 679.

25. 27 August 1903, BL Add. Ms. 45925.

26. Vanbrugh, op. cit., 68–69.

27. Pinero had his lecture, "Robert Louis Stevenson: The Dramatist," privately printed by the Chiswick Press in London in 1903.

28. "Musings Without Method," *Blackwood's Magazine*, April 1903, 561.

29. *OTN*, vol. 2, 83.

30. "Preface to *Three Plays by Brieux*," reprinted in *Collected Prefaces of Bernard Shaw* (London: Constable, 1934), 205.

31. Programme, TM.

32. Unpublished letter to Archer (20 October 1903), BL Add. Ms. 45294.

33. *Daily Express*, 13 October 1904, 5.

34. *Times*, 13 October 1904, 4.

35. *Evening News*, 14 October 1904, 1.

36. *Actor Illustrated*, January 1905, 18.

37. *Evening News*, 13 October 1904, 1.

38. *Saturday Review*, 29 October 1904, 546.

39. *Dramatic Mirror*, 31 December 1904, 16.

Chapter 14: England's Premier Dramatist

1. A.E.W. Mason, *Sir George Alexander and the St James's Theater* (London: Macmillan, 1935), 174.

2. Unpublished letter to Archer, BL Add. Ms. 45294.

3. Clayton Hamilton, "Critical Preface to *His House in Order*," in *The Social Plays of Pinero*, vol. 3 (New York: AMS Press, 1967 reprint), 245.

4. Mason, op. cit., 175.

5. Ibid., 174.

6. *CL*, 199.

7. *CL*, 200.

8. Mason, op. cit., 176.

9. Irene Vanbrugh, *To Tell My Story* (London: Hutchinson, 1948), 74.

10. Mason, op. cit., 176.

11. Ibid.

12. Vanbrugh, op. cit., 75.

13. *Daily Telegraph*, 2 February 1906, 5 (as well as reviews in *Times, Morning Leader, Daily Mail*, and *Daily Express* also dated 2 February 1906, TM).

14. *Saturday Review*, 10 February 1906, 168.

15. " 'No Pleasure in the Theatre for Me,' says Pinero," *Theatre Magazine*, September 1906, 234.

16. Unpublished letter from Wyndham (4 April 1906), TM.

17. Edith Craig and Christopher St John, eds., *Ellen Terry's Memoirs* (London: Gollanz, 1933), 281.

18. Unpublished letter, BL Add. Ms. 45294.

19. *Scotsman*, 26 February 1903, 6.

20. Unpublished letter (14 April 1904), BL Add. Ms. 45294.

21. A. W. Pinero, "My Speech at the Lyceum Theatre Meeting," BL Add. Ms. 45294.

22. *Era*, 20 March 1909, 21.

23. Unpublished letter (1 February 1907), BL Add. Ms. 52586.

24. *Daily Telegraph*, 11 May 1908, 7.

25. George Rowell, ed., Introduction to *Plays by A. W. Pinero* (Cambridge: Cambridge University Press, 1986), 10.

26. Clayton Hamilton, "Critical Preface to *Mid-Channel*," in *Social Plays*, vol. 4, 280–281.

27. Vanbrugh, op. cit., 78.

28. Mason, op. cit., 196.

29. Ibid., 195.

30. *BSCL 1898–1910*, 885.

31. Unpublished letter, BL Add. Ms. 45926.

32. *CL*, 214.

33. *BSCL 1898–1910*, 801.

34. Ibid.

35. Ibid., 843.

36. "Queen's Dolls Have Priceless Library," *New York Times*, 24 August 1924, Section 8, 3.

Act 4: Resolution

Chapter 15: Shaw and Pinero

1. Sir George Arthur, *From Phelps to Gielgud* (London: Chapman and Hall, 1936), 187.

2. Unpublished letter from Shaw (20 November 1908), Texas.

3. Unpublished letter from Shaw (24 November 1908), Texas.

4. Unpublished letter from Shaw (7 January 1909), Texas.

5. *BSCL 1898–1910*, 848.

6. Ibid.

7. Ibid., 909–911.

8. Ibid., 912.

9. Cited by C. B. Purdom, *A Guide to the Plays of Bernard Shaw* (London: Methuen, 1963), 98.

10. *Era*, 29 February 1908, 14.

11. Unpublished letter from Barrie to Archer (4 November 1907), BL Add. Ms. 45290.

12. Michael Holroyd, *Bernard Shaw, vol. 2: The Pursuit of Power* (London: Chatto & Windus, 1989), 233.

13. *Times*, 25 September 1907, 7.

14. *Morning Leader*, 2 December 1911, 4.

15. Unpublished letters from Brookfield (20 and 22 December 1908), Rochester.

16. Unpublished letter from Barker to Archer (23 September 1908), BL Add. Ms. 45290.

17. See "Bancroft Babble," *Saturday Review*, 22 May 1909, 662; and Bancroft's (that is, Shaw's) reply in the following issue, 29 May 1909, 688.

18. *Era*, 27 March 1909, 17.

19. *BSCL 1898–1910*, 841–842.

20. *Times*, 20 June 1910, 10.

21. Ibid., 23 June 1910, 13.

22. Ibid., 27 June 1910, 12.

23. Ibid., 28 June 1910, 13.

24. Ibid., 30 June 1910, 12.

25. Ibid., 2 July 1910, 14.

26. *BSCL 1898–1910*, 887.

Notes

27. *CL*, 234.

28. *Stage*, 25 Janaury 1911, 18.

29. *CL*, 227.

30. *Times*, 19 February 1912, 11.

31. E. B. Charteris, *The Life and Letters of Sir Edmund Gosse* (London: Heinemann, 1931), 332.

32. Unpublished letter from Shaw (15 May 1912), Texas.

33. Dunkel, 87.

34. Unpublished letter from Shaw (25 June 1912), Texas.

35. *CL*, 243.

36. *CL*, 244.

37. Unpublished letter from Shaw (13 September 1912), Texas.

38. Unpublished letter to Shaw (26 August 1912), BL Add. Ms. 50547.

39. Previously unpublished letter from Shaw (15 October 1912), Texas.

Chapter 16: Public Ordeals, Private Griefs

1. Angus Hamilton, *Korea* (London: Heinemann, 1904), 300.

2. *Pall Mall Gazette*, 16 June 1913, 8.

3. *Times*, 21 June 1913, 11.

4. *CL*, 248.

5. Alan Dent, ed., *Bernard Shaw and Mrs Patrick Campbell: Their Correspondence* (London: Gollanz, 1952), 19.

6. *BSCL 1898–1910*, 884.

7. Blanche Patch, *Thirty Years with G.B.S.* (London: Gollanz, 1951), 238.

8. Unpublished letter, Garrick.

9. *CL*, 249.

10. Austin Brereton, *"H.B." and Laurence Irving* (London: Grant Richards, 1922), 214.

11. *Daily Telegraph*, 2 September 1915, 3.

12. Preface to Arthur Pinero, *The Big Drum* (London: Heinemann, 1915), viii.

13. Unpublished letter from Shaw (22 October 1915), Texas.

14. Unpublished letter to Shaw (30 October 1915), BL Add. Ms. 50547.

15. Unpublished letter from Shaw (13 November 1915), Texas.

16. "Queen's Dolls Have Priceless Library," *New York Times*, 24 August 1924, Section 8, 3.

17. *Times*, 28 February 1916, 11.

18. Report by G. S. Street, 20 December 1916. Lord Chamberlain's Plays, BL.

19. *Tatler*, 13 March 1918, 345.

20. *CL*, 269.

21. Dunkel, 92.

22. *Times*, 15 September 1917, 13.

23. *CL*, 262; unpublished letter, Myra Pinero to Alexander (18 March 1916), the Lilly Library, Indiana University.

24. *Kinematograph Monthly Film Record*, vol. 5 (January–June 1916), 87.

25. *Bioscope*, 16 March 1916, 1132.

26. *Kinematograph Monthly Film Record*, op. cit.

27. Unpublished letter from Shaw (5 November 1915), Texas.

28. *CL*, 262.

29. Irene Vanbrugh, *To Tell My Story* (London: Hutchinson, 1948), 117.

30. Unpublished letters, Myra Pinero to Alexander (18 March 1916, undated), the Lilly Library, Indiana University.

31. Unpublished letter, May Bright to Pinero (25 August 1919), Rochester.

32. Dunkel, 92.

Chapter 17: A Voice from the Past

1. Sir Arthur Pinero, "Lady Hare," *Times*, 6 October 1931, 15.

2. *CL*, 274.

3. *Times*, 28 May 1921, 13.

4. Ibid.

5. Ibid., 23 February 1922, 13.

6. *CL*, 274.

7. *Times*, 2 March 1922, 10.

8. *Pall Mall Gazette*, 16 June 1913, 8.

9. Carlton Miles, "Jaunts into Brightest England: Sir Arthur Wing Pinero," *Theatre*, April 1923, 25.

10. *Evening News*, 5 June 1922, 3

11. *Evening Standard*, 13 June 1922, 4.

12. *Times*, 23 March 1925, 12.

13. Ibid., 15 December 1922, 10.

14. Ibid., 2 June 1925, 10.

15. Ibid., 31 October 1922, 10.

16. Ibid., 24 November 1926, 12.

17. Ibid., 15 May 1928, 14.

18. William Archer, *The Old Drama and the New* (London: Heinemann, 1923), 285–286.

19. Ibid., 330.

20. George Pleydell Bancroft, *Stage and Bar* (London: Faber, 1939), 278–279.

21. Sean O'Casey, *Autobiographies II* (London: Macmillan, 1963), 263.

22. Ibid., 265.

23. Unpublished letter, Myra Hughes to Shipman (c. November 1927), NYPL.

24. Dunkel, 94.

25. Dunkel, 95–96.

26. Unpublished letter, Barker to Pinero (20 July 1928), Rochester.

27. "The Theatre in the 'Seventies," in *The Eighteen-Seventies*, ed. H. Granville-Barker (Cambridge: Cambridge University Press, 1929), 141–142.

28. Ibid., 159.

29. *Stage*, 30 May 1929, 14.

30. *Times*, 20 February 1932, 11–12.

31. Hesketh Pearson, *The Last Actor-Managers* (London: Methuen, 1974), 29.

32. Carlton Miles, op. cit.

33. W. Somerset Maugham, *The Summing Up* (New York: Literary Guild of America, 1938), 154–155.

34. A. W. Pinero, "Foreword," *Two Plays* (London: Heinemann, 1930), vi.

35. *CL*, 283.

36. *Two Plays*, 209.

37. "Foreword," *Two Plays*, ix–x.

38. *Evening News*, 18 May 1932, 6.

39. *Sunday Times*, 22 May 1932, 6.

40. James Agate, *Ego* (London: Hamish Hamilton, 1935), 164.

41. *Daily Telegraph*, 20 May 1932, 3.

42. BL.

43. Unpublished letter, Harold Child to Pinero (9 January 1932), Rochester.

44. Unpublished letter, Pinero to St John Ervine (17 October 1932), Texas. Replies from Granville-Barker (22 October 1932), Texas; Max Beerbohm (17 October 1932), Edinburgh University Library; and Shaw (16 June 1932), Texas.

45. Dunkel, 119.

46. Unpublished letter to Wagstaff (21 June 1934), Royal Society of Literature.

47. Unpublished letters to Farren (26, 28, and 29 September), NYPL, Berg Collection.

Bibliography

Primary Sources

Plays

The plays are listed in order of composition. After each title, where applicable, is the following information:
- The place and date of the first London (unless otherwise stated) production. (The number of performances, where ascertained, is given in parentheses.)
- Notable revivals, including films and musicals.
- Publication details.

£200 a Year (one-act comedy)
- Globe Theatre, 6 October 1877 (36).
- Unpublished. Manuscript copy in British Library, Lord Chamberlain's Plays (LCP).

La Comète; or, Two Hearts (three-act drama with prologue)
- Theatre Royal, Croydon, 22 April 1878.
- Unpublished. British Library (LCP).

Two Can Play at That Game (one-act comedy)
- Lyceum Theatre, 20 May 1878 (40).
- Unpublished. British Library (LCP).

Daisy's Escape (one-act comedy)
- Lyceum Theatre, 20 September 1879 (31).
- Unpublished. British Library (LCP).

Hester's Mystery (one-act comedy-drama)
- Folly Theatre, 5 June 1880 (308).
- London: T. H. Lacy, 1893.

Bygones (one-act comedy)
- Lyceum Theatre, 18 September 1880 (89).
- Unpublished. British Library (LCP).

The Money-Spinner (two- [originally three-] act comedy)
- Prince of Wales's Theatre, Manchester, 5 November 1880.
- London, St James's Theatre, 8 January 1881 (98). New York, Wallack's Theatre, 21 January 1882.
- London: T. H. Lacy, 1900; Samuel French, 1910.

Imprudence (three-act farce)
- Folly Theatre, 27 July 1881 (54).

- Privately printed. London: Walter Smith, 1881.

Bound to Marry [alternative titles: "The Breadwinner," "The Captain"] (three-act comedy)
- Unperformed.
- Unpublished. Typescript in Garrick Club library.

The Squire (three-act play)
- St James's Theatre, 29 December 1881 (170).
- New York, Daly's Theatre, 10 October 1882 (47).
- London: Samuel French, 1905.

Girls and Boys: A Nursery Tale (three-act comedy)
- Toole's Theatre, 1 November 1882 (53).
- New York, Daly's Theatre, 5 December 1883 (7).
- Unpublished. British Library (LCP).

The Rector: The Story of Four Friends (four-act play)
- Court Theatre, 24 March 1883 (16).
- Unpublished. British Library (LCP).

The Rocket (three-act farce)
- Prince of Wales's Theatre, Liverpool, 30 July 1883.
- London, Gaiety Theatre, 10 December 1883 (51).
- London: Samuel French, 1905.

Lords and Commons (four-act comedy)
- Haymarket Theatre, 24 November 1883 (70).
- New York, Daly's Theatre, 15 November 1884 (10).
- Unpublished. British Library (LCP).

Low Water (three-act comedy)
- Globe Theatre, 12 January 1884 (7).
- Unpublished. British Library (LCP).

The Ironmaster (four-act play, trans. from Georges Ohnet's *Le Maître des Forges*)
- St James's Theatre, 17 April 1884 (200).
- Unpublished. British Library (LCP).

In Chancery (three-act farce)
- Lyceum Theatre, Edinburgh, 19 September 1884.
- London, Gaiety Theatre, 24 December 1884 (36). New York: Madison Square Theatre, 8 June 1885 (24). Musical: *Who's Hooper?* (book by Fred Thompson, music by Howard Talbot and Ivor Novello), Adelphi Theatre, 13 September 1919 (350).
- London: Samuel French, 1905.

The Magistrate (three-act farce)
- Court Theatre, 21 March 1885 (363).
- New York, Daly's Theatre, 7 October 1885 (75). Chichester, Festival Theatre, 21 May 1969. London, Cambridge Theatre, 18 September 1969. London, Old Vic, 18 March, 1959. National Theatre (Lyttelton), 24 September 1986. Musical: *The Boy* (book by Fred Thompson, music by Lionel Monckton and Howard Talbot), Adelphi Theatre, 14 September 1917 (803). Films: Samuelson, 1921; *Those Were the Days*, Elstree Studios, 1934.

- London: Heinemann, 1892; Samuel French, 1936. Also in *Pinero: Three Plays*, introduced by Stephen Wyatt (London: Methuen, 1985).

Mayfair (five-act play adapted from Victorien Sardou's *Maison Neuve*)
- St James's Theatre, 31 October 1885 (53).
- Privately printed. London: J. Miles & Co., 1885.

The Schoolmistress (three-act farce)
- Court Theatre, 27 March 1886 (291).
- New York, Standard Theatre, 7 December 1886 (28). London, Savoy Theatre, 8 April 1964. Manchester, Royal Exchange Theatre, 8 February 1979.
- London: Heinemann, 1894. Also in George Rowell, ed., *Plays by A. W. Pinero* (Cambridge: Cambridge University Press, 1986).

The Hobby-Horse (three-act comedy)
- St James's Theatre, 23 October 1886 (109).
- London: Heinemann, 1892.

Dandy Dick (three-act farce)
- Court Theatre, 27 January 1887 (262).
- New York, Daly's Theatre, 5 October 1887. London, Mermaid Theatre, 18 August 1965. Chichester, Festival Theatre, 25 July 1973. London, Garrick Theatre, 17 October 1973. Film: Elstree Studios, 1935.
- London: Heinemann, 1893 and 1959; Samuel French, 1936.

Sweet Lavender (three-act comedy)
- Terry's Theatre, 21 March 1888 (684).
- New York, Lyceum Theatre, 13 November 1888. London, Ambassador's Theatre, 14 December 1922 (90). Films: Hepworth, 1916; Paramount, 1920.
- London: Heinemann, 1893.

The Weaker Sex (three-act comedy)
- Theatre Royal, Manchester, 28 September 1888. Revised version: Court Theatre, London, 16 March 1889 (61).
- London: Heinemann, 1894.

The Profligate (four-act play)
- Garrick Theatre (inaugural production), 24 April 1889 (129).
- Film: Ideal Company, 1917.
- London: Heinemann, 1891.

The Cabinet Minister (four-act farce)
- Court Theatre, 23 April 1890 (199).
- New York, Daly's Theatre, 12 January 1892 (6). Manchester, Royal Exchange Theatre, 17 December 1987. London, Albery Theatre, 21 November 1991.
- London: Heinemann, 1892; Birmingham: Oberon Books, 1987.

Lady Bountiful (four-act play)
- Garrick Theatre, 7 March 1891 (65).
- New York, Lyceum Theatre, 15 November 1891 (53).
- London: Heineman, 1891.

The Times (four-act comedy)
- Terry's Theatre, 24 October 1891 (155).
- London: Heinemann, 1891.

Bibliography

The Amazons (three-act farce)
- Court Theatre, 7 March 1893 (114).
- New York, Lyceum Theatre, 19 February 1894. Film: Paramount, 1917.
- London: Heinemann, 1894.

The Second Mrs Tanqueray (four-act play)
- St James's Theatre, 27 May 1893 (225).
- New York (Kendal's production), Star Theatre, 9 October 1893 (18). London, Playhouse, 3 June 1922 (220); Haymarket Theatre, 29 August 1950 (206); National Theatre (Lyttelton) 15 December 1981. Films: Ideal Film Company, 1917; Vandyke, 1952.
- London: Heinemann, 1895; Samuel French, 1936. Also in Clayton Hamilton, ed., *The Social Plays of Arthur Wing Pinero*, vol. 1 (New York: AMS, 1967 reprint); *Pinero: Three Plays*; and *Plays by A. W. Pinero*.

The Notorious Mrs Ebbsmith (four-act play)
- Garrick Theatre, 15 March 1895 (86).
- New York, Abbey's Theatre, 23 December 1895.
- London: Heinemann, 1895. Also in *The Social Plays*, vol. 1.

The Benefit of the Doubt (three-act comedy)
- Comedy Theatre, 16 October 1895 (74).
- New York, Lyceum Theatre, 6 January 1896 (30).
- London: Heinemann, 1895.

The Princess and the Butterfly; or, The Fantastics (four-act comedy)
- St James's Theatre, 29 March 1897 (97).
- New York, Lyceum Theatre, 23 November 1897 (79).
- London: Heinemann, 1898.

Trelawny of the "Wells' (four-act comedy)
- Court Theatre, 20 January 1898 (135).
- New York, Lyceum Theatre, 22 November 1898 (131). London, Old Vic, 1 June 1925; National Theatre (Old Vic), 17 November, 1965; Comedy Theatre, 7 December 1992; National Theatre (Olivier), 18 February 1993. Musical: *Trelawny* (adapted by Aubrey Woods, George Rowell, and Julian Slade), Bristol, Old Vic, 12 January 1972; London, Sadler's Wells, 3 August 1972. Films: Hepworth, 1916; *The Actress*, 1928.
- London: Heinemann, 1899; Samuel French, 1936. Also in *Pinero: Three Plays*; *Plays by A. W. Pinero*.

The Beauty Stone (light opera; with J. Comyns Carr; music by A. S. Sullivan)
- Savoy Theatre, 28 May 1898 (50).
- London: Chapell & Co., 1898.

The Gay Lord Quex (four-act comedy)
- Globe Theatre, 8 April 1899 (300).
- New York, Criterion Theatre, 12 November 1900 (67). London, Albery Theatre, 16 June 1975. Film: Ideal Company, 1918.
- London: Heinemann, 1900. Also in *The Social Plays*, vol. 2.

Iris (five-act play)
- Garrick Theatre, 21 September 1901 (115).
- New York, Criterion Theatre, 23 September 1902 (77). London, Adelphi Theatre, 21 March 1925 (150). Films: Hepworth, 1916; *A Slave of Vanity*, 1920.

- London: Heinemann, 1902. Also in *The Social Plays*, vol. 2.

Letty (four-act play with epilogue)
- Duke of York's Theatre, 8 October 1904 (123).
- New York, Hudson Theatre, 12 September 1904 (64).
- London: Heinemann, 1904. Also in *The Social Plays*, vol. 3.

A Wife Without a Smile (three-act farce)
- Wyndham's Theatre, 12 October 1904 (77).
- New York, Criterion Theatre, 19 December 1904 (16).
- London: Heinemann, 1905.

His House in Order (four-act play)
- St James's Theatre, 1 February 1906 (430).
- New York, Empire Theatre, 3 September 1906 (127). London, New Theatre, 6 July 1951 (114). Films: Paramount, 1920; Ideal Company, 1928.
- London: Heinemann, 1906. Also in *The Social Plays*, vol. 3.

The Thunderbolt: An Episode in the History of a Provincial Family (four-act play)
- St James's Theatre, 9 May 1908 (58).
- London, Arts Theatre, 12 September 1945.
- London: Heinemann, 1909. Also in *The Social Plays*, vol. 4; *Plays by A. W. Pinero*.

Mid-Channel (four-act play)
- St James's Theatre, 2 September 1909 (58).
- New York, Empire Theatre, 31 January 1910 (96). London, Royalty Theatre, 30 October 1922. Film: Equity Pictures, 1920.
- London: Heinemann, 1911. Also in *The Social Plays*, vol. 4.

Preserving Mr Panmure (four-act farce)
- Comedy Theatre, 19 January 1911 (99).
- New York, Lyceum Theatre, 27 February 1912 (31). London, Arts Theatre, 15 November 1950. Chichester, Festival Theatre, 5 August 1991.
- London: Heinemann, 1912.

The "Mind the Paint" Girl (four-act comedy)
- Duke of York's Theatre, 17 February 1912 (126).
- New York, Lyceum Theatre, 9 September 1912 (136).
- London: Heinemann, 1913.

The Widow of Wasdale Head (one-act comedy)
- Duke of York's Theatre, 14 October 1912 (26).
- In Barrett H. Clarke, ed., *Representative One-Act Plays* (Boston: Little, Brown, 1921).

Playgoers: A Domestic Episode (one-act comedy)
- St James's Theatre, 31 March 1913 (70).
- London: Samuel French, 1913; and in Constance M. Martin, ed., *Fifty One-Act Plays* (London: Gollanz, 1934).

The Bulkley Peerage: A Very Grand Guignolette (farcical sketch)
- No professional performance.
- *Pearson's Magazine* 38 (December 1914): 654–658.

The Big Drum (four-act play)
- St James's Theatre, 1 September 1915 (111).

- London: Heinemann, 1915.

Mr Livermore's Dream: A Lesson in Thrift (propaganda sketch)
- Coliseum, 15 January 1917 (12).
- Privately printed. London: Chiswick Press, 1917.

The Freaks: An Idyll of Suburbia (three-act comedy)
- New Theatre, 14 February 1918 (51).
- London: Heinemann, 1922.

Monica's Blue Boy: A Wordless Play (music by Sir Frederick Cowen)
- New Theatre, 8 April 1918 (38).
- Unpublished. Typescript in Garrick Club library.

Quick Work: A Story of a War Marriage (three-act comedy)
- Stamford Theatre, Stamford, Conn., 14 November 1919.
- Privately printed. London: Chiswick Press, 1918.

A Seat in the Park: A Warning (one-act play)
- Winter Garden, 21 February 1922 (1).
- London: Samuel French, 1922.

The Enchanted Cottage: A Fable (three-act comedy)
- Duke of York's Theatre, 1 March 1922 (64).
- New York: Ritz Theatre, 31 March 1923. Films: 1924; RKO, 1945.
- London: Heinemann, 1922.

A Private Room (one-act play)
- Little Theatre, 14 May 1928 (23).
- London: Samuel French, 1928.

Dr Harmer's Holidays (play in nine scenes)
- Shubert-Belasco Theatre, Washington, D.C., 16 March 1931.
- In *Two Plays* (London: Heinemann, 1930).

Child Man (three-act farce)
- Unperformed.
- In *Two Plays*.

A Cold June (three-act comedy)
- Duchess Theatre, 29 May 1932 (19).
- Privately printed. London: Chiswick Press, 1932.

Late of Mockford's (three-act play)
- Unperformed.
- Typescript in British Library.

Fiction and Verse

"Capel and Capello," *The Era Almanac and Annual 1880*. London: *Era*, 1880, 105–110.

"Consulting the Oracle," *The Era Almanac and Annual 1886*. London: *Era*, 1886), 86–87.

"Confessions of a Theatrical Swindler," *The Era Almanac and Annual 1882*. London: *Era*, 1882, 102–105.

Bibliography

"A Fairy," *The Era Almanac and Annual 1883*. London: *Era*, 1883, 65.

"A Fallen Star," *The Era Almanac and Annual 1881*, London: *Era*, 1881: 119–124; reprinted in Leopold Wagner, ed., *20 Stories by 20 Tellers*. London: Fisher and Unwin, 1905.

"The Inverness Cape," *Theatre* (August 1880): 77–84.

"One Day," *Theatre* (January 1884): 50.

"The Riddle," *Theatre* (September 1883): 168.

"A Theatrical Art Union," *The Era Almanac and Annual 1879*: 52–54.

Articles, Prefaces, Speeches, and Addresses

"At the Beginning," *The Era Almanac and Annual 1903*. London: *Era*, 1903, 25–26.

"Foreword," *Two Plays*. London: Heinemann, 1930.

"Introduction," in L. N. Tolstoi, *The Fruits of Enlightenment*. London: Heinemann, 1891.

"Introduction," in Leonard Merrick, *The Position of Peggy Harper*. London: Hodder & Stoughton, 1918.

"Introductory Note," in A. W. Pinero, *The Times*. London: Heinemann, 1891.

"J. L. Toole: A Great Comic Actor," *Times*, (12 March 1932): 13.

"Letter" (on Lady Bancroft as an actress), in Squire Bancroft, *Empty Chairs*. London: John Murray, 1925.

"Mathews and Sothern," *The Era Almanac and Annual 1884*. London: *Era*, 1884, 86–88.

"The Modern British Drama" (Speech to the Royal Academy, 3 May 1895), *Theatre* 25 (June 1895): 346–368.

"My Speech to the Garrick Club," in Wilbur Dwight Dunkel, *Sir Arthur Pinero*. Chicago: University of Chicago Press, 1941.

"Prefatory Letter," in William Archer, *The Theatrical World of 1895*. London: Walter Scott, 1896.

"Prefatory Note," in W. L. Courtney, *The Idea of Tragedy in Ancient and Modern Drama*. London: Constable, 1900.

"Robert Browning as a Dramatist," *Transactions of the Royal Society of Literature*, second series, 31 (1932): 255–268.

"Robert Louis Stevenson as a Dramatist," in Brander Matthews, ed., *Papers on Playmaking*. New York: Hill and Wang, 1957.

"The Theatre in the 'Seventies," in Harley Granville-Barker, ed., *The Eighteen-Seventies: Essays by Fellows of the Royal Society of Literature*. Cambridge: Cambridge University Press, 1929.

"The Theatre in Transition," *Times* (20 February 1922): 11, 15. Reprinted in *Fifty Years: Memories and Contrasts: A Composite Picture of the Period 1882–1932 by Twenty-Seven Contributors to The Times*. London: Butterworth, 1931.

"Theatrical Byways," *Theatre*, 2 (May 1879): 234–237.

Bibliography

"Tom Robertson's Pals," *Theatre Guild Magazine*, 6 (1929): 19–21, 47–49.

Interviews

"Arthur Wing Pinero," *Era* (3 September 1881): 6.

"How I Construct My Plays: A Chat with Mr Pinero," *Sketch* (15 March 1893): 412–413.

"Jaunts into Brightest England: Sir Arthur Wing Pinero," by Carlton Miles, *Theatre* (April 1923): 25, 56.

"A Morning with Mr. Pinero," *Era* (12 November 1892): 11.

""No Pleasure in the Theatre for Me," Says Pinero," *Theatre Magazine* (September 1906): 234–237.

"Personal Portraits by Walter Tittle: Sir Arthur Pinero," *Illustrated London News* (4 April 1925): 601.

"A Talk with Pinero," *New York Times* (5 April 1925): section 9, 2.

Secondary Sources

Agate, James. *Ego: The Autobiography of James Agate*. London: Hamish Hamilton, 1935.

———. *Ego 2*. London: Gollanz, 1936.

Allen, Percy. *The Stage Life of Mrs Stirling*. London: T. Fisher Unwin, 1922.

Archer, Charles. *William Archer: His Life, Work and Friendships*. London: Allen and Unwin, 1931.

Archer, William. *About the Theatre*. London: T. Fisher Unwin, 1886.

———. *English Dramatists of Today*. London: Sampson Low & Co., 1882.

———. *The Old Drama and the New*. London: Heinemann, 1923.

———. *Playmaking: A Manual of Craftsmanship*. London: Chapman and Hall, 1912.

———. *Real Conversations*. London: Heinemann, 1904.

———. *Study and Stage: A Year-Book of Criticism*. London: Grant Richards, 1899.

———. *The Theatrical "World" of 1893, 1894, 1895, 1896, 1897*. 5 vols. London: Walter Scott, 1894–1898.

Archer, William, and H. Granville-Barker. *A National Theatre: Scheme and Estimates*. London: Duckworth & Co., 1907.

Arliss, George. *On the Stage*. London: John Murray, 1928.

Arthur, George. *From Phelps to Gielgud*. London: Chapman and Hall, 1936.

Arundell, Dennis. *The Story of Sadler's Wells*. London: Hamish Hamilton, 1965.

Ashwell, Lena. *Myself a Player*. London: Michael Joseph, 1936.

Bibliography

Baker, Michael. *The Rise of the Victorian Actor*. London: Croom Helm, 1978.

Bancroft, George Pleydell. *Stage and Bar*. London: Faber, 1939.

Bancroft, M. E., and S. Bancroft. *Mr and Mrs Bancroft on and off the Stage*. London: Richard Bentley and Son, 1891.

Bancroft, Squire. *Empty Chairs*. London: John Murray, 1925.

Barnes, J. H. *Forty Years on the Stage*. London: Chapman and Hall, 1914.

Beerbohm, Max. *Around Theatres*. London: Rupert Hart-Davis, 1924.

———. *Last Theatres*. London: Rupert Hart-Davis, 1970.

———. *More Theatres*. London: Rupert Hart-Davis, 1969.

Behrman, S. N. *Conversation with Max*. London: Hamish Hamilton, 1960.

Blow, Sydney. *Through Stage Doors*. Edinburgh and London: W. & R. Chambers, 1958.

Booth, Michael. *Theatre in the Victorian Age*. Cambridge: Cambridge University Press, 1991.

Brahms, Caryl. *Gilbert & Sullivan*. Boston: Little, Brown, 1975.

Brandon, Thomas. *Charley's Aunt's Father*. London: MacGibbon & Kee, 1955.

Brereton, Austin. *"H.B." and Laurence Irving*. London: Grant Richards, 1922.

———. *The Life of Henry Irving*. London: Longmans, 1908.

Brookfield, Charles. *Random Reminiscences*. London: Edward Arnold, 1902.

Burnand, Francis C. *Records and Reminiscences*. London: Methuen, 1905.

Campbell, Mrs Patrick. *My Life and Some Letters*. London: Hutchinson, 1922.

Cecil, David. *Max: A Biography*. London: Constable, 1964.

Chapelow, Allan. *Shaw: The Chucker-Out*. New York: AMS Press, 1968.

Charteris, E. B. *The Life and Letters of Sir Edmund Gosse*. London: Heinemann, 1931.

Cook, Dutton. *Nights at the Play*. London: Chatto & Windus, 1883.

Cooper, Gladys. *Gladys Cooper*. London: Hutchinson, 1931.

Davies, Cecil W. "Pinero: The Drama of Reputation," *English* 14 (Spring 1962): 13–17.

Dawick, John. "The "First" *Mrs Tanqueray*," *Theatre Quarterly* 35 (Autumn 1979): 77–93.

Denison, Patricia D. "Drama in Rehearsal: Arthur W. Pinero's *Trelawny of the 'Wells,'" Modern Drama* 31 (1988): 141–156.

Dent, Alan, ed. *Bernard Shaw and Mrs Patrick Campbell: Their Correspondence*. London: Gollanz, 1952.

———. *Mrs Patrick Campbell*. London: Museum Press, 1961.

Donaldson, Frances. *The Actor-Managers*. London: Weidenfeld and Nicolson, 1970.

Drew, John. *My Years on the Stage*. New York: E. P. Dutton, 1922.

Bibliography

Drinkwater, John, ed. *The Eighteen-Sixties: Essays by Fellows of the Royal Society of Literature*. Cambridge: Cambridge University Press, 1929.

Duncan, Barry. *The St James's Theatre*. London: Barrie and Rockcliff, 1964.

Dunkel, Wilbur Dwight. *Sir Arthur Pinero: A Critical Biography with Letters*. Chicago: University of Chicago Press, 1941.

Eliot, W. G. *In My Anecdotage*. London: Phillip Allen & Co., 1925.

Ellman, Richard. *Oscar Wilde*. London: Penguin, 1988. Reprint.

Ervine, St John. *The Theatre in My Time*. London: Rich & Cowan, 1933.

Filon, Augustin. *The English Stage*. Trans. Frederick Whyte. London: John Milne, 1897.

Forbes-Robertson, Johnston. *A Player Under Three Reigns*. London: T. Fisher Unwin, 1925.

Foulkes, Richard. *The Calverts: Actors of Some Importance*. London: Society for Theatre Research, 1992.

Frohman, Daniel. *Memories of a Manager*. London: Heinemann, 1911.

Fyfe, Hamilton. *Arthur Wing Pinero, Playwright: A Study*. London: Greening & Co., 1902.

———. *Sir Arthur Pinero's Plays and Players*. London: Ernest Benn, 1930.

Girton, Tom. *The Abominable Clubman*. London: Hutchinson, 1964.

Granville-Barker, Harley, ed. *The Eighteen-Seventies: Essays by Fellows of the Royal Society of Literature*. Cambridge: Cambridge University Press, 1929.

Griffin, Penny. *Arthur Wing Pinero and Henry Arthur Jones*. London: Macmillan, 1991.

Grossmith, George. *GG*. London: Hutchinson, 1933.

Hamilton, Clayton, ed. *The Social Plays of Arthur Wing Pinero*. 4 vols. New York: AMS Press, 1967. Reprint.

Hamilton, J. Angus. "Arthur Wing Pinero," *Munsey's Magazine* (October 1894): 247–251.

———. *Korea*. London: Heinemann, 1904.

———. *The Siege of Mafeking*. London: Methuen, 1900.

Hamilton, Myra. *Fancy-Far Land*. London: Chapman and Hall, 1901.

———. *The Pinero Birthday Book*. London: Heinemann, 1898.

Hardwicke, Cedric. *A Victorian in Orbit*. London: Methuen, 1961.

Harker, Joseph. *Studio and Stage*. London: Nisbet & Co., 1924.

Hendrickx, Johan R. "Pinero's Court Farces: A Revaluation," *Modern Drama* 26 (1983): 54–61.

Hibbert, H. G. *A Playgoer's Memory*. London: Grant Richards, 1920.

Hicks, Seymour. *Between Ourselves*. London: Cassell & Co., 1930.

———. *Hail Fellow, Well Met*. London: Staples Press, 1949.

————. *Me and My Missus.* London: Cassell & Co., 1939.

Holroyd, Michael. *Bernard Shaw,* vol. 1: *The Search for Love.* London: Chatto & Windus, 1988.

————. *Bernard Shaw,* vol. 2: *The Pursuit of Power.* London: Chatto & Windus, 1989.

————. *Lytton Strachey: The Unknown Years, 1880–1910.* London: Heinemann, 1967.

Irving, Laurence. *Henry Irving.* London: Faber, 1951.

————. *The Successors.* London: Rupert Hart-Davis, 1967.

Jenkins, Anthony. *The Making of Victorian Drama.* Cambridge: Cambridge University Press, 1991.

Jones, Doris Arthur. *The Life and Letters of Henry Arthur Jones.* London: Gollanz, 1930.

Kaplan, Joel H. "Edwardian Pinero," *Nineteenth Century Theatre,* 17 (Summer and Winter 1989): 20–49.

————. " 'Have We No Chairs?': Pinero's *Trelawny* and the Myth of Tom Robertson," *Essays in Theatre* (May 1986): 119–133.

Kendal, M. *Dame Madge Kendal, by Herself.* London: John Murray, 1933.

Laurence, Dan H., ed. *Bernard Shaw Collected Letters 1874–1897; 1898–1910.* London: Reinhardt, 1965, 1972.

Lawrence, Arthur. *Sir Arthur Sullivan: Life, Story, Letters and Reminscences.* London: James Bowden, 1899.

Lazenby, Walter. *Arthur Wing Pinero.* New York: Twayne Publishers, 1972.

Leggatt, Alexander. "Pinero: From Farce to Social Drama," *Modern Drama* 17 (September 1974): 329–344.

Mander, Raymond, and Joe Mitchenson. *The Lost Theatres of London.* London: Rupert Hart-Davis, 1968.

————. *The Theatres of London.* London: Rupert Hart-Davis, 1963.

Mackail, Denis. *The Story of J.M.B.* London: Peter Davies, 1963.

Martin-Harvey, John. *The Autobiography of Sir John Martin-Harvey.* London: Sampson Low, n.d.

Mason, A.E.W. *Sir George Alexander and the St James's Theatre.* London: Macmillan, 1935.

Maude, Cyril. *Behind the Scenes with Cyril Maude.* London: John Murray, 1927.

Maugham, W. Somerset. *The Summing Up.* New York: Literary Guild of America, 1938.

Meisel, Martin. *Shaw and the Nineteenth Century Theatre.* New York: Limelight Editions, 1984. Reprint.

Merrick, Leonard. *The Position of Peggy Harper.* London: Hodder & Stoughton, 1918.

Bibliography

Miles, Carlton. "Jaunts into Brightest England: Sir Arthur Wing Pinero," *Theatre* (April 1923): 25, 56.

Millgate, Michael. *Thomas Hardy*. Oxford: Oxford University Press, 1982.

Miner, Edmund J. "The Limited Naturalism of Arthur Pinero," *Modern Drama* 19 (June 1976): 147–159.

———. "The Novelty of Arthur Pinero's Court Fraces," *English Literature in Transition* 19:4 (1976): 299–305.

———. "The Theme of Disillusionment in the Drama of Arthur Pinero," *Contemporary Review* 226 (April 1975): 184–190.

Newton, H. Chance ("Carados"). *Cues and Curtain Calls*. London: Bodley Head, 1927.

Nicoll, Allardyce. *English Drama 1900–1930. The Beginnings of the Modern Period*. Cambridge: Cambridge University Press, 1973.

———. *A History of English Drama*, vol. 5: *Late Nineteenth Century Drama* (rev. ed.), and vol. 6: *Alphabetical Catalogue of Plays*. Cambridge: Cambridge University Press, 1959.

O'Casey, Sean. *Autobiographies*. London: Macmillan, 1963. Reprint.

Orme, Michael [Mrs Grein]. *J. T. Grein: The Story of a Pioneer 1862–1935*. London: John Murray, 1936.

Patch, Blanche. *Thirty Years with G.B.S.* London: Gollanz, 1951.

Pearson, Hesketh. *Beerbohm Tree: His Life and Laughter*. London: Methuen, 1956.

———. *The Last Actor-Managers*. London: Methuen, 1974.

———. "Pinero and Barrie," *Theatre Arts* (July 1958): 56–59.

Pemberton, T. Edgar. *John Hare, Comedian*. London: Routledge, 1895.

———. *The Kendals*. London: C. A. Pearson, 1930.

Peters, Margot. *Mrs Pat*. London: Hamish Hamilton, 1984.

Playfair, Nigel. *Hammersmith Boy*. London: Faber, 1930.

Pope, W. MacQueen. *Ghosts and Greasepaint*. London: Robert Hale, 1951.

Purdom, C. B. *A Guide to the Plays of Bernard Shaw*. London: Methuen, 1963.

Purdy, Richard. *Thomas Hardy: A Bibliographical Study*. Oxford: Oxford University Press, 1954.

Purdy, Richard, and Michael Millgate, eds. *The Collected Letters of Thomas Hardy*, vol 1: *1840–1892*. Oxford: Clarendon Press, 1978.

Robertson, Graham. *Time Was*. London: Quartet Books, 1981. Reprint.

Robins, Elizabeth. *Both Sides of the Curtain*. London: Heinemann, 1940.

Ronning, R. J. "The Eccentric: The English Comic Farce of Sir Arthur Pinero," *Quarterly Journal of Speech* 63 (February 1977): 51–58.

Rothenstein, William. *Men and Memories*. London: Faber, 1931.

Rowell, George, ed. *Plays by A. W. Pinero*. Cambridge: Cambridge University Press, 1986.

Bibliography

————. "Sullivan, Pinero and 'The Beauty Stone,' " *Sir Arthur Sullivan Magazine* 21 (Autumn 1965): 4–14.

————. *Theatre in the Age of Irving*. Oxford: Basil Blackwell, 1981.

————, ed. *Victorian Dramatic Criticism*. London: Methuen, 1971.

————. *The Victorian Theatre 1792–1914*. 2nd ed. Cambridge: Cambridge University Press, 1978.

Salaman, Malcolm C. "Arthur Wing Pinero: The Man and the Dramatist," *Cassell's Magazine* (1899): 354–362.

Sawin, Lewis. *Alfred Sutro: A Man with a Heart*. Niwot, Colo.: University Press of Colorado, 1989.

Scott, Clement. *The Drama of Yesterday and Today*. London: Macmillan, 1899.

Scott, Margaret. *Old Days in Bohemian London*. London: Hutchinson, 1899.

Shaw, Bernard. *Our Theatres in the Nineties*. 3 vols. London: Constable, 1932.

Spong, Hilda. "Working with Pinero, Barrie and Shaw," *Theatre* (July/August 1920): 32–33.

Stoker, Bram. *Personal Reminiscences of Sir Henry Irving*. London: Heinemann, 1906.

Stottlar, James F. "Hardy v. Pinero: Two Stage Versions of *Far from the Madding Crowd*," *Theatre Survey* 18 (November 1977): 22–43.

Sutro, Alfred. *Celebrities and Simple Souls*. London: Duckworth, 1933.

Taylor, John Russell. *The Rise and Fall of the Well-Made Play*. London: Methuen, 1967.

Terriss, Ellaline. *Just a Little Bit of String*. London: Hutchinson, 1955.

Terry, Ellen. *The Story of My Life*. London: Hutchinson, 1933.

Tittle, Walter. "Personal Portraits: Sir Arthur Pinero," *Illustrated London News* (4 April 1925): 601–602.

Toole, J. L., and Joseph Hatton. *Reminiscences of J. L. Toole*. London: Hurst and Blackett, 1889.

Vanbrugh, Irene. *To Tell My Story*. London: Hutchinson, 1948.

Walkley, A. B. *Drama and Life*. London: Methuen, 1907.

Ward, Genevieve, and Richard Whiting, *Both Sides of the Curtain*. London: Cassell & Co., 1918.

Wearing, J. P. "Arthur Wing Pinero," in Stanley Weintraub, ed., *Dictionary of Literary Biography*, vol. 10. Detroit: Gale Research Co., 1982.

————, ed. *The Collected Letters of Sir Arthur Pinero*. Minneapolis: University of Minnesota Press, 1974.

————. *The London Stage 1890–1899* (2 vols.); *1900–1909* (2 vols.); *1910–1919* (2 vols.); *1920–1929* (3 vols.). Metuchen, N.J.: Scarecrow Press, 1976, 1981, 1982, 1984.

————. "Pinero the Actor" and "Pinero's Professional Dramatic Roles, 1874–1884," *Theatre Notebook* 26 (Summer 1972): 133–144.

Bibliography

————. "Pinero's Letters in the Brotherton Collection of the University of Leeds," *Theatre Notebook* 24 (1969–1970): 74–79.

————. "Two Early Absurd Plays in England," *Modern Drama* 16 (December 1973): 259–264.

Weaver, Jack W., and Earl J. Wilcox. "Arthur Wing Pinero: An Annotated Bibliography of Writings About Him," *English Literature in Transition* 23 (1980): 231–259.

Webster, Margaret. *The Same, Only Different*. London: Gollanz, 1969.

West, E. J. "The Playwright as Producer: Sir Arthur Pinero, the Autocrat Dictator," *University of Colorado Studies in Languages and Literature* 6 (1957): 79–102.

Wyatt, Stephen. "Introduction," in *Pinero: Three Plays*. London: Methuen, 1985.

Index

Note: Theatres that are located in cities other than London are indexed under the name of that city. London theatres are indexed under the name of the theatre.

Index

Index

Index

Index

School (Robertson), 19
School for Scandal, The (Sheridan), 32, 45, 248, 292
Schoolmistress, The (Pinero), 137–38, 139, 141, 145, 146–48, 356
Schwartz, Maria Sophia, 117
Scott, Clement, 58, 125, 127, 132, 137, 149; on Archer's review of The Profligate, 159; on British drama and the influence of Ibsen, 173, 175; on Bygones, 75, 78; Dandy Dick reviewed by, 144; The Gay Lord Quex reviewed by, 247; The Hobby-Horse reviewed by, 140; Imprudence criticized by, 91; Lady Bountiful reviewed by, 168; Lords and Commons reviewed by, 119–20; The Magistrate reviewed by, 129, 130; and Mrs Campbell, 185; The Money-Spinner reviewed by, 79; and The Notorious Mrs Ebbsmith, 208, 212; Pinero accused of plagarism by, 197–200, 207; on Pinero's acting, 53; and The Second Mrs Tanqueray, 191, 194; and The Squire, 102; on Sweet Lavender, 154–55
Scott-Siddons, Mary Frances, 32
Scribe, Eugene, 270
Seat in the Park, A (Pinero), 353–54
Second Mrs Tanqueray, The (Pinero), 155, 203, 209, 211, 219, 372; accusation of plagarism against, 197–200; casting and plot of, 179–81, 183, 184–86; film productions of, 345–46; manuscript of, sold at auction, 374; opening night of, 191–94; in Paris, 230–31; publication of, 210; rehearsals for, 186–88, 190; response to, 181, 191, 192, 193, 194–202, 205–7; revivals of, 287, 332, 334, 356, 375; as revolutionary, xvii, 181, 213, 312; and Shaw's Mrs Warren's Profession, 205–6; as a "well-made play," 270; writing of, 173, 178–79
Shakespeare, William, xix, 17, 265, 323, 359, 363; memorial of, 293, 296

Shaw, George Bernard, 66, 204 (illus.), 229, 317, 326 (illus.), 371; and Archer, 203, 205, 271, 301–2, 303; The Benefit of the Doubt reviewed by, 219; and censorship, 311–12, 313, 314, 315; and the Dramatic Subcommittee, 302, 308–9, 310, 314, 342; and the Dramatists' Club, 310, 311, 341–42; in the epilogue to Masks and Faces, 348–49; on the film version of Iris, 348; friendship with Pinero of, 315–16, 342; Guy Domville reviewed by, 210; The Importance of Being Earnest reviewed by, 210–11; Iris reviewed by, 263, 266; Jones's The Physician reviewed by, 226–27; knighthood sought for Pinero by, 303–4, 307; on Mid-Channel, 318–19, 323; on The "Mind the Paint" Girl, 322–23; The Notorious Mrs Ebbsmith reviewed by, 212–13; Pinero viewed by, 59, 90, 202, 203, 204, 205, 210, 213–14, 221–22, 239, 264, 266, 301–2, 323, 375; The Princess and the Butterfly reviewed by, 226–27; reading editions published by, 177; on realism, 271–72; and the repertory scheme in the West End, 316–17; on the St James's audience, 300–301; and The Second Mrs Tanqueray, 205–6; Slaves of the Ring reviewed by, 210; social mores viewed by, xvii, xviii–xix, 104, 216; and the split between old and new dramatists, 302; on Trelawny, 241–42; in a triple bill of one-act plays with Pinero and Barrie, 324–25, 326–28; and World War I, 341–42, 343
Sheep in Wolf's Clothing, A (Taylor), 79
Shepperson, Claude, 344
Sheridan, Richard, 123–24, 226, 248, 337
She Stoops to Conquer (Goldsmith), 94, 105
Shewing-up of Blanco Posnet, The (Shaw), 312

431

Index